Truth and Revolution:
A History of the Sojourner Truth Organization, 1969–1986

Michael Staudenmaier

AK PRESS
OAKLAND, EDINBURGH, BALTIMORE

Truth and Revolution:
A History of the Sojourner Truth Organization, 1969–1986
By Michael Staudenmaier

© 2012 Michael Staudenmaier
Foreword © 2012 John H. Bracey, Jr.

This edition © 2012 AK Press (Edinburgh, Oakland, Baltimore)

ISBN-13: 978-1-84935-097-6
Library of Congress Control Number: 2012937711

AK Press
674-A 23rd Street
Oakland, CA 94612
USA
www.akpress.org
akpress@akpress.org

AK Press UK
PO Box 12766
Edinburgh EH8 9YE
Scotland
www.akuk.com
ak@akdin.demon.co.uk

The above addresses would be delighted to provide you with the latest AK Press
distribution catalog, which features several thousand books, pamphlets, zines,
audio and video recordings, and gear, all published or distributed by AK Press.
Alternately, visit our websites to browse the catalog and find out
the latest news from the world of anarchist publishing:
www.akpress.org | www.akuk.com
revolutionbythebook.akpress.org

Printed in the United States on 100% recycled, acid-free paper.

Cover by Josh MacPhee | www.justseeds.org
Interior by Margaret Killjoy | www.birdsbeforethestorm.net

Contents

Foreword v

Acknowledgements ix

"A Donation for Anarchy" 1

Part One: **The Working Life** **9**

1969: The Revolution That Didn't Happen 11

The Petrograd-Detroit Proletariat 37

"A Science of Navigation" 79

Part Two: **Dreams Found and Lost** **113**

Reorganization in Difficult Times 115

Iran and Cleveland:

Anti-Imperialism in Theory and Practice 147

The Politics of Culture and the Culture of Politics in a Revolutionary

Organization 191

Part Three: **The River is Dry** **231**

Building a Tendency, but How? 233

Autonomy in STO: From Dialectics to Diabolics 267

Reading STO Politically 307

Bibliography 335

Index 348

Foreword By John Bracey

As time passes, and events that one participated in decades ago have become the stuff of history, one often faces the reality that too many accounts by younger scholars bear scant resemblance to one's memories. Too often scholars ignore the recollections of participants that do not buttress their own preconceived conclusions. I am pleased that Michael Staudenmaier's *Truth and Revolution: A History of the Sojourner Truth Organization* (STO) breaks from that mold. I was active in Chicago Black and left politics during the 1960s. I knew or worked with several of the key figures discussed in this study, and met others of them during subsequent years. Staudenmaier's account as far as possible gets it right.

Staudenmaier recounts how the STO attempted over a decade and a half to hold on to their principles while confronting an increasingly inhospitable environment. Staudenmaier makes a case without rancor, but with great care and sympathy, that their efforts to achieve any lasting change was a failure and that the organization's demise was a tragedy, though largely, it is hard to see how the outcome could have been otherwise.

The political and economic trajectories taken by the United States and capitalism on a global scale during the past four decades have made a shambles of any simplistic teleology positing inevitable passage through stages of history. Who can say with any certainty how to characterize the current era or its place in some larger historical process?

The STO, like many of the most prominent left organizations, grew out of the specific circumstances of the 1960s. None survived as the country moved steadily to the right and the ruling class worked to smash, intimidate, or coopt such groups as the Black Panther Party, League of Revolutionary Black Workers, SDS, Revolutionary Action Movement, etc. They all share a story of internal debates—especially over issues of gender, family and sexuality, fragmentation, turnover and loss of membership, burnout, and eventual demise. The lesson of the STO may be more in the depth of their commitment to understanding the world in all its complexities than in their relative successes or failures in changing it.

On a personal note, it is good that the lives and works of old friends and comrades not be lost or forgotten. I remember meeting Ken Lawrence (Berg at that time) and his future wife Pat at the sit-in demonstrations at 73rd and Lowe on Chicago's south side in 1963. They both were in high school I believe and seemed so very young. I was surprised that they became active in Facing Reality. It was to their apartment that I brought C.L.R. James to meet with a group of young Black activists so that James could take the measure of their goals and beliefs. One of the achievements of the Black student movement at Northwestern University was to hire James as one of the first faculty in a budding Black Studies Department and we helped to fulfill all of his requests to meet with youth and activists in the Chicago area.

Macee Halk I knew through organizing efforts among the students and street gangs on the South and West sides. We both were members of the Revolutionary Action Movement. Like Malcolm X, Macee evolved beyond an earlier life that had resulted in his incarceration and transformed himself into one of the smartest most courageous persons that I have ever encountered. My memory of talks with Macee about his work with the STO confirm Staudenmaier's account. In fact, I met Carole Travis when she made a trip to Amherst, Massachusetts to see Macee whom I had invited to participate in an anti-war, anti-imperialist conference. Noel Ignatiev I had known through various audio tapes he sent me from time to time. I respected him as a fellow admirer of the Marxism of C.L.R. James, and I later accepted his invitation to serve on the editorial board of *Race Traitor*. Staudenmaier's portrayal of Noel again seems accurate and fair.

The STO has left behind important traces of their thoughts and practice. The special issue of *Urgent Tasks* on "C.L.R. James: His Life and Work" is still a useful antidote to the flood of new works that have tried to redefine James as a founder of "cultural studies," "postcoloniality," and the like. Noel Ignatiev and John Garvey's *Race Traitor* stands as an approach far beyond the platitudes of multicultural dialogue, etc. The STO's emphasis on popular culture as sites of resistance was thoroughly Jamesian. After the publication of *Beyond a Boundary*, the left, as Staudenmaier relates, was free to break loose from the strictures of folk music and the elitism of Frankfurt School theoreticians, and to engage with the sights and sounds of the world they lived in.

Staudenmaier offers a valuable cautionary account of the STO's difficult and complex attempts to struggle against male supremacy in both its institutional and interpersonal manifestations. It is a welcome relief from the often over generalized and not very useful accounts in most histories of the left. The discussion on parenting and the role of children by members of the STO is insightful and unique. Many of the internal struggles are an indication of the strong influence on the U.S. left of Leninist forms of organization dictated by the conditions of Czarist Russia. The contrast with the very full, interesting, chaotic lives of Karl Marx's family is telling. The letters of Marx's daughters portray Marx as a loving and supportive father, and the Marx household as a place not without fun and laughter. The fight for socialism does not have to be boring.

Staudenmaier has done a great service in walking past the obvious big game targets on the left and has given us an extremely valuable history of how one can be of the left, yet not live in despair. There was much work to be done and many ways to do it. The value in this study is not to present formulas or to engage in nostalgia. It is to document the experiences of a group of people who, acting on a clearly defined set of ideas, engaged in a variety of forms of struggle that were in concert with their ultimate goal of the empowerment of working people and a transition to socialism. When, how, or even if this takes place, knowledge of past experiences can provide both insights and inspiration as well as caveats and warnings. Future generations, not us, will decide what use will be made of the history of the STO. Staudenmaier has done his part by preserving and analyzing that experience so that it will be there if wanted and needed. My experience in watching the impact of lectures by Noel Ignatiev and Selma James on youthful audiences, the popularity of *Race Traitor*, and the interest excitement generated by a seminar on James' writings among students active in the Occupy movement indicates that the ideas and efforts of the STO still have resonance.

As capitalism (not neoliberalism, whatever that is) continues the relentless expansion across the globe that Marx outlined in the *Communist Manifesto*, it well might be that the actions of workers in China, India, Nigeria, and Brazil will have a greater impact on the prospects for socialism than that of workers in Europe and the United States. The study of the STO demonstrates that the site of struggle is in our everyday lives, against the obtsacles that working people face there, not in books about their lives. To do that for over a decade, to involve real people in real struggles is never a lost cause. That activity and those experiences are part of human history and are worthy of our attention. There is a Black Gospel hymn that says "I may never reach perfection, but I tried." That is the story of the STO that Michael Staudenmaier has told so well in the book you hold in your hands.

Amherst, Mass, March 2012

Acknowledgements

This book took just under seven years to complete, and for all but the last few months of that time I was an independent historian. As such, I experienced both an unusual sense of isolation in researching and writing this book, as well as a heightened feeling of reliance upon those who actively supported my work. One result of this contradiction is a rather lengthy list of acknowledgements.

First and foremost, none of what I have accomplished would have been possible without the incredible support of my wife Anne Carlson, as well as that of our children, Sofia and Nico. Anne is a gifted teacher who invariably brings a thoughtful and passionate eye to my work as well as to her own. In particular, her approach to questions of race and class in daily life has been immeasurably influential on my efforts to deal with such issues in this book.

A handful of other friends and comrades have supported me so completely in this project that they deserve special recognition. Kingsley Clarke, a former member of Sojourner Truth Organization (STO), saw the real-world political importance of my project very early on, and I might well have abandoned the job years ago had he not been so encouraging. Long ago, my brother, Peter Staudenmaier, set me on my path toward anarchism. Though he has pursued a slightly different trajectory as a radical historian, we regularly compare notes on our respective research, and he has always seen the very best in what I have accomplished. Christian Ogilvy has remained one of my very best friends and my closest political comrade during the entire time I've worked on this project, and his honest feedback has kept me grounded in the twenty-first century rather than the dusty seventies. Dan Berger offered the benefit of his experience as an independent scholar writing about the Weather Underground, and also gave me my first taste of peer-reviewed publishing. Krisna Best and Rob O'Dell, who initiated the online archive of STO publications (www.sojournertruth.net) before they knew anything about my project, have been constant reminders that a concern for the legacy of STO is shared more broadly than I initially imagined.

My efforts benefitted immensely from my interactions over the past sixteen years with former members of the Sojourner Truth Organization. Since my research began in earnest in 2005, I have interviewed, corresponded with, or otherwise communicated with the following former members (an asterisk indicates that at least one "formal" interview was conducted): *Hal Adams, *Guillermo Brstovsky, *Leslie Byster, *Jim Carrillo, *Ira Churgin, *Lee (Holstein) Churgin, *Kingsley Clarke, Linc Cohen, *Allison Edwards, Lynn French, Michael Goldfield, *Randy Gould, *Don Hamerquist, *Carol Hayse, *Noel (Ignatin) Ignatiev, *Bill Lamme, *Marcia LaRose, *Ken Lawrence, Caroline Levine, *Lowell May, Mike Morgan, Nick Paretsky, *Janeen (Creamer) Porter, *Dave Ranney, *Alan Rausch, *Marcia Rothenberg, *Mel Rothenberg, *George Schmidt, Cecile Singer, *John Strucker, *Carole Travis, *Ed Voci, *Kathan Zerzan, *Elias Zwierzynski. Thanks to every one of them. Hal Adams, one of the first veterans of STO that I met, and much later one of my first interviewees, was possibly the nicest former member I ever got to know, as well as one of the most dedicated. He died on March 16, 2011, and is sorely missed.

Beyond former members, I also interviewed a small number of people who were contemporaries of STO. Their critical insights into an organization they never joined were essential to my research. Thanks to John Garvey, Macee Halk, Jose Lopez, J. Sakai, and Ethan Young. Sadly, Macee, about whose life and activities an entire book could (and should!) be written, died before this book was finished. When I interviewed him at his home on the south side of Chicago in 2006, his grandchildren Clifton and Kalynn politely requested that I mention them by name in the book I was writing; several years later, I'm happy to oblige.

Most of the archival research for this project was done in the basements, offices, storage closets, and filing cabinets of former members of STO. The book would never have come to be had it not been for the willingness of Janeen Porter and Don Hamerquist to allow me (and many other young anarchists) access to the dusty overstock piles at C&D Printshop in Chicago in the mid-nineties; my initial collection of STO publications came from there. Special thanks to Ed Voci, J. Sakai, and Noel Ignatiev in particular, each of whom gave me access to and/or copies of a large number of documents that would have likely been impossible to obtain anywhere else. Kingsley Clarke, Alan Rausch, and Carole Travis provided additional items, while Dave Ranney and Pat Wright provided most of the photos that appear on the cover. Among non-members, Steve Wright in Australia, Kevin McDonnell in England, and Vic Speedwell in Chicago provided me with copies of documents I did not encounter elsewhere. Certain internal items, including some that former members would perhaps prefer I had never seen, were provided by Alexander Van Zandt Akin at Bolerium Books in San Francisco.

Reference librarians at four libraries were responsive to obscure requests sent via email, often mailing me photocopies of useful documents. Thanks to William Lefevre at Wayne State University (the Detroit Revolutionary Movements Collection), Peter Nelson at Amherst University (the Marshall Bloom Alternative Press Collection), Rukshana Singh at the Southern California Library for Social Studies and Research in Los Angeles (the Mike Conan Collection), and Evan Matthew Daniel of the Tamiment Library and Robert F. Wagner Labor Archives in New York City. Traci Harris deserves special thanks for spending an entire day off visiting the Southern California Library, looking through folders, summarizing her findings for me over email, and then scanning dozens of documents for me.

One significant area of overlap between STO's history and my own experience was work done in solidarity with the Puerto Rican independence movement. For many years, I worked at the Dr. Pedro Albizu Campos Puerto Rican High School in Chicago, and I still consider my time there to be among the most profound educational experiences of my life. This book, especially Chapter Five, benefitted immensely from years of conversation with Marvin Garcia, Michael Hannan, Jose Lopez, Lourdes Lugo, Alejandro Molina, and Michelle Morales, among many, many others.

During part of the time I worked on this book I was an active member of the Four Star Anarchist Organization, which along with Bring the Ruckus, the First of May Anarchist Alliance, Miami Autonomy and Solidarity, the Kasama Project, the Black Orchid Collective, and Unity and Struggle, reminds me that contemporary revolutionary groups are still learning from the legacy of STO, a quarter-century after its demise.

As my project neared completion, my life as an independent historian came to an end and I entered the PhD program in History at the University of Illinois at Urbana/Champaign. A special thanks goes to Dave Roediger for his encouragement of both my independent research and my pursuit of graduate study. Thanks as well to Sundiata Cha-Jua, Zach Sell, and the participants in the Working Class History Reading Group, which gave me great feedback on a draft of Chapter Five.

Beyond those already identified, the list of people who gave me assistance, support, and encouragement during this project is substantial.

For every person below there are any number of great stories to tell; each of them deserves my thanks: Aaron Barnhart, Gregor Baszak, Jesse Cohn, Cloee Cooper, Daniel Curtis, Geert Dhondt, Tony Doyle, Ferd Eggan (RIP), Diane Eickhoff, Max Elbaum, Carlos Fernandez, Geoff, Gio, Paul Glavin, Maria Gluzerman, Beau Golwitzer, Sharlyn Grace, Rebecca Harris, Nate Holdren, Bree Johnson, Kieran Knudson Frazier, Peter Little, B. Loewe, Matthew Lyons, Josh MacPhee, Cindy Milstein, Chuck Morse, S. Nappalos, Michael Novick, Danny Postel, Margaret Power, Lauren Ray, Becca Sandor, Jason Serota-Winston, Joe Sexauer, Jaggi Singh, Sprite, John Steele, Kerry Taylor, Brian Tokar, Beverly Tomek, James Tracy, Daniel Tucker, Mabel Constanza Valencia and her partner Juan Diego Castrillon as well as their children Santiago and Adriana, and Adam Weaver.

Charles Weigl, Kate Khatib, and all the folks at AK Press have been wonderful to work with. John Bracey graciously agreed to pen the brief foreword, for which I am extremely grateful. Special thanks to Josh MacPhee for his fantastic cover design, and for being a good friend and comrade for many, many years. Dara Greenwald, Josh's partner of many years and one of the most gifted cultural organizers I have ever personally known, passed away as the editing process for this book was in its final stages; the legacy of art and activism she has left behind is immense.

Portions of Chapters Two and Five, as well as parts of the Introduction and the Conclusion, appeared in altered form in my essay "Unorthodox Leninism: Workplace Organizing and Anti-Imperialist Solidarity in the Sojourner Truth Organization," which was included in Dan Berger's edited anthology on the movements of the seventies, *The Hidden 1970s: Histories of Radicalism*, published by Rutgers University Press in 2010. A small amount of additional material appeared previously in the entry on STO that I authored for inclusion in the *International Encyclopedia of Revolution and Protest*, edited by Immanuel Ness and published by Wiley-Blackwell in 2009.

I have always been very close to my family. My dad, L. William Staudenmaier, was my first editor, and still one of the toughest I've ever had; he is also a big part of the reason I love long bike rides, nice beer, and the Green Bay Packers. My siblings, Ann Marie, Bill, Terry, Peter, and Suzanne, along with their spouses, partners, kids and pets, have always been a source of joy and strength. Finally, my mother, Kathleen Marie Staudenmaier, died before my book was completed. She was an absolute rock in my life, a brilliant and endlessly caring individual. I miss her every day. This book is dedicated to her memory.

Introduction:
"A Donation for Anarchy"

In 1996, I was part of the collective that ran the Autonomous Zone, an anarchist "infoshop" in Chicago. Our biggest project that year was hosting a conference and a set of protests against the Democratic National Convention, held in our city that August. We called it "Active Resistance, a Counter-Convention," and in the end it drew more than seven hundred young revolutionaries from all corners of North America to strategize and to mingle. Early on in the planning process, we decided to produce a poster that could be widely distributed in advance of the event. Tony Doyle, the most gifted artist in our collective, created a beautiful design, and Vic Speedwell was assigned the task of shopping it around to find an affordable print shop. When she arrived at the innocuously named C&D Printshop on the near west side, she had no idea the owners had a radical background, much less that the business had originated two decades prior as the in-house printing press for the Sojourner Truth Organization. So it was quite a surprise when Janeen Porter looked at the poster, then looked at her husband and co-owner Don Hamerquist, and said, "I think we could make a donation for anarchy, don't you?" As a result, the Autonomous Zone only had to pay for materials; all labor was donated.

At the time, I had vaguely heard of STO, but knew very little about the group or its history. (I had never heard of Janeen or Don, even though Don had helped found the organization, was one of its leading theoreticians, and was the only person to remain a member from beginning to end of the group's history.) That would change over the next few years as a number of us younger Chicago anarchists became friends and comrades not only with Janeen and Don, but also with a range of other veterans of STO. Along the way, I realized that Janeen's spontaneous decision to offer discounted printing services was not exactly exceptional in the context of her former group's history. Throughout its existence, STO was committed to a pragmatic view of revolutionary struggle, looking for promising forms of activity and materially supporting them while offering critical perspectives and advice. Whether the terrain was the factory floor, the anti-imperialist milieu, or new social movements, the group demonstrated its firm commitment to revolution despite the dramatically changing circumstances of the seventies and eighties.

* * *

STO was a font of new and challenging ideas, as well as a fulcrum for revolutionary action. Among the areas of work in which the group immersed itself were (and this list is by no means exhaustive): workplace organizing, GI resistance, community-based antipolice efforts, women's and especially reproductive rights, anti-imperialist solidarity, international networking with like-minded revolutionaries in Europe and Latin America, antifascist organizing, antinuclear and disarmament struggles, radical responses to state repression, opposition to US intervention in Central America and the Middle East, and youth and student radicalism. This book places special emphasis on some of these, while effectively ignoring others. In all cases, this was the result of difficult decisions made due to space constraints when organizing a monograph that was inevitably going to be too long.

Despite this wide range of activities, it is possible to create a rough but coherent narrative arc that categorizes STO's trajectory into three distinct periods: a workplace-organizing period lasting approximately from 1970 through 1975, an anti-imperialist-solidarity era running more or less from 1976 through 1980, and a direct-action, tendency-building phase beginning at the end of the seventies and continuing through the group's demise in the mid-eighties. These demarcations are not exact, as all three sorts of organizing continued at some level during all three periods. They also neglect a range of other essential components of STO's work, including a continuing commitment to autonomous organizing by working-class women and an intense focus on theoretical development and internal education. Nonetheless, this book approximately follows such a scheme, with each phase being covered by a section of the text, in order to help shed light on STO's unique place within the political movements that emerged in the aftermath of the sixties.

At its inception in Chicago at the end of 1969, STO was heavily influenced by the work of the Detroit-based League of Revolutionary

Black Workers. STO's early emphasis was on organizing at the point of production, especially in large factories in the steel, auto, and manufacturing sectors. In contrast to many other groups of the same period also engaged in workplace organizing, STO rejected mainstream labor unions as a venue for struggle, to which it counterposed the option of "independent mass workers' organizations." The group's members participated in the creation of several such organizations, in both unionized and non-union factories, always agitating for demands that challenged what STO described as the "bourgeois legality compromise." This compromise doomed traditional unions, which necessarily were in the business of negotiating functional relationships between workers and management. STO's activities within dozens of factories around the Chicagoland area resulted in hundreds of job actions during the early seventies, ranging from short-term sit-down work stoppages to longer wildcat strikes and sabotage at the worksite.

As the sixties receded further into the past and the independent labor upsurge of the early seventies waned, conflicts within STO over ideology and strategy led to a series of splits that nearly destroyed the group. The rebuilding process preserved the core commitments of the organization ideologically, but two shifts manifested. First, the group extended its reach geographically, becoming a regional organization and eventually growing to include members in a dozen states across the US. Second, STO began to emphasize the importance of national liberation struggles. Solidarity with, most prominently, the Puerto Rican independence movement and the Iranian student movement in the US, became central components of the group's practical work. This transition produced a number of side effects, including an unorthodox take on the theoretical aspects of what Marxists called "the national question," as well as an enhanced appreciation of the need for internal political and philosophical study.

As the eighties dawned, STO altered its strategy once again, distancing itself from the Stalinism of many of the national liberation movements it had previously supported, and turning its attention to building a revolutionary tendency within the so-called new social movements—the antinuclear movement and anti-Klan organizing, as well as youth/student, anti-intervention, and reproductive rights struggles, among others. Within this context, the group consistently encouraged militant direct action as a strategic orientation and emphasized the autonomy of all such movements. However, internal confusion about the implications of autonomy and the external pressures of the Reagan era led to a new series of splits and departures that undermined STO's viability as a formal organization. By the late 1980s the group was defunct.

* * *

On an intellectual level, several key themes recur throughout the group's history. In every area and at every point in time, STO emphasized the importance of mass action, the rejection of legal constraints on struggle, the question of consciousness within the working class, the central role of white supremacy to the continued misery of life under capitalism, and the necessity of autonomy for exploited and oppressed groups, not only from capitalism and white supremacy but also from their supposed representatives, various self-proclaimed vanguards, and any other "condescending saviors."[1]

Two essential theoretical innovations in particular marked STO's contribution to the revolutionary left. First, the group re-articulated Italian Marxist Antonio Gramsci's understanding of hegemony as an analysis of "dual consciousness," arguing that the working class displayed both a broad acceptance of the status quo and an embryonic awareness of its own revolutionary potential as a class.[2] An early pamphlet produced by

---

1   The latter phrase comes from the standard US translation of the lyrics to the "Internationale," and was also part of the title of an STO pamphlet from the mid-seventies, *"…no condescending saviors"* by Noel Ignatin. The full stanza is:

> We want no condescending saviors
> To rule us from their judgment hall,
> We workers ask not for their favors
> Let us consult for all:
> To make the thief disgorge his booty
> To free the spirit from its cell,
> We must ourselves decide our duty,
> We must decide, and do it well.

2   The source of this term, in its usage by STO, is somewhat murky. Gramsci discusses the hypothetical worker as having "two theoretical consciousnesses (or one contradictory consciousness)." *Prison Notebooks* (New York: International Publishers, 1991), 333. W.E.B. Du Bois used the phrase "double consciousness" in his classic work *The Souls of Black Folk* (New York: Signet Classic, 1995 [1903]), 45, to describe the experience of black people living in a white supremacist society. Despite the group's obvious debt to Du Bois, there is no clear evidence that his work was the source of STO's usage. Don Hamerquist, who first introduced the term within STO, recalls Lenin's critique of trade union consciousness as an important influence in how the organization used the term

STO suggested that "what is in the worker's head is a source of power insofar as it reflects the worldview of the working class—and a source of weakness—insofar as it reflects the world view of the capitalist class."[3] The task of revolutionaries was to help expand the level of proletarian consciousness through participation in mass struggle, while challenging the acquiescence to bourgeois consciousness. STO believed that this process required the creation of a revolutionary party, but it rejected what it called the "Stalin model" of party building in favor of an eclectic mix of organizational ideas drawn from Lenin and, especially as the eighties arrived, from the Trinidadian Marxist C.L.R. James.

The second quintessential aspect of STO's revolutionary theory was its analysis of white-skin privilege as a bulwark of white supremacy. A founding member of the group, Noel Ignatin (now Ignatiev), helped pioneer the concept by reframing ideas initially advanced by W.E.B. Du Bois, especially in his classic work, *Black Reconstruction in America, 1860–1880*. According to the theory, people identified as "white" benefit from material and psychological advantages that people of color are denied. STO argued that white workers must "actively and militantly reject their partial, selfish and counterfeit interests as part of a group which is favored in relation to blacks, on behalf of their total, broad and true interests as part of a class which is coming alive."[4] As a largely white group, STO saw its role as spurring the white working class in this direction and supporting organizing efforts emerging from black, Puerto Rican, and other nonwhite communities.

As the group moved closer to its own demise, a third key concept gained prominence within its theoretical universe: autonomy. Conceptually, autonomy was applied to a wide range of social groups—black people, other oppressed nations, women, youth, the working class as a whole. The list of those from whom autonomy must be sought and defended was similarly broad—capitalism and the state, but also trade unions, political parties, and even in many cases STO itself. This intense

---

"dual consciousness" in its work. Hamerquist, email to the author, October 26, 2009.

3   Sojourner Truth Organization (STO), *Toward a Revolutionary Party: Ideas on Strategy and Organization* (Chicago: STO, 1976 [1971]), available at www.sojournertruth.net/tarp.html (accessed February 18, 2009).

4   STO, *The United Front Against Imperialism?* (Chicago: STO, 1972), available at www.sojournertruth.net/unitedfront.html (accessed February 18, 2009).

awareness of the need for real independence at the level of mass movements marked the final period of the group's existence, and facilitated both high and low points in its existence. Closely tied to the theoretical focus on autonomy was a practical demand for militancy and a willingness to challenge legal boundaries in order to build a revolutionary movement. While there was a certain conceptual incoherence built into this constellation of ideas, most of STO's clear-cut "successes" reflected a careful balance between acting as a radical pole inside broader struggles, on the one hand, and ensuring that mass movements had the freedom to determine their own trajectory. This was just as true in the factories of 1972 as it was in the antiwar protests of 1982. When STO failed—which was often—it was frequently because the balance was tipped too far in one direction or the other.

* * *

A brief explanation of the title of this book is perhaps in order. For a long time, the working title was the unwieldy mouthful "Revolutionaries Who Tried to Think," which was drawn from Ignatiev's reflections on STO's distinctiveness within the US left of its era. Eventually, *Truth and Revolution* was chosen both for its play on the group's name and for the way in which it calls attention to fundamental questions of radical theory and practice. In the hands of the historical left, "truth" and "revolution" have too often had a troubled relationship. STO's critique of Stalinism reflected the rejection of a methodology that presented the revolutionary party as the source of scientific knowledge and revolutionary truth. Much more recently, Hamerquist has called for "organizational forms that are mobile and flexible, and that are looking to intervene, not because they have the truth, but as a part of the development of the will to create new truths."[5] At the same time, STO itself was sometimes

---

5   Don Hamerquist, "Lenin, Leninism, and Some Leftovers" (2009). Available online at http://sketchythoughts.blogspot.com/2009/09/lenin-leninism-and-some-leftovers.html (accessed September 8, 2011). Hamerquist's recent writings have engaged the work of Alain Badiou, a French radical philosopher with a Maoist background. Badiou's approach to truth can be glimpsed throughout his work, most notably in the essays "Truths and Justice" and "Politics as Truth Procedure," both of which appear in the book *Metapolitics* (London and New York: Verso, 2005). Thanks to John Steele for bringing these pieces to my attention.

less than saintly in its own attempts to demarcate the supposed truth of its own positions. "Truth" is a difficult and complicated idea to define, but it is precisely this complexity and ambiguity that make the term apt as a bookend with "revolution" when conceptualizing the history of STO.[6] The chapters that follow address questions of truth only obliquely, but contemporary revolutionaries have much to gain in viewing STO through the dual prism suggested by the title.

* * *

This book covers a lot of terrain. It describes events that took place during three different decades, in locations all over the world, from Chicago, New York, and Kansas City to Puerto Rico, Italy, and Iran. While focusing on the specific trajectory of a single, small organization, it attempts to shed light on the broader history of the international revolutionary left over the last half century. STO was both exemplary and exceptional when considered in the context of the movements that emerged from the end of the sixties. It grappled with a set of problems that were nearly universal—the contradictions of race and class, the failure of revolutionary struggles to establish or maintain free and egalitarian societies, the need to incorporate the work of conscious revolutionaries into mass struggles, and so forth. Yet its proposals for dealing with these problems were proudly unorthodox, drawing on a range of sources in the Marxist, revolutionary nationalist, feminist, and other radical traditions. While claiming the mantle of Leninism, STO diverged sharply from most standard interpretations of that term.

In the pages that follow, I attempt to balance an intellectual history of STO's theoretical innovations with a social history of the group's real world activities. This task is, of course, more easily identified than accomplished, in part because the available written materials (both published and internal) tend to focus on theory at the expense of practice. Oral history interviews with former members only partially redressed this imbalance. But for me, as for STO, it remains a fundamental premise that ideas can only obtain their value, and indeed their validation,

---

6   The philosophical and political literature on truth is vast and often contradictory. Two productive if quite different starting points would be Hans-Georg Gadamer, *Truth and Method* (London and New York: Continuum, 2004 [1975]), and Patricia Hill Collins, *Black Feminist Thought: Knowledge, Consciousness and the Politics of Empowerment* (New York: Routledge, 2009 [2000]).

in the messy world in which we actually live. As a result, in addition to discussions of consciousness and white skin privilege and autonomy, these pages include stories of getting, keeping, and losing jobs, reflections on popular music and spectator sports, descriptions of protests and conferences, and commentary on organizational questions that may on first glance seem needlessly obscure. The goal is not to be eclectic, but to be true to the complex life of any revolutionary group. Considered as a whole, the historical arc of the Sojourner Truth Organization has much to teach contemporary radicals, especially those aspiring to be revolutionaries who try to think as well as act. This book is intended as a modest contribution to the creation of a framework for moving forward by looking closely at a small slice of the past.

Part One:
The Working Life

Factory takes his hearing, factory gives him life,
The working, the working, just the working life.

Bruce Springsteen, "Factory"

Chapter One:
1969: The Revolution That Didn't Happen

Nineteen sixty-nine was a difficult year for North American revolutionaries. Black radicals, in the Black Panther Party and other groups, were under direct attack by the FBI and local police across the United States. Students for a Democratic Society (SDS), the flagship organization of the white new left, imploded at its annual convention in Chicago. The war in Vietnam was intensifying, as Richard Nixon reinforced and expanded the imperialist foreign policy that Lyndon Johnson had previously administered. Everywhere the initiatives championed by the new left were on the defensive, as capital and the state dug in their heels to defend the status quo.

At the same time, 1969 was also a year of great optimism for North American revolutionaries. Enormous numbers of young people across the country embraced the term "revolution." In the eyes of many, the wheat was being separated from the chaff, as the gulf between culturally oriented hippies and ideologically committed militants grew ever greater. The collapse of SDS was viewed as a symbol of the limits of student-centered radicalism, and attention turned to the growing wave of wildcat strikes in a variety of industries where workers were openly rejecting the sweetheart deals that mainstream unions had established with employers. An increasingly radical women's movement was growing by leaps and bounds, challenging male supremacy within both mainstream society and the established left. If the bad guys were digging in for a fight, the good guys were getting more sophisticated, more determined, and more energized in their efforts to turn the world upside-down.

In this contradictory context, a small number of revolutionaries in Chicago spent the fall of 1969 discussing the state of the movement and the prospects for radical social change. The process culminated, sometime between Christmas and the New Year, in the founding of the Sojourner Truth Organization, a group that would spend most of the next two decades critically engaged in revolutionary struggles. In order to better understand the origins of STO, it is useful to briefly review the circumstances in which its founding members found themselves in the year leading up to the group's inception.

* * *

The black movement was both huge and diverse in 1969, although signs were already visible of the pressures, both external and internal, that would decimate it as the seventies progressed. The civil rights movement had been torn for some time between the reformist approach of most of the major southern organizations and the increasing radicalism of the urban rebellions that began in the mid-sixties.[1] By the time Martin Luther King, Jr. was assassinated in 1968, the organized face of the black movement included groups like the Black Panther Party (BPP), the Republic of New Afrika, and the Revolutionary Action Movement. These and other organizations advocated black power and favored a revolutionary approach to the problem of white supremacy, in contrast to the reformism of more established formations, such as the Southern Christian Leadership Conference and even the Congress of Racial Equality. But as the number of radical black groups proliferated, so did the tensions between them, and in some cases inside them. Some of these conflicts were the result of government repression and COINTELPRO tactics, while in other cases the FBI and local police exploited already-existing disagreements between groups to further fracture the movement.[2] For a time, the problems at the organizational level were more than outweighed by the vibrant mass movement of black people everywhere against the daily

---

1   For more on the shift from civil rights to black power modes of the black freedom movement, see Peniel E. Joseph, *Waiting 'Til the Midnight Hour: A Narrative History of Black Power in America* (New York: Henry Holt and Company, 2006).

2   For more on COINTELPRO operations against the black movement, the white left, and the far right, see David Cunningham, *There's Something Happening Here: The New Left, the Klan, and FBI Counterintelligence* (Berkeley, CA: University of California Press, 2004).

experience of racism in all arenas of life. As this momentum dissipated over the succeeding decade, the difficulties plaguing the organized black left served as both cause and effect of the decline. But even before the movement as a whole was in trouble, the conflicts and the repression had a ripple effect on the rest of the left.

The Panthers, in particular, had ties to SDS and other largely white groups, so their internal tensions and the government attacks they suffered had a demoralizing effect on the section of the white movement that took inspiration from their bold rhetoric and deep commitment to social change.[3] Over the course of 1969, the BPP was on the receiving end of just about every form of government repression one can think of. Activities and communications were subject to surveillance, key leaders were arrested on trumped-up charges, and the Panthers' public commitment to armed self-defense was used as an excuse for police to conduct violent assaults on their offices and the homes of members. On April 2, the "Panther 21" were arrested in New York City and charged with conspiracy, arson, and attempted murder; although they would eventually be acquitted, their legal defense put significant strain on the BPP's east coast operations.[4] Then on December 4, the Chicago Police Department invaded the home of Illinois Black Panther Party Chairman Fred Hampton, murdering him in his bed and also killing BPP leader Mark Clark.[5] Internally, these and other attacks did nothing to diminish the growing divide between the Huey Newton and Eldridge Cleaver factions of the BPP, which by early in 1971 had turned into a full-blown split in the Party.[6]

It was impossible at the time to predict the coming decline in the black movement. In part, this was due to other developments that were much more encouraging. The most impressive of these was the emergence of the League of Revolutionary Black Workers (LRBW) in Detroit during the

---

3   The influence of the Panthers, and black radicalism generally, on the white left of the late sixties is detailed in David Barber, *A Hard Rain Fell: SDS and Why It Failed* (Jackson, MS: University Press of Mississippi, 2008).

4   On the Panther 21, see Murray Kempton, *The Briar Patch: The Trial of the Panther 21* (Cambridge, MA: Da Capo Press, 1997 [1973]).

5   The best work on Hampton's killing is Jeffrey Haas, *The Assassination of Fred Hampton: How the FBI and the Chicago Police Murdered a Black Panther* (Chicago: Lawrence Hill Books/Chicago Review Press, 2010).

6   The split in the Party is detailed by Peniel Joseph, *Midnight Hour*, 261–269.

summer of 1969.[7] The League represented an alternative to the Black Panther Party, both in its organizing methods and in its constituency. Where the Panthers advocated the rhetorical flourish, the open show of firearms, and the establishment of direct service antipoverty programs, the League preferred grassroots organizing in the workplace, the use of legal defense as a form of propaganda, and the creation of alternative media institutions like publishing houses. In each case, the means chosen reflected the segment of the population targeted by the group: the BPP aimed its efforts at the black underclass, including unemployed and semicriminal elements, while the League attempted to engage sectors of the black working class, especially in the auto industry and in community colleges. These differences held enormous significance for the future members of STO, who were much more interested in the LRBW than they were in the Panthers.[8]

The League was always an unstable combination of organizers with different agendas and strategies, but it symbolized a convergence of the black movement with the promise of workplace rebellions like the wildcat strike at the Dodge plant in Hamtramck, Michigan in May, 1968. This strike led to the creation of the Dodge Revolutionary Union Movement (DRUM), from which came some of the founding members of the League a year later.[9] Others came out of the black student movement and from a loose collection of slightly older activists in Detroit. The unique situation of Detroit as a heavily black and heavily industrialized city limited the applicability to other locales, but the example of the League was certainly inspiring to a cross-section of the white left, just at a moment when the problems facing the Panthers were becoming difficult to ignore.

The LRBW was not the only positive news from the black movement, either. The legacy of the civil rights movement as a militant, grassroots struggle with an undeniable base of support in black communities nationwide was still strong, despite King's death and the organizational splintering described above. As early as 1967, Carl Davidson, a leading member of SDS, argued that

> the black ghetto rebellions this summer fundamentally
> altered the political reality of white America, including the

---

7   The classic assessment of the League is Dan Georgakas and Marvin Surkin, *Detroit: I Do Mind Dying: A Study in Urban Revolution (Updated Edition)* (Cambridge, MA: South End Press, 1998 [1975]).

8   See Chapter Two for more on the LRBW's influence on STO.

9   Georgakas and Surkin describe the rise of DRUM and its connection to the emergence of the LRBW. *Detroit: I Do Mind Dying*, 20–41.

white left. The black liberation movement has replaced the civil rights and anti-poverty movements, revealing the utter bankruptcy of corporate liberalism's cooptive programs. The events of this summer marked not only the possibility, but the beginning of the second American revolution.[10]

Two years later, despite all their difficulties, the Panthers remained a highly visible organization that at least initially seemed to hold up well under increasing government repression. Smart revolutionaries understood that any serious attempt to overthrow capitalism would face the harshest possible attacks from the power structure, and the black movement was perceived as the segment of the US population most prepared for these attacks and most committed to resisting them.

* * *

One result of the League's activities, especially its commitment to self-promotion through alternative media, was that, as the sixties came to a close, increasing numbers of young leftists began to pay attention to the industrial workplace as a site of social struggles. Several factors had previously kept the new left from investigating workplace struggles. The dominance of SDS within the white new left led to an overwhelming emphasis on student issues and campus-based struggles. Even when they turned their attentions outward, most student radicals focused their efforts on community organizing and antipoverty campaigns, rather than labor issues. Many SDS members felt nothing but disdain for the old left politics of groups that had historically emphasized work within organized labor. The Communist Party USA, the Socialist Workers' Party, and others were widely perceived as reformist at best and corruptly reactionary at worst.

And of course the "official" labor movement was subject to even more stinging criticism and dismissal. As Carole Travis, a founding and long-time member of STO, emphasized, "no one thought that they [unions]

---

10   Carl Davidson, "Toward Institutional Resistance," *New Left Notes*, November 13, 1967, quoted in David Barber, "'A Fucking White Revolutionary Mass Movement' and Other Fables of Whiteness," *Race Traitor* no. 12, Spring 2001, 35. Davidson subsequently participated in the New Communist Movement throughout the seventies, including several years spent in the Harpers Ferry Organization, a small New York City group aligned with STO.

were valuable to social change at all."[11] A lengthy campaign to bureaucratize the labor movement simultaneously purged almost all major unions of openly radical voices, a process eagerly supported by the US government under the auspices of anti-Communism.[12] The merger of the American Federation of Labor (AFL) and the Congress of Industrial Organizations (CIO) in 1955 had cemented the commitment of mainstream labor unions to labor peace. By the late sixties, the AFL-CIO was one of the most reactionary entities in US politics, with a membership that largely supported the Vietnam War, opposed civil rights and women's liberation, and routinely tolerated corrupt sweetheart agreements with employers. The leadership had ties to the CIA and to the mafia, and the rank and file was largely dismissed by the left as having no revolutionary potential. Weatherman, the wing of SDS that would later be known as the Weather Underground, argued in its initial political statement that "unionized skilled workers" had "a higher level of privilege relative to the oppressed colonies, including the blacks, and relative to more oppressed workers in the mother country; so that there is a strong material basis for racism and loyalty to the system," and by the fall of 1969 the group had embraced the slogan "fight the people," with only a tinge of irony.[13] While other radicals harshly criticized this line, it was in many ways only a slightly exaggerated reflection of the positions held by much of the revolutionary left at the end of the decade.

Against this backdrop, only a small number of radicals gave any serious thought to engaging in workplace organizing. Nonetheless, under the very noses of a largely ignorant new left, explosive labor struggles were taking place in an array of industries across the country. Many, perhaps most, of these fights pitted rank and file workers against *both* the management and the union leadership, resulting in a growing wave of wildcat strikes like the one that spawned DRUM in 1968.[14] From bus

---

11   Carole Travis, interview with author, June 6, 2006.

12   This process is outlined in Kim Moody, *An Injury to All: The Decline of American Unionism* (New York: Verso, 1988), 45–51.

13   Karen Ashley, Bill Ayers, et. al., "You Don't Need a Weatherman to Know Which Way the Wind Blows" (June 18, 1969), in Harold Jacobs, ed., *Weatherman* (Berkeley, CA: Ramparts Press, 1970), 66. "Fight the people" is discussed in favorable terms in Bill Ayers, "A Strategy to Win" (September 11, 1969) in Jacobs, 192.

14   For more on labor unrest in the late sixties and early seventies, see Aaron Brenner, Robert Brenner, and Cal Wislow, eds., *Rebel Rank and File: Labor Militancy and Revolt from Below During the Long 1970s* (New York: Verso, 2010).

drivers and postal workers to machinists and longshoremen, the working class was becoming increasingly aware of its own power, as opposed to the supposed power of its self-proclaimed representatives. This was true both in the US and elsewhere, as the French general strike of 1968 and the Italian Hot Autumn of 1969 indicated.[15] To the small minority of the left that was paying attention, workplace struggles began to seem full of revolutionary potential.

One factor that influenced this assessment was the relatively integrated character of many larger workplaces in the United States, especially in heavy industry and some service-sector work (such as hospitals and transportation). Racism was certainly an inescapable reality for black and latino workers, who routinely received the worst paid, least safe, and least secure jobs in any factory, assuming they were able to find employment at all in the face of double-digit unemployment for nonwhites, especially youth.[16] Once on the job, however, workers of color brought with them the lessons learned from two decades of the civil rights movement. And in many cases, they were able to teach these lessons to disaffected younger whites who increasingly saw the limits of individual attempts at rebellion in the form of long hair and dope smoking.

For both black and white young men in the working class, the war in Vietnam represented the ever-present threat of draft and death. For those who survived their tour of duty, factory bosses often became the object of residual anger that had previously been targeted at commanding officers. The result was an increase in shop floor militancy, a willingness to confront perceived injustice and demand change, and an openness to radical perspectives. It's likely that only a handful of the workers involved in wildcats and other struggles went into them with anything like an anticapitalist worldview, but more than a few emerged as committed revolutionaries with remarkable organizing experience and a strong sense of solidarity.

One segment of the new left, including many of the people who would go on to found STO at the end of 1969, took an interest in this

---

15 These events are described in greater detail in Chapter Two.

16 According to economists Peter Jackson and Edward Montgomery, the unemployment rate for black men between the ages of eighteen and nineteen was 19 percent, more than double the 7.9 percent for white men of the same ages. Peter Jackson and Edward Montgomery, "Layoffs, Discharges and Youth Unemployment," in Richard B. Freeman and Harry J. Holzer, eds., *The Black Youth Employment Crisis* (Chicago: University of Chicago Press, 1986), 116.

underpublicized movement, especially once groups like DRUM and the LRBW used recognizably revolutionary rhetoric to describe struggles that might otherwise have seemed reformist in spite of their militancy. Upon reflection, the wave of wildcats could be seen as a validation of two traditional insights of Marxism. First, the fact that they took place outside the union structure was a confirmation of the longstanding radical claim that "the emancipation of the working classes must be conquered by the working classes themselves," rather than the work of trade union bureaucracies.[17] Second, the factory was able to "discipline" workers, teaching them solidarity and cooperation even while it imposed competition and division. Insurgent organizing efforts served as experience that helped prepare the working class to run society. While few if any of the wildcats of the late sixties and early seventies resulted in factory occupations, much less the continuation of production under worker control, this was a presumptive next step that was much discussed by revolutionaries both inside and outside the workplace.

* * *

If conflict at the point of production was intensifying as the sixties came to a close, conflict around the war in Southeast Asia was even more explosive. This was perhaps the only arena in which the momentum of the new left did not falter in 1969, despite the confused character of the increasingly disparate antiwar movement. Demonstrations continued to draw enormous crowds, just as they had in preceding years. Direct actions against draft boards and military recruitment offices became more frequent and more violent. The number of draft resisters continued to rise as young men fled to Canada and elsewhere to avoid induction. Perhaps more important, resistance within the military became more pronounced and more radical. The number of fraggings (violent assaults on commanding officers, often using fragmentation grenades with intent to kill) skyrocketed in 1969, and the number of desertions increased dramatically over the previous year.[18]

---

17   This particular phrasing comes from the "General Rules" of the International Workingmen's Association, adopted in October 1964. Available online at http://www.marxists.org/archive/marx/iwma/documents/1864/rules.htm (accessed January 7, 2012).

18   The classic work on GI resistance in Vietnam remains David Cortright, *Soldiers in Revolt: GI Resistance During the Vietnam War* (Chicago: Haymarket Books, 2005 [1975]). For a thorough, if pro-military, look at

In short, the antiwar movement was becoming more proletarian in its orientation, as young working-class enlisted men and their families began to question the war effort. Just a few years before, opposition to the Vietnam War had been confined to the middle class, and especially to student radicals at more or less prestigious universities and to religiously oriented progressives. There had always been a strong moral component to the antiwar movement, partly inherited from the pacifist legacy of previous movements during Korea and World War Two.[19] But as the Vietnam War became less and less popular with mainstream Americans, the moral basis of the antiwar movement became something of a stumbling block. Draft dodging and counter-recruitment, for instance, could be ridiculed as middle-class escapism and patronizing missionary work, respectively.

The increasing radicalism of the student left, coupled with its rapid expansion into the realm of second tier state universities and community colleges, provided an opening in which connections could be built across the class divide. Once again, the black movement was the fulcrum point, as civil rights veterans began to turn their attentions to the racism of the draft and the parallels between the experience of African Americans and that of the Vietnamese. Martin Luther King famously spoke out in opposition to the war shortly before his assassination in 1968, and the world champion boxer Muhammad Ali refused military service as early as 1966, saying "I'm not going 10,000 miles from home to help murder and burn another poor nation simply to continue the domination of white slave masters of the darker people the world over."[20] Racism inside the military may also have helped to radicalize the GI resistance movement: some activists believed that white enlisted men were being forced to choose between white supremacy and class solidarity as they decided whether to side with largely black deserters or their mostly white commanding officers.[21]

Unfortunately, the radical potential of a broad-based antiwar movement was undercut at the end of the sixties by several factors, chief among them the internalized white supremacy of the white working class and the

---

fragging, see George Lepre, *Fragging: Why US Soldiers Assaulted Their Officers in Vietnam* (Lubbock, TX: Texas Tech University Press, 2011).

19   James Tracy, *Direct Action: Radical Pacifism from the Union Eight to the Chicago Seven* (Chicago: University of Chicago Press, 1996) describes this historical development through the end of 1969.

20   Quoted in Mike Marqusee, *Redemption Song: Muhammad Ali and the Spirit of the Sixties* (New York: Verso, 1999), 214–215.

21   George Schmidt, interview with the author, March 26, 2006.

ascension of Richard Nixon to the presidency in 1969 on a supposedly antiwar platform. In contrast to the student movement, which was headed toward the pro-Vietcong stance best typified by Weathermen marching at the Days of Rage in Chicago with Vietnamese National Liberation Front (NLF) flags, the mainstream antiwar movement was always couched in the language of patriotism.[22] On one level this was yet another legacy of the civil rights movement, which had, for the most part, considered inclusion of blacks as full citizens to be a truly American goal. But a bigger issue was the insidious nature of white supremacy and imperialism. Except for a small core of revolutionaries, most white people opposed the war out of concern for the safety and well-being of young white men in the US military. The cost of the war on the people and land of Vietnam, and even upon black and latino soldiers, were of only marginal concern at best. This racism also influenced mainstream responses to draft dodging and GI resistance. Young men fleeing to Canada (mostly white) received a fair bit of positive press coverage, while those participating in army rebellions (often black) were either ignored or denounced.[23]

Richard Nixon was elected president in 1968, and his "southern strategy" of appealing to white racial resentment of the civil rights movement only reconfirmed the tight grip of white supremacy on the electoral process.[24] In the context of the campaign, however, Nixon actually came to represent a certain type of antiwar sentiment. Without any specifics, he promised a new approach to the war in Vietnam, which was known as the "secret plan." Given the growing distaste among white liberals for the war's rising death toll, Nixon represented a change from five years of escalating involvement in Vietnam under Lyndon Johnson. Despite some late efforts to distance himself from Johnson's policy, Hubert Humphrey represented, for many people, a Democratic Party committed to staying the course. While mainstream opposition to the war was increasing, it found an unfortunate outlet in support for Nixon.

The result was a confused antiwar movement, which in 1969 encompassed both white, racist Nixon supporters in the south and black revolutionaries killing their CO's in Vietnam, white revolutionaries flying

---

22   Dan Berger, *Outlaws of America: The Weather Underground and the Politics of Solidarity* (Oakland, CA: AK Press, 2006) 99–104, describes Weather's support for the NLF; the cover of the book features a photo of Weatherman women marching with NLF flags in 1969.

23   George Schmidt, interview with the author, March 26, 2006.

24   James Boyd, "Nixon's Southern Strategy: 'It's All in the Charts'," *New York Times*, May 17, 1970.

Vietcong flags in Chicago and black civil rights leaders across the country still tied to a floundering Democratic Party. Great opportunities were overlaid with huge internal disagreements, and the radicals who would found STO at the end of the year were most likely at a loss for how best to proceed.

* * *

One social movement of the late sixties, the women's movement, cut across the grain of the others. Initially an outgrowth of women's involvement in the civil rights movement and the new left, by 1969 feminists had begun to challenge male supremacy not only in mainstream society but also within the left as well. The available targets were so many and varied that the result was a women's liberation movement whose ideological diversity nearly matched that of the antiwar milieu. It included everyone from lesbian separatists to revolutionary communists to budding capitalist functionaries. While these internal contradictions wouldn't become unresolvable until the early seventies, they were already exerting a complicated effect on the new left as a whole.

There were at least three versions of feminism in the United States during the late sixties, which might be termed liberal feminism, radical feminism, and feminist radicalism.[25] The first of these was to become in many ways the defining aspect of the movement, as middle-class, white women struggled to gain entry to the male power structure. Corporate jobs, professional careers, access to the military, and the right to work full time instead of being at home with the children—these were the primary goals of liberal feminists. The presumption was that women—at least, white, middle-class women—could be integrated successfully into the economic sphere without jeopardizing the health of capitalism. It turns out that they were right, even though wage disparities persist for women

---

25 These distinctions are artificial and a bit arbitrary, but are largely consistent with the taxonomy offered by the philosopher Alison Jaggar in her pioneering work *Feminist Politics and Human Nature* (Totowa, NJ: Rowman and Littlefield, 1988 [1983]). My usage of "feminist radicals" tracks generally with Jaggar's category of "socialist feminists." Ellen Willis, in a fascinating memoir-style reflection on the twists and turns of sixties and seventies feminism, uses the title "Radical Feminism and Feminist Radicalism." While she fails to define the latter term, her analysis is similar to mine. Ellen Willis, "Radical Feminism and Feminist Radicalism," *Social Text* no. 9/10 (1984), 91–118.

and men in equivalent jobs. With the possible exception of some Marxists who viewed this integration as a stepping stone toward the creation of a fully bourgeois society that would then inevitably be toppled by proletarian revolution, almost no one in the new left, men or women, had any use for liberal feminism.

The distinction between radical feminism and feminist radicalism, as the names suggest, was largely one of emphasis. Both camps rejected liberalism and looked toward fundamental social change as a necessity for women's liberation. But where feminist radicals tied the success of feminism to the broader project of social revolution, radical feminists saw the oppression of women as the root of social ills ranging from war to capitalism. This led radical feminists to criticize, and in some cases to reject outright, the rest of the left as a bastion of male supremacy and a detour from the essential work of freeing women as women.[26] This approach was always double-edged. On the one hand, it produced brilliant insights into the nature of oppression and resistance: the claim that "the personal is political," for instance, and the use of consciousness raising as a way to organize women in all spheres of life. Similarly, the critique of sexism and macho behavior within the new left, typified in essays like Marge Piercy's "Grand Coolie Damn," was clearly on target. She began her essay by noting that

> the Movement is supposed to be for human liberation. How come the condition of women inside it is no better than outside? We have been trying to educate and agitate around women's liberation for several years. How come things are getting worse? Women's liberation has raised the level of consciousness around a set of issues and given some women a respite from the incessant exploitation, invisibility, and being put down. But several forces have been acting on the Movement to make the situation of women actually worse during the same time that more women are becoming aware of their oppression.[27]

---

26   For a key example of this line of thinking, see Robin Morgan, "Goodbye to All That" (1970), in Rosalyn Baxandall and Linda Gordon, eds., *Dear Sisters: Dispatches From the Women's Liberation Movement* (New York: Basic Books, 2000), 53–57.

27   Marge Piercy, "The Grand Coolie Damn," *Leviathan Magazine*, November, 1969. Available online at http://www.cwluherstory.com/the-grand-coolie-damn.html (accessed January 8, 2012). Piercy is one of

At the same time, the prioritization of women's supposedly common experience as women underplayed the divisions between the lives of women of different backgrounds (black and white, poor and rich, young and old, lesbian and straight, etc.). This blindspot alienated many working-class women who otherwise might well have been open to the insights feminism had to offer. As a result, the work of radical feminists began to reflect more and more narrowly the lived experience of white, middle-class, educated women.[28] The trajectory from here to liberalism was never foregone, but neither is it hard to divine.

By contrast, feminist radicals emphasized the need to include women's issues within the overall analysis of the new left. Without ignoring the problems of sexism in broader social movements, they argued that women's problems could not be solved without simultaneously addressing racism, the war, and what new leftists called "the system."[29] For a number of women, including several founders of STO, this meant first and foremost addressing the concerns of working-class women, women of color, and the women of Vietnam. In doing so, it became clear that many of these issues—poverty and discrimination in the black community, for instance, or war crimes in Southeast Asia—were primarily about race and class, and only secondarily about sex. From this perspective, the limits of the radical feminist worldview seemed increasingly frustrating to the feminist radicals. In some cases, this led to a baby and bathwater sort of reaction, where even the important lessons of consciousness raising were dismissed as middle-class diversions.[30] The personal might be

---

many feminists of the era whose complex views highlight the limits of the distinction between the feminist radicals and the radical feminists.

28 The historian Alice Echols frames this problem in terms of the rise of cultural feminism during the early seventies. Alice Echols, *Daring to Be Bad: Radical Feminism in America, 1967–1975* (Minneapolis: University of Minnesota Press, 1989). Some of the internal struggles around questions of class and race within the feminist movement are described on pages 204–210 and 291–293.

29 Heather Booth, Evi Goldfield, and Sue Munaker, *Toward a Radical Movement* (Somerville, MA: New England Free Press, 1968) represents an early version of this analysis. Goldfield was subsequently a founding member of STO. Available online at http://www.cwluherstory.com/toward-a-radical-movement.html (accessed January 8, 2012).

30 Carole Travis, a founding and long-time member of STO, attributes this view to herself at the end of the sixties. Interview with the author, June 6, 2006.

political, but women doing ten-hour piecework shifts in textile factories have more urgent problems than being forced to conform to men's standards of beauty. The solution, according to the feminist radicals, was social revolution with a feminist twist.

Another, tangentially related development in 1969 was the birth of the modern gay rights movement during the Stonewall rebellion in New York City. On the night of June 27, police raided the Stonewall Inn in Greenwich Village, continuing a longstanding tradition of harassing gay men, lesbians, and drag queens in one of the only places they could then congregate.[31] For reasons that are still disputed today, the patrons resisted the police, and successfully forced them to retreat in fear for their own safety. In one of the most heavily queer neighborhoods in the United States, this small altercation quickly blossomed into a full scale riot during which 2,000 or more angry gays and lesbians fought several hundred police officers for control of the streets. At least two more nights of fighting followed, and the movement for gay and lesbian liberation burst upon the scene, taking obvious inspiration from both the black and feminist movements in its combination of consciousness raising and militant street tactics.

In later years, the lesbian and gay liberation movement would fracture under the strain of divisions similar to those encountered by the women's movement of the late sixties. Nonetheless, both gay and lesbian liberation and feminism were sources of great enthusiasm and optimism (as well as dread and derision) on the left as the decade came to a close. The strategic choices implied by the various tendencies within both movements ensured that no one could predict what the seventies had in store for feminism or for the gay movement.

* * *

A striking number of feminists, if only a limited segment of the gay and lesbian movement, cut their teeth on the student movement of the sixties, especially within Students for a Democratic Society.[32] SDS had grown dramatically over the course of the decade, from a small organization of progressive students at mostly elite universities to a massive network of

---

31   For more on Stonewall, see Martin Duberman, *Stonewall* (New York: Dutton, 1993) and David Carter, *Stonewall: The Riots that Sparked the Gay Revolution* (New York: St. Martins Griffin, 2005).

32   The most comprehensive historical account of SDS remains Kirkpatrick Sale, *SDS* (New York: Random House, 1973).

radical youth from all walks of life, including many who were not even students. But expansion led also to heightened disagreement over politics and strategy. Regular meetings of the group in the late sixties were marked by ever more bitter argument between two leading factions: the Worker Student Alliance and the Revolutionary Youth Movement. At the annual SDS convention in Chicago in June of 1969, the conflict split the group, effectively destroying what had been the largest formation within the new left and leaving the student movement in near total disarray.

The Worker Student Alliance was a front group for the Progressive Labor (PL) Party, which was the newest of the old left parties, having been founded in 1961 by dissidents leaving the CPUSA.[33] From the start, PL had prioritized work on campuses, and by the mid-sixties it had begun sending members into SDS. Around the same time, the leadership of PL began to advocate a pro-working-class strategy (hence the name "Worker Student Alliance") that criticized nationalism both in the black community and in Vietnam. Instead, PL argued for a combination of unite-and-fight approaches to labor struggles in the US and Maoist internationalism abroad. Their deference to Mao and to the working class brought them a certain amount of credibility within SDS, but their version of antiracism led to significant criticism. Among the initial opponents of PL's strategy was Noel Ignatin, later to become one of the founders of STO, whose open letter to PL was published—along with a sympathetic response from Ted Allen to Ignatin—under the title "The White Blindspot" in 1967.[34] Ignatin argued that PL inappropriately separated the struggle for black liberation from the efforts of the working class to overthrow capitalism, as if the former were merely a set of liberal reforms needed before the latter could be fully implemented.

---

33   In addition to Sale, background on the origins of PL and its subsequent involvement in SDS can be found in Dan Berger, *Outlaws of America*, 75–91, and Max Elbaum, *Revolution in the Air: Sixties Radicals Turn to Lenin, Mao and Che* (New York: Verso, 2002), 63–64 and 69–72. My account of these events is based on these three renderings.

34   Noel Ignatin and Ted Allen, "The White Blindspot," in *Understanding and Fighting White Supremacy* (Chicago: STO, 1976). This document was published repeatedly between 1967 and the mid-seventies. Sometime after his departure from STO in the mid-eighties, Noel Ignatin changed his name to Noel Ignatiev. For the sake of consistency, I will use "Ignatin" in reference to any document or activity that he was associated with during his time in STO, and reserve "Ignatiev" for statements made after his departure from the group.

"The White Blindspot" was the first written formulation of the analysis of white supremacy that would characterize STO throughout its existence. In it, Ignatin and Allen argued for the centrality of struggles against white supremacy in any working-class context. In particular, emphasis was placed on the need to combat white skin privileges, which in the view of the authors poisoned the well of working-class solidarity. The burden was squarely on the shoulders of white workers to adopt the demands of black workers as their own, not simply incorporate some antiracist rhetoric into otherwise white-led efforts.

While certainly controversial in its own right, Ignatin's view was welcomed by the anti-PL forces within SDS. In fact, Ignatin was recruited to join SDS partly on the basis of his letter, despite the fact that he was a factory worker not enrolled in any school.[35] By the time of the fatal conference two years later, one or another version of the white skin privilege line had been more or less adopted by a variety of people in SDS, including a small but significant faction of the SDS leadership, which coalesced primarily around opposition to PL and support for black movements. This faction took the name Revolutionary Youth Movement (RYM), and managed briefly to paper over its own glaring disagreements, long enough to expel the PL members from SDS through a set of procedural moves that were awkward at best and antidemocratic at worst.

Once the split in SDS was final, the conflicts within RYM came to the surface, with the Weatherman faction (briefly known as RYM I) retaining control of the formal apparatus of the group long enough to finally run it into the ground on their way to clandestinity. Opposing their efforts, if only half-heartedly, was the RYM II faction, which agreed on opposition to PL and Weather, and support for an orientation toward the working class, but not on much else. The collapse of SDS had soured RYM II on student struggles, and attention increasingly turned toward workplace and community organizing. But once again, political differences made RYM II short-lived, as it disintegrated after its only conference, in Atlanta in November, 1969 (which was attended by several of the soon-to-be founders of STO). Putting to one side the continuing efforts of PL to maintain what it called the "real" SDS, the organized student movement was dead by the end of the year, and even though hundreds of campuses would erupt the following spring in anger over the bombing of Cambodia, the linkages between STO and the campus left had been more or less permanently sundered before the group was even founded.

---

35   Noel Ignatiev, interview with the author, January 27, 2006.

* * *

In many ways, Chicago represented a microcosm of the left at the end of the sixties. Each movement described here was on display, and in several cases Chicago was something of an advanced laboratory for left trajectories that would later become more widespread. The city's large size, economic vitality, and geographic location between the coasts helped ensure that it was a place people moved to from elsewhere in the country. For the new left, this centrality was augmented by two factors: first, the presence of the SDS National Office in Chicago guaranteed that participants in the most advanced sectors of the white left visited frequently, and in many cases moved there temporarily or permanently.[36] Second, the infamous events surrounding the 1968 Democratic National Convention put Chicago on the map as an important center for militant social struggles. Not surprisingly, the founding members of STO represented something of a cross-section of the movements of the sixties, all based in the city of big shoulders.

Among the leaders of the RYM II faction of SDS who called Chicago home in 1969 was Noel Ignatin, who, as mentioned previously, was responsible for the initial articulation of what became STO's line on white supremacy and white skin privilege. His background included time spent in old left cadre organizations, and, as he recalled later, "I myself was still a Stalinist, with several important reservations."[37] He was heavily influenced by the writings of W.E.B. Du Bois, especially the landmark study *Black Reconstruction*, from which he drew the title for his polemic against PL.[38] Ignatin's attachment to Stalinism was challenged by C.L.R. James, who was living temporarily in Chicago in 1968. At the invitation of his friend Ken Lawrence (who would himself join STO in the mid-seventies), Ignatin attended a public speech by James and came

---

36   Sale describes the role of Chicago's SDS head office repeatedly in his book, beginning in the "Fall 1965" section and continuing throughout.

37   Noel Ignatin, "The POC: A Personal Memoir," *Theoretical Review* #12, September/October 1979. Available online at http://www.marxists.org/history/erol/1956-1960/ignatin01.htm (accessed January 9, 2012) The Provisional Organizing Committee to Reconstitute the Marxist Leninist Communist Party USA (or POC) was a small Stalinist splinter from the CPUSA formed in the late fifties.

38   W.E.B. Du Bois, *Black Reconstruction in America, 1860–1880* (New York: Free Press, 1998 [1935]).

away impressed.[39] James had made the opposition to Stalinism one of the two pillars of his political outlook, along with the opposition to white supremacy.[40] Ignatin agreed with the latter, and as the decade ended he found himself more and more in agreement with the former. As late as fall 1969, he could still criticize the Weatherman faction of SDS by favorably referencing the leading role of "Marx, Engels, Lenin, Stalin, and Mao."[41] Nonetheless, given his encounters with PL, his experience inside SDS, and the rapidly changing political environment, Ignatin's move toward anti-Stalinism was swift.

In addition, Ignatin had years of direct experience with factory work, which gave him additional prestige as RYM II moved closer to a working-class orientation. By 1969, he was working at the International Harvester (IH) Plant on the southwest side of Chicago.[42] When IH announced the impending closure of the plant (in a little-noticed sign of the massive deindustrialization that was to come), Ignatin attempted to combine in-plant organizing with the support of movement people. On the same weekend in October that the Weatherman faction had called for Days of Rage, the RYM II faction held a series of nonconfrontational protests designed to showcase their commitment to the working class.[43] One of these protests was held at the gates of the IH plant, which nonetheless closed its doors for good some months later and was eventually replaced by an expansion of the Cook County Jail.[44]

Three other founding members of STO, Marilyn Katz and Evie and Mike Goldfield, were also veterans of SDS. Katz had been actively involved in planning the protests at the 1968 Democratic Convention, as part of the tactical team that coordinated security and demonstration

---

39   Noel Ignatin, "Meeting in Chicago," *Urgent Tasks* #12, Summer 1981, 126–127.

40   C.L.R. James, *State Capitalism and World Revolution* (Chicago: Charles H. Kerr Publishing Company, 1986 [1950]), written in collaboration with Raya Dunayevskaya and Grace Lee, represents the most comprehensive of James's many attacks on Stalinism.

41   Noel Ignatin, "Without a Science of Navigation We Cannot Sail in Stormy Seas, or, Sooner or Later One of Us Must Know," in *The Debate Within SDS: RYM II vs. Weatherman* (Detroit: Radical Education Project, September, 1969).

42   Noel Ignatiev, interview with the author, January 27, 2006.

43   Sale details this sequence of actions in the section "Fall 1969."

44   Noel Ignatiev, interview with the author, January 27, 2006.

marshals.[45] She was specifically identified by prosecution witnesses during the Chicago Seven trial, although she was never charged.[46] Her expertise in the area of movement defense was enhanced by her relationship with another founding member, Bob Duggan, a martial arts trainer whose background supposedly included extensive experience in semi-underground revolutionary formations in Latin America.[47]

The Goldfields had lengthy experience with SDS, including work with the Radical Education Project (REP) of the mid-sixties, and active involvement in the student protests against the firing of feminist radical professor Marlene Dixon from the University of Chicago in late 1968.[48] These protests had led to the occupation of an administration building in early 1969 and the expulsion of dozens of students. Mike Goldfield was also employed at the International Harvester plant with Ignatin, and was enthusiastic about organizing at the point of production.[49]

In addition to her participation in SDS, Evie Goldfield was also active in the feminist movement, both within and outside of SDS. She was the co-author of a number of pamphlets and essays, including *Toward a Radical Movement*, published in April 1968.[50] The perspective of this piece is clearly aligned with that of feminist radicalism, as the pamphlet

---

45   John Kifner, "28-Year-Old Snapshots Are Still Vivid, and Still Violent," *New York Times*, August 26, 1996.

46   The testimony of William Frapolly, an undercover investigator and prosecution witness during the trial, presents the government's view of Katz's role in the protests. Available online at http://www.law.umkc.edu/faculty/projects/FTrials/Chicago7/Chi7_trial.html (accessed January 9, 2012)

47   Duggan subsequently became publicly identified with right-wing politics and founded a training school for elite bodyguards serving corporate executives and government officials, Executive Security International. A hagiographic capsule biography can be found online at http://www.esi-lifeforce.com/about-us/faculty/bob-duggan.html (accessed January 9, 2012). Duggan's apparent political shift may have been more extreme than that of any other former member of STO.

48   Sale identifies both Goldfields as participating in the REP in the fall of 1966. For more on the struggles around Marlene Dixon, see Arthur Hochberg, "U of Chicago Students Seize Building, Protest Woman's Firing," *New Left Notes*, February 5, 1969.

49   Noel Ignatiev, interview with the author, January 27, 2006.

50   Heather Booth, Evi Goldfield, and Sue Munaker, *Toward a Radical Movement* (Somerville, MA: New England Free Press, 1968).

ties together "women's liberation and the liberation of all people." Further, the essay highlights the plight of working-class women and women of color, while still addressing the concerns of middle-class alienation and general issues of women's oppression by social roles.

At least one other founding member of STO was involved in the women's movement in Chicago: Hilda Vasquez Ignatin, wife of Noel, was a contact person in the late sixties for a Chicago-based newsletter called *The Voice of the Women's Liberation Movement*.[51] Despite being of Mexican ancestry, she was also a prominent member of the Young Lords, a Puerto Rican revolutionary organization that had been founded as a street gang in Chicago in the early sixties.[52] By the time Vasquez Ignatin was involved, the group had undergone its political transformation and had expanded geographically to include radical Puerto Ricans in New York City and elsewhere. Her role in leadership was indicated by her selection to speak on behalf of the Young Lords at a rally during the RYM II demonstrations that fall.[53]

On the other hand, at least two female founders of STO, Lynn French and Carole Travis, did not have extensive involvement with the women's movement, although they had their own areas of experience on the left. French was a member of the Illinois Black Panther Party, headed by Fred Hampton until his murder in December, 1969. Under Hampton, the Illinois BPP was one of the most vibrant sections of the Party nationwide. It developed ongoing (though not always smooth) relations with the SDS national office, and with activist groups in other communities that were modeled in part on the Panthers, such as the Young Lords Organization in the Puerto Rican community, and the Young Patriots, who were active in the community of Appalachian whites who had immigrated to Chicago over the course of the sixties.[54] French recalls that she had been arrested

---

51 Ignatin's name appears on the inside front cover of Beverly Jones and Judith Brown, *Toward a Female Liberation Movement* (Somerville, MA: New England Free Press, 1968), in author's possession.

52 Her role in the Young Lords is confirmed in both Jeffrey Haas, *The Assassination of Fred Hampton*, 47, and Lilia Fernandez, *Latina/o Migration and Community Formation in Postwar Chicago: Mexicans, Puerto Ricans, Gender, and Politics, 1945–1975* (PhD Diss., University of California, San Diego, 2005), 196. Fernandez's dissertation represents the most detailed account of the origins and early development of the Young Lords in Chicago.

53 *Young Lords Organization* 1, no. 5 (January, 1970), 3.

54 See Amy Sonnie and James Tracy, *Hillbilly Nationalists, Urban Race*

shortly before Hampton was killed, "so I was in Cook County Jail and did not get out until some time after the funeral. I'd been beaten and sustained leg injuries that still cause me problems. I went east to [stay with] my parents for a few weeks, and gave a lot of thought to whether or not I would return to the BPP.… Although I ultimately returned to the Party, I was involved in the founding of [STO] during the interim."[55] She also proposed the name "Sojourner Truth Organization," after the former slave, abolitionist, and women's rights activist of the nineteenth century.[56] The name stuck with the group long after French departed, and despite the almost all-white demographics of the membership throughout its history.

Carole Travis was an antiwar activist whose main frame of reference was antiracism and a commitment to the working class. For a time she was on staff at the National Mobilization Committee to End the War in Vietnam.[57] Travis's father was Bob Travis, an active militant in the Communist Party who had led the Flint Sit-Down Strike of 1937, which was pivotal in organizing the auto industry and gave incredible momentum to the newly founded CIO.[58] "I grew up with my mother," Travis recalls. "She was more of a New Deal Democrat, although she was a genius and critical of everything, and she had a good sense of humor and was crazy."[59] She embraced her mother's opposition to racism, but she also retained her father's commitment to the industrial working class. The militant struggles at the grassroots that characterized the Flint strike and other early CIO efforts were a major influence on the initial workplace organizing of STO in the early seventies.

Sometime in the late sixties, Travis met and married Don Hamerquist, who was to become the only person involved with STO throughout the group's existence. At the time of their meeting, Hamerquist

---

Rebels, and Black Power: Community Organizing in Radical Times (Brooklyn, NY: Melville House Publishing, 2011), 66–100, for more on this process, normally labeled the original Rainbow Coalition.

55   Lynn French, email to the author, November 27, 2006.

56   Lynn French, email to the author, November 28, 2006. For more on Sojourner Truth, see Nell Irvin Painter, *Sojourner Truth: A Life, A Symbol* (New York: W.W. Norton, 1996).

57   See the capsule biography of Travis used to honor her at an awards ceremony in 1994. Available online at http://www.chicagodsa.org/d1994/index.html (accessed January 9, 2012)

58   Studs Terkel, *Hope Dies Last: Keeping the Faith in Difficult Times* (New York: The New Press, 2003), 102–108.

59   Carole Travis, interview with the author, June 6, 2006.

was an emerging young star of the CPUSA. He had recently relocated from the west coast to Chicago in order to participate in the planning of the protests around the 1968 Convention.[60] He had been favorably profiled in *Time* magazine, and was rumored to be Gus Hall's pick to replace him as head of the Party.[61] But things changed: Hamerquist was profoundly influenced by the new left, and was dismayed by the Soviet invasion of Czechoslovakia. His biggest political influence was Italian Marxist Antonio Gramsci, whose writings were newly translated into English in the mid-sixties.[62] Gramsci's analysis of hegemony and consciousness, and his commitment to the workers' councils as the basis of communist power, were to be hallmarks of STO's analysis throughout its existence.

Hamerquist and others briefly attempted the equivalent of a coup in the Party, advancing an alternative political program and convincing many younger radicals to join the party in an attempt to elect a new leadership slate. Having lost this effort, he quit before the Party could expel him, and set his sights on next steps.[63] He and Travis remained in Chicago, immersed themselves in factory work, and began developing the analysis of dual consciousness that would mark STO from the start. Their disillusionment with the CPUSA also led them to a critique of Stalinism that meshed well with the Jamesian approach that Ignatin was developing around the same time.

One additional person deserves mention here. Ken Lawrence, as mentioned above, was not a founding member of STO, partly because in 1969 he was still a member of the not-yet-defunct Facing Reality Organization, led by James and coordinated by Martin Glaberman in Detroit.[64] Lawrence had also played a role in the small resurgence of the Industrial Workers of the World (IWW) a few years earlier, and found himself profoundly influenced by the legacy of the original Wobblies.[65]

---

60   Don Hamerquist, interview with the author, September 14, 2006.

61   "Oregon: Marxist From Multnomah," *Time*, October 13, 1967.

62   Gramsci's *The Modern Prince* had been available in English as early as 1957, but his pivotal essay "Soviets in Italy" appeared in *New Left Review* no. 51 (September/October, 1968), 28–58. STO would subsequently reprint this selection as a pamphlet.

63   Don Hamerquist, interview with the author, September 14, 2006.

64   Ken Lawrence, interview with the author, August 24, 2006.

65   J. Sakai, interview with the author, November 9, 2006. For more on Wobbly resurgence, see Franklin Rosemont and Charles Radcliffe, eds., *Dancin' in the Streets!: Anarchists, IWWs, Surrealists, Situationists and*

This connection no doubt had some responsibility for the development of STO's initial "Call to Organize," which begins by quoting the famous first sentence of the Preamble to the IWW Constitution: "The working class and the employing class have nothing in common."[66] Lawrence also had extensive experience in the civil rights movement, and through Facing Reality was familiar with the development of the League of Revolutionary Black Workers. By the late sixties, Lawrence was a familiar face to several of those who did participate in the creation of STO, and his influence was significant on the early trajectory of the group.

In short, the founding members of STO were in some ways as diverse as the movements from which they emerged: men and women, mostly white but with black and latino participation as well, largely young and inspired by the new left of the sixties, but also with ties to the old left of the CPUSA and its various splits and imitators. The result was an eclectic mix of experiences and perspectives, which bore some similarity to the emergence of other groups in what became known as the New Communist Movement, while retaining a uniqueness that persisted over the course of the next two decades.[67]

* * *

The initial rumblings of what became the Sojourner Truth Organization lie in the RYM II conference in Atlanta, over Thanksgiving weekend of 1969. In advance of the conference, a small grouping of revolutionaries, including the people described above, had begun meeting in Chicago to discuss the future of the movement, broadly speaking.[68] As indicated, they took inspiration from the Leninist tradition, both in the US and around the world. The grouping drafted a paper to distribute at the Atlanta convention, advocating the creation of a Marxist-Leninist party as

---

Provos in the 1960s, as Recorded in the Pages of The Rebel Worker *and* Heatwave (Chicago: Charles H. Kerr Publishing Company, 2005).

66 Don Hamerquist and Noel Ignatin, "A Call to Organize," in *Workplace Papers* (Chicago: STO, 1980), 2.

67 For background on the New Communist Movement, see Max Elbaum, *Revolution in the Air*.

68 Much of what follows comes from two "Outline History of STO" documents, one from 1972, the other from 1981, both written largely by Noel Ignatin. The 1972 version is available online at http://www.marxists.org/history/erol/ncm-1/sto.htm (accessed January 9, 2012). The latter document in author's possession.

a key task for the coming period. The Atlanta paper identified several key attributes that were necessary if the new party was to succeed. It needed a theory and a line that could guide a comprehensive revolutionary strategy for the United States; that theory was Marxism-Leninism, and the line was the emerging analysis of white skin privilege. The line had to be tested in practice, and in particular it was necessary to be sure that success was a result of the line, not of the efforts made by individual leaders of the party. The party had to succeed in recruiting workers, not simply students or middle-class intellectuals, and including these workers in the leadership. The membership needed to reflect the demographics of the US population, and it had to be a presence in "the most important industrial centers of the country." Finally, it needed a sizeable and supportive periphery, people who wouldn't join the party but "were happy to see it formed."[69]

In this, the Chicago grouping was on the same page as most of the other RYM II formations. The hosts in Atlanta, for example, were in the process of forming the Georgia Communist League, which also looked toward the creation of a new party. But the similarities largely stopped there, as the Chicago grouping took far greater interest than any other RYM II groupings in mass (as opposed to cadre) revolutionary formations, in the development of revolutionary consciousness through collective action, and in the repudiation of Stalinism.[70] Further, STO's understanding of the white skin privilege line differed significantly from the analysis adopted by most of the other RYM II groups, some of which eventually repudiated the line completely as the seventies progressed.[71]

The Chicago grouping continued to meet after the Atlanta conference, despite the fact that RYM II was clearly doomed. By the end of the year, the collective decided to act on the paper it had produced and constitute itself as a formal organization that would act like a party on a small scale.[72] Just after Christmas, the Sojourner Truth Communist Organization was born. (The word "Communist" was "allow[ed] … to fall

---

69   "Outline History of STO" (1972).

70   These positions are clearly outlined in *Toward a Revolutionary Party* (Chicago: STO, 1976 [1971]), one of STO's earliest political statements.

71   Kingsley Clarke recalls Bob Avakian, then of the Revolutionary Union, denouncing the white skin privilege line as "bankrupt, bankrupt, bankrupt" at a conference in 1974. Clarke, interview with the author, July 6, 2005.

72   "Outline History of STO" (1972).

into disuse" about a year later.)[73] A meeting schedule was agreed upon, dues were collected, and two areas of work were prioritized: workplace organizing focused on producing an underground in-factory newsletter as part of the campaign to keep the International Harvester plant open, and community organizing efforts were dedicated to winning the release of a young black man who had been framed on a murder charge. The SDS/RYM/RYM II experience had left a bitter aftertaste in the mouths of STO's founders, and initially the group avoided contact with the rest of the self-identified left, preferring direct immersion in working-class communities. Although this policy was soon reversed, the insistence on mass work as opposed to a simplistic reliance on left coalition-building efforts was a continuing theme within the organization.

Over the course of the next fifteen or more years, STO would go through innumerable changes in membership; only Hamerquist, Ignatin, Travis, and Katz (as well as Lawrence) would play any significant role after 1973. The political transformations the group would undergo as the years progressed were even more important. The first major period of the group's existence, roughly from 1970 until 1975, saw the development of STO's initial ideas around the centrality of working-class experience (Chapter Two) and the opposition to white supremacy (Chapter Three), as well as the group's initial efforts to develop an organization that could sustain the fight for revolution in changing circumstances. It is to the practical and theoretical implications of these concepts, workers and whiteness in the context of revolutionary strategy, that we turn next.

---

73   "Outline History of STO" (1972). "Communist" was still in use as late as the publication of *Bread and Roses* in late 1970 or early 1971, but was missing from the first issue of the *Insurgent Worker* in May 1971.

Chapter Two:
The Petrograd-Detroit
Proletariat

In the fall of 1973, a six-day long wildcat strike took place at the Western Electric Hawthorne Works in the Chicago suburb of Cicero, Illinois.[1] About 150 men, mainly black and latino, refused to work in the twister department of the cable plant, where telephone cables were wound together by machine. Although the strikers were officially members of the International Brotherhood of Electrical Workers (IBEW), they viewed the union with total disdain because of its cozy relationship with the company. When the company laid off several employees and told the remaining workers they would need to pick up the slack, union officials counseled the men to accept the changes while their concerns were investigated. No doubt thinking of the many accidents caused by previous management speed-ups, the workers instead decided to shut down the department and walk out.

The strikers organized themselves well, and in addition to demanding a reduction in the work load back to its previous level, the removal of a racist foreman, the creation of a rest area near their department, and access to better medical facilities, they also demanded a permanent

---

1   Most of the information in this section, including the two direct quotes, is derived from an unsigned article entitled simply "Wildcat at Western Electric," *Insurgent Worker*, Spring 1974, 14–17, in author's possession. Author interview with Noel Ignatiev, January 28, 2006, provided additional context.

negotiating committee for the department, elected by the workers to deal directly with the company when grievances arose (thus bypassing the union altogether). The men elected a temporary negotiating committee made up of one black and one latino worker from each shift, and they immediately established a picket line to raise plant-wide awareness of their actions. The company was willing to meet with the negotiating committee, but no concessions were forthcoming, and the workers were told to return to work by the following week or be fired en mass. IBEW officials told the workers their strike was illegal and that no aid would come from the union if they didn't end the walkout by the company's stated deadline.

A total of 26,000 workers were employed at the massive facility, and in living memory there had never been any sort of organized work stoppage at the plant, whether authorized or wildcat. Given the miniscule numbers in the twister department, the strike was hardly major news to the outside world. For much of Chicago's left, however, the implications were significant. The walkout was seen as more evidence of the growing militancy of workers in heavy industry, and as a prime opportunity to distribute radical literature and recruit new members. But there was a problem: the strikers weren't interested. As one worker explained, "We don't want any communists, socialists, movies, raps, leaflets, newspapers, newspaper interviews, photographs, lectures or anything else."[2] Most Marxist organizations viewed this sort of rejection as a kind of working-class anticommunism and abandoned the struggle in frustration.

One of the only left groups that established ongoing communication with the strikers was the Sojourner Truth Organization, which had been observing the Hawthorne Works since at least May 1971. That month, the first issue of the *Insurgent Worker* focused heavily on problems there and, in an editorial provocatively entitled "Western Electric: We Shall Bury You," opined that "if there is any crime against the working people for which Western Electric can escape responsibility, we haven't been able to discover it."[3] Two years later, when the twister department workers asked the Labor Committee of the Chicago branch of the National Lawyers Guild (NLG) for advice on the legality of the strike, several STO members on the Committee were able to establish contact with the strikers.[4] The men

---

2   "Wildcat at Western Electric," 16. Noel Ignatiev remembered almost exactly the same phrasing during an interview in January, 2006.

3   "Western Electric: We Shall Bury You," *Insurgent Worker*, May 1971, 2.

4   At the time, several members of STO were lawyers, and as a result the

accepted both legal assistance and an offer to print leaflets on STO's press. According to one STO member, "in this situation, one in which we had no direct influence, we felt the best we could do was to ready ourselves to help execute any plans the workers would come up with, putting our full resources and ideas at their disposal if they desired."[5] Ten thousand leaflets, written by the strikers and printed by STO, were distributed to other workers at the plant, and having received some key legal advice from the NLG Labor Committee, the men found themselves negotiating from a position of strength.

After six days, and with the pressure building, the company management agreed to every one of the workers' demands, but in exchange they required that the men stop discussing the situation with other workers. Unfortunately, this "code of silence" proved to be the undoing of the strike gains, as the company proceeded to transfer the most militant workers—including the original members of the permanent negotiating committee—to other departments and otherwise disrupt the momentum gained from the immediate victory. Having deliberately accepted the limits the men placed on outside involvement in the strike, STO could only stand by and watch this final act play out, despite its assessment that broad solidarity efforts, within the factory and outside it, were the only chance for long-term success in the plant.

There are literally hundreds of stories much like this one, describing various workplace interventions made by the Sojourner Truth Organization during the early seventies. In this case, the course of events reflects both what STO had in common with other left groups—an emphasis on organizing at the point of production—and what made the group unique—a commitment to the autonomy of workers in struggle. At the same time, the course of the Western Electric wildcat strike is representative of both the strengths and the weaknesses of STO's approach to workplace organizing. Before assessing these aspects of the group's work, however, it is essential to understand why STO (and other left groups) were drawn to situations like the twister department walkout in the first place.

* * *

group exerted significant influence on the local NLG chapter, and the Labor Committee in particular. Author interview with Kingsley Clarke, July 6, 2005.

5   "Wildcat at Western Electric," 17.

The interest of seventies radicals in heavy industry has its roots deep in the Marxist tradition, in Karl Marx's theory of history. Marx believed that the development of human history was a dialectical process that necessarily went through several distinct stages, including primitive communism, feudalism, capitalism, and finally socialism and communism.[6] Each stage made the next one possible (or inevitable, according to some versions of Marxism), so that capitalism grew out of the internal contradictions of feudalism and could not have simply emerged spontaneously from early class societies like ancient Rome. At its core, this theory of history recognizes the interplay between objective conditions like the available level of technology, and subjective conditions such as social norms and modes of organization.

Consistent with this theory, Marx argued that capitalism necessarily produced the seeds of its own destruction in the form of the working class.[7] One distinctive element of capitalist economics is industrial production in the context of the factory. The creation of a class of workers whose lot in life is to staff the factories is a double-edged sword, however. As Marx argued,

> The development of the industrial proletariat is, in general, conditioned by the development of the industrial bourgeoisie. Only under its rule does the proletariat gain that extensive national existence which can raise its revolution to a national one, and only thus does the proletariat itself create the modern means of production, which become just so many means of its revolutionary emancipation. Only bourgeois rule tears up the material roots of feudal society and levels the ground on which alone a proletarian revolution is possible.[8]

---

6   The classic work on Marx's theory of history is G.A. Cohen, *Karl Marx's Theory of History: A Defence* (Princeton, NJ: Princeton University Press 2000 [1978]). A valuable critique from the left of Marx's theory (written prior to Cohen's book) can be found in Cornelius Castoriadis, *The Imaginary Institution of Society* (Cambridge, MA: The MIT Press, 1987), especially pp. 15–54.

7   For simplicity's sake, but contrary to some Marxist terminological approaches, I will use "working class" and "proletariat" interchangeably, and will use "industrial" as an adjective attached to either phrase to indicate factory workers in particular.

8   Karl Marx, *The Class Struggles in France 1848–1850*, (1850) "Part I: The Defeat of June 1848," available online at www.marxists.org/archive/

One key way in which capitalism conditions the development of the industrial working class, says Marx, is through the imposition of discipline in the factory. Workers are forced to conform to various schedules, and they are also obligated to cooperate in order to complete their tasks. As a result, the proletariat is "a class always increasing in numbers, and disciplined, united, organized by the very mechanism of the process of capitalist production itself."[9] Further, in an era before rapid transit, factory workers necessarily lived near their workplace, and thus near each other. And as Lenin later noted, this "concentration of the industrial proletariat" "enhances their class consciousness and sense of human dignity and enables them to wage a successful struggle against the predatory tendencies of the capitalist system."[10]

As a method, Marxism's value lies in its ability to predict the future course of events by analyzing history. From this perspective, the experiences of the Russian Revolutions of 1905 and 1917 were seen by later Marxists as a confirmation of the importance of the industrial working class.[11] The centrality of the Petrograd workers to the inspiring but abortive events of 1905, and the correlation between the subsequent expansion of industrialization in Russia and the success of the revolution in 1917, convinced many revolutionaries in all parts of the world that, as Antonio Gramsci put it, "the industrial proletariat [is] the only class of the people that is essentially and permanently revolutionary."[12] The

---

marx/works/1850/class-struggles-france/ch01.htm (accessed September 15, 2011).

9   Karl Marx, *Capital: A Critique of Political Economy* (1867), Volume 1, Chapter 32. Available online at www.marxists.org/archive/marx/works/1867-c1/ch32.htm (accessed September 15, 2011). This passage can be found on page 929 of the Penguin edition (1990), which translates "trained" instead of "disciplined." Nate Holdren originally pointed me to this quotation.

10 V.I. Lenin, "On the So-Called Market Question" (1893). Available online at www.marxists.org/archive/lenin/works/1893/market/06.htm (accessed September 15, 2011).

11 For a thoughtful and idiosyncratic history of the 1905 and 1917 Russian Revolutions, see Murray Bookchin, *The Third Revolution, Volume 3* (London: Continuum, 2004).

12 Antonio Gramsci, "Parties and Masses," unsigned editorial in *L'Ordine Nuovo*, September 25, 1921, in Gramsci, *Selections From Political Writings, 1921–1926* (Minneapolis: University of Minnesota Press, 1990), 72.

universality of this claim was later challenged by the experiences of the Chinese revolution and the writings of Mao, but the lessons of the Russian experience were still seen by most Marxists as applicable to advanced industrialized countries such as the United States.

* * *

In the late sixties, at a point when many North American revolutionaries had turned their backs on working class, three major experiences brought renewed attention to the idea that the industrial proletariat was the revolutionary agent: the French General Strike of 1968, the Italian "Hot Autumn" of 1969, and the early successes of the Revolutionary Union Movements (RUMs) and the League of Revolutionary Black Workers in Detroit. In each case, the militant actions of factory workers reverberated across a society in the midst of great upheaval, and in the French and Italian cases, the strikes came close to fomenting revolution.

The French events of May and June 1968 began innocuously enough as a student strike at an elite university in Paris on May 2, not unlike the occupation of Columbia University in New York City that took place the same month.[13] Unlike at Columbia, however, the French strike spread quickly to other universities and other parts of the country. Cycles of increasing confrontation between students and police led to street fighting and the creation of barricades in many parts of the city, which quickly brought the conflict national attention. Young workers began to fraternize with the student strikers, and as the police repression became more outrageous, popular support swung toward the students, resulting in a massive demonstration of almost a million people in Paris on May 13. The next day, a series of factory occupations began, with workers striking initially in solidarity with the students, while also adding their own demands. By late May, nearly 10 million workers were on strike, at least 100 workplaces were occupied, and France seemed on the verge of revolution.

---

13   For more on the French events, see Daniel Singer, *Prelude to Revolution: France in May 1968* (Boston: South End Press, 2002 [1970]), as well as Andree Hoyles, "The Occupation of Factories in France: May 1968," in Ken Coates, Tony Topham, and Michael Barrett Brown, editors, *Trade Union Register* (London: Merlin Press, 1969). This latter essay was reprinted by STO in the early seventies as a pamphlet entitled *General Strike: France 1968* (Chicago: STO, n.d.).

Sadly, the momentum of the French general strike dissipated quickly in early June. The primary reason for this about-face was the state's carrot-and-stick strategy. On the one hand, the major unions, including especially the powerful Communist Party-led General Confederation of Labor (CGT), continuously badgered the workers into making concrete—and "reasonable"—demands that were then partially granted by the various plant managers. At the same time, French president General Charles de Gaulle made it publicly clear that a continuation of the strikes would result in a military occupation of the country, with deliberate, if unstated, echoes of the bloody repression that crushed the Paris Commune of 1871. Fear combined with partial victory to undermine the revolutionary potential of the May–June events, and by the end of summer there was little evidence to remind visitors of the uprising that had just concluded. Nonetheless, among Marxist radicals in North America, the broad importance of the general strike was considered reminiscent of the Petrograd experience of 1905, while the actions of the trade union bureaucracies reinforced left-wing skepticism of the official labor movement.

A little more than a year after the French general strike ended, the Italian industrial working class rose up in a widespread rebellion known as the Hot Autumn.[14] When a number of major union contracts came up for renewal simultaneously in the fall of 1969, the collaboration between the company bosses and the union bureaucrats was plain to see. At the same time, the Italian government was in the beginning stages of a lengthy campaign to foment fascist paramilitary violence against leftists and working-class militants. For instance, the left charged that clandestine organizations of the far right with ties to the Italian state were responsible for a series of terrorist attacks in and around Milan over the course of 1969. But in contrast to the French situation, where partial concessions and the fear of repression had helped pacify the workers, major Italian factories like Fiat and Pirelli were in large part staffed by internal migrants from southern Italy, whose agrarian backgrounds included extensive experience with direct action and sometimes violent confrontation, but only limited previous interaction with trade unions. As a result, maneuvering by union officials failed to impress the rank and

---

14 The single best source on the Hot Autumn remains Robert Lumley, *States of Emergency: Cultures of Revolt in Italy, 1968–1978* (London: Verso, 1990). Much of the text of this book is available online at http://libcom.org/history/states-emergency-cultures-revolt-italy-1968-1978 (accessed September 15, 2011).

file, while incidents of fascist terror to a great extent only reinforced the militancy of the working class.

The Hot Autumn featured a number of factory occupations, and ultimately resulted in enormous concessions from management, including an average wage increase of almost 25 percent. More importantly, however, the Italian events highlighted the role of a type of permanent organization of workers outside the trade unions. The two most important of these organizations were Potere Operaio (Workers' Power) and Lotta Continua (Continuous Struggle). Both groups attempted to intervene as conscious revolutionaries in the wide range of working-class struggles typified by the Hot Autumn, but did so neither as representatives of a vanguard party nor as partisans of the traditional labor unions. In the process they built networks of factory committees on a city-wide and even regional basis. This new form of organization was paralleled by the development of new theories of revolution based on the experiences of Italian workers in struggle. These theories were grouped under the general heading of *operaismo*, or "workerism."[15] The key theoretical innovation to come out of the Italian context was "autonomy," meaning the autonomy of the working class not only from capital, but also from its "official" representatives in the unions and from its would-be vanguards in the Leninist left. In the North American context, most of the New Communist Movement took inspiration from the Hot Autumn's factory occupations, while ignoring or rejecting its organizational and theoretical innovations.[16] For STO, however, these elements were to prove decisive in the creation of a novel approach to workplace organizing.

---

15   This use of "workerism" must be distinguished from the more common English usage as (more or less) a synonym for syndicalism. The latter usage was for a time in the early seventies much more common within the New Communist Movement, and within STO. I will use "operaismo" to describe the former, and "workerism" to describe the latter.

16   On the positive response of US leftists to the Italian Hot Autumn, see Max Elbaum, *Revolution in the Air: Sixties Radicals Turn to Marx, Che and Mao* (London: Verso, 2002), 88. For contemporaneous US responses to the Hot Autumn and the Italian far left of that era, see two issues of *Radical America* 5, no. 5, September/October, 1971, and 7, no. 2, March/April, 1973. For a marvelously comprehensive analysis of the theoretical universe within which the Hot Autumn erupted, including background on both Lotta Continua and Potere Operaio, see Steve Wright, *Storming Heaven: Class Composition and Struggle in Italian Autonomist Marxism* (London: Pluto Press, 2002).

Closer to home, the trajectory of the various Revolutionary Union Movements (RUMs) and later the League of Revolutionary Black Workers in Detroit was perhaps even more inspiring than the Italian and French events, even though it was much smaller in its impact and even more fragile in its outcomes. The inspiring aspect of the Detroit experience was precisely in its location: Detroit was a) in the United States rather than in Europe, and b) largely black in a country where all recent radical movements had either emerged from the black community or else in response to movements within the black community. The radicals who subsequently formed the League had in fact established direct contact with many of the Italian radicals in the winter before the Hot Autumn, when John Watson, who was later to serve on the League's Executive Committee, traveled to Rome for a conference on anti-imperialism.[17] As was noted in Chapter One, Detroit was hardly unique in producing militant rank and file labor struggles, but the sophistication of the LRBW gave the city enough national prominence on the left that, decades later, Noel Ignatiev could still speak of the "Petrograd-Detroit industrial proletariat" as the model for STO's initial forays into workplace organizing.[18]

* * *

Having recognized the importance of Detroit, and of the general wave of wildcat strikes and other workplace struggle of the late sixties and early seventies, the question remained, how to explain them? Why was the labor peace of the post-World War II era eroding so quickly? For much of the Marxist left, the answer lay in a combination of Leninist dogma and romantic admiration for the black liberation movement. For the Sojourner Truth Organization, however, the reasons were more complex, and provided the key to a proper revolutionary strategy.

In attempting to understand the seemingly spontaneous militancy of industrial workers as the sixties progressed, STO and in particular Don Hamerquist turned to the theories of the Italian Communist Antonio Gramsci.[19] Gramsci was a gifted organizer and thinker who was active

---

17   Dan Georgakas and Marvin Surkin, *Detroit: I Do Mind Dying* (Boston: South End Press, 1998 [1975]), 49–51.

18   Telephone interview with Noel Ignatiev, July 16, 2005.

19   Much of the information that follows comes from Quintin Hoare and Geoffrey Nowell Smith, "General Introduction," in Antonio Gramsci, *Selections from the Prison Notebooks* (New York: International Publishers, 1971).

in Marxist politics in Italy throughout most of his relatively short life. After the Russian Revolution he helped create the Communist Party of Italy (PCI), and partly as a result, he was imprisoned by Mussolini in 1926, where he remained until his death in 1937 at age forty-six. While confined, he wrote regularly, and produced a series of works, known collectively as *The Prison Notebooks*, that went unpublished until long after his death. Here, Gramsci developed his signature contribution to revolutionary theory, the idea of "hegemony." In general terms, hegemony describes the hold that bourgeois consciousness exerts over the worldview of all who live under capitalism. That is, the parameters of a capitalist economy—wage labor, exploitation, and so forth—are seen as permanent and unchangeable, impervious to challenge by the working class or by anybody else. On one level, this was simply a reformulation of Marx's famous dictum that "The ideas of the ruling class are in every epoch the ruling ideas."[20] Nonetheless, Gramsci's analysis of hegemony represented a significant innovation in Marxist theory, because it provided a basis for understanding the continued survival of capitalism while simultaneously opening a path to its overthrow. If bourgeois hegemony could be challenged, then the willingness of workers to accept partial concessions would give way to a generalized revolutionary consciousness and struggle. For Hamerquist, hegemony helped describe the contradictory experience of working-class life in the United States, which he reformulated as "dual consciousness."[21] According to this framework, "The working class as it exists under capitalism has two conceptions of the world. One is essentially capitalist. It accepts private property as necessary; sees competitiveness, acquisitiveness, and selfishness as basic characteristics of 'human nature'; and does not challenge the notions of right, justice, and freedom which serve to maintain the dominance of the capitalist class."[22] In contrast, proletarian consciousness presaged the potential for a new organization of society, communism. According to *Toward a*

---

20   Karl Marx, *The German Ideology* (1846), Chapter One, Part B. Available online at http://www.marxists.org/archive/marx/works/1845/german-ideology/ch01b.htm (accessed September 15, 2011).

21   See Sojourner Truth Organization, *Toward a Revolutionary Party: Ideas on Strategy and Organization* (Chicago: STO, 1976 [1971]). Hereafter, *TARP*. This pamphlet was officially signed by STO, but was largely written by Hamerquist. The full text is available online at http://sojournertruth.net/tarp.html (accessed September 15, 2011).

22   Hamerquist, "Reflections on Organizing" (1970), in Sojourner Truth Organization, *Workplace Papers* (Chicago: STO, 1980), 11.

Revolutionary Party, one of STO's earliest pamphlets, "The second factor determining the content of working-class ideology is the potential of that class to become a ruling class. This potential is manifested in, and demonstrated by, ideas and actions which run counter to the capitalist conception of the world. As has been said, these ideas and actions become mass phenomena during periods of sharp struggle...often being articulated as the explicit basis of the struggle."[23] Hamerquist maintained that this process was possible only in and through the collective actions of the working class itself: in particular, moments of intense class struggle at the point of production can help accelerate the process of replacing bourgeois with proletarian consciousness.

According to STO, bourgeois consciousness in North America was manifested in a variety of ways, including the limits placed on radical organizing by the commitment to trade unions and to general notions of legality. However, the most important example of bourgeois consciousness was white supremacy, and in particular the attachment of white workers to the privileges of white skin. This issue will be discussed in greater detail in Chapter Three, but for now it is important to note that STO identified white skin privilege as symptomatic and exemplary of a broader obstacle to revolution, not simply as an isolated question of racist ideas. Similarly, white supremacy was never viewed as primarily an issue of attitudes and opinions, because Marxism maintained that consciousness was the result of material conditions. The group argued strongly for the position that white supremacy had a material basis in the development of capitalism in North America, and regularly reprinted the writings on this topic by Ted Allen (who was never himself a member of STO).[24]

This conception of consciousness and the revolutionary potential of the working class was unusual, to say the least, within the developing New Communist Movement of the early seventies. Most other groups involved in point-of-production work, whether based in the Trotskyist or Maoist traditions, maintained the traditional position associated with Lenin's well-known tract *What is to be Done?*: workers themselves can only obtain the sort of "trade union consciousness" that leads them to accept partial concessions from management in a permanently reformist cycle.

---

23   *TARP*, 32. Ellipsis in original.
24   See, for example, Ted Allen, "White Supremacy in US History" (1973), in the collection *Understanding and Fighting White Supremacy* (Chicago: STO, 1976). This text is available online at http://www.sojournertruth.net/whitesupremushist.html (accessed September 15, 2011).

Thus, the class will remain divided and ineffectual until the intervention of organized, conscious revolutionaries transforms the perspective of the workers from the outside, creating the "revolutionary consciousness" that is necessary for the overthrow of capitalism.[25] This line of thinking led to the creation of multiple self-appointed vanguard parties throughout the seventies, including the Revolutionary Communist Party (previously the Revolutionary Union, or RU) and the Communist Party Marxist-Leninist (initially the October League, or OL). Both of these organizations at their respective heights were far larger than STO, each including hundreds of members spread across the country, and depending upon one's perspective, could be viewed as having been more "successful" in their workplace interventions. But their theoretical approach was never the only one available.

Hamerquist was a committed Leninist and certainly did not reject the importance of organized revolutionaries—or else he would never have participated in STO—but he believed that Lenin's original analysis of consciousness had been transformed by the experiences of 1905 and 1917.[26] In the context of radical agitation within the working class, STO's *Toward a Revolutionary Party* argues that "The connection between mass struggle and socialism must be organic and political, not a mechanical or literary gimmick like making the last demand on every program a demand for socialism. Unless socialist agitation and propaganda can be linked to the learning context of the mass struggle, it will amount, at best, to lecturing the workers on issues which their own experiences have not yet made real, and it will not take root."[27] In striking a necessary balance between mass struggles and small group revolutionary organizing, STO tended to emphasize the former, while its larger competitor organizations prioritized the latter.

One corollary to this contrast was that where other left groups focused first on the development of theory and political line, which could then be implemented in practical ways, STO looked first to the realm of practice as the place where provisional theories could be put to the test and evaluated. This difference should not be overstated, since all Marxist

---

25   V.I. Lenin, *What is to be Done? Burning Questions of our Movement* (1902), available online at http://www.marxists.org/archive/lenin/works/1901/witbd/ (accessed September 15, 2011).

26   This is sometimes portrayed as the contrast between the Lenin of *What is to be Done?* and the Lenin of *State and Revolution*, which was written in 1917, on the eve of the Bolshevik seizure of power in Russia.

27   *TARP*, 13.

groups recognized the need to integrate both theory and practice in their efforts. Nonetheless, the distinctiveness of the STO approach is reflected in an assessment of the group's incredible breadth of actual organizing experiences during the first half of the seventies.

* * *

The guiding principle of STO's attempts at workplace organizing was the rejection of trade unions as the vehicle for their efforts. Following the *What is to be Done?* strategy, most other left groups of the era (especially the OL, as well as several Trotskyist organizations) emphasized the creation of opposition caucuses that could eventually take over the unions and turn them into fighting organizations of the working class. But for STO, the very concept of "trade union consciousness," combined with the Italian and Detroit experiences, as well as the overall arc of organized labor's increasingly corrupt history in the twentieth century, implied profound limits to the radical potential of the unions.[28] In this context, the classic experiences of the Industrial Workers of the World, from its inception in 1905 to its decline in the mid-twenties, provided an example of the alternative to the AFL-CIO. STO referred to this alternative as "independent mass workers' organizations," which more or less paralleled the Wobbly concept of "one big union." In its prime, the IWW had organized thousands of workplaces, led hundreds of strike actions, and throughout had shown complete disregard for bourgeois niceties like legality, reasonableness, and respectability.[29] The Wobblies reflected and crystallized the revolutionary aspirations of a vast cross section of semiskilled and unskilled industrial workers all across the United States. Beginning with Chicago more than half a century later, STO optimistically hoped to accomplish something similar.

In the early months of 1970, the influence of the IWW could be seen not only in the text of STO's first official publication, "A Call to Organize," which quoted the preamble to the IWW constitution, but also in

---

28 For an analysis of the conservative and corrupt character of the North American labor movement at the end of the sixties, see Stanley Aronowitz, *False Promises: The Shaping of American Working Class Consciousness* (New York: McGraw-Hill, 1973).

29 For more on the IWW, see Joyce Kornbluh, ed., *Rebel Voices: An IWW Anthology* (Chicago: Charles H. Kerr, 1998); and Paul Buhle and Nicole Schulman, eds., *Wobblies! A Graphic History of the Industrial Workers of the World* (New York: Verso, 2005).

two abortive efforts made by STO to intervene in industrial contexts. First, Noel Ignatin drafted a constitution he hoped would be adopted by a Chicago-wide federation of such independent organizations, "based on the expectation that it would shortly have chapters in all the major plants in Chicago and be widely recognized as a major force in industry. Fortunately," Ignatin noted sardonically in 1980, "that document has been lost."[30] Second, Hamerquist wrote a call for a Chicago-wide, all-industry general strike to be held on May Day, 1970, taking a page directly from the IWW playbook of six decades previous.[31] Needless to say, the strike did not come off as planned. Beyond demonstrating STO's initial naïveté concerning the immediate prospects for industrial organizing and revolution, these first efforts also clearly outline the group's refusal to work within the established trade unions. While subsequent organizing work was less grandiose, it was no less confrontational.

For the most part, STO's strategy took one of two approaches: either the group provided support to independent organizations as they developed in workplaces like Western Electric, or members of STO took jobs in specifically targeted factories and attempted to organize independent organizations directly, with and alongside other militant coworkers. The flagship factory for this sort of industrial concentration was the Stewart-Warner facility on the north side of Chicago, although similar efforts were made at Motorola, at the International Harvester Plant in Melrose Park (once the Chicago plant had closed), and in the steel mills of South Chicago and northwestern Indiana. In the early years, the organization was structured into multiple branches, and for a time each branch was associated with a major factory concentration, although in no case did every member of a branch work in the target plant.[32] In each instance, however, several STO members obtained work in each factory and set about organizing rank and file groups that always included nonmembers as well.

---

30   Noel Ignatin, "Preface," in *Workplace Papers*, iii.

31   Author interview with Don Hamerquist, September 14, 2006. Perhaps unsurprisingly, this document has also been lost. For more on the concept of the general strike within a wobbly context, see *The General Strike for Industrial Freedom* (Chicago: IWW, 1946).

32   See the unsigned *Outline History of Sojourner Truth*, September 1972, in Detroit Revolutionary Movements Collection, Subseries F, box 15, Reuther Library, Wayne State University. This document is available online at http://www.marxists.org/history/erol/ncm-1/sto.htm (accessed September 15, 2011).

The first part of building an industrial concentration was obtaining employment in the chosen factories. This was not always easy, especially for middle-class radicals with years of university experience in their recent past. Lies had to be told, job applications had to be fudged, and eyebrow-raising aspects of personal histories had to be rewritten for the benefit of hiring agents. When John Strucker, for example, applied for work at the Stewart-Warner factory, he needed to explain away the seven years he had spent pursuing his undergraduate and masters degrees full time. He concocted an elaborate tale, wherein he had completed high school but then had been obligated to take over the family hardware store in New Jersey when his father became ill. Being good with his hands but not much as a manager, the store had struggled for several years and eventually went under, after which he had headed to Chicago in search of factory jobs. This story was good enough to get him work as a lathe operator, a position he held for more than a decade. Early on, however, he was identified as a trouble-maker, and the company eventually researched his back story. Once they determined that no such hardware store had ever existed, management attempted to fire him. With help from STO's contingent of lawyers, Strucker appealed his case to the National Labor Relations Board (NLRB). Upon consideration, the NLRB ruled in his favor, noting that although he had in fact lied on his job application, he had lied "down," underplaying his credentials rather than overstating them.[33]

In the early seventies, the Stewart-Warner factory employed several thousand people, more or less evenly split between black, white, and latino (largely Puerto Rican) workers, of whom perhaps one half were women.[34] The plant manufactured a variety of electrical components for use in cars, boats, and other vehicles. It had a range of military contracts that were lost in the aftermath of the Vietnam War.[35] As many as a dozen STO

33 Telephone interview with John Strucker, February 5, 2006.

34 Kathy and Lynn, "Organizing in an Electrical Plant in Chicago," in *Collective Works* 1, no. 1, October 1974, 11–20. This piece pseud-onymously refers to the "AC" plant, and changes the names of STO members and ex-members then working there, in order to protect the then-ongoing organizing efforts. However, the description of the plant and STO's efforts there clearly match the descriptions offered in interviews with several former STO members, especially John Strucker, February 5, 2006.

35 This information comes largely from my interviews in 2006 with John Strucker, Don Hamerquist (who worked there for a time), and Noel Ignatiev (who never worked there).

members had jobs in various departments, and were thus able to slowly build a factory-wide presence for the group's politics. (Many other radical groups also sent members to work at the plant, resulting in something of a hot-house for testing competing approaches.) The first step was the initiation of a shop newsletter called *Talk Back*, which was published at least occasionally for close to a decade, well after the last STO members still working at Stewart-Warner left the organization (but not the factory) in 1978. Initially, *Talk Back* was published and distributed anonymously to prevent the company from punishing those responsible. As time went on, however, the members began to publicly distribute the newsletter as a way to build solidarity within the factory. In addition, STO members also produced and distributed a range of stickers in and around the factory, which were used as propaganda and as morale boosters.

This initial phase of propaganda and semi-anonymous agitation was paralleled in all the plants where STO had a physical presence. Newsletters called *Workers' Voice* were published and distributed at Melrose Park and at Motorola, where the name was later changed to *Breakout!*, and similar efforts were made elsewhere.[36] All these publications shared a common approach, using to-the-point arguments and avoiding obscure political jargon, while stoking controversy whenever possible. Issues specific to particular departments were given as much coverage as plant-wide problems, in an attempt to broaden worker interest and solidarity. Particularly corrupt union officials and especially hated foremen and managers were routinely criticized, insulted, and mocked by name. Instances of collective worker action, be they spontaneous or well planned, were reported as models to emulate. But STO understood that the goal of publishing such shop sheets went beyond simply providing information to workers. Hamerquist worked at Stewart-Warner when *Talk Back* was first initiated, and in an early analysis of the group's workplace efforts, he argued that "Since the function of leaflets and newsletters is not just general education or agitation, but to help create a base of independent organization, they must aim toward mobilizing the workers for certain specific struggles. It can easily happen that the literature can make threats, pledges, and calls to action that it can't back up with a base of real strength. This hurts. When something is put on paper, the authors are committed to it; and if they can't deliver, the credibility of their organizing work is damaged."[37]

---

36   See the "shop sheets" appendix at the end of *Workplace Papers*. Noel Ignatiev provided me with photocopies of dozens of additional shop sheets.

37   Hamerquist, "Reflections on Organizing," 10.

Recognizing this relationship between publications and organizing, an outside phone number or address was often included in the shop sheets, in an effort to include other interested workers. In most cases the newsletters either started out as or eventually became collaborative efforts rather than purely STO projects. This interactive aspect also allowed some of the publications to become limited forums for political debate, as when *Talk Back* printed a series of exchanges with a militant but racist worker who sent in letters criticizing working conditions in her or his department while also castigating Puerto Ricans for supposedly being lazy.[38] This provided the STO members and editors of the newsletter an opportunity to challenge the white supremacy that characterized even more militant white workers.

Another aspect of STO's approach to propaganda was the production of an agitational newspaper for mass distribution. Beginning in late 1970 with a single issue of *Bread and Roses*, a paper aimed specifically at working-class women, the organization consistently (if irregularly) distributed such newspapers to workers across the Chicago area until at least 1974. *Bread and Roses* depicted the struggles of working mothers, reported on labor struggles at a variety of hospitals, analyzed the causes of inflation, retold the history of the IWW-led textile strike in Lawrence, Massachusetts in 1912 that popularized the demand for "bread and roses," and criticized mainstream labor unions as unresponsive to the needs of women workers. In an editorial statement, the group popularized its views on unions and on white supremacy: "If we are ever going to get anywhere, white women must support the struggles of black and Latin workers for an end to racism and for equality. We cannot rely on the existing unions to fight for us. The unions do nothing for women workers. They are content to let us work for slave wages. They don't care if we are excluded from the better jobs. They don't even fight for our job security."[39] The paper also contained a four-page section in Spanish. Apart from the exclusive emphasis on women workers, *Bread and Roses* set the pattern for most of the agitational publications put out under STO's name over the next several years.

---

38   Kathy and Lynn, "Organizing in an Electrical Plant in Chicago," 13.

39   "What We Want," in *Bread and Roses: A Paper by and for Working Women* 1, no. 1 (n.d., but late 1970), 2. Amherst College Archives and Special Collections, Bloom Alternative Press Collection. *Bread and Roses* was also apparently the last publication to be put out under the name "Sojourner Truth Communist Organization." The May 1971 edition of the *Insurgent Worker* was attributed simply to the "Sojourner Truth Organization."

The group's next agitational paper was the *Insurgent Worker*, which was published regularly as a tabloid-size paper in 1971 and 1972, and sporadically in magazine size during the next two years. During 1973, STO members in Gary published the smaller and more Indiana-focused *Calumet Insurgent Worker*, which primarily covered news from the steel mills as well as other workplaces in Gary and the surrounding area. All these papers featured news STO considered to be of interest to working-class people, including updates on rank-and-file struggles at factories across the United States and abroad, advice on dealing with the legal aspects of on-the-job conflicts such as National Labor Relations Board hearings and unemployment claims, and analysis of major news stories like the wage and price controls instituted by Nixon in 1971, the prison uprising at Attica, and the course of the war in Vietnam.[40]

The distribution of shop sheets and agitational newspapers was a common tactic for seventies leftists involved in workplace organizing, and there is no evidence that STO was any more successful than, for example, the October League, either at integrating workers into their papers' preparation or at tying them to specific struggles. The distinctiveness of STO's approach to the workplace became more clear when, building upon the initial work of producing shop sheets, in-plant efforts graduated to supporting and even initiating organizing efforts within the factory.[41] These campaigns ran the gamut from small-scale attempts to remove particularly mean-spirited or racist foremen to plant-wide struggles around improving working conditions and health and safety precautions. Three elements helped clarify the differences between STO's efforts and those of the OL, the RU, and other groups involved in factory work.

First, one common example of left work in factories was missing from the STO approach: attempts to change the union leadership. In contrast to other left groups that focused their efforts on developing oppositional caucuses that could challenge corrupt union bureaucrats, STO argued that the institution of the trade union was itself the problem, and that changing the names on the leadership slate would, at best, have no effect, or, at worst, make workers even more complacent than they had previously been. At Stewart-Warner, for example, *Talk Back* mocked the

---

40   See *Insurgent Worker* Nov–Dec. 1971 on the controls and on Attica, and *Insurgent Worker* June/July 1972 on Vietnam and GI resistance.

41   In some cases the progression was in the opposite direction: campaigns first, publications second, although in most of the major points of concentration, and certainly at Stewart-Warner, the publications came first. Kathy and Lynn, "Organizing in an Electrical Plant in Chicago."

inner-union caucus efforts by promoting a garbage can, "Filthy Billy" Trash, as a "CANdidate" for president of the local.[42]

This abstention, which was criticized by skeptics both inside and outside STO, extended even to the level of departmental steward, which represented to many leftists both a winnable and a meaningful position in the union hierarchy. Stewards have responsibility for pursuing worker grievances, and the choice between a responsive steward and a corrupt one can make the difference between success and failure in any number of meaningful on-the-job crises. Nonetheless, STO's critical perspective on trade unions led the group to decide that no STO member could run for steward, although members did sometimes support, and shop sheets periodically reported on, the candidacies of militant coworkers.[43] As we shall see, this position did not go unchallenged within the group as the seventies progressed.

Of course, not all workplaces were unionized. In nonunion plants, a different set of problems presented themselves, but the contrast between STO and other left groups attempting to organize workers remained. At the Motorola factory on the west side of Chicago, for example, STO members were involved in the creation of the Motorola Organizing Committee and the publication of the newsletter *Breakout!* For a group like the International Socialists this might have been a prelude to an organizing drive to bring in a progressive but mainstream union and demand a first contract. But even after several years of activity in the plant, the editors of *Breakout!* could write: "We do not work for any union. We are not against unions, but mostly we are for people fighting the company."[44] Just as in unionized factories, the STO members at Motorola didn't think unions were a productive way to fight the company, so they never attempted to bring one in.

---

42 *Talk Back* 2, no. 5, February 25, 1974, in author's possession. Sections of this issue, including documents from the "Filthy Billy" union election campaign, as well as other leaflets STO distributed on shop floors at other factories, are available online at http://sojournertruth.net/shopleaflets.pdf (accessed September 21, 2011).

43 In one case, an STO member at Stewart-Warner helped initiate a campaign to unseat a particularly corrupt steward, only to be forced to abandon the effort when no other candidate was forthcoming from the department, despite his co-workers attempts to convince him to run himself. Kathy and Lynn, "Organizing in an Electrical Plant in Chicago."

44 "Who We Are," *Breakout!* 1, no. 4, December 11, 1973, 2.

Another major difference between STO's approach and that of other left groups committed to industrial concentration related to the kinds of demands that were put forward in organizing projects. Many left groups pushed campaigns that promised to improve working conditions for all workers equally, such as across-the-board pay raises, in a version of the argument that a rising tide lifts all boats. STO members, by contrast, involved themselves first and foremost in struggles to improve the situations of the most oppressed workers, typically minorities and women. For example, the *Talk Back* group helped coordinate an eventually successful campaign at Stewart-Warner to eliminate a particular pay grade that was being used by the management as an excuse to pay black and Puerto Rican women significantly less than white women for similar work.[45] Organizing workers around this demand meant convincing the majority of the workers—all men and white women—to back a demand that had no immediate effect on their working conditions. The arguments advanced by STO members and their allies in campaigns like this were both moral and strategic, and, win or lose, they helped define the approach taken by STO to workplace organizing.

The third key difference between STO's work in factories and that of other left groups concerned recruitment. All Leninist organizations agreed on the need to create a new and truly revolutionary party that could serve as the vanguard of all struggles against capitalism; this included STO, which had made party-building a part of its initial self-conception as far back as 1969. Further, all these groups recognized that any such party needed to be demographically representative of the working class it claimed to represent. For the OL, the RU, and most other New Communist groups, this implied a significant emphasis on recruitment of workers, and especially nonwhite workers, to their organizations. For STO, however, the defense of workers' autonomy implied in the critical view of the trade unions meant that the involvement of workers in independent organizations in the workplace was *not* normally a first step toward recruitment into the group, but first and foremost a way to build the experience and self-confidence of workers. Further, the analysis of white supremacy and white skin privilege led STO to be even more leery of attempts to recruit workers of color (or "third world workers" as they were commonly known in the seventies).[46] In the end, few people joined STO directly from the shopfloor, and of those who did, almost none maintained their membership

---

45 Telephone interview with John Strucker, February 5, 2006.
46 Kingsley Clarke, interview with author, July 6, 2005.

for longer than a year or two.[47] On the whole, STO was less interested in recruitment than in supporting the autonomy of the working class. Thus, the group attempted to intervene in struggles that it believed might eventually result in the creation of a revolutionary party in the United States, but it did not generally consider itself the organizational kernel around which that party would develop.

* * *

This emphasis on autonomy was also reflected clearly in the effort the Sojourner Truth Organization put into supporting independent rank-and-file struggles in workplaces where the group had no physical presence, like the cable plant at the Western Electric factory in Cicero. STO intervened, in its unique fashion, in dozens of such workplace campaigns, attempting in every case to aid in the creation of the same independent mass workers' organizations that were mentioned previously. In addition to the twister department experience, two other examples provide substantial insight into the successes and failures of the organization's approach: the Gateway struggle and the nationwide independent truckers' strike of 1974.

Gateway Industries ran a small factory on the southeast side of Chicago that for unknown reasons manufactured the odd pairing of dishwasher detergent and seatbelts.[48] In many ways, the plant was the opposite of a factory like Stewart-Warner: it was small (seven hundred employees at most), it had never been unionized, the workers were almost entirely immigrant women from Mexico, and STO had no physical presence in the plant at any time. STO members who operated a Workers' Rights Center in the neighborhood made initial contact with disgruntled former workers at the plant. The Center was primarily a legal clinic where workers from the surrounding community could get free advice from sympathetic lawyers and paralegals, who were members of STO. Among other programs, volunteers at the Workers' Rights Center helped people who had recently been laid off apply for unemployment benefits. In this process, STO members encountered a number of Mexican women who

47   Author interviews with Noel Ignatiev, January 22, 2006; Don Hamerquist, September 14, 2006; and Carole Travis, June 6, 2006.

48   Much of the information that follows comes from an unpublished memoir by Beth Henson, in author's possession, as well as the interviews with Noel Ignatiev, January 22, 2006; and Kingsley Clarke, July 6, 2005.

had been put out of work when the Gateway factory closed its doors in preparation for a move to Mexico. Then-member Beth Henson was their primary contact at the Center, and she recalls their anger about the situation:

> Estela, a formidable woman in her forties, who had worked there for over a decade, told me how management had brought in new machines a year before shutting down in Chicago. "We taught them how to run those machines; they didn't teach us. They sent us their so-called experts but their experts didn't know how to run production, *we* knew how to run production. We were the ones who were there every day, not them. They were in the front office, drinking coffee. We showed them how to do it and then they took it away and went to teach it to someone else. They left us here with nothing, after we showed them how."[49]

With a little prompting from STO, the women decided to fight the plant closure. They called a demonstration and distributed leaflets (again, written by the workers and printed by STO), which succeeded in getting the attention of Gateway's management. The personnel officer contacted the Workers' Rights Center and agreed to meet with Kingsley Clarke, the main attorney at the Center, to discuss the situation. Clarke was also a member of STO, and with his help Henson was able to gather the women for a sneak attack: when the Gateway manager arrived for his one-on-one, fifty angry, out-of-work women came in through the side door and cornered him. Under pressure, he offered the women jobs at a new factory Gateway was about to open. The new plant was an hour's drive away, but as Henson remembers, "Kingsley and I thought it was a good offer and a kind of victory, but after some heated discussion, in a mixture of English and Spanish, the women refused. They even went so far as to tear up the contract we had drawn up."[50]

Was this refusal a victory or a defeat? This vexing question can be asked about almost all the workplace efforts STO undertook. In this case, the women remained without work, and even their sense of collective power was short-lived. But, to quote Henson again,

---

49   Henson, *Memoir*, 3.

50   Ibid., 5. Clarke remembers the same sequence of events. Author interview, April 2, 2006.

I'd seen a glimpse of a new world in the way they gathered themselves together and cohered, with their affectionate teasing and the way they made room for one another, the way they surmounted their condition as wives and mothers, leaving their families to fend for themselves (the table set, dinner in the oven). One of them had been so resistant to her husband's demand that she stay at home that the battle escalated into a petition for divorce. They became actors in the drama, lifted out of the daily routine. The struggle gave them a glimpse of power, a crack in a world whose order could be overturned. They had recognized again the way the company had exploited them, finally replacing them as if they were interchangeable units, and they had regained, too, their unity, discipline, and organization, brought about by the same common experience. I had never seen anything like it; it was a living demonstration of the development of the proletariat into a class. Our intervention had been incidental; we had provided only the frame and the occasion.[51]

Another such living demonstration was provided by a very different set of workers, the independent, owner-operator long-distance truck drivers, who went out on a several-day-long wildcat strike at the end of January and beginning of February 1974. The truckers were almost entirely white men, and in contrast to the women of Gateway, they each, theoretically, owned their own small businesses in the form of their cabs. Nonetheless, STO saw in the truckers' strike a kernel of working-class autonomy and power that was not so dissimilar to that glimpsed by Henson in the context of the Gateway struggle.

By early 1974, inflation in the US was rapidly driving up the prices of a range of basic necessities, including food, utilities, and fuel.[52] The last of these, the price of gas, was forced even higher by the Middle East conflict and the energy crisis of 1973. For owner-operator long-distance truckers, a small change in the price per gallon of diesel fuel made the difference between a comfortable profit and the threat of bankruptcy. In this context, a number of independent truckers' organizations sprang up and demanded an immediate reduction in fuel prices. It may seem odd

---

51 Henson, *Memoir*, 5–6.
52 For a useful analysis of inflation as a capitalist tactic during the seventies, see Harry Cleaver, *Reading Capital Politically* (San Francisco: AK Press, 2000 [1979]), especially 157–158.

now that a price reduction could even be a negotiable demand, but in 1974 Nixon's wage and price controls were a recent memory, so it did not seem impossible that the federal government would comply, if enough pressure was brought to bear. Pressure arrived on January 31, in the form of a nationwide shut down in long-distance trucking; across the country, truck stops filled up and didn't empty out as drivers stopped their rigs wherever they happened to be on the chosen day.

Gary, Indiana was home to a major truck stop, and STO took full advantage of this proximity. In addition to the members of the organization who already lived in Gary, at least two Chicago-based STO members temporarily moved to the truck stop itself to work directly with the strikers. Predictably, one of the group's first actions was to help the truckers design a poster, which was then printed on STO's press. The poster showed a photo of an actual striker's truck in the Gary truck stop, with a sign in the driver's side window that read "Shut down or shut up! Jan. 31st until …"[53] Around the photo were printed the words "Simon says … 'Get 'em rolling!' Truckers say … Hell NO!!" At the time, William Simon was the Federal Energy Czar and Deputy Secretary of the Treasury, and he designed the government's response to the strike, which was to order the truckers back on the road, but allow them to charge their customers more in order to offset the high diesel prices.[54] Many of the strikers opposed this because it would contribute to inflation and hurt working people across the board, whereas a reduction in the price of diesel would only inconvenience the oil companies. The "Simon Says" poster was distributed not only at the truck stop, but also to workers across Chicago, wherever STO had contacts. *Talk Back* also published a piece in late February entitled "TB Supports Truckers," as a way of continuing the discussion among Stewart-Warner workers even after the strike had ended.[55]

In addition to printing the poster, STO members offered the truckers technical assistance on organizing meetings, and helped them make contact with women living in Gary whose husbands, brothers, or sons were truckers who had shut down in other parts of the country. As Carole Travis remembers, "We were trying to extend their own sense of their own power, and give them tools to extend it. That's why we helped them come up with the idea of going to the community and using the radio to get women to come out who were from the area … even though maybe

---

53   An image of this poster is reproduced in the Spring 1974 edition of the *Insurgent Worker*, 19.

54   See "Payoff for Terror on the Road," *Time*, February 18, 1974.

55   *Talk Back* 2, no. 5, Feb. 25, 1974.

their husbands were in Missouri."[56] As the strike continued, pressure built on the truckers, both from the government—who had called out the National Guard in some states after strikers were accused of assaulting scab truckers who were still on the highways—and from families who were under greater economic strain the longer their husbands and fathers were away from home. In this context, STO members attempted to paint a bigger picture for the strikers, so that they could see the broader implications of their action. "So we would talk with them," recalls Travis, "'What are you doing? What do you hope for?'" These conversations had at least as much impact on STO as they did on the truckers themselves. Three decades later, according to Travis, "It's hard to really even remember in some ways, but we felt like we were connected—and we were connected—to some workers who were spontaneously taking on the power structure, and acting … It was wonderful."

STO was quite possibly the only left group in the United States to take the truckers' strike seriously. For most other Marxists, the truckers weren't of interest, largely because in traditional Marxist terms they weren't part of the working class. Further, even if they were included in the proletariat, as white men they reflected a highly privileged stratum of the working class. None of this kept STO from recognizing the incredible potential of independent organization in the transportation industry. The strike dramatically impeded the normal operation of capitalism, with both factories and stores feeling the shortage of goods that were sitting idle in truck stops across the country. Several major auto plants shut down temporarily, as did a number of coal mines. In addition, the truckers' status as owner-operators meant that they couldn't establish a trade union, even if they wanted to, while STO's alternative model of independent mass workers' organizations was spontaneously being implemented. The need for the National Guard highlighted the fact that the truckers made direct action a central part of the strike, even going so far as to dynamite a bridge in Pennsylvania.[57] In the end, however, the strike was lost, as one-by-one the truck stops emptied and rigs returned to the road. A handful of strike attempts were made in the ensuing years, but none was anywhere near as successful in shutting down interstate transit.

* * *

56   This and subsequent quotes are from the interview with Carole Travis, June 6, 2006. Ellipses mine.

57   See "Payoff for Terror on the Road," *Time,* February 18, 1974.

It was no accident that STO was well-positioned to support strik-ing truckers camped out in Gary, Indiana. From the beginning, STO's geographic base of operations was deliberately limited to the Chicago metropolitan area. Nonetheless, from early on the group placed a pri-ority on expanding its mass work to other regions whenever this was feasible. An early effort in this direction was the decision to send mem-bers to Gary, where they were to seek work in the steel industry. This was initially conceived as part of an attempt to build a working rela-tionship with the Black Workers' Congress (BWC), one of the succes-sor organizations to the League of Revolutionary Black Workers from Detroit. The League split in 1971, drawn apart by a combination of personal conflicts and political differences over the proper direction for the group. The Black Workers' Congress faction was interested in using the workplace organizing model pioneered by DRUM as a basis for radical activity across the country.[58] The first venue for this effort was the steel industry in Gary, Indiana, which resembled Detroit insofar as it was heavily industrialized and heavily black. Sensing an opportunity to build meaningful connections based on a shared interest in point-of-production organizing and an opposition to white supremacy, Noel Ignatin and several other members of STO moved to Gary.[59] While the BWC project barely got off the ground before the group changed direc-tion yet again—this time toward party-building efforts at the expense of mass work—STO maintained a modest presence in the steel mills for the next several years.

Once the steel connection had been established, STO looked to ex-pand its horizons further by publishing a special edition of the *Insurgent Worker* that focused entirely on the steel industry. This one-off project was a collaboration between STO and like-minded comrades in the steel mills of Detroit and Buffalo.[60] In a parallel vein, the group published a series of pamphlets over the course of 1972 that were intended for na-tional distribution. Some of them, like the criticism of the Revolution-ary Union's attempts (along with the now party-oriented Black Workers' Congress) to build a "United Front Against Imperialism," were aimed at

---

58   See Georgakas and Surkin, *Detroit: I Do Mind Dying*, esp. Chapter 7. The *Insurgent Worker*, May 1971, contains an optimistic description of the founding of the Black Workers' Congress.

59   Interview with Noel Ignatiev, January 22, 2006.

60   I have been unable to locate a copy of this paper, which is described in the "Outline History of Sojourner Truth Organization" (1972).

a narrow left audience.[61] Others, however, were pitched as how-to manuals on a variety of topics, and were somewhat more broadly applicable. One of these was a pamphlet entitled *Organizing Working Class Women*, which argued that women occupied key roles in the struggle against capitalism, even while it recognized that most women did not work in heavy industry.[62] This pamphlet was part of a continuing emphasis STO placed on women's issues, although it clearly positioned itself within the framework established by the feminist radicals. One of the pamphlet's major contentions is that "working women's power lies with their class, with the growth of working-class consciousness, and the development of concrete challenges to bourgeois society and bourgeois ideas. Through the development of dual power organizations of workers, proletarian women can identify where their power lies as a class, even though they may not be directly involved in production."[63]

Although the immediate effects of such efforts to project STO politics on a national scale were limited, the idea of intervening in a small way in mass struggles outside the Chicago area remained central to the group's strategy for the rest of its existence, even after workplace organizing had ceased to be a priority. A much more complicated attempt to implement STO's approach to point-of-production work arose in the form of the Farah Strike in El Paso, Texas. Four thousand garment workers at the Farah Manufacturing Company were on strike for almost two years, from May of 1972 until March of 1974, initially because several workers had been fired for attending a pro-union rally.[64] What began as a local labor dispute quickly became a nationwide fixation for labor and left movements, partly because Farah-brand blue jeans were sold across the country, but also because the workforce was overwhelmingly Mexican-American, and overwhelmingly female.

Like most other New Communist Movement organizations, not to mention the mainstream labor movement, STO took an immediate interest in the strike. The group organized fundraising events as a way to educate and involve factory workers in Chicago, and many of the shop sheets reported sympathetically on the women's struggles. In addition,

---

61 STO, *The United Front Against Imperialism?* (Chicago: STO, 1972).

62 STO, *Organizing Working Class Women* (Chicago: STO, n.d., but probably 1972).

63 *Organizing Working Class Women*, 4–5.

64 For more on the Farah strike, see Laurie Coyle, Gail Hershatter, and Emily Honig, *Women at Farah: An Unfinished Story* (El Paso: Reforma, 1979).

however, STO took the extra step of sending people to El Paso, first on an investigative trip and later on a long-term assignment to work directly with the strikers.[65] At the time, STO included a number of native Spanish speakers, and at least two of them spent much of 1973 living in El Paso, providing direct assistance to the strikers.[66] While other left groups may have sent similar delegations, STO's unique politics around trade unions ensured that its approach was distinctive. From early on, the garment workers had been officially members of the Amalgamated Clothing Workers of America (ACWA), but as usual STO encouraged the women not to place their trust in the union. For a brief period the prospects for collaboration seemed good, but internal problems in Chicago contributed to a sluggish response. A small number of members, including those who traveled to El Paso, were inspired by the possibilities of the struggle, but the majority of the membership was unfamiliar with the issues and apparently unwilling to be distracted from their own immediate organizing responsibilities in order to focus on a campaign taking place a thousand miles away.[67] As a result, the Farah strike remained on the back burner for the organization as a whole, and in the end the women put their faith in the ACWA rather than in STO.

* * *

Another problem area for the Sojourner Truth Organization during its workplace period was the cultural realm. Certainly, the group understood on a basic level the importance of popular culture as a motivating force in people's lives, but STO was for the most part unable to harness its power. Several former members recall a certain woodenness to the group's cultural work. Events planned for after-work hours tended to be educationals or fundraisers (on Farah, for example, or other important struggles from across the country), rather than simply arenas for the building of affinity and solidarity among workers. Former member Guillermo Brzotowski remembers a handful of dance parties that

---

65   Kathy W., "A Lesson in What Democratic Centralism Is Not, or How a Representative-Democratic Exec Did Not Work in a Revolutionary Organization," unpublished paper in author's possession, n.d, but approximately November, 1973.

66   This is described in the unsigned "Letter From El Paso," in the *Insurgent Worker*, July 1973, 10–13. Additional information came from author interview with Guillermo Brzotowski, October 10, 2008.

67   Kathy W., "A Lesson."

brought together workers from several of the factories where STO had a presence, but this was clearly the exception rather than the rule.[68] The fact that most early STO members did not themselves have children may have contributed to a blind spot in the organization around the concept of the working-class family.[69] Partly as a result, the group's members shared with many other New Communist groups a single-mindedness as organizers and political militants that partially alienated them from their target audience of coworkers, who were often impressed with their dedication but in most circumstances were unwilling to replicate it.

The root of much of this disconnection was probably the class division between STO members, who were generally university-educated and in many cases from bourgeois backgrounds, and their coworkers at factories like Stewart-Warner. One former member describes himself and his then-comrades as having no sense of "the richness of working-class life."[70] In reaction, many members of the group attempted to adopt certain cultural forms that they identified as appropriate to the working class, such as musical interests. Long-time member John Strucker maintains that "most of the time I was in STO, we were way into whatever music the working-class people we were with, liked. And, basically, Chicago being Chicago, that meant soul and blues on the one hand, and country and western on the other."[71] Similarly, Kingsley Clarke remembers "a certain shit-kicking Johnny Cash-like culture," that he encountered early on: "my first exposure to STO was in Gary, and on the second day they invited me to eat breakfast, and they were drinking whiskey for breakfast. And I think that was a bit of a posture."[72]

For some members, the posture transformed into a more developed political stance. One tendency within STO was labeled "workerist" because of the emphasis placed on integrating as fully as possible with the working class. In many cases, this manifested itself in the adoption of common working-class attitudes, including eventually a willingness to work with the trade unions. Noel Ignatiev recalls "the people who really

---

68   Author interview, Guillermo Brzotowski, October 10, 2008.

69   This problem was emphasized in author interview with Mel and Marsha Rothenberg, October 12, 2006, as well as in correspondence from George Schmidt, May, 2006.

70   Mel Rothenberg, Interview, October 12, 2006. It is worth noting that Rothenberg himself was a university professor and never worked in a factory during his time as a member of STO.

71   Interview with John Strucker, March 26, 2006.

72   Author interview with Kingsley Clarke, July 6, 2005.

dug in, got a house and wife and kids in Gary … some are probably re-
tired by now, if they didn't destroy their lungs."[73] From the perspective of
those who remained in STO for the long-haul, these people were inevitably lost to the struggle, as they made their peace with the unions, and
with the day-to-day realities of working-class life. On the other hand,
the workerist attitude was an important corrective to the woodenness
or posturing that characterized much of STO's early work. In the end, a
split in the organization over these issues would mark the conclusion of
STO's initial workplace period.

* * *

Internal disagreements over workerism were just one example of the
dynamic evolution of STO's perspective on workplace organizing: it was
never static, and was in fact subject to regular evaluation, challenge, and
reformulation within the group. STO's first formal publication was "A
Call to Organize," which was drafted by Ignatin and Hamerquist in early
1970. This leaflet summarizes the initial approach taken by STO, as well
as the optimism that characterized its earliest work. The text was subsequently revised and expanded as a pamphlet called *Mass Organization
in the Workplace*, which was reprinted multiple times. As early as the
beginning of 1972, however, it included a prefatory note to the effect
that it was "not a full and accurate picture of the production organizing
perspective of the Sojourner Truth Organization."[74] This cautionary note
exemplified the group's constant attempts to improve on its prior theory
in the light of accumulated experience.

By the same token, STO's internal discussions of the appropriate trajectory for workplace interventions were quite sophisticated, and often quite
heated. In the fall of 1970, STO held its first evaluation-of-work meeting.
Don Hamerquist presented a paper entitled "Reflections on Organizing,"
which articulated some necessary corrections to the group's initial conception.[75] In Hamerquist's view, STO's first efforts had been characterized by a simplistic understanding of the class forces involved in workplace

---

73   Author interview with Noel Ignatiev, January 22, 2006.

74   Note on page 0 of the January 1972 edition of STO, *Mass Organization
in the Workplace* (Chicago: STO, 1972).

75   Don Hamerquist, "Reflections on Organizing" (1970), in STO, *Workplace Papers* (Chicago: STO, 1980). This piece was also published in
edited form, and signed by "Members of Sojourner Truth," in *Radical
America* 6, no.2, March/April, 1972.

organizing, as well as a naïve understanding of the risks and benefits of direct action at the job site. For instance, he challenges the notion that younger workers, black and latino workers, and established rank-and-file militants shared a common openness to revolutionary ideas. Instead,

> The initial cadre of workers [within an independent orga-
> nization] must have a number of different characteristics
> which show up among different social groups in the fac-
> tory. It must be open to a general revolutionary critique of
> capitalism; it must be aware of the importance of organiza-
> tion; it must be able to provide leadership for the struggles
> that develop on the job. Workers radicalized outside of the
> job [e.g. black and latino workers and younger, counter-
> cultural whites] are more likely to accept a radical critique
> than they are to see the possibility and necessity of building
> mass struggle and organization. The trade union opposition
> might want to get organized and even accept a few revolu-
> tionary propositions, but they won't see why this should go
> beyond a struggle for control of the union. The leader of job
> actions is likely to be great whenever a spontaneous struggle
> arises, but to have no idea of what to do in other situations
> or how to relate job issues to general political issues. Each
> of these limitations in areas of possible support for our
> perspective help spell out the sort of political problems that
> are involved in implementing it.[76]

Similarly, just as different sorts of workers exhibited different potentials, so too did different sorts of job actions. In this case, however, a
single type of action, such as a strike, could take on completely different meanings depending upon its character. Thus, "some strikes involve
mass participation in struggle, but most clearly do not. No alternative
conception of the world is manifested in those strikes where the union
and management cooperate in the orderly closure of operations; where
picketing is only a dull and tiring public-relations chore; and where the
bulk of workers just disappear till a new contract is signed. And this is
the character of most present-day strikes."[77] The alternative to this dismal outlook was direct action at the job site. But one universal difficulty
of implementing STO's perspective was the tension between the need

---

76 Hamerquist, "Reflections on Organizing," 9.
77 Ibid., 12.

for direct action, and the risk of job loss or even criminal prosecution. This tension was paralleled by a similar conflict between the requirement that independent organizations be mass in character and the necessity that they be politically cohesive. The terrain on which these contradictions played themselves out was the question of openness and secrecy. In Hamerquist's view, "though the difficulties in functioning openly are certainly real, there is no alternative to using whatever possibilities exist and working to expand these possibilities as rapidly as possible. This follows from the absolutely essential role of direct action…. There is no way that direct action can be developed if a conspiratorial cadre grouping becomes a substitute for, rather than a means to, a mass organization."[78] Building on these reflections, and on the concrete experiences of members, the group progressively shifted its emphasis toward greater openness on the shop floor. In 1973, in particular, the organization prioritized mass work to the exclusion of most other concerns, including the internal functioning of the group as a whole, which suffered as a result.

* * *

Once this transition was underway, conflicts arose within STO around the implications of mass organizing. While the majority of members, including both the formal and informal leadership, stood firm in opposition to participating in intra-union reform efforts, a growing minority began to question the logic of this position. The disagreement manifested itself in the form of a debate over the right of members to run for shop steward. As indicated above, stewards were the lowest rung of the union bureaucracy, and in many cases replacing a bad steward with a good one led directly to improvements in working conditions as well as organizing prospects. In fact, more than a few STO members in multiple factories were asked by their rank-and-file workmates to run for steward, most often against particularly hated union hacks. In most cases, these members refused, citing an organizational policy that was often difficult for their coworkers to fathom. This process could be frustrating for all involved, although in many situations compromises could be arrived at, where non-STO militants ran for steward instead.

The frustration was perhaps most intense in the Westside STO branch, which was concentrated around the International Harvester plant in Melrose Park. In contrast to the undeniably corrupt IBEW local that controlled Stewart-Warner, a somewhat more progressive faction of

---

78   Ibid., 14–15.

the United Auto Workers was in charge at Melrose. Further, the radical origins of the UAW and its liberal reputation throughout the sixties and early seventies encouraged the STO members employed by International Harvester to pursue some tentative engagement with the union.[79] The branch established a Workers' Voice Committee, which straddled the line between being an independent organization and functioning as a dissident union caucus.[80] Michael Goldfield, who had helped found STO and was one of its most experienced workplace organizers, was drawn to the possibility of becoming a departmental steward; both his coworkers and his branch mates supported him, while other STO members were harshly critical. As early as the fall of 1972, such criticisms led Goldfield and his supporters to feel as if they were being marginalized within the organization.[81]

By late 1973, conflict came to a head at the meeting where members reviewed the previous year's work, which was held over Thanksgiving weekend at a retreat center in Michigan. In advance of the meeting, Goldfield and another STO member named Mel Rothenberg drafted a paper entitled "The Crisis in STO," which was subsequently signed by seven additional members of the group, including the entire Westside branch. In many ways, this document skirts the trade union issue, preferring instead to argue its points on the plane of STO's party-building efforts and the question of correct interpretations of Leninism (these issues will be dealt with in more detail in Chapter Four). However, the early sections of the piece contain an assessment of the organization's mass work, including thinly veiled criticisms of the extra-union orientation that guided STO's approach to workplace struggles. "The Crisis" begins by asking a number of critical questions about difficulties that the Westside branch had encountered in organizing at the International Harvester plant: "Why has so much direct action at Melrose not contributed towards the development of a growing, stable, independent

---

79   Author interview with Marsha and Mel Rothenberg, October, 2006. Similar perspectives are put forward in Al, Evi, Gary, Hilda, Jim C., Marsha, Mel, Mike and Pauline, "The Crisis in STO" (n.d., but fall 1973), unpublished paper in author's possession.

80   George S., "Critique of the Paper Entitled 'The Crisis in STO'," unpublished paper in author's possession (n.d., but fall 1973).

81   Author interview with Marsha and Mel Rothenberg, October, 2006. Nonetheless, Goldfield's proposals to prioritize mass work were accepted by STO in its annual review at the end of 1972. George S., "A Critique."

organization?… Why have we been unable to build a sustained, coherent, credible alternative to trade unionist forms of struggle?"[82]

In answering these questions, the paper identifies two factions of the organization that, while superficially opposed to each other, formed a unified obstacle to STO's success in the workplace. The authors label these factions the "workerist tendency" and the "bureaucratic tendency." The former is consistent with the earlier description of total immersion in mass work and an attempt at complete integration with the working class. The latter represents an approach that prioritized organizational growth and structure above mass work. According to "The Crisis," "these two antagonistic tendencies can co-exist and complement each other, not only in the organization, but at various times in the minds of the same individuals."[83] In contrast, the signers of "The Crisis" position themselves as a faction advancing the Maoist position of "politics in command," within which the theoretical line would determine everything. This they opposed to the "technique in command" stance supposedly shared by the workerists and the bureaucrats, all of whom, according to "The Crisis," emphasized a mechanistic devotion to tactics instead of theory.[84]

According to the paper, the roots of STO's crisis were to be found in the theoretical incoherence of the group's line on class consciousness, as expressed primarily in *Toward a Revolutionary Party*. The idea of "leading workers into an organizational form where they can 'experience' socialism in action," as implied by Hamerquist's dual consciousness theory, "shows a contempt for workers' immediate interests, refuses to rely on workers' ability to think and develop politically, and poses a behavioristic shortcut to class consciousness."[85] The question of a "shortcut" is key: dual consciousness theory ignores the necessary developmental process by which workers internalize the transformative vision put forward by conscious revolutionaries. By contrast, "The Crisis" advocates a return to the more traditionally Leninist theory of trade-union and revolutionary consciousness, which not coincidentally offered greater latitude to those

---

82   "The Crisis in STO" p. 2. Ellipsis mine.

83   Ibid., 4.

84   Ibid., 8. The phrases "politics in command" and "technique in command" were popularized in English by William Hinton, a North American farmer sympathetic to the Chinese Communist Party and the Cultural Revolution. See William Hinton, *The Turning Point: An Essay on the Cultural Revolution* (New York: Monthly Review Press, 1972).

85   "The Crisis in STO," 10.

interested in union reform efforts. In a follow-up paper with the telling title "The Role of a Proletarian Party in the Development of Mass Socialist Consciousness," this contrast is clarified:

> The difference between Lenin's conception of the development of socialist consciousness and the view put forth by the pamphlet [*Toward a Revolutionary Party*] is profound. While Lenin insists upon the difference between spontaneous consciousness, growing out of labor struggles, and socialist consciousness, and in fact makes the contradiction between the two forms of consciousness the raison de etre of the party, the STO pamphlet sees in the first the unclear and fragmentary articulation of the second."[86]

Two different sets of practical implications resulted from this disagreement. One concerned the internal character of STO as a revolutionary organization, which we'll deal with in Chapter Four. The other centered on the question of mass work and the trade unions. From the perspective of the signers of "The Crisis," STO's understanding of dual consciousness led to the view that "there are some features of the everyday struggle of labor against capital that are *intrinsically* revolutionary," presumably those that take place outside the trade union structure.[87] The documents associated with "The Crisis" never explicitly advocate union reform efforts, or any other concrete alternative to the independent organization approach they criticize. In interviews, however, many former STO members, from both sides of the conflict, remember the stewardship question as having been central to the dispute over the "Crisis" document.[88] A two-part shift was thus suggested, which challenged both the optimism that had characterized STO's approach to production work, and the perceived purity of the group's methods. Ironically, in down-grading the revolutionary potential of workplace struggles, "The Crisis" simultaneously restored union reform efforts to the central role in the struggle for working-class revolution that they played for the rest of the left.

---

86   Al, Evie, Gary, Hilda, Jim C., Marcia, Mel, Mike and Pauline, "The Role of a Proletarian Party in the Development of Mass Socialist Consciousness" (n.d, but fall 1973), unpublished paper in author's possession, 3.

87   "The Role…," 9. Emphasis in original.

88   Author interviews with Noel Ignatiev, John Strucker, Kingsley Clarke, Carole Travis, Don Hamerquist, and Marsha & Mel Rothenberg all confirm this perception.

The "Crisis" paper was hardly the only document drafted in advance of the end-of-year review. Some others were designed specifically to refute the charges leveled therein. One of these, with the less-than-scintillating title "A Critique of the Paper Entitled 'The Crisis in STO,'" challenged nearly every assumption made and conclusion offered in "The Crisis."[89] Maintaining throughout that the organization was going through a predictable series of ups and downs characteristic of any revolutionary organization, the "Critique" identifies the authors of "The Crisis" as the source of any pending crisis in STO. In particular, it argues that the "demagogy" of the "Crisis" document undermines the potential for resolving what the author concedes are "serious problems which are the result of positive aspects of our political line, our work and our growth."[90] The "Critique" hews closely to the official organizational policy on abstaining from intra-union struggles, while acknowledging that the previous year's intense emphasis on workplace organizing had hampered the group's ability to resolve internal problems in the short term. On the topic of trade unions, it argues that "The Crisis" was "posing a caucus strategy in practice and now in theory in opposition to the line of the organization [STO] on building independent organizations at the workplace," and that "there is a fundamental difference between this line and the line of Sojourner Truth."[91] The issue is posed in stark terms: "Either our theory has to change, or the people who insist on practicing a trade union position have to leave the organization."[92]

In the end, the latter is precisely what happened. By the time the review-of-work conference was over, more than a quarter of the membership had left the organization, never to return. Among the departed were some of the group's most seasoned workplace organizers, including the only person of color then active as a member, Hilda Vasquez. After nearly four years of existence, complete with organizing victories and defeats, slow but steady growth in membership, and carefully targeted geographic expansion, STO had suffered its first real split. It would not be the last one.

* * *

Goldfield and Rothenberg were not the only people to identify problems in STO's approach to workplace organizing as 1973 came to a close.

---

89   George S., "A Critique."
90   Ibid.
91   Ibid., 14.
92   Ibid.

That fall, the group hosted a visitor from across the Atlantic Ocean, a member of the British group Big Flame.[93] Big Flame had been founded in Liverpool in 1970, though by 1973 they had a presence in many parts of England. Like STO, Big Flame took inspiration from the Italian movements highlighted by the Hot Autumn, and, again like STO, Big Flame focused its work in factories. Thus it was understandable that the two groups would establish contact despite the distance between them. For Big Flame, STO as a group was important because it was "the biggest of its kind (our kind) in the States."[94]

Nonetheless, the visitor was not overly impressed with STO's theory or its practice. In a sometimes harshly critical report to Big Flame, the author excoriates STO for "being dominated by an informal hierarchy" and for lacking an educational program for new members. "The internal life of the group," according to the report, "is consequently full of problems—administratively, politically and personally." One such problem concerned the limitations of STO's heavy emphasis on workplace organizing. As the author notes, "The group also has problems understanding any political practice not tied to the workplace. They have no perspective (apart from a possible verbal acknowledgement) on community struggle. There is no understanding of the totality of capitalist oppression—sex roles, the family, personal relations—and therefore the need for socialists to have a *total* theory and practice, taking in all aspects of capitalist society." Although STO would eventually develop some theoretical and practical insights into this nexus, the issue would recur over the years, as described in Chapter Six.

The biggest concern expressed in the Big Flame report had to do with STO's problems in understanding its own role in workplace struggles. Despite STO's interest in questions of autonomy, the report argues that "although they've heard of the concept of autonomy, they haven't yet learned how to use it." Focusing on the early influence of C.L.R. James within the group, the report echoes some of the criticisms offered by "The Crisis": "there is no process or dynamic involved" in STO's conception of

---

93 The single best source for information on Big Flame is a website that contains both archival documents and contemporary reflections on the group's activities and legacy. http://bigflameuk.wordpress.com (accessed September 27, 2011).

94 This and subsequent quotations in the next four paragraphs come from the "Report on the Sojourner Truth Group in Chicago," unpublished paper in author's possession, n.d., but probably early 1974. Thanks to Kevin McDonnell for providing me with a copy of this document.

workers, "no dialectic which pushes the working class forward," leaving only the prospect of spontaneous revolutionary upsurge. On one level, this critique seems inattentive to the complexities of the dual consciousness theory that was then jostling for position within STO with the Jamesian "seeds of socialism" analysis, since dual consciousness as articulated by Hamerquist did at least imply a dialectical interplay between the bourgeois and proletarian aspects of workers' self-understanding.

Nonetheless, in practical terms, the report to Big Flame was not far off the mark. In the absence of any developed conception of autonomy, claims the report, "they fall back on the Leninist model of the party leading and educating the class, which adds further to their confusion, because it then becomes impossible to understand the dialectic between organization and spontaneity." Of course, to the extent that "The Crisis" advocated an unambiguous embrace of traditional Leninist strategy, Big Flame was even less sympathetic to this alternative. At the level of activity, the report points out that "any strategy is really based on exemplary action, that is [STO] trying to establish these [independent workplace] groups, and then in some kind of confused way handing them over to the workers." From the perspective of "The Crisis," the solution to this was intra-union reform efforts, but Big Flame shared with STO an extra-union perspective. Instead, the report seems to identify the source of the problem in the more general difficulty of attracting non-politicized workers to any sort of permanent left workplace structure. The only solution implied is the development and application of working-class autonomy, although it is not clear exactly how the author believed this would help resolve STO's difficulties.

* * *

Meanwhile, back in Chicago, Don Hamerquist also drafted a paper for the Thanksgiving conference, and while his contribution was not able to prevent the "Crisis" split, it did challenge some prevailing attitudes within the group while attempting to address some of the issues later noted in the report to Big Flame. "Trade Unions/Independent Organizations" directly acknowledges the sorts of difficulties the Westside branch had experienced in challenging the former and establishing the latter. In attempting to explain these problems, Hamerquist turns not to a criticism of his own theory of dual consciousness, but to an assessment of two underexamined factors: the flexibility of the trade unions and the instability of the independent, revolutionary, mass workplace organizations that STO championed. The unions, for their part, are not irreparably corrupt, as the group had previously tended to assume. According to Hamerquist, the organization's earlier writings on production work suggest "that the US trade unions cannot absorb a major insurgency because they are so corrupt that they cannot and will not even handle the routine defense of their members' interests. The evidence does not support this assumption."[95] As examples, he points to the AFL's recuperation of the CIO upsurge of the thirties, the British trade unions' cooptation of the militant shop stewards' movement of the middle twentieth century, and most intriguingly, the success of the Italian trade unions in absorbing the factory assemblies popularized during the Hot Autumn of 1969. The source of this flexibility has to do with the nature of the trade unions themselves. Whereas STO had previously argued that "unions are basically just a police arm of the employer that is given some legitimacy by workers' illusions," Hamerquist maintains that "The general function of trade unions is not the suppression of class struggle, it is the containment of it within the framework of capital. The conservative role of unions is not typically manifested through their becoming an immediate barrier to the initiation of struggle, but through their mediation of the struggle to prevent it from developing in revolutionary directions."[96] In other words, the problems of the Westside branch, for instance, resulted at least in part from the somewhat responsive character of the UAW at Melrose, when STO had been expecting a more obviously regressive union like the IBEW locals at the Hawthorne Works or Stewart-Warner.

As for the independent organization model, the solution to challenges like those faced by the Westside entailed an acknowledgement of the limitations of these organizations, which the document refers to as "workers' councils" despite their obvious differences from the traditional meaning of this term. Specifically, it was important to view them as inherently unstable, especially when confronting the hegemonic position of the established trade unions. Because consciousness is developed in the course of struggle, the independent organizations were expected to be small and primarily focused on reflection and communication among militant workers. "But even at the abnormal moments," claims Hamerquist, "so long as the struggles are isolated and sporadic, the council will be narrower than the total constituency of the struggle. We will have to go further along the road to revolution before councils will or can become the legitimate and organic mode of self-organization of the class

---

95   Don Hamerquist, "Trade Unions/Independent Organizations" (1973) in *Workplace Papers* (Chicago: STO,1980), 38.

96   Ibid.

even in the most developed instances."[97] Short of a broadly revolutionary situation, independent organizations could have only the most limited success in drawing in masses of workers, in part because, in an isolated workplace conflict, they would, at best, function as less corrupt and more militant unions.

In many ways, "Trade Unions/Independent Organizations" can be seen as an attempted compromise with the faction that produced the "Crisis" document. In particular, Hamerquist specifically acknowledges the immediate value to workers of responsive unions: "Since there is a valid role for trade unions short of a revolutionary situation, and since the potential for revitalizing US unions cannot be written off, it would be absolutely wrong for communists to regard the trade union-ist sentiment within the independent organization as reactionary."[98] At the same time, however, the intra-union approach advocated in "The Crisis" is still rejected, albeit in a more cautious way than before: "In no way should we put ourselves in a position of opposition to union reform. What we can do is try to explain why that is not our priority."[99] In the event, Hamerquist's concessions to those who wanted to participate in intra-union struggles were insufficient, and the "Crisis" split went forward regardless.

At the same time, Hamerquist's reflections indicated a growing awareness, common throughout the radical left as the seventies advanced, that a revolution was no longer on the immediate horizon. STO was hardly the only organization during this period to suffer acrimonious splits and frustrating organizing setbacks. The sixties were over, the mass movements of that decade had dissipated instead of intensifying, and in every corner revolutionaries were struggling to grapple with the proper strategy for changing times. Similar considerations may have motivated the departure of the "Crisis" faction as well. Kingsley Clarke was a new member of STO at the time, and he recalls Goldfield and others arguing "that STO had no influence either in the communist movement or in the workers' movement by virtue of its ultra-left position on independent organizations in the workplace, and that we had better get on board with October League, the New Communist Movement, because they were gaining greatly and we should be moving in that direction."[100] Hamerquist's strategy for dealing with the organization's difficulties was

97   Ibid., 45.
98   Ibid., 52.
99   Ibid.
100 Author interview with Kingsley Clarke, April 2, 2006.

fundamentally different, but he too defended the need for a revolutionary organization that could help catalyze workers' struggles in a nonrevolutionary situation.

But just when the organization believed it had moved beyond the real crisis precipitated by the "Crisis" document, another dissenting faction emerged. These were the "workerists" who had been criticized in "The Crisis": advocates of complete integration with the working class, they challenged the need for a separate organization of communist militants constructed on the Leninist model. Led by two experienced labor organizers of Polish descent and Argentine upbringing, Guillermo Brzotowski and Elias Zwierzynski, this faction argued that STO's proper role was to be a service organization to workers, not a leading body of any kind. In line with this analysis, they proposed renaming the *Insurgent Worker* the *Workers' Toolbox*.[101] From their perspective, Hamerquist's reflections in "Trade Unions/Independent Organizations" conceded too much to the worst aspects of the "Crisis" document. This didn't necessarily mean the "workerists" were opposed to trade union work, however. Since their whole approach involved direct immersion in working-class struggles, and because these struggles often took place within the unions, many of the people in this faction took a position on stewardship and the trade unions that was strikingly similar to that outlined by "The Crisis."

In the summer of 1974, less than one year after the departure of the "Crisis" faction, the "workerists" produced their own lengthy critique of STO, a paper known as "The Head is a Balloon." The title was a reference to the overly inflated sense of self-importance that the signers attributed to the leadership of the organization, and to its pretensions to leadership of the workers' movement.[102] This problem was only exacerbated by the "Crisis" split, since it led to a situation where, as the report to Big Flame puts it, STO "is now dominated by one or two heavies," especially

---

101 Author interview with Don Hamerquist, September 14, 2006. Telephone interviews with Elias Zwierzinski, January 1, 2007, and Guillermo Brzotowski, October 10, 2008, corroborate the basic outline though neither of them recalled the specific debate over the title of the publication.

102 Telephone interviews with Elias Zwierzinski, January 1, 2007, and Guillermo Brzotowski, October 10, 2008, provided context and insight into the paper, which I have been unable to obtain. While most former members attribute authorship to Zwierzinski and Brzotowski, Brzotowski himself denies having been central to drafting it.

Hamerquist and Ignatin.[103] "The Head is a Balloon" accused STO of "being dogmatically Leninist, and called for the dissolution of the group into a federation of autonomous work groups."[104] This restructuring was intended to serve both an ideological purpose, opening the group to the independent political perspectives of the workers themselves, and an organizational purpose, sidelining the power of the informal hierarchy. Once again, the organization was plunged into conflict, and again the outcome was a split. The cumulative result was a devastating reduction in size and influence for a group that one year before had been one of the leading left organizations in the Chicago area, at least in the arena of workplace organizing. The acrimony of these two consecutive rifts also drove away a number of individuals who were frustrated with both the slow pace of movement building and the infighting that had come to characterize STO.

In the end, perhaps a half-dozen members remained in an organization that had not long before numbered close to fifty. In a particularly poignant scene, Noel Ignatiev recalls a walk along the Indiana dunes in the summer of 1974 with Don Hamerquist and Carole Travis, the remaining founders of the organization.[105] They reminisced about the experiences they had shared over the previous five years, and contemplated an uncertain future. While things had not gone as they had planned, none of them wanted to throw in the towel. They dedicated themselves to the rebuilding the Sojourner Truth Organization from the ground up, a task that they managed to accomplish in a little more than a year, as described in Chapter Four. One basis for this regroupment was a stronger emphasis on theoretical development and ideological agreement. This agreement was based on a number of principles, but one of the most important was the opposition to white supremacy as viewed through the theory of white skin privileges. An examination of the origins and development of this concept comprises the next chapter.

---

103 "Report on the Sojourner Truth Group in Chicago."

104 Noel Ignatin, "Outline History of STO," unpublished manuscript in author's possession.

105 Author interview with Noel Ignatiev, January 22, 2006.

Chapter Three:
"A Science of Navigation"

The November/December 1971 issue of the *Insurgent Worker* featured a fairly typical lead article about a recent job action at the Melrose Park International Harvester plant. IH Melrose was a massive factory that produced, among other things, bulldozers and other tractors. Entitled "Harvester Workers Walk Off Over Discrimination," the piece told an inspiring story of worker solidarity in an antiracist context.[1] The incident began when a "notorious racist" foreman in the small tractor department reassigned an older black worker—referred to throughout only as "Tiny"—into a job where he was responsible for work that had previously been handled by two white workers. Having set the worker up for failure, the foreman twisted the knife: Tiny would not receive the same bonus as his coworkers because he had not kept up with the work load. This sort of petty power-play was a daily occurrence at any large factory, and the racial aspect was hardly unusual. The official response from the union, United Auto Workers Local 6, was decent enough, if unexceptional: the departmental steward accompanied Tiny to the foreman's office to initiate a grievance for racial discrimination.

"What happened next," in the words of the article, "was beautiful," but it was not exactly predictable. Tiny's coworkers shut down their assembly line, and then proceeded to inform other nearby departments and lines about the incident. In solidarity with Tiny's grievance, workers in at least four other departments walked off their lines, and hundreds of them gathered spontaneously outside the office of the racist foreman.

---

1   The information for this vignette, including all direct quotes, comes directly from the *Insurgent Worker*, Nov/Dec 1971, 1, 12.

This action clearly violated the standard procedure for handling grievances, and management representatives threatened the workers with suspension if they didn't return to their stations. No one complied. At this point the UAW representatives stepped in to broker a compromise: if the workers went back immediately, only the steward on Tiny's line would be suspended. This too was unacceptable to the assembled workers, and they stood their ground until the company agreed to settle Tiny's grievance on the spot and pay him his bonus. Having won their demand, the workers returned to their jobs.

The *Insurgent Worker* does not indicate whether or not any STO members were involved in this action, but it certainly reflects the group's approach to fighting white supremacy within the framework of the workplace organizing described in the previous chapter. By struggling, and winning a victory (however modest), around the demands of a black employee, the workers had enhanced their collective sense of power while taking a stand against racism. As the article noted: "A significant thing about this walkout was that it was initiated and led by black workers over the issue of white supremacist discrimination, and the majority of white workers supported the action and joined the walkout. All the workers regarded Tiny's problem as their problem. This is the meaning of class solidarity." In this sort of situation, STO's primary objective was to draw white workers into such struggles, despite the hesitation of many whites to view discrimination as an issue that affected them. These efforts were not driven exclusively, or even primarily, by moral considerations. Instead, the organization's opposition to white supremacy was rooted in a detailed theory of US history, a sophisticated analysis of world affairs, and a precise strategy for revolution, each of which deserves careful examination.

* * *

Just as Don Hamerquist had taken the lead in articulating the theories that grounded STO's approach to workplace organizing, so in turn did Noel Ignatin pioneer the group's understanding of white supremacy. Where Hamerquist took his cues from Antonio Gramsci, Ignatin rooted his analysis in the work of W.E.B. Du Bois. Du Bois was a black intellectual and historian from Massachusetts, long-time editor of *The Crisis*, the magazine of the National Association for the Advancement of Colored People, and a proudly unorthodox Marxist throughout most of his life. His 1935 masterwork, *Black Reconstruction in America: 1860– 1880*, challenged the traditional white historiography that viewed the post-Civil War era as an unfortunate blot on the otherwise glorious history of the United States. Instead, said Du Bois, Reconstruction represented the most radically democratic period in US history, and the closest the country had yet come to working-class rule. Just as the *Prison Notebooks* served as the ur-text of STO's theory of consciousness and thus of its workplace campaigns, so did *Black Reconstruction* function as the pivot of the group's theory of US history, which in turn was the first building block of its analysis of white supremacy.

Almost alone among historians of his era, Du Bois placed the experiences of black people at the very center of the history of the United States. The contradiction between the rhetoric of democracy and the reality of slavery "was the great and primary question which was in the minds of the men who wrote the Constitution of the United States."[2] Slavery was the central experience of black workers, who constituted "the ultimate exploited."[3] It was also an indispensable component of the developing economic power of the US after the Revolution. This combination of misery and success was explosive: "It was thus the black worker, as the founding stone of a new economic system in the nineteenth century and for the modern world, who brought civil war in America. He was its underlying cause, in spite of every effort to base the strife upon union and national power."[4] These efforts included not only those of the leading political and military figures during the war, but also those of historians—whether of the right or of the left—who in later years recorded and interpreted the causes, course, and consequences of the war.

If the black experience had been the essential trigger of the Civil War, it naturally followed that the actions of black people during the war were pivotal in determining its outcome. Here, Du Bois highlighted the importance of the mass escapes that steadily depleted the slave population of the South over the course of the Civil War, as blacks fled toward the Union lines. This was "the quiet but unswerving determination of increasing numbers no longer to work on Confederate plantations, and to seek the freedom of the northern armies."[5] Even before the Emancipation Proclamation of 1863, the geographic movement of black people damaged the Confederacy's ability to function while simultaneously offering the Union army additional, and often

---

2   W.E.B. Du Bois, *Black Reconstruction in America: 1860–1880* (New York: The Free Press, 1998 [1935]), 13.

3   Ibid., 15

4   Ibid.

5   Ibid., 65.

enthusiastic, laborers (and in some cases soldiers). In describing these events, Du Bois gave a novel twist to a traditional concept of working-class radicalism by naming the process a "general strike" of slave laborers. Such an interpretation, equally unacceptable to right-wing and left-wing historians of his era, represented a bold re-interpretation of the Civil War as an economic conflict in which the conscious decisions of masses of slaves were decisive factors.

Similarly, Du Bois sketched a vision of the post-Civil War Reconstruction era far different from that offered in standard histories. While acknowledging the ineptness and even corruption of some black leaders of the era, he argued strenuously that Reconstruction represented the most democratic and progressive era in United States history. Partly this was a question of the new freedoms, including the vote, granted to black men, and of the deliberate attempt to eliminate racial distinctions in public matters. But this was not all: state and local governments of the Reconstruction period also instituted free public education and took steps toward providing health care to the poor. Once again, Du Bois borrowed from the lexicon of the radical left, initially describing the black-led government of one state as "the dictatorship of the black proletariat in South Carolina."[6] In providing a detailed account of the accomplishments of the various Reconstruction governments, Du Bois extended even further his argument that black activity was the key element determining the course of US history.

But racism did not die with slavery, and Reconstruction was replaced with the brutal, white regime later known as Jim Crow.[7] How to explain the persistence of white supremacy in the post-Reconstruction era? To answer this question, Du Bois examined the interaction between black workers and white workers, and his conclusions were again contentious. Building upon his unorthodox usage of terms like "general strike" and "dictatorship of the proletariat," he directly challenged the white left's tendency to separate the struggles of working people—who were assumed to be white—from the black movement, before, during and after the Civil War. In particular, *Black Reconstruction* identified the source of

6   Ibid., 381. Upon consideration, Du Bois dropped the word "dictatorship," largely because the government of South Carolina was never sufficiently anticapitalist to merit the term Marx used to describe the transitional stage between capitalism and socialism.

7   The classic work on the history of Jim Crow is C. Vann Woodward, *The Strange Career of Jim Crow* (New York: Oxford University Press, 2002 [1955]).

this false distinction in the different treatment given to white workers and black workers after the end of Reconstruction:

> It must be remembered that the white group of labor-ers, while they received a low wage, were compensated in part by a sort of public and psychological wage. They were given public deference and titles of courtesy because they were white. They were admitted freely with all classes of white people to public functions, public parks, and the best schools. The police were drawn from their ranks, and the courts, dependent upon their votes, treated them with such leniency as to encourage lawlessness. Their vote selected public officials, and while this had small effect upon the economic situation, it had great effect upon their personal treatment and the deference shown them."[8]

These same opportunities were all systematically denied to black people on the basis of their race. Thus a sharp difference in social status existed even when black and white workers shared roughly equivalent economic circumstances. The continued existence of white supremacy was the result of the willingness of white workers, especially but not exclusively in the South, to side with their class enemies (the capitalists) and accept continued economic exploitation in exchange for the "public and psychological wage" of being able to look down upon black people.

Du Bois also detailed the way in which the "wage" prevented the white-led labor movement from living up to its full potential in spite of militant campaigns like the struggle for the eight-hour day. Speaking of attempts to unionize in the aftermath of Reconstruction, he wrote: "One can see for these reasons why labor organizers and labor agitators made such small headway in the South. They were, for the most part, appealing to laborers who would rather have low wages upon which they could eke out an existence than see colored labor with a decent wage. White labor saw in every advance of Negroes a threat to their racial prerogatives ..."[9] This psychological wage was sufficient to divide the working class when it most needed unity, and the revolutionary opportunity presented by Reconstruction was lost.

* * *

---

8   Du Bois, *Black Reconstruction,* 700–701.
9   Ibid., 701. Ellipsis mine.

The grand narrative offered by Du Bois, of slavery, Civil War, Reconstruction, and Jim Crow, served as the fulcrum of STO's theory of US history, but it left two key topics unaddressed: the origins of white supremacy and racial slavery, and the post-New Deal rise of the black freedom movement. To address the former, STO looked to the pioneering research being done by Ignatin's long-time comrade Ted Allen. Allen, a white communist militant from New York, had been a member, along with Ignatin, of the CP splinter known as the Provisional Organizing Committee, and the two had long shared a common interest in Du Bois and his theory of US history. In between day jobs as diverse as coal mining, mail delivery, and teaching high school, Allen managed to conduct impressive original research on the historical origins of racial slavery in North America.[10]

Allen's work reflected the influence of Du Bois both in his stark challenge to mainstream historiography and in his deliberately unorthodox twists on left analysis. Arguing first that "the capitalist system of production was in force from the beginning" in the slave-holding colonies, he followed *Black Reconstruction* in rejecting popular Marxist notions of slavery as a semifeudal economic system displaced only in 1865 with the victory of the industrial North in the Civil War.[11] But Allen went further, declaring provocatively that slavery had not always been racially based, and that white supremacy as we know it was the result of strikingly conscious decisions made by colonial slave-holding capitalists almost two centuries before the Civil War. In assessing the colonial history of Virginia in particular, Allen focused on the second half of the seventeenth century as the period when a previously multiracial population of bond servants was divided into a pool of white workers indentured for a limited term of several years and a pool of black workers who were converted into permanent and hereditary chattel slaves.[12] This division was, accord-

---

10   For biographical background on Allen, see Jeffrey B. Perry, "In Memoriam: Theodore W. Allen" (2005), available online at http://clogic. eserver.org/2005/Perry.html (accessed September 29, 2011).

11   Allen, "White Supremacy in US History" (1973), in *Understanding and Fighting White Supremacy: A Collection* (Chicago: STO, 1976), 1.

12   See Theodore William Allen, *Class Struggle and the Origin of Racial Slavery: The Invention of the White Race* (Somerville, MA: New England Free Press, 1976). A slightly different version of this text is presented under the title "…They Would Have Destroyed Me," available online at http://sojournertruth.net/destroyedme.html (accessed September 29, 2011).

ing to Allen, the result of uprisings like Bacon's Rebellion, in which black and white bond servants sacked Virginia's colonial capital of Jamestown in 1676.[13] Allen's research produced significant evidence, from primary documents such as the colonial records, demonstrating that, fearing the power of such a unified group, the colonial elite intentionally granted specific privileges to white servants—especially the eventual prospect of freedom—that were denied to blacks. The unstated quid pro quo was that white workers were expected to help police the black population, rather than unite with them in subsequent rebellions. This often took the form of white bond servant participation in armed slave patrols and militias that repressed any spark of resistance. Here, said Allen, was the origin of white supremacy as an ideology, and of the "public and psychological wage" identified by Du Bois. Colonial Virginia was the birthplace of the white skin privilege.

As for the other end of the arc of US history, both its publication date of 1935 and its stated topic prevented *Black Reconstruction* from addressing the inspiring trajectory of the black freedom movement in the period extending from the New Deal through the post-war era. The bridge between Du Bois's psychological wage and the white skin privilege analysis of the late sixties was precisely the civil rights movement, and in particular the evolution of the Student Nonviolent Coordinating Committee. The origins of the civil rights movement lay in the cross-pollination between long-standing black demands for freedom and the strategic orientation toward direct action that had come to prominence through the CIO organizing drives of the thirties and forties. The exigencies of World War Two had made it clear that the ruling class commitment to white supremacy could at least be modified if sufficient pressure was brought to bear. For instance, A. Phillip Randolph's March on Washington Movement used the threat of a major demonstration by African Americans and organized labor to force the US government to prohibit racial discrimination in both military and civilian spheres of the defense industry.[14] Beginning in the mid-fifties, the civil rights movement attempted to replace the external pressures of war with the internal

---

13   Ibid. Bacon's Rebellion has been the subject of much dispute within the far left. For a strident criticism of the anti-indigenous basis of the Rebellion, see J. Sakai, *Settlers: The Mythology of the White Proletariat* (Chicago: Morningstar Press, 1989 [1983?]), 12–16.

14   For more on Randolph and the March on Washington Movement, see Andrew E. Kersten, *A. Phillip Randolph: A Life in the Vanguard* (Lanham, MD: Rowman & Littlefield, 2007).

one of direct action. From the beginning, the movement was black-led, but the commitment to the goal of ending racial segregation ensured an integrated movement. Cofounder Ella Baker brought Du Bois's influence into SNCC, which developed as a multiracial organization of young radicals so devoted to direct action that an arrest record quickly became a badge of honor.[15] As the sixties progressed, however, the interaction between predominantly southern blacks and largely northern whites led to a growing awareness of the relative privileges experienced by the white students: those from the North could leave the struggle whenever they chose simply by returning home, but even those from the South received less harsh treatment from the white power structure. None of this made white activists necessarily less committed to the cause, but eventually the black leadership of SNCC came to a realization: if freedom for black people was ever to be achieved, two parallel struggles were needed, one in which blacks fought for their liberation, and another in which progressive whites struggled with other white people in order to convince them to support black liberation.[16]

Large numbers of white radicals, especially those centered around SDS, took this perspective seriously, and began to act on it with little, if any, conscious awareness of Du Bois's concept of the psychological wage or Allen's notion of white skin privilege. At the same time, the antiwar movement provided another resonant theme for radicals of the late sixties, who watched anti-imperialist movements develop throughout the third world, most famously in Vietnam and Cuba. For many, white

---

15   Author interview with Ken Lawrence, August, 2006. Lawrence describes attending the first SNCC convention in 1960: "I think it was Ella Baker who had helped everybody organize, but basically nobody knew how to organize a convention in those days, so they had organized it like a national Democratic or Republican convention. It was in a chapel, but everybody was arranged by the places they were from. So they were trying to figure out how to take the vote, and they decided to call the roll by states. And some young man stood up and shouted, 'No! You can't do that. If you haven't been to jail, you can't vote. Everybody has the right to speak, but in this organization if you haven't been to jail you can't vote.'" For more on Ella Baker and SNCC, see Barbara Ransby, *Ella Baker and the Black Freedom Movement: A Radical Democratic Vision* (Chapel Hill: The University of North Carolina Press, 2003).

16   On the departure of white activists from SNCC, see Clayborne Carson, *In Struggle: SNCC and the Black Awakening of the 1960s* (Cambridge, MA: Harvard University Press, 1995 [1981]), 204–206.

supremacy could be viewed as the domestic manifestation of imperialist capitalism. In this context, white skin privileges were one aspect of a broader oppression of the global majority of humanity. Further, the development of youth culture (both pop- and counter-) over the course of the fifties and sixties provided another pillar for the antiracist sentiments of the white new left. As the historian Paul Buhle notes,

> Subjectively, the role of Black culture in the teenage lives of the future New Left prepared the way. Only Communist or very racist parents, it is safe to say, perceived the breadth of this influence from sports to music to sexual fantasy.... To affirm solidarity with Blacks in any political sense was a minority act; but the sympathy towards Black culture reached further among millions of ordinary teenagers than any previously Left-orchestrated effort could have envisioned.[17]

The convergence of specifically North American experiences—both cultural and political—and a global assessment of revolutionary momentum contributed to the openness shown by many white radicals to some form of the white skin privilege analysis as the sixties progressed.

* * *

His connection to Allen, his reading of Du Bois, and his experiences within SDS provided a lens through which Ignatin could view this broad arc of US history, from Bacon's Rebellion through the Civil War all the way up to the black power movement that emerged in the late sixties. This historical sketch was not simply an academic exercise; it held precise theoretical and strategic implications, embedded in the phrase "white skin privilege." The term itself was first used in print by Ted Allen, in a 1965 commemoration of John Brown's raid on Harper's Ferry.[18] Allen and Ignatin reconceptualized the psychological wage described by Du Bois as a set of privileges granted to people who were perceived as having white skin. These privileges covered a wide terrain, including the opportunity to be first hired and last fired in an employment context,

---

17   Paul Buhle, *Marxism in the United States: Remapping the History of the American Left* (New York: Verso, 1991 [1987]), 224. Ellipsis mine.

18   See Ignatin's introduction to "The White Blindspot," in *New Marxist Forum: A Journal of Debate and Theory for Marxist-Leninists*, Issue #1, January 1973, 8.

access to preferential treatment at the hands of police and government bureaucrats, and the same general sort of deference and courtesy that had been described in *Black Reconstruction*. The privileges were relative rather than absolute: first hired and last fired, for instance, meant that whites could expect that they would always get jobs more easily than blacks, not that there were always jobs available for any whites that wanted them.

In proper Marxist fashion, the white skin privilege represented a material basis for the ideology of white supremacy. While rejecting the notion that racist ideas and attitudes were hardwired into white people, Ignatin and Allen refused to accept the liberal position that racism could be eliminated simply by changing people's minds. Further, despite the use of the word "skin" in white skin privilege, Allen, Ignatin, and others argued strenuously that "whiteness" itself was a political rather than a fixed biological category.[19] Since political identities were subject to repeated contestation and change, whiteness could be understood to have a certain fluidity that allowed groups of people, such as various immigrant communities, eventual access to "whiteness" and its privileges, contingent upon their willingness to reject any solidarity with black people.[20] This was a dynamic historical process, not some abstract permanent feature of genetics. Thus, according to Ignatin and Allen, what could be done could also be undone. White skin privileges could be repudiated in struggle, and this created the possibility of a reunified proletariat capable of overthrowing capitalism. Herein lay the basis for the strategic approach to fighting white supremacy that was to characterize STO throughout its existence. This understanding, when combined with the workplace organizing discussed in Chapter Two, was another key element of the comprehensive strategy of revolution that guided the group during its first several years of activity.

* * *

On one level, white supremacy and white skin privileges represented just one example among many of the false divisions imposed on the proletariat by the hegemonic power of the ruling class in the perpetual struggle to prevent revolution, alongside trade unions, elections, and

---

19   For a more detailed examination of this now somewhat commonplace understanding, see Theodore W. Allen, *The Invention of the White Race* (New York: Verso, 1994, two volumes).

20   One of the classic case studies of this process is Ignatiev's *How the Irish Became White* (New York: Routledge, 1995).

other obstacles. At the same time, however, Ignatin argued powerfully that white supremacy was *the* main roadblock to working-class unity in the United States. And since unity of the working class was an essential precondition to any revolutionary upsurge, the repudiation of white skin privileges by white workers was a necessary first step on the road to revolution. This reasoning was already clearly articulated three years before STO was founded. As indicated previously, the development of the group's version of the white skin privilege line began with the publication of Ignatin and Allen's "The White Blindspot" in early 1967. Here, Ignatin updated the analysis offered by Du Bois in assessing the failure of the labor movement after Reconstruction:

> As long as white supremacy is permitted to divide the working class, so long will the struggle of the working class remain on two separate planes, one concerned with their "own" class demands and the other, on a more elementary plane (but with a much higher degree of class consciousness) fighting first for the ordinary bourgeois rights which were won long ago for the rest of the workers. As soon as white supremacy is eliminated as a force within the working class, the decks will be cleared for action by the entire class against its enemy.[21]

Ignatin's strategy reflected the theory of history that had been pieced together from the work of Du Bois, Allen, and others; not surprisingly, "The White Blindspot" opened with two quotes from *Black Reconstruction*, one of which described the "blindspot in the eyes of America" that inspired the piece's title.[22]

Ever the Marxist, Ignatin grounded his analysis not only in the work of Du Bois and Allen, but also specifically laid claim to the position held by Karl Marx himself, going so far as to quote a famous passage from the first volume of *Capital*: "In the United States of North America, every independent movement of the workers was paralysed so long as slavery disfigured a part of the Republic. Labour cannot emancipate itself in

---

21 Ignatin, "White Blindspot," in *Understanding and Fighting White Supremacy*, 29.

22 Ignatin, "White Blindspot," 26. The quote from Du Bois reads in full: "It is only the blindspot in the eyes of America, and its historians, that can overlook and misread so clean and encouraging a chapter of human struggle and human uplift." *Black Reconstruction*, 577.

the white skin where in the black it is branded."[23] In this way, Ignatin attempted (in vain, as it happened) to pre-empt the inevitable criticism of his position as anti-Marxist. Despite its critical tone, however, "The White Blindspot" was also clearly informed by the immediately subsequent passage from *Capital*, even though Ignatin didn't quote it: "But out of the death of slavery a new life at once arose. The first fruit of the Civil War was the eight hours' agitation, that ran with the seven-leagued boots of the locomotive from the Atlantic to the Pacific, from New England to California."[24] This optimistic view of the relationship between antiracist struggles and the prospects for working-class radicalism ensured that, contrary to the charges of utopianism leveled by his opponents within the white left, Ignatin was thinking strategically and not just offering criticism without alternatives.

"The White Blindspot" offered not only a general strategy for working-class unification, but also precise instructions to revolutionaries, especially white revolutionaries, on how to help facilitate this unification:

> Communists (individually this is the task primarily of white communists, although collectively it is the responsibility of the whole party) must go to the white workers and say frankly: you must renounce the privileges you now hold, must join the Negro, Puerto Rican and other colored workers in fighting white supremacy, must make this the first, immediate and most urgent task of the entire working class, in exchange for which you, *together with* the rest of the workers will receive all the benefits which are sure to come from one working class (of several colors) fighting together.[25]

This understanding of the work required of revolutionaries informed the decision of the *Insurgent Worker* to highlight the actions of the IH Melrose workers who backed Tiny's struggle against his racist foreman. It also confused, alienated, and angered a range of radical groups and activists during the years after its initial publication. First the Progressive Labor Party, then the *Guardian* newspaper and a variety of smaller Marxist

---

23   Karl Marx, *Capital* Volume 1, Chapter 10 ("The Working Day"), 414 in the Penguin edition; quoted in Ignatin, "White Blindspot," in *Understanding and Fighting White Supremacy*, 26.

24   Ibid.

25   Ignatin, "White Blindspot," 29. Emphasis in original.

groupings of the seventies, criticized Ignatin's approach to revolutionary strategy as moralistic, petty-bourgeois, antiworker, and otherwise undesirable.[26] As we shall see below, these objections surfaced within STO as well.

∗ ∗ ∗

During the three years between the initial publication of "The White Blindspot" and the founding of STO, Ignatin advanced his theories through a variety of articles and essays. In 1968, Ignatin produced "Learn the Lessons of US History," which addressed the historical questions in more detail, identifying multiple situations—including Reconstruction, the Populist era at the turn of the century, and the capitulation of the CIO to New Deal liberalism at the end of the thirties—where the white-led labor movement had chosen white supremacy over class solidarity. The piece was originally published in *New Left Notes*, the weekly magazine of SDS, and Ignatin, perhaps acknowledging the growing antiwar and anti-imperialist turn of the student movement, expanded his horizons. Instead of conceiving of white skin privilege as primarily a domestic issue of whites and blacks, he now spoke of the division between white workers and "the nonwhite majority of the earth's population."[27] Nonetheless, the strategy was unchanged, since Ignatin's target remained the hearts and minds of white workers in the United States, who needed to be won to the renunciation of their privileges; otherwise, "I will point to 1877, 1904, and 1940, and say that if this task is not tackled and achieved, we will see the same thing over again."[28] The piece concluded with a plea that the student movement not take the same road.

The quick collapse of SDS the following year arguably kept it from making this particular error, although this hardly exempted the various factions from charges of racism. In the chaotic period following the final SDS convention in June of 1969, Ignatin continued to highlight the centrality of the fight against white supremacy. But circumstances

26 For a summary of criticisms leveled by other left groups at "The White Blindspot" and subsequent statements of the argument, see Don Hamerquist, *White Supremacy and the Afro-American National Question* (Chicago: STO, 1978 [1976]), 25–34.

27 Ignatin, "Learn the Lessons of US History," in *New Left Notes*, March 25, 1968, 4–5. Quoted in David Barber, "'A Fucking White Revolutionary Mass Movement' and Other Fables of Whiteness," in *Race Traitor*, #12, Spring 2001, 38.

28 Ibid., 39.

had changed dramatically since the original publication of "The White Blindspot" two and a half years earlier. Suddenly, the main problem was no longer PL's outright rejection, but the attempted embrace of the white skin privilege analysis by the Weatherman faction of SDS. This group's founding document, "You Don't Need a Weatherman to Know Which Way the Wind Blows"— named for a line in the Bob Dylan song "Subterranean Homesick Blues"—articulated a version of the white skin privilege line that superficially resembled the position advanced by Ignatin and Allen. It argued that white support of black demands was essential, and it made mention of the need for working-class revolution. Nonetheless, the piece was quickly denounced by both men for a variety of reasons. Without naming Weatherman in particular, Allen criticized the way in which some white radicals wrote off the white working class and put their faith exclusively with the global national liberation movements, calling this approach "wrong, dishonest, and cowardly."[29]

Ignatin, meanwhile, wrote a scathing critique under the ponderous title "Without a Science of Navigation we Cannot Sail in Stormy Seas, or, Sooner or Later One of Us Must Know," which challenged the "Weatherman" document on a variety of levels.[30] This essay may have been the last piece published by Ignatin before founding STO, and it still bears the marks of his original Stalinism, not least in his glowing reference to "the teachings of Marx, Engels, Lenin, Stalin and Mao."[31] It is perhaps the most dated of Ignatin's sixties writings, and the first part of the title also betrays the scientist version of Marxism that would occasionally crop up within STO even as it pursued its anti-Stalinist trajectory. At the same time, the subtitle, taken from a Dylan song of the same name (found on the album *Blonde on Blonde*), reads today as a clumsy and unsuccessful attempt to compete with the pop-cultural hipness of the "Weatherman" title. The piece reflects Ignatin's commitment to at least one specific position—one associated directly with Stalin—that he (along with the entirety of STO) later rejected: the idea that only "in the

---

29   Ted Allen, "Can White ~~Workers~~ Radicals Be Radicalized?" in *New Marxist Forum: A Journal of Debate and Theory for Marxist-Leninists*, Issue #1, January 1973, 23.

30   Noel Ignatin, "Without a Science of Navigation we Cannot Sail in Stormy Seas, or, Sooner or Later One of Us Must Know," in *The Debate Within SDS: RYM II vs. Weatherman* (Detroit: Radical Education Project, September, 1969), 31–44. Thanks to both Dan Berger and Geoff in Portland for bringing this Ignatin essay to my attention.

31   Ibid, 42.

deep South, where Black people constitute a majority" do "the conditions for Black nationhood exist."[32] In contrast, the "Weatherman" document drew on the analysis of the Republic of New Afrika (RNA) in arguing that black people constituted a nation throughout the United States, a position that would later come to be associated with STO, which for many years in the middle seventies prioritized solidarity work with the RNA. (This question will be discussed in greater detail in Chapter Five.)

Regardless, Ignatin's piece reiterated his longstanding position on white supremacy and refocused his approach in order to address the changed circumstances and salvage his version of the white skin privilege analysis from those who would use it to write off the white working class entirely. He criticized a certain conception of imperialism, under which, according to the "Weatherman" document, "virtually all of the white working class also has short-range privileges from imperialism, which are not false privileges but very real ones which give them an edge of vested interest and tie them to a certain extent to the imperialists."[33] In response, Ignatin drew on three contemporary examples from the labor movement—auto, mining, and textiles—to demonstrate that even the short-term interests of white workers are harmed by the embrace of white skin privilege. "*The greater and more firmly established the privilege, the greater the misery.*"[34] "If the acceptance of white-skin privilege is in their interests," Ignatin asks sarcastically, "what would the white workers have to do to run counter to their interests?!"[35]

Lest his position be misunderstood as simply defending the honor of white workers, Ignatin argued that the real problem with the "Weatherman" analysis was that it let white workers off the hook: "'Weatherman' is in fact telling white workers that they do not have to fight white supremacy now, since they benefit from it, but at some point in the future they will have to."[36] Indeed, according to Ignatin, the Weatherman faction was engaged in "the *practical* abandonment of the fight against white supremacy. All their documents and speeches show a clear tendency to substitute calls for 'support of national liberation' for the struggle against white supremacy which is the basic and indispensable expression

---

32 Ibid., 38.

33 "You Don't Need a Weatherman to Know Which Way the Wind Blows," in Harold Jacobs, ed., *Weatherman* (San Francisco: Ramparts Press, 1970), 65. Quoted in Ignatin, ibid., 32–33.

34 Ignatin, ibid., 34. Emphasis in original.

35 Ibid.

36 Ibid.

of such support on the part of whites."[37] Further, "the line of denying the identity of interests of white and Black workers is anti-working class. In being anti-working class, it is, of necessity, anti-Black!"[38] And, finally, "'Weatherman' does not believe in the class struggle."[39] For a group like Weatherman, which openly stated its commitment to black liberation and world revolution, these sorts of criticisms must have been hard to bear. Nonetheless, they accurately reflected the perspective that Ignatin brought into STO from the beginning, that the class struggle depended first and foremost on the fight against white supremacy, and that, absent this combination, revolution was impossible.

* * *

When STO came into existence at the end of 1969, Ignatin's ideas were certainly prominent within the organization, and from the start his public profile helped distinguish the group from other post-SDS organizations that differed on the proper understanding of the white skin privilege line. Nonetheless, a diversity of approaches to the question of white supremacy characterized STO throughout its first several years of existence. This was in keeping with the group's early commitment to a general policy of "refusing to impose discipline on matters of theory and fighting for discipline on matters of practice."[40] Lynn French, for example, brought to the group her lifetime of experiences as a black woman, and in particular the lessons she learned during her time with the Black Panther Party. Despite the fact that all but two founding members were white, she wanted STO's membership to reflect "the multiracial success of the Underground Railroad" in which Sojourner Truth, the group's namesake, had participated.[41] Other members of the group were drawn to the concept of separate organizations for white and nonwhite revolutionaries, and conceived of STO as primarily oriented toward the white working class. Partly as a result of these disagreements, French left the group after only a few months. The issue of STO's existence as a multiracial organization, which would recur multiple times over the ensuing years, was a source of debate from the very start.

---

37   Ibid., 36. Emphasis in original.
38   Ibid.
39   Ibid.
40   "Outline History of Sojourner Truth Organization," September 1972, 1.
41   Lynn French, email to author, November 28, 2006.

A related question concerned the group's decision to place a priority on the kind of militant community organizing that the Panthers and SDS had both emphasized in the late sixties. STO's initial choice of campaigns reflected this: alongside the doomed effort to keep the International Harvester McCormick Reaper Works from closing, the group also committed itself to a more successful community campaign: "the fight to win freedom for Joe Green, a black youth framed up on a murder charge."[42] Although this campaign, unlike the workplace struggle, was successful, the group still decided, "around the summer of 1970," to "dissolve the community branch. This did not mean that we considered community work unimportant, but that for us, given our resources and the problems and possibilities at this time, it should not be a major concentration on an equal footing with production work."[43] It is unclear whether this decision was related to French's decision to leave the group, but given her experience with the Panthers and her disinterest in factory organizing, some connection seems likely. Regardless, the move did reflect one of the first practical changes in the organization's strategy. Rather than emphasize direct organizing work within the black community, STO shifted its sights to the racially diverse arena of heavy industry, where blacks and whites were in close contact on a daily basis. In this context, the group could attempt to implement its theoretical understanding of the fight against white supremacy in direct engagement with white workers.

* * *

Once inside the factories, STO had little difficulty organizing across racial lines, developing independent organizations open to all while still respecting the frequent desires of nonwhite workers to build independent structures such as black caucuses. In some cases, both sorts of groupings existed in the same factory, with overlapping participation. Elsewhere, a single independent organization existed, but maintained a membership that was overwhelmingly black or latino; in these situations, STO members and a handful of other radicals, often members of competing revolutionary groups like the October League, frequently constituted the only white participants. Similar things could be said for factories where STO had no presence but provided assistance to workers on an ad hoc basis. For example, the twister department wildcat at the Western Electric Hawthorne Works, mentioned in Chapter Two, was led by black

42   "Outline History of Sojourner Truth Organization," September 1972, 2.
43   Ibid.

and latino militants, with little apparent participation from their white coworkers, while the brief walkout in the small tractor department at IH Melrose was also led by blacks, but was supported by a large number of white workers.

A fundamental ambiguity characterized STO's workplace efforts: as a revolutionary organization committed to workers' autonomy and proletarian revolution, their interventions tended to focus on the most militant workers, who were often black, while the group's largely white make-up led its membership to prioritize engagement with white workers. This tension reflects the issue raised earlier regarding STO's demographic makeup. For an organization with a highly developed theoretical position on white supremacy and white skin privilege, it is perhaps surprising that STO was never able to formally resolve the practical question of whether it was multiracial or all-white.[44] At times, the issue threatened to alienate both black and white workers, but in some ways the tension was actually productive, insofar as it challenged the framework of white skin privilege while emphasizing the need for unified action by workers. This was reflected in the various shop sheets and agitational newspapers produced by STO, which highlighted the central role of black workers in struggle without targeting primarily white or black audiences. Of course, difficulties arose in workplaces where competing black factions demanded support for opposed strategic outlooks, although in no case does it appear STO found itself forced to pick sides in a sectarian struggle between black organizations. Again, this was partly the result of the multiracial composition of the industrial working class, which imposed limits on the sort of narrow factionalism that too often characterized the white left, and partly a result of decisions—whether deliberate or unconscious—made by STO itself.

The major problem associated with this dynamic was the confusion it caused, both within the organization and outside it. In particular, this ambivalence plagued the group's interaction with black revolutionaries throughout the early seventies. The decision to send STO members to Gary in 1971, for instance, was initially the result of the group's desire to work more closely with the Black Workers' Congress.[45] The nature of this hoped-for collaboration was never explored, as the BWC's political trajectory quickly proved different than that of STO. The following year,

---

44   Kingsley Clarke, in multiple interviews and discussions, initially focused my attention on this paradox.

45   See the article "International Congress of Black Workers," in the *Insurgent Worker*, May 1971, 4, which lauds the creation of the BWC.

the group made contact with another group of black communists, this time in Chicago. Known as the League of Revolutionary Black Workers, it is unclear whether the group was directly related to the Detroit group of the same name (which was in any event largely defunct, with its remaining members well on their way toward joining the Communist League), or merely inspired by them. In Chicago, the League had a significant presence at the Hotpoint factory, where ovens and other household appliances were manufactured. STO had no presence at the plant, so direct ties were largely the result of personal interactions between members of the two groups.[46] One of the leading members of the League in Chicago was Macee Halk, an experienced black militant who maintained close ties with STO until its demise. When contact was initially made, the question of STO's demographic makeup was pivotal; according to one assessment: "It became fairly clear that there was a necessity to formalize relationships with [Halk]. The question was raised in the context of recruiting him."[47] In the event, the group decided to develop fraternal ties with the League rather than recruit one or more of its members into STO. Unfortunately, this effort never really got off the ground before the "Crisis" and "Balloon" splits decimated the group, and the relationship remained ambiguous in a way that may have limited STO's organizing opportunities. Nonetheless, looking back on it later, Halk remembered frequent interactions with STO over the years, and maintained that what he liked best about the group was that "they never tried to recruit me."[48]

Similar ambiguities characterized much of STO's early workplace organizing, partly because membership in STO was not always seen to be as important as membership in the various independent organizations set up at different factories. As former member Kingsley Clarke recalls: "Were we a 'white' organization?… This is where you get into subtleties. What does it mean when Macee's coming to every meeting and speaking—not every meeting, to many significant meetings. Or you're down there in Gary and you've got [black] workers coming to

---

46   Kathy W., "A Lesson in What Democratic Centralism Is Not: Why a Representative-Democratic Exec Did Not Work in a Revolutionary Organization," unpublished document in author's possession, n.d., but c. fall 1973, esp. 5. Also, author interview with Macee Halk, March 8, 2006. The Kathy W. document refers to Halk simply as "M."

47   Kathy W., "A Lesson…," 5.

48   Author interview, Macee Halk, March 8, 2006.

meetings."[49] Other former members of STO recall early participation by Native American and Puerto Rican factory workers.[50] At the same time, the group's emphasis on workers' autonomy was paralleled by a defense of racial (or national, in later formulations) autonomy that necessarily impeded any move toward actual recruitment of nonwhites into STO. In the end, despite an incredibly sophisticated and nuanced analysis of the nature of white supremacy and the need to struggle against it, the Sojourner Truth Organization of the early seventies was unable to implement a coherent internal practice regarding the issue of multiracial membership.

* * *

It is important to note that, rhetoric aside, STO never saw North American race relations as a simple question of black and white; from the very start the group clearly understood that latinos, specifically Mexicans and Puerto Ricans, suffered under white supremacy, albeit in ways different than African Americans. The membership of Hilda Vasquez Ignatin no doubt contributed to this early awareness, but so too did the demographic reality of Chicago, which featured established and growing Mexican and Puerto Rican communities from the fifties onward. The largely working-class makeup of these communities, and the presence of significant numbers of Puerto Ricans and Mexicans at many of the factories where STO members worked, made it imperative that STO develop an analysis of white supremacy that acknowledged the unique experiences of latinos.

One manifestation of the group's commitment in this direction was the regular appearance of Spanish-language sections in STO's agitational newspapers. Beginning with the single issue of *Bread and Roses* (*Pan y Rosas*) and continuing through several issues of the *Insurgent Worker* (*El Obrero Insurgente*), Spanish readers of STO's publications were treated to both translations of the English language articles and the occasional Spanish-language exclusive, such as "Chicanos en Huelga contra Farah Pants" in the October/November 1972 issue.[51] The group's pamphlets were produced entirely in English, but many of the shop sheets and agitational leaflets prepared for distribution at job sites

---

49   Author interview, Kingsley Clarke, April 2, 2006.

50   Author interview, Don Hamerquist, September 12, 2006.

51   "Chicanos en Huelga contra Farah Pants, N.M., Texas," in *El Obrero Insurgente* October/November 1972, 2.

were at least partially bilingual, including the leaflet prepared by the twister department strikers at the Hawthorne Works, mentioned in Chapter Two.[52]

STO's interest in the struggles of Spanish-speaking workers went beyond mere propaganda. John Strucker remembers working at the Stewart-Warner factory on a day when the Immigration and Naturalization Service (INS) raided the plant looking for undocumented Mexican workers.[53] Most of the latinos at Stewart-Warner were Puerto Rican, and thus US citizens from birth, but a small number were Mexicans actually subject to deportation for being in the US without papers. In the face of this raid, STO members and others in the *Talk Back* grouping proceeded to hide these workers within the plant, in dumpsters and other unlikely spots, thus helping them avoid arrest and deportation. This sort of action resonated on several levels, not only with the group's opposition to white supremacy but also with its enthusiasm for direct action and the challenge to bourgeois legality. Similarly, the successful evasion of arrest was a classic example of the real knowledge and power of workers acting collectively: they secured their coworkers in hiding places that neither the management nor the police were able to locate, all within a closed campus only one block square. In fact, the failure of other, more conservative workers to aid the INS in their efforts demonstrated that white supremacy and anti-immigrant sentiment, no matter how deeply entrenched in white workers (and, in the case of anti-immigrant sentiment, even in black and Puerto Rican workers), were countervailed by a nascent tendency toward solidarity with coworkers and the common working-class prohibition on snitching.

The INS raid at Stewart-Warner, and similar raids at other factories, eventually induced STO to produce literature specifically dealing with the special problems faced by Mexican workers in the US. The most developed example was the unsigned pamphlet *"Since When Has Working Been a Crime?" The Deportation of Mexicans Without Papers*, written largely by Noel Ignatin.[54] The pamphlet compares the treatment of un-

---

52 A reproduction of the Spanish version of the leaflet appears in *Breakout! by and for Motorola Workers* 1, no. 4, December 11, 1973, 2.

53 Author interview with John Strucker, February 8, 2006.

54 *"Since When Has Working Been a Crime?" The Deportation of Mexicans Without Papers* (Chicago: South Chicago Workers Center [STO], n.d., but c. 1977). While this pamphlet was published after STO had begun to de-emphasize factory organizing, its themes emerged directly from that earlier period. For more on the intended distribution of the

documented immigrants—who, then as now, were largely but not exclusively from Mexico—to the experience of escaped slaves in the northern United States after the passage of the Fugitive Slave Act in 1850. But this is no academic treatment of historical parallels. The pamphlet begins with a scenario clearly reminiscent of the Stewart-Warner raid: two non-immigrant factory workers discuss a recent raid of their workplace by the INS and wonder about the fates of two latino coworkers who were taken away for deportation. Later, one of the workers discusses the issue with his wife, who suggests that the raid, arrests, and deportations are unjust.

As this introduction makes clear, the target audience for the pamphlet was factory workers, both black and white, who were unsure of how to feel about their latino coworkers and the problems they faced. After sketching out the basics of immigration policy and the economic situations that led to northward migration by Mexicans looking for jobs, the pamphlet, in an unusual turn, takes "a page from history."[55] Examining the history of the Fugitive Slave Act of 1850, under which escaped slaves living in northern free states could be arrested and returned to their previous owners in the South, the pamphlet draws direct parallels between white supremacy in the pre-Civil War period and white supremacy in the seventies. This connection was especially important in attempting to convince black workers to support their Mexican comrades, despite the common accusation that undocumented workers were "stealing" jobs. A key aspect of this parallel concerned resistance to the Fugitive Slave Act, which necessarily took the form of direct and mass illegal action, because slaves had no legal rights. One particularly successful response is described as follows:

> On February 15, 1851, waiter Fred Wilkins, or Shadrach, as he was known, was seized from his job and rushed to the Boston courthouse. While Shadrach was still in court, a group of 50 black people from the neighborhood pushed into the courtroom, lifted him in the air, and spirited him to a carriage. Shadrach and his rescuers moved away "like a black squall." The rescue was so fast, nobody even pursued Shadrach. His rescuers were all eventually found not guilty by a sympathetic jury.[56]

---

pamphlet, see Chapter Five.
55   *"Since When Has Working Been a Crime?,"* 11.
56   Ibid., 15.

An inspiring connection is made between these sorts of organized efforts and actions like those at the Stewart-Warner factory.

Although the pamphlet was produced by STO, it was officially published by the South Chicago Workers Rights Center, which also worked with the women fired by Gateway Industries, discussed in Chapter Two. South Chicago was (and remains, to a certain extent, today) one of the few areas of the city of Chicago where sizeable populations of working-class blacks, whites, Mexicans, and Puerto Ricans all reside in close quarters, often working in the same factories—although the steel mill that employed some forty thousand people has long since shut its doors, leaving behind nothing but a mile-long stretch of concrete, garbage, and weeds along Lake Michigan. At one point, plans were discussed within STO to go door-to-door distributing the pamphlet and talking with residents about the issues of immigration and workers' rights.[57] This never happened, largely because of a quickly developing crisis in the Puerto Rican community that will be further discussed in Chapter Five. Nonetheless, the mere existence of the pamphlet reflects the seriousness with which STO took the problems of Mexican workers. This seriousness was also manifested in the group's efforts to support the striking Farah workers in El Paso. The Farah strikers were all Mexican women, and their experience of white supremacy obviously differed from that of black workers at Stewart-Warner or in the steel mills of Chicago and Gary. Regardless, STO was able to incorporate these various lived realities into the analysis of white supremacy and white skin privilege that continued to characterize the group's politics.

* * *

By 1972, STO's line on white supremacy and white skin privilege was fully developed, to the point that it could be used to differentiate the group's strategic approach to working-class organizing from that advocated by other left groups. One of the largest of these competing groups was the Revolutionary Union (RU), which had a nationwide presence and had made deliberate attempts to organize in heavy industry. In the early seventies, the RU, along with a number of other groups (including the Black Workers Congress) put forward a strategic orientation built around the creation of a "united front against imperialism." STO was one of many organizations invited to participate in the formation of the united front, and it used the opportunity to decline the invitation as a

---

57 Author interview, Kingsley Clark, April 2, 2006.

means to differentiate itself from the politics of the RU. The unsigned pamphlet *The United Front Against Imperialism?* offered the most comprehensive programmatic view of the STO position on white supremacy yet published under the group's name. Along with a host of other criticisms of the RU, it maintains that

> Since the influence of white supremacy is at present the greatest barrier to proletarian unity and class consciousness, and since the black movement today represents the most effective challenge to the selfish, racist, opportunistic tendencies of white workers, the most urgent task of the revolutionary movement as a whole is to remove the obstacles that stand in the way of the black movement. For white revolutionaries in particular, this means a special responsibility to win the support of the white workers for the aspirations of the black masses, to help the white workers actively and militantly reject their partial, selfish and counterfeit interests as part of a group which is favored in relation to blacks, on behalf of their total, broad and true interests as part of a class which is coming alive. For us, the central point of reference on any issue is the need to tear down the walls of white supremacy and achieve equality for black people.[58]

While the general line of argument was not much changed from Ignatin's sixties writings, his analysis had now become a central element of the political program of a revolutionary organization, rather than simply an abstract theory. Indeed, the black struggle had become a strict litmus test for STO.

> If, in regard to education, equality for blacks requires that children be bused, then we support busing; if it requires that they not be bused, then we are against busing. If equality in housing requires open-occupancy laws, then we are for open-occupancy laws. If it requires black control of black communities, we are for that. If it requires both open-occupancy laws and black control of black communities, then we are for both. If equality in employment means that the seniority system must be destroyed, then we are for

---

58   *The United Front Against Imperialism?* (Chicago: STO, 1972), 24–25.

scuttling it. If it requires the preservation of the seniority system, then we defend it. Organizations, whatever their defects, that fight for equality for black people are worthy of support, in our eyes. Organizations that reinforce white supremacy, whatever their virtues, we regard as reactionary. And so forth. The reader will note that we have advanced a somewhat different criterion for determining friends from enemies from the one put forward by the RU. Our stand on this matter flows directly from our strategic perspective, which places top priority on efforts to unify the workers as a class.[59]

With this publication, the lines had been clearly drawn, and STO was publicly identified with support for black struggles for liberation and against white supremacy, as well as with the ongoing effort to convince white workers to support black demands in much the same fashion as STO did.

If *The United Front Against Imperialism?* represented STO's official program in regards to white supremacy, another document attempted to flesh out the subjective aspects of this program in the context of the working-class life. This document was a speech given by Ignatin in 1972 to a group of student radicals in Portland, Oregon. Originally untitled and subsequently known as "Black Worker, White Worker," the talk is peppered with real-life examples of race relations in the steel mills and in other heavy industrial settings.[60] It takes these seemingly isolated vignettes and weaves them into a thoughtful examination of the complexities and contradictions of white supremacy and resistance to it in a working-class context. Thus, for example, Ignatin describes "a large farm equipment manufacturing plant in Chicago," where

a Black worker was being tried out for a repair job on an assembly line. The foreman had been harassing the man, trying to disqualify him during his three-day trial period. After two days of this, the majority of the workers on the line, Black and white, walked off their jobs demanding that the man be accepted for the job. The company backed

59 Ibid., 25–26.
60 The title "Black Worker, White Worker" is an additional homage to Du Bois' *Black Reconstruction*, which begins with two chapters, one entitled "The Black Worker," the other "The White Worker."

down and work resumed. Later on, some of the same white
workers took part in racist demonstrations at a Chicago
high school. The demonstrations were called against "over-
crowding" in an attempt to keep out several hundred Black
students who had been transferred to the school as a result
of redistricting.[61]

While the term itself remains unused, this scenario clearly depicts a
common manifestation of dual consciousness, as described in Chapter
Two. Fully aware of the historical resonance, Ignatin reformulates this
internal conflict as "a civil war in the mind of the white worker."[62] The
two sides in this conflict are, on the one hand, the "drive to reorga-
nize society so that they [workers] become the masters of production
instead of the servants of production—the essential meaning of socialism," and, on the other hand, the selfish pragmatism of "the white-skin
privilege system."[63] The task for (white) revolutionaries is to demonstrate to white workers the contradiction between these two world-
views, and encourage the embrace of the former and the rejection of
the latter. In this context, the "the daily activities of the Black people,
especially the Black workers, are the best existing model for the aspirations of the workers generally as a distinct class of people."[64] Thus, there
is a direct correlation between resistance to white supremacy and the
push toward working-class self-emancipation, because "the activities of
the Black workers are the most advanced outpost of the new society we
seek to establish."[65] Indeed, "white revolutionaries must understand,
and help the masses of white workers to understand, that the interests
of the entire working class can only be served by standing firmly with
the Black workers."[66]

Ignatin's speech deliberately focuses on real-world examples where
the perceived interests of "workers" (read, white workers) conflict with
the efforts of black people to improve their position in society. Only in

---

61   Noel Ignatin, "Black Workers, White Workers," in *Understanding and
      Fighting White Supremacy: A Collection* (Chicago: STO, n.d., but c.
      1976), 5. The same piece was later republished under the name "Black
      Worker, White Worker," in *Workplace Papers* (1980).

62   Ibid.

63   Ibid., 6.

64   Ibid., 7.

65   Ibid.

66   Ibid., 8.

situations like these can white workers be forced to make a decision between stark alternatives: fighting to defend the small gains that separate them from even more exploited black workers, or abandoning their own privileges in order to make common cause with black workers fighting for equality on the shop floor. Revolutionaries who accept this approach clearly have their work cut out for them. Ignatin readily agrees that this is not the most optimistic scenario: "The course I advocate offers great difficulties—no doubt about it. It is likely that the repression directed against a radical group that relentlessly fought racial discrimination would be greater than against a more moderate group.... I freely concede all the difficulties. But then," he concludes, reasonably enough, "who ever said that making a revolution was easy?"[67]

In addition to continuing the development of STO's strategic outlook on white skin privilege, the Portland speech also reflected the growing influence of C.L.R. James on Ignatin's thought, not only in its approach to working-class self-activity and the struggle against white supremacy, but also in its methodology. James was a black revolutionary from Trinidad, who spent almost seventy years immersed in working-class radical movements in the West Indies, Great Britain, and the United States. While living in the US from 1938 until his forced departure in 1953, he was profoundly affected by the developing struggle for black liberation in North America.[68] He wrote extensively on the topic, and his 1949 classic essay "The Revolutionary Answer to the Negro Problem in the USA" articulated a relationship between black militancy and working-class emancipation that foreshadowed the development of Ignatin's own position two decades later.

* * *

In the end, Ignatin's Portland speech represented a high point in STO's efforts to grapple with the contradictions and opportunities of life within a capitalist and white supremacist society. Today, the speech

---

67   Ibid., 10.

68   Since the demise of STO a veritable James industry has emerged, with possibly dozens of books focused on assessing his life and political legacy. Among these, two stand out: Kent Worchester, *C.L.R. James: A Political Biography* (Albany, NY: State University of New York Press, 1996), and Matthew Quest, *In the Shadow of State Power: C.L.R. James, Direct Democracy, & National Liberation Struggles* (unpublished manuscript).

is one of the best known publications associated with STO, having been reprinted and widely distributed over the years by radical groups such as Anti-Racist Action. Nonetheless, its initial circulation inside STO prompted a contentious debate within the group around the version of white skin privilege analysis it contained. Not long after the talk was given, the text was proposed to STO's Literature Committee for distribution as "a mass pamphlet that formalized our strategy for the struggle against white supremacy."[69] The Committee unanimously rejected this proposal, in a two-page document entitled "Critique of Noel's Portland Speech." The Committee argued both that "the paper projects a moralistic and unprogrammatic approach to the fight against white supremacy," and that "its conceptualization of socialism and how to win it is untenable in a document of a Leninist organization committed to a Leninist strategy for socialist revolution."[70] This latter argument dovetails with the critique of STO's theory of dual consciousness advanced by the "Crisis" grouping, and indeed the representative of the Literature Committee who penned the official response was Pauline, subsequently a signer of the "Crisis" documents.

The first argument, that the Portland speech was "moralistic and unprogrammatic," was hardly a novel criticism. Pauline herself noted that much of the rest of the left characterized the STO position on white supremacy in exactly these terms. But for these claims to be made within the group itself represented a fundamental challenge. The "Critique" argues that "Noel fails to demonstrate the immediate interests whites have in fighting against the system of white-skin privileges."[71] In particular, Ignatin "ignores the contradiction in these privileges. Not only do they divide the workers in struggle over immediate class issues, but they are often disadvantages disguised as privileges."[72] Further, "the line he puts forward is unprogrammatic. It requires white workers to make a commitment to socialism in order to repudiate their white-skin privileges…. Noel presents no program based on repudiation of concrete privileges that the white worker can be won to in the daily battles of the class struggle."[73] Thus, the "Critique" was not strictly speaking a repudiation of the white skin privilege analysis, but rather an attempt to reformulate

---

69   Pauline, "Critique of Noel's Portland Speech," unpublished manuscript in author's possession, n.d., but c. 1973.

70   Ibid., 1.

71   Ibid.

72   Ibid.

73   Ibid. Ellipsis mine.

it so that it appealed to the perceived self-interests of white workers. On one level, this was not entirely dissimilar from Ignatin's own critique of the Weatherman version of white skin privilege a few years previous. At the same time, however, the "Critique" could be perceived as an attempt to evade the real difficulties encountered in attempting to win white workers to STO's politics and strategy. The very real examples of contradictory behavior by white workers offered in the Portland speech could not be resolved simply by showing these workers the contradictions; as Ignatin maintained, "White working people aren't stupid. They don't act in a racist fashion simply out of blind prejudice. There are much more substantial causes—the system of white-skin privileges—which lead them to behave in a selfish, exclusionary manner."[74] Facing this problem squarely did not make Ignatin's position moralistic, but it did demand that revolutionaries avoid easy answers.

The second argument advanced in the "Critique," that Ignatin's vision of socialism and the strategy for achieving it were unworkable, represented a more fundamental challenge to STO's political outlook. The line of reasoning here was more or less identical to the criticisms discussed previously in regards to the "Crisis" faction. Thus, Ignatin "rejects Lenin's argument in *What Is to Be Done* that by itself the experience of workers cannot produce socialist consciousness…. To Lenin's approach Noel counterposes the 'gardener approach.' Discover the seeds of socialism in workers' self-activity, identify them, nurture them…. This approach is spontaneist and syndicalist."[75] In particular, the "Critique" argues that Ignatin's Portland speech romanticized the revolutionary potential of the black community: "he presents black culture as a model for the new society. He idealizes black consciousness and the social relations among black people. His 'program' for fighting white supremacy is for whites to recognize black culture and the black movement as the best expression of socialism."[76] The obvious alternative, from the perspective of the Literature Committee, was the embrace of the traditional *What is to be Done* approach prioritizing the ideological intervention of revolutionary cadre, such that "the development of this revolutionary class consciousness is the job of conscious communists armed with Marxist-Leninist theory."[77]

This criticism represented a direct attack on the Jamesian element in the Portland speech. The Portland speech (and, before it, the pamphlet

---

74 Ignatin, "Black Workers, White Workers," 5.
75 Pauline, "Critique," 2. Ellipses mine.
76 Ibid.
77 Ibid.

The United Front Against Imperialism?) was certainly open to criticism for romanticizing black struggles, but this aspect, as well as the concept of the seeds of socialism implicit in working-class life, both show the influence of James, whose political trajectory was almost defiantly unorthodox in terms of his approach to Leninism. One striking characteristic of James's analysis was his attentiveness to the daily life of workers and black people. Thus, years before the emergence of the modern Civil Rights Movement in the US South, he admonished,

> Let us not forget that in the Negro people, there sleep
> and are now awakening passions of a violence exceeding,
> perhaps, as far as these things can be compared, anything
> among the tremendous forces that capitalism has created.
> Anyone who knows them, who knows their history, is
> able to talk to them intimately, watches them at their own
> theatres, watches them at their dances, watches them in
> their churches, reads their press with a discerning eye, must
> recognise that although their social force may not be able to
> compare with the social force of a corresponding number of
> organised workers, the hatred of bourgeois society and the
> readiness to destroy it when the opportunity should present
> itself, rests among them to a degree greater than in any
> other section of the population in the United States.[78]

This attentiveness to cultural forms and daily life as potential sites of mass resistance to oppression was clearly echoed in Ignatin's analysis of the workplace and of black struggles against white supremacy.

Despite their common Jamesian roots, these two criticisms—the romanticization of black culture and the rejection of the seeds of socialism analysis—must be distinguished if for no other reason than that the former was insightful, while the latter was an unthinking regurgitation of Stalinist methodology. The projection of revolutionary potential

---

78   C.L.R. James, "The Revolutionary Answer to the Negro Problem in the USA" (1948), in Scott McLemee, ed., *C.L.R. James on the "Negro Question"* (Jackson, MS: The University Press of Mississippi, 1996), 146. Available online at http://www.marxists.org/archive/james-clr/works/1948/revolutionary-answer.htm (accessed October 10, 2011). Like many pieces published by James during his time in the United States, this document was originally published under a pseudonym, in this case "J. Meyer."

onto the black community was indeed a problem that characterized STO throughout most of its existence, although it was by no means the only radical group of its era to make this mistake. Even Ignatiev himself now considers this to have been one of STO's main shortcomings, lamenting the fact that the group couldn't see the difference between black revolution and proletarian revolution. He draws a parallel to the early IWW's failure to see the difference between industrial unionism and revolution.[79] At the same time, James himself cannot take all the blame here, since he argued only that black struggles had greater *potential* to be revolutionary than other movements, not that they were *necessarily* revolutionary. The biggest culprit was the context of the early seventies, following upon two full decades during which every progressive movement in the United States had either emerged from or taken direct inspiration from the black community. In this context, it is easy to see how such romanticization could have developed, although the "Critique" was certainly correct in challenging it.

On the second question, however, concerning the seeds of socialism idea, Ignatin's Portland speech holds up four decades later. A significant part of what made STO unique politically within its milieu was precisely the rejection of traditional understandings of the *What Is to Be Done* strategy, as has been described in greater detail in Chapter Two. Nonetheless, a tension always existed within STO regarding the relative importance of Leninist party-building measures and what the "Critique" describes as the "gardener approach." The latter element had clear roots in political experiences of STO's founding members, especially those who, like Ignatin and Hamerquist, had been disillusioned with the traditional methods of the Communist Party and its imitators. In the case of Hamerquist, this approach was largely influenced by Gramsci's analysis of the Italian soviets after World War One, while Ignatin was more closely drawn to James and his analysis. In this context, the obvious precursor to "Black Worker, White Worker" was the 1947 pamphlet *The American Worker*, by Paul Romano and Ria Stone, originally published by a group of Trotskyist militants centered around James. Romano was himself a politicized auto worker, and his analysis of the day-to-day reality of work in heavy industry reflected many of the same insights Ignatin brought to the Portland speech. For instance, Romano maintained that

> The worker expresses his hatred of the incentive system by
> saying he should write the union contract. This is no less

---

79 Author interview, Noel Ignatiev, January 27, 2006.

than saying that the existing production relations must be overthrown. It is also much more. It means that he wants to arrange his life in the factory in such a way that it satisfies his instincts for doing a good job, knowing that it is worthwhile, and living in harmony with his fellow men. It is deeply rooted in the worker that work is the foundation of his life. To make his work a meaningful part of life, an expression of his overall individuality, is what he would attempt to put into reality.[80]

Ignatin's experiences two decades later in farm implement factories and steel mills confirmed this understanding, and led him to similar conclusions. At the same time, however, Pauline and the other members of the "Crisis" faction were hardly alone in wanting STO to develop into a Marxist-Leninist party. This objective, as has been noted previously, marked STO from its founding in late 1969. Indeed, by the mid-seventies, STO would begin to place primary emphasis on this development, although as a group it was always convinced that any such party would necessarily be led primarily by revolutionaries of color. In this context, James himself was largely overshadowed, not just within STO but within the entire North American left, by the prominence of Maoism and Stalinism within the black movement. From the League of Revolutionary Black Workers (many of whom had direct or indirect exposure to James and his ideas in Detroit) to the Black Panther Party, and from the Republic of New Afrika to the African People's Socialist Party, black radical organizations of the early seventies almost invariably aligned themselves with the Maoist tradition within Marxism.[81] Thus,

---

80   Paul Romano and Ria Stone, *The American Worker* (Detroit: Bewick Editions, 1972 [1947]). Available online at http://libcom.org/history/ american-worker-paul-romano-ria-stone (accessed October 10, 2011). Ria Stone was a pseudonym for Raya Dunayevskaya, co-leader with C.L.R. James of the "Johnson-Forest Tendency" that emerged within the Workers Party and the Socialist Workers Party in the forties. "F. Forest" was another of Dunayevskaya's pseudonyms, while "J.R. Johnson" was one of several pen names for James. For more on Johnson-Forest, see Loren Goldner, "Introduction to the Johnson-Forest Tendency and Background to "Facing Reality" (2002), available online at http://home. earthlink.net/~lrgoldner/johnson.html (accessed October 10, 2011).

81   Thanks to Ethan Young for framing the question in these terms. Correspondence, September 14, 2006. See also Robin D.G. Kelley and Betsy

Ignatin's conceptual interest in the Jamesian "gardener approach" was more than counterbalanced by the practical requirements of STO's efforts to combat white supremacy within the context of the New Communist Movement. The result, in terms of the Portland speech, was a contradictory view of organization, one that placed a high value on both mass self-determination and Leninist cadre structures. STO's evolving perspective on this subject would oscillate over the next decade between party building and autonomy, as will be explored further in Chapters Four and Eight. The tension between these two poles was not to be easily resolved within STO.

* * *

Such debates could have continued indefinitely within STO, due to the group's previously noted policy of "refusing to impose discipline on matters of theory and fighting for discipline on matters of practice."[82] However, the "Crisis" split of late 1973 included the departure of Pauline, and presumably other members of the Literature Committee, who had declined to publish the Portland speech. At the same time, however, STO's analysis of white skin privilege faced a challenge, of an entirely different sort, from the people aligned with the "workerist" faction that was shortly to split under the banner of the "Head Is a Balloon" statement. In this case, the disagreement was not over proper interpretations of the line on white supremacy, or even about strategic questions emerging from the line. Rather, the leadership of the "Balloon" faction, in particular Zwierzynski and Brzostowski, for the most part did not believe the white skin privilege analysis was relevant within the context of extra-union organizing.[83] Key members of the "Balloon" faction were centrally involved in the independent truckers' strike, which mobilized an almost entirely white and male workforce, and in the Farah strike, which centered around the efforts of Mexican women. But apart from questions of language (English

---

Esch, "Black Like Mao: Red China and Black Revolution," in *Souls: A Critical Journal of Black Politics, Culture and Society* 1, no.4 (1999), 6–41. A PDF of this article is available online at http://www.columbia. edu/cu/ccbh/souls/vol1no4/vol1num4art1.pdf (accessed October 10, 2011).

82 "Outline History" (1972), 1.

83 Veterans of three different factions from the 1973–1974 era, Kingsley Clarke, Mel and Marcia Rothenberg, and Guillermo Brzostowski, all agreed on this point in interviews with the author.

in Gary, Spanish in El Paso), the "workerists" saw no important differences in terms of organizing. Confronting the truckers on questions of white skin privilege seemed counterproductive from this perspective, while in the Farah context it was entirely unnecessary. No doubt Ignatin and others would have disagreed with these assessments, but this debate was also truncated by the departure of the "Balloon" faction in mid-1974. In the end, Ignatin's view of white skin privilege became universal within STO, not so much via a protracted ideological struggle among the membership but through a process of attrition. By the time the dust had settled, the only people remaining in STO were people who agreed with the perspectives advanced in the Portland speech.

Strangely, however, the speech itself had not yet been published, almost two years after Ignatin had first given it in 1972. In fact, it was first published for a mass audience not by STO, but in the magazine *Radical America*, in the summer of 1974, under the title "Black Workers, White Workers."[84] This reflected not only the political disagreements within STO, but also its decreasing logistical capabilities as the group shrank dramatically. Nonetheless, once initial publication had finally been achieved, Ignatin's speech was widely republished and broadly distributed on the left, appearing both in collections relating to workplace organizing and in those focused on questions of white supremacy and resistance to it. As STO grew again in the mid-seventies, its approach to these questions would shift somewhat into a national liberation framework, but never again would any member fundamentally challenge the white skin privilege analysis contained in "Black Worker, White Worker."

---

84   Noel Ignatin, "Black Workers, White Workers," in *Radical America* 8, no. 4, July/August 1974, 41–60.

Part Two:
Dreams Found and Lost

Lives on the line where dreams are found and lost

I'll be there on time and I'll pay the cost

Bruce Springsteen, "Darkness on the Edge of Town"

Chapter Four:
Reorganization in Difficult Times

The way Noel Ignatiev tells the story, one of the key turning points in his political life took place during a conversation with Don Hamerquist in the fall of 1969, not long before the founding of STO.[1] At the time, Ignatin was still within the orbit of Stalinism, although he was already well on his way to the unorthodox Leninism that would characterize his future path. Hamerquist had only recently left the CPUSA, but his own political shift had begun a few years previous. Both men were well versed in the endless debates that dominated the new left as the decade came to a close, including the question of the Sino-Soviet split.[2]

The Soviet Union and the People's Republic of China were the largest and the third largest countries in the world, respectively, and they both claimed leading roles in the world communist movement. Tensions between their Communist Parties had reached a boiling point in the early sixties, several years after Nikita Khrushchev succeeded Joseph Stalin as

1   Noel Ignatiev, author interview, January 2006. As indicated previously, Ignatin changed his name to Ignatiev after his departure from STO. I use Ignatiev when describing his current positions (including relaying this story) and Ignatin when describing his activities and the positions he held before and during his time in STO.

2   A comprehensive scholarly treatment of the Sino-Soviet conflict can be found in Lorenz M. Luthi, *The Sino-Soviet Split: Cold War in the Communist World* (Princeton, NJ: Princeton University Press, 2008).

head of the Soviet Union. Khrushchev had initiated a significant shift in Soviet foreign policy that included substantial accommodation with the United States and other western powers, while Mao Tse-Tung was propelling the Chinese government into a series of confrontations with the US and its allies. One side effect of this conflict was China's posthumous embrace of Stalin as a great revolutionary who had defeated Hitler and dramatically expanded the reach of the international communist movement while challenging post-war US global hegemony. From this perspective, Stalin's legacy had been repudiated by Khrushchev's efforts at "peaceful co-existence."[3] As was the case in any number of contexts, much of the North American new left took its cues from Mao and China, leading to a hagiographic treatment of Stalin that continued throughout the seventies and into the eighties.

In this context, Hamerquist dropped a bombshell: according to Ignatiev, he argued that Khrushchev was not a repudiation of Stalin, but a continuation of his politics.[4] The implication was clear: Stalin had not been a revolutionary icon worthy of the admiration of the new left. Rather, he—like Khrushchev—had been an opportunist, a bureaucrat, a dictator above and against the proletariat, a brake on the engine of revolution. This view of Stalin was not without precedent, of course, but within non-Trotskyist versions of Leninism it was highly unusual.[5]

---

3   A number of writers have indicated that the public embrace of Stalin's legacy by the Chinese Communists was not entirely genuine, and that Mao and other leaders of the CPC had a number of private reservations about Stalin's role. See Ignatin, *"…no condescending saviors,"* as well as Russell Jacoby, "Stalinism and China," in *Radical America* 10, no.3 (May/June 1976), 7–24.

4   Interview with Noel, January 2006. Hamerquist does not remember this precise conversation, but has indicated that Ignatiev's narrative does accurately portray his (Hamerquist's) views at the time.

5   Trotskyists, of course, built an entire analysis around opposition to Stalin and his legacy, while anarchists and assorted ultraleft sectors of the left rejected not only Stalin and Khrushchev but the entire trajectory of Leninism. The literature here is enormous, but the basic outline of the Trotskyist critique of Stalin can be gleaned from A. Belden Fields, *Trotskyism and Maoism: Theory and Practice in France and the United States* (New York: Autonomedia, 1988), 14–16. Various ultraleft criticisms of Leninism are detailed in Richard Gombin, *The Radical Tradition: A Study in Revolutionary Thought* (New York: St. Martin's Press, 1979), while the general anarchist response to Bolshevism is

Hamerquist had come to this perspective after intense personal experience inside the CPUSA, extensive study of the Communist history and theory, and much exposure to social movements outside the Party's direct control. In essence, he had determined that in order to advance the cause of revolution, it was necessary to leave behind the organizational forms and strategies he grouped under the heading "the Stalin model."[6]

Ignatin was convinced, and he was not alone. The initial work of the Sojourner Truth Organization was devoted above all else to the development and implementation of revolutionary strategies that could overcome the obstacles presented not only by capital and the state, but also by the dominant revolutionary traditions of the era, including especially Stalinism. But in its early years, STO devoted relatively little attention to the organizational questions implied by its rejection of Stalinism. As previously noted, the group initially adopted a policy of "refusing to impose discipline on matters of theory and fighting for discipline on matters of practice." One practical result of this approach was a lack of theoretical coherence and, as we have seen, a series of debilitating splits. Only after its near collapse in 1974 did STO begin to seriously address issues of revolutionary organization. Nonetheless, to understand the resurrection of STO in the mid-seventies, it is necessary to back up slightly and assess the state of the US left in the early part of the decade.

* * *

By 1972, the New Communist Movement (NCM) had become one of the most vibrant tendencies to emerge from the ashes of the sixties new left, and within the NCM, the Revolutionary Union (RU) and the October League (OL) were recognized as the largest and most influential organizations. STO, among others, had already attacked the politics of both the RU and the OL, but these political criticisms did not automatically result in the growth of an organizational alternative. Movement toward developing such a tendency took the form of a conference outside of Cincinnati, Ohio in October 1972.[7] Known subsequently as the Grailville Conference (for the suburb where the conference took

---

summarized in Michael Schmidt and Lucien van der Walt, *Black Flame: The Revolutionary Class Politics of Anarchism and Syndicalism* (Oakland, CA: AK Press, 2009), 100–105.

6   This formulation recurs in Hamerquist's writings, but one of the earliest occurrences is found in *TARP*, 43.

7   For more on Grailville, see Elbaum, *Revolution in the Air*, 106.

place), it brought together a few hundred "independent" Leninists, some individuals and some in smaller collectives, who for one reason or another had not joined one of the larger organizations. STO was heavily involved in planning the conference, which it initially viewed as a likely framework for unifying the participants. In the event, however, the political differences among the attendees proved overwhelming. STO retreated back to its ongoing work in Chicago, and left the post-conference networking to others.

Over the next two years, while STO suffered through the "Crisis" and "Balloon" splits, a number of other Grailville veterans developed a loose network of like-minded groups, largely but not exclusively located in Midwestern cities: St. Louis, Kansas City, Louisville, Danville, IL, New York, and Boston, as well as Chicago. The looseness was even reflected in the name(s) given to the grouping, which was sometimes referred to as the "Coalition," sometimes the "Confederation," and sometimes the "Midwest Federation" (despite the participation from two east coast cities); similarly, the member groups were sometimes "Independent Marxist Collectives," and at other points "Independent Marxist-Leninist Organizations." Regardless of the name, however, the participants were united largely by their rejection of the politics advanced by the RU and OL (as well as Trotskyist groups like the International Socialists (IS) and other left organizations outside the New Communist Movement), by their embrace of the white skin privilege analysis, and by their emphasis on mass work in factories, hospitals, the military, and other venues.

In the aftermath of the "Balloon" split, STO was reduced to a handful of members, and for a brief time even lost its franchise on the name "Sojourner Truth" to a coalition of splitters who technically constituted a majority.[8] Both versions of STO participated in the Federation. Until the new grouping disintegrated in 1975, the once-and-future STO was known within the Federation as "STO(X)," or simply "the (X)." The (X) was more active, partly because its small numbers made its previous forms of mass work impossible to maintain. As a matter of survival, STO(X) focused its efforts on rebuilding its membership, and building links with like-minded revolutionaries outside Chicago was an important part of this process. By 1975, STO(X) was heavily involved in the Federation's discussions around the creation of a coherent revolutionary organization. The debate over whether and how to accomplish this task provides substantial insight into the strategic approach taken by STO—the (X),

---

8   Noel Ignatiev, email to the author, May 3, 2006.

to be precise—in its middle period, from the mid-seventies through the end of the decade.

* * *

The question of organizational unification among the various groups within the Federation was quite contentious from the start. One pole, led largely by the then-unnamed "Boston Group," argued that "it is only around theoretical positions, organizational principles, strategic and tactical line that communist unity can be achieved."[9] In other words, theoretical unity necessarily preceded organizational unity. In support for this view, the Boston Group marshaled a famous quote from Mao himself: "The correctness or otherwise of the ideological and political line decides everything."[10] This position was counterposed to the argument that "a more centralized organizational structure will more readily permit struggle over programmatic and theoretical differences."[11] In this scenario, the practical work of building a democratic centralist organization would precipitate further theoretical unification. This was STO(X)'s position. What appeared at first glance to be a chicken-and-egg question around

9 Boston Group, "A Perspective on Organizational Structure," in *Collective Works* #2, March 1975, 5. The "Boston Group" later became the Proletarian Unity League (PUL), and eventually helped form the Freedom Road Socialist Organization. In this context, there is a certain irony to PUL's later (1981) autobiographical description: "When it first formed, the group had not settled all the major questions, or even all the most important ones." PUL, "Proletarian Unity League: Where We Came From, What We Look Like, What We Do" (1981). Available online at http://www.freedomroad.org/index.php?option=com_content&view=article&id=237:family-tree-proletarian-unity-league&catid=171:our-history&Itemid=264&lang=en, accessed October 18, 2011.

10 *Collective Works* #2, 4. Originally from Mao Zedong, "Summary of Chairman Mao's talks with Responsible Comrades at Various Places during his Provincial Tour from the Middle of August to 12 September 1971," in Stuart Schram, editor, *Chairman Mao Talks to the People: Talks and Letters: 1956–1971* (New York: Pantheon Books, 1974), 290. Hamerquist's tart response to the Mao quote was to opine that "Luckily Mao will not be judged on the basis of this one statement because it is wrong on its face." Hamerquist, "Further Criticisms of Boston Position," in *Collective Works* #2, 18.

11 Ibid., 3.

theory and practice revealed, on a deeper level, the divisions between the highly unorthodox Leninism of the (X) and the more traditional positions put forward by the Boston Group. At the root, the dispute revolved around differing understandings of the classic Leninist organizational principle known as "democratic centralism."[12]

While most of the participating groups in the Federation embraced some version of democratic centralism, they disagreed profoundly about the proper definition of this important term. Once again, the strongest advocates of the opposing positions were the Boston Group and STO(X). Boston argued that "democratic centralism is precisely the organizational form recognizing the necessity for a single direction of the proletariat and disciplined democratic discussion of its strategic and tactical options."[13] In counterposing this to what it called "federalism," the Boston Group further defined democratic centralism by clarifying what it was *not*: "federalism also implies the equality and inviolable integrity of different political lines … but liberalism of this kind is incompatible with an organization seeking to serve the interests of the oppressed and the exploited."[14] Although the Boston Group did not believe that there was sufficient unity within the Federation to establish democratic centralism as its internal operating system, it made clear its political disdain for the alternatives.

In response to Boston, STO(X) unleashed its two biggest intellectual guns, Ignatin and Hamerquist, to present a very different vision of democratic centralism. Ignatin characterized the (X)'s critique of the Boston position as two-fold: "1. Differences [within a democratic centralist organization] cannot be anticipated and eliminated solely through a process of pure reason. 2. The party will always contain differences, even important ones, within it. This is not a 'weakness' to be 'eliminated' through struggle.'"[15] Hamerquist went even further, arguing that

> when Boston treats democratic centralism as a desirable, but remote, goal for the [Federation], they are applying a very mechanical, almost arbitrary, notion of what democratic

---

12 A straightforward explanation of democratic centralism and its historical development as a concept can be found in the online "Marxist Encyclopedia" project, available here: http://www.marxists.org/glossary/terms/d/e.htm#democratic-centralism accessed October 18, 2011.

13 Boston Group, "A Perspective on Organizational Structure," 6.

14 Ibid.

15 Ignatin, "Critical Notes on Boston Paper," in *Collective Works* #2, 11.

centralism must be. It must be that internal regimen known popularly as "Stalinism": assumption of leadership infallibility; assumption that Marxism has already answered all important questions; the banning of "factions"; strict limits on internal debate; and the prohibition of any public manifestations of internal division.… [A]ll these points … have little or nothing to do with democratic centralism, in my opinion.[16]

This critique, especially the negative view of Stalinism, represented a continuation of STO's longtime opposition to the orthodox Leninism of groups like the RU and the OL, now focused on a member group of the Federation itself.

Rather than reject democratic centralism, STO(X) put forward a competing definition that focused heavily on the importance of practical work in determining political line. Again, Hamerquist took the lead:

For the [Federation], democratic centralism means a decision to carry out joint activity … without such a decision, and such activities, it is quite possible to continue to function as if every position and tendency had equal status. Second, it means implementation of divisions into clear majorities and minorities on all disputed questions with the understanding that the majority "rules." Third, it means that a minimum concern with developing our political position into a coherent perspective entails the organizational purging of elements which consistently adopt minority positions which are closer to that of other political tendencies than to the [Federation]. Fourth, it means a very careful and reasoned concern with not mechanically imposing a majority decision on the minority, for the simple reason that no minority that is serious will accept such treatment in a grouping so new and so weak. Fifth, it means definite protections of the right of minorities to argue their position.[17]

This exhaustive detailing of democratic centralism served multiple purposes: it not only articulated a coherent alternative to the more

---

16   Hamerquist, "Further Criticisms of Boston Position," in *Collective Works* #2, 22.

17   Ibid. Ellipsis in original.

traditional understanding of democratic centralism that was no doubt widespread within the Federation, it also served as a shot across Boston's bow in the form of the "organizational purging" clause, and it set forth the basic short-term organizational goals of the (X)'s participation in the Federation.

As these political disputes continued over the course of 1975, it became increasingly clear that the Boston Group was losing the battle of opinion within the Federation. Most of the Midwestern groups, despite a variety of other disagreements, sided with STO(X) on the definition of democratic centralism and its immediate applicability to the Federation. By the summer, the Boston Group withdrew from the Federation, along with the collective based in New York, but not before Hamerquist launched one more salvo against Stalinism as a general proposition. In advancing a set of "Discussion Points on the Party and Revolutionary Strategy," he offered the most direct rejection of Stalinism STO had yet put forward:

> The Leninist conception of the party must be recaptured from Stalinist distortion. We take this to involve the following points (at least): (A) Party life must emphasize clear, sharp and critical debate over points of principle. Furthermore, the maximum effort must be extended to make this debate accessible to the working class. Fear of public differences and of "factions" is no part of Leninist theory or practice on the question of the party. (B) The ability of a party to play a vanguard role (and thus to truly be able to exercise discipline) is not given a priori. It is gained through a process of demonstrating to the masses of people that it is able to define and attack the burning questions of the day, that it is able to articulate and organize popular aspirations in a framework of class struggle, that it can recognize and correct mistakes before they lead it to catastrophe or irrelevance. (C) The notion that the party leads by virtue of being the guardian of the "science of Marxism-Leninism" inevitably leads to distortion of the scientific character of Marxist theory, and a misunderstanding of the potential of the party to operate "scientifically." (D) The so-called "party principle" must be cleared of any implication that runs contrary to the central Marxist thesis that the emancipation

of the working class is the task of the working class itself.[18]

In a way, this analysis, offered at the midpoint of the decade, can be seen as a pivot in the theoretical development of STO's approach to organization. From 1970 to 1975, the group had moved closer and closer to a traditional party-building model, progressively abandoning the more spontanist aspects of its early embrace of mass work in the factories as the labor upsurge declined. The winnowing process within the Federation represented the closest STO ever came to creating "the Party." As much as Hamerquist's indictment of Stalinism assumed the validity of the party-building idea, it also contained the kernels of STO's eventual rejection of that model, especially in its final assertion regarding the class and the party. As the decade came to a close, STO would edge ever closer to a version of autonomist Marxism heavily influenced by C.L.R. James, which tended to view the class and the party as antagonists rather than partners. But the process that led to this conclusion was complicated, and began with the death of the Federation and the rebirth of a new, expanded Sojourner Truth Organization.

* * *

Once the Boston group departed from the Federation, the remaining collectives were largely united in their strategic approach to revolution. After shedding the St. Louis and Danville groups in a series of conflicts over relations with the growing anti-imperialist trend within the North American left, the three remaining member organizations—STO in Chicago, Workforce in Kansas City, and the Haymarket Organization in Davenport, Iowa—agreed in early 1976 to merge into a single organization, adopting Hamerquist's version of democratic centralism along the way. Chicago was identified as the "center" of the organization, and STO's name was retained for the group as a whole, which was possible because the other version of STO had ceased to exist.[19]

---

18 Hamerquist, "Discussion Points on the Party and Revolutionary Strategy," in *Collective Works* #3 (June, 1975), 8–9.

19 There is some disagreement about the basis for this decision. The pre-eminence of Ignatin and Hamerquist as both experienced organizers and as major theoreticians, and their location in the Chicago area, may have played the decisive role. However, Alan Rausch, then a member of the Haymarket Organization, recalls that the naming decision was not a result of deference to the Chicago comrades, and more the outcome

At a conference in Iowa early that summer, a series of position papers were adopted, known later as the "Coe Resolutions," after the college campus that hosted the meeting. These resolutions addressed everything from the organizational principles of the newly restructured group (for example, the clause that allowed the expulsion of "consistent minorities" was formally approved) to an analysis of the short-term prospects for revolutionary movements. On this subject, the group made a significant departure from its previous approach, in essence decentering the workplace as a site of social struggle, while acknowledging the rising momentum of a range of anti-imperialist movements within the United States, especially those for Puerto Rican independence, New Afrikan liberation, and revolution in Iran (see Chapter Five for more on this). The theoretical justification for this strategic shift was an analysis that the industrial working class in the United States was entering a period STO called "the lull," which the group expected to last for several years before a re-surgent working-class radicalism would re-invigorate shop-floor efforts. In the mean time, the group decided its efforts were better focused on internal education (especially around the theoretical topics we'll discuss in Chapter Six) and on direct support for third world revolutionaries. While many members of STO still worked in factories, there was no longer any organizational encouragement to concentrate in particular worksites or industries.

Structurally, the new version of STO was based around a regular "General Membership Meeting" (GMM) which debated political issues, set policy, and determined strategic priorities, normally via a majority vote of members on a series of resolutions. Between GMMs, the leadership body was the National Committee (NC), which was elected by the membership at each GMM and was supposed to meet face-to-face on a quarterly basis. The NC was responsible for guiding internal discussions on political and strategic questions, and for ensuring the implementation of decisions made at each GMM. To deal with travel and communication difficulties, members of the National Committee who resided in Chicago constituted a Central Committee (CC), which was tasked with making certain tactical decisions between NC meetings. This arrangement reinforced the traditional leading role of several Chicago members of the group, especially Hamerquist and Ignatin, although they were not consistently members of the National or Central Committees. In general,

---

of a general satisfaction with the historical and political resonance of the name "Sojourner Truth." Conversation with the author, August 1, 2009.

the organizational structure adopted at the Coe Conference was designed to reflect the version of democratic centralism advocated with the Federation by Hamerquist and others. In practice, it resulted in a somewhat flawed hybrid of democratic control and informal hierarchy. Even when certain leading members of STO were not in formally elected positions on the NC or CC, their base of power within the group was still substantial.

In an attempt to behave more like a party-building organization, STO began to use the National Committee as a framework for addressing the political implications of personal decisions facing individual members. This approach had long been common within the group for questions of employment, but as the organization expanded geographically, it came to be applied more broadly to life decisions. For instance, if a member in one city was considering leaving that city for any of a variety of personal reasons (personal conflicts, lack of work, etc.), the NC would weigh in with a recommendation on where that person should move. While these decisions were not normally binding on the members in question, they were almost always agreed to. As a result, in the mid- to late seventies, STO members were "sent to" cities as diverse as Denver, Portland, Philadelphia, and New York, as well as more traditional "placements" in Chicago and Kansas City.

Another aspect of the Coe Resolutions that was to become significant in the coming period concerned the racial composition of STO's membership. While the group had always been open to members regardless of race, it had also traditionally been overwhelmingly white, partly as a result of its commitment to autonomy for radical movements of people of color. The Coe Resolutions for the first time approved an organizational position on the recruitment of members of color (or "third world members," in the terminology of the resolutions). Given STO's strong commitment to autonomy and national liberation, it was unsurprising that the Coe Resolution focused on "Third World Revolutionary Organizations and the Party Building Process."[20] Beginning with the premise that "a multinational communist party in this country will develop mainly through the gradual merging of Third World communist groups with organizations that are largely white," the resolution advocated for nonwhite members of STO to shift toward membership in revolutionary groups of their specific race or nationality whenever appropriate. Thus,

---

20   The Coe Resolution of this name is attached as "Appendix I" to the unpublished document "The Reasons for the Split in STO: White Chauvinism in Practice," in author's possession. Subsequent quotes are from the resolution as presented in this appendix.

"it is the policy of STO to encourage Third World cadre to join and take discipline from Third World revolutionary organizations if they perceive that joining such organizations will enhance the development of these organizations." With this substantial caveat, STO was formally open to accepting members of color, and within a year of the Coe Conference the group had indeed added four members of color (two black women, a latino man, and a latina woman), a small but substantial number for a group that still numbered fewer than fifty people.

This new policy inevitably exacerbated a long-standing tension within STO, between the belief in the necessity of a multiracial revolutionary movement and the support for autonomous organizing within communities of color. In contrast to other largely white revolutionary groups that deliberately recruited members of color at least partly in order to diversify their demographic composition, STO was always gun-shy about this approach, with several ex-members recalling a shared disdain for the tokenism they saw in the recruitment efforts of groups like the RU/RCP.[21] Indeed, STO's practice during the period after the Coe conference was to avoid "recruiting TW [third world] members without [first] consulting with national liberation organizations to which they might belong and with which STO had working relationships."[22] In formalizing the view that the coming revolutionary party would develop from the merger of several revolutionary groups with different demographics and largely under the leadership of radicals of color, the newly restructured STO gained a justification for remaining overwhelmingly white. But at the same time, the support for "third world" autonomy necessarily resulted in an openness to admitting members of color who directly expressed an interest in STO's political direction and practical work. This Coe Resolution attempted to bridge the gap by suggesting that membership in STO should be a transitional phase for black or latina/o revolutionaries on their way to eventual membership in their "appropriate" national liberation movements, but this perspective discounted the possibility that such revolutionaries might feel more at home politically within STO than in other organizational structures. The seeds of eventual conflict were more or less built into the self-conception that emerged from the Coe Conference.

---

21   Author interviews with Kingsley Clarke, Don Hamerquist, David Ranney.

22   "The Reasons for the Split in STO: White Chauvinism in Practice," unpublished document dated January 28, 1978 and signed by twelve ex-members of STO, 1. In author's possession.

* * *

Regardless of any subtle tensions, STO emerged from Coe stronger and more vital than it had been in some time. With established branches in a variety of locations, and with a refocused set of strategic priorities, the group was able to engage in many different areas of work. In addition to solidarity work with national liberation movements, the group undertook the substantial task of developing a theoretical pole within the North American left. Now straddling the New Communist Movement and the anti-imperialist white left, STO resumed an aggressive publishing schedule, issuing a series of pamphlets on key topics and using its network of contacts to distribute them nationally and even overseas.[23] This included re-issuing the classic piece *Toward a Revolutionary Party*, producing a collection of pieces themed around *Understanding and Fighting White Supremacy*, and introducing important new pamphlets on topics like *White Supremacy and the Afro-American National Question* and *Rape, Racism, and the White Women's Movement*. STO produced so many publications during this period that, shortly after the Coe Conference, it distributed a trifold leaflet advertising fourteen different pamphlets under the heading "Literature from Sojourner Truth Organization." Including sections on "General Strategy," "White Supremacy and the National Question," and "Production Organizing," the leaflet was representative of the group's ongoing political transformation. "Despite some changes in our strategic conceptions," according to the leaflet, "we continue to reprint all of our literature that we feel is relevant to current revolutionary concerns so that our development is open for examination."[24] The trifold even contained an order form for interested readers, and an offer to waive shipping costs if "payment accompanies your order."

This flurry of publications was a direct result of STO's declaration of the "lull," which meant that limited energies were better spent organizing the left itself rather than attempting to organize the class. It was also made possible by STO's earlier investment in a printing press, which by the mid-seventies had been incorporated into a full-scale printshop that

---

23 British radical Kevin McDonnell indicates that STO pamphlets were available for sale in a variety of radical bookshops in London during the mid-seventies. Email to author, May 8, 2009.

24 Untitled leaflet (n.d., but c. 1976). The Tamiment Library and Robert F. Wagner Labor Archives, New American Movement Records (TAM051), Box 1. Thank you to Evan Matthew Daniel for providing me with a copy of this document.

provided continuous employment to one or more STO members until the group's final demise in the mid-eighties.[25] This in-house press allowed STO to produce substantial print runs of a large number of pamphlets with an increasingly professional design. Where early STO publications were routinely based on text produced on typewriters, by the mid-seventies the printshop had incorporated typesetting equipment that looked quite sharp by the pre-computer standards of the era.

In contrast to many other left groups that engaged in regular publication, STO's efforts in this arena were not normally focused on proclaiming official organizational position papers. Instead, a number of the main documents published in 1976 were openly billed as "discussion papers," meaning that they were intended to argue for claims that were not just controversial within the left but were contentious inside STO as well. Hamerquist's *White Supremacy and the Afro-American National Question* fell into this category, as did Ignatin's long essay published under the title *"...no condescending saviors"*, which amounted to an extended argument for the position that the then-existing "socialist" governments of the world—especially the Soviet Union, China, and Cuba—were actually implementing a version of "state capitalism." Drawing heavily on the analysis of C.L.R. James in his classic work *State Capitalism and World Revolution*, but built largely around Ignatin's review of the relevant literature, the pamphlet was not only not a formal position paper, it probably never reflected a majority position within STO.[26] This reflected both the group's commitment to airing internal political disputes in public, as well as the high level of influence wielded by Ignatin personally within STO.

The crux of Ignatin's argument, at least in terms of the Soviet Union, amounts to a restatement of Hamerquist's revelatory reframing of the issue in 1969, as described early in this chapter. Ignatin argues that the classic Maoist line on Russia—that capitalism was "restored" there by Khrushchev in 1957—is illogical and inconsistent with the known facts. Instead, he proposes, "There are only two opinions on this matter that meet minimum standards of reasonableness: *either* socialism exists in the Soviet Union, in spite of any backward steps that may have been taken by the revisionists; *or* socialism was never attained there, and the

---

25   The printshop continued to operate as a commercial enterprise until approximately 2002, largely under the direction of two former members of STO, printing a variety of materials for various left, community-based, commercial, and music-oriented projects.

26   See C.L.R. James (with Raya Dunayevskaya and Grace Lee), *State Capitalism and World Revolution* (Chicago: Charles H. Kerr, 1986 [1950]).

Khrushchev-Brezhnev policies represent, in the most fundamental sense, not a reversal but a continuation of previous policies."[27] Ignatin makes it clear that he endorses the latter scenario, and much of his pamphlet focuses on documenting this line of argument with extensive use of Lenin's own writings, as well as references to the historiography of the Russian Revolution.

According to Ignatin, Lenin himself advocated for the necessity of state capitalism as a response to the economic crises facing the Soviet Union in the years immediately following the revolution. Under this analysis, the New Economic Policy (NEP), introduced in 1921, "was an alliance between the Soviet state and large-scale capitalism, against the petty capitalism which then prevailed."[28] The real question, however, concerns not economic policy but political issues around the structure of the Soviet state. Lenin believed that the danger of state capitalism could be contained by the increasingly powerful and revolutionary state apparatus. But instead of "broaden[ing] the base of participation in state affairs," the Bolsheviks "chose another course, to rely increasingly on the Party to perform the administrative tasks of the new state."[29] Stalin's innovation was not the single-party state as such, but the attending "theory of the party as the repository of all knowledge, whose task was to mobilize the population to carry out its directives."[30]

His critique of Soviet state capitalism notwithstanding, Ignatin defends Lenin's political integrity to a great extent, arguing that the Bolsheviks were "forced" to follow such a course, and further claiming that in Lenin's last year of life he saw the error of the NEP and attempted to combat the new scourge of state capitalism with a "damning criticism of the Soviet regime."[31] But it was too late; Lenin died in 1924 and was replaced by Stalin, who dramatically expanded the reach and depth of Soviet state capitalism and its attendant bureaucracies. In Ignatin's analysis, Lenin's theory of the party bears no responsibility for the "subsequent degeneration of the Soviet Union."[32] This maneuver to absolve Lenin of the sins of Stalin was by now familiar to those who followed STO's political development, and it was certainly of a piece with Hamerquist's earlier defense of democratic centralism.

---

27   Ignatin, *"…no condescending saviors"* (Chicago: STO, 1976), 9.
28   Ibid., 13.
29   Ibid., 18.
30   Ibid.
31   Ibid., 14.
32   Ibid., 18.

Ignatin also pays considerable attention to the twists and turns of both Soviet and Chinese foreign policies, but within a framework where "a country's foreign policy is an extension of its domestic one."[33] Thus, neither Soviet efforts to constrain the revolutionary efforts of subordinate Communist parties in the third world (what the Maoists called "social-imperialism"), nor the notorious support of the Chinese Communists for reactionary forces in Africa and Latin America, were in themselves the central problem. They were instead symptomatic of the continued power of capitalism in the two largest so-called Communist countries in the world. Ignatin issues a direct challenge to other US revolutionaries, such as the October League, who had an unfortunate tendency to pursue to the extreme the logic of "my enemy's enemy is my friend," defending China and excoriating the Soviet Union, even when such a position was functionally identical to that of the United States government itself. In contrast, argues Ignatin, "we remain firmly committed to the traditional stance of communists in an imperialist country—for American workers, the enemy is at home!"[34] Despite substantial differences over the nature of the Soviet and Chinese regimes, this strategic conclusion was one that all members of STO would have strongly embraced.

* * *

Pamphlets weren't the only publishing method STO used to heighten its political profile. Less than a year after the Coe Conference, the first issue of *Urgent Tasks* appeared, heralding one of STO's lasting contributions to the US left. *UT*, as it was often known, was a well-produced, well-written, and well-distributed magazine that promoted STO's political stance in a consistent fashion in fourteen issues over the course of the next five years. The title was drawn, unsurprisingly, from Lenin, specifically from the title of the editorial in the first issue of the pre-Bolshevik newspaper *Iskra*, published in 1900, "The Urgent Tasks of Our Movement." Every issue contained the same brief quotation from its namesake document: "… not to serve the working class at each of its stages, but to represent the interests of the movement as a whole, to point out to this movement its ultimate aim and its political tasks, and to safeguard its political and ideological independence."[35] From

---

33   Ibid., 2.

34   Ibid.

35   Quoted from *Urgent Tasks* #1, May, 1977, inside front cover. The original can be found (with a slightly different translation) in V.I. Lenin,

the fifth issue onward, the subtitle "Journal of the Revolutionary Left" was appended. The editorial board was elected by STO's membership on a regular basis, and Ignatin served as editor for almost every issue after the fifth. Each issue of the magazine was designed, typeset, and printed at STO's printshop.

Early issues of *UT* contained a series of strident polemics by STO members against erstwhile allies and opponents like the Prairie Fire Organizing Committee and the Philadelphia Workers' Organizing Committee.[36] But the range of topics and authors began to broaden, and the quality of design and layout improved substantially, allowing *UT* to develop into a solid and nondogmatic publication that was taken seriously by a significant section of the left by the end of the decade. The journal regularly featured new translations of important documents from revolutionaries in places like Iran, Italy, Poland, and Puerto Rico. When STO approved organizational position papers on various topics, normally under the rubric of "theses," these were published in *UT* for maximum distribution. Thus the "Theses on White Supremacy and the National Question," approved by the GMM in May 1977, were published in Number Two (October 1977), while the "Theses on Fascism," approved by the GMM in April 1981, were published in the penultimate issue, Number Thirteen (Spring 1982).

Beginning with Number Three (Spring 1978), a clarification was printed alongside the listing of the editorial board: "Signed articles do not necessarily express the views of Sojourner Truth Organization."[37] Only rarely were author biographies provided, so it was impossible for most outsiders to know whether a signed piece had been penned by an STO member or not. As time went on, a significant number of items in almost every issue were written by nonmembers, although behind the

---

"The Urgent Tasks of Our Movement" (1900), in *Collected Works*, Volume 4, 366–371.

36 The Prairie Fire Organizing Committee (PFOC) was one of the leading groups in the white, anti-imperialist solidarity movement of the seventies, while the Philadelphia Workers' Organizing Committee (PWOC) was a relatively late arrival in the New Communist Movement. By 1977, when the first issue of *UT* was published, both groups were quite prominent in the US left. For more on PFOC, see Chapter Five of this book, as well as Dan Berger, *Outlaws of America: The Weather Underground and the Politics of Solidarity* (Oakland, CA: AK Press, 2006). For more on PWOC, see Elbaum, *Revolution in the Air*.

37 Quoted from *Urgent Tasks* #3, Spring 1978, inside front cover.

scenes, members were being strongly encouraged to contribute.[38] Some pieces in *UT* addressed theoretical issues such as Marx's law of value, some were concerned with historical topics like the nature of slavery before the Civil War, and some focused on strategic questions that spoke directly to the ongoing work of STO. This last category, over the duration of *UT*'s lifespan, included articles on factory organizing, antinuclear work, fascism and antifascism, and the nature of the movement for gay liberation, among other topics. Most of these articles were written by STO members, as were the periodically published study guides on topics like Reconstruction and dialectics.

The twelfth issue of *UT* was almost certainly the most well-received by the left outside of STO, even though it lacked any articles with immediate implications for strategy. This issue, guest edited by the founding and longtime editor of *Radical America*, Paul Buhle, was a celebration of "C.L.R. James: His Life and Work."[39] James had been an ever-growing influence on the politics of Ignatin and other members of STO as the seventies progressed. The 132-page tome dwarfed all other issues of the magazine, and may have earned Ignatin as much scorn inside STO as it garnered praise in the outside world. Dozens of well-known radicals from several continents contributed reminiscences, reflections, and assessments of various aspects of James's written output, his organizing work, and his personal life. Of the authors, however, only two—Ignatin and Ken Lawrence—were members of STO; though the organization was clearly influenced by James and his politics, most of the membership was not engaged with the project. This unusual and decidedly unrepresentative publication went on to become one of the most widely known items ever produced by STO; its contents were even subsequently republished as a book in Great Britain. Ironically, while Ignatin and STO were drawn to James largely because of his major contributions to revolutionary theory and his unorthodox approach to organizational and cultural questions, the publication of the special issue of *UT* coincided almost perfectly with the rise of James as an acceptable and safe topic for academic study.

* * *

While considerations of general revolutionary theory and strategy were certainly important to STO during this period, the organization remained

---

38   See, for example, Noel Ignatin, "Even More Urgently on *UT*," in *Internal Discussion Bulletin* #7, Jan/Feb 1979, 39–40.

39   See *Urgent Tasks* #12, Summer 1981.

concerned about a number of issues that might be seen as more immediate. Foremost among these, of course, were white supremacy and patriarchy, which together helped worsen the misery of capitalism for the vast majority of the world's population. The same flurry of publication that led to "… *no condescending saviors"* also produced one of STO's most widely distributed, and most controversial, pamphlets, Allison Edwards's *Rape, Racism, and the White Women's Movement: An Answer to Susan Brownmiller*. Brownmiller was a well-known white feminist writer and activist who, in 1975, published a best-selling book entitled *Against Our Will: Men, Women and Rape*. Widely regarded as a key text in the mainstream acceptance of the feminist movement, *Against Our Will* positions rape as a central weapon in the continued oppression of women by men. "From prehistoric times to the present," argues Brownmiller, "rape has played a critical function. It is nothing more or less than a conscious process of intimidation by which *all men* keep *all women* in a state of fear."[40] In terms of race, the book maintains that "interracial rape remains a huge political embarrassment to liberals."[41] It examines in some detail the ways in which the US left, especially the CPUSA, chose to highlight the plight of black men wrongfully charged with raping white women—such as the defendants in the 1931 Alabama trial known popularly as the Scottsboro case—instead of focusing on the experience of white women who were victims of interracial rape.[42]

Edwards's pamphlet launches a frontal attack on Brownmiller's book, accusing it of capitulation to a racist, law-and-order mentality that did nothing to advance the legitimate cause of feminism. After painting a picture of rising crime amidst the general economic crisis of the mid-seventies, Edwards argues that "to focus on the increase in rape, particularly black on white rape, in isolation from the entire pattern and its causes, can only contribute to the repression and terror against black people."[43] Describing Brownmiller's position as "racist, reactionary, and

---

40 Susan Brownmiller, *Against Our Will: Men, Women and Rape* (New York: Simon and Schuster, 1975), 15. Italics in original.

41 Ibid., 254.

42 On Scottsboro, see Hayward Patterson and Earl Conrad, *Scottsboro Boy* (New York: Collier Books, 1969 [1950]), as well as James Goodman, *Stories of Scottsboro* (New York: Pantheon, 1994). Edwards says of Patterson's memoir, "it should be required reading for everyone who has read *Against Our Will.*" Allison Edwards, *Rape, Racism and the White Women's Movement: An Answer to Susan Brownmiller* (Chicago: STO, 1976), 10. All quotes are from the first edition.

43 Edwards, 8.

terribly dangerous," Edwards goes on to criticize "her inevitable law-and-order conclusions on how to stop rape."[44] Thus, maintains Edwards, "A solution to rape that calls for more prosecutions is a solution that is designed to put more black men in jail, whether or not they have committed any crimes."[45] *Against Our Will* suggests that female parity in police employment would be the "ultimate testing ground" for "full equality for women," leading Edwards to sarcastically question whether women should also demand the right "to plot 50% of the assassinations of leaders of third world countries engaged in struggles for national liberation."[46] From a revolutionary perspective, Brownmiller's analysis was anathema.

For Edwards, the critique of Brownmiller becomes a launching pad for criticizing the rightward (and whiteward) trajectory of the women's movement during the seventies. Combining STO's traditional emphasis on the struggle against white supremacy with an immanent critique of feminism's prospects, Edwards argues that "a women's movement without black women will not free itself of bourgeois domination and become a revolutionary movement. In fact, a white women's movement that does not align itself with black women's struggle for liberation cannot be considered a women's movement at all."[47] Drawing on the historical parallel of how the women's movement of the nineteenth century responded to black leadership in the movement for the abolition of slavery before the Civil War, Edwards suggests a framework that would allow white feminists to link their efforts to those of black communities for freedom and self-determination. She summarizes the importance and potential of a truly radical feminist movement:

> A proletarian revolution is an absolute necessity for the liberation of women. Conversely, an autonomous women's movement is an absolute necessity as part of a strategy for proletarian revolution. Without an independent women's movement, there is no guarantee that the male supremacy now rampant in bourgeois society or, for that matter, within the proletarian movement or in any party, will be challenged. Thus, without a women's movement there is no assurance that even under socialism the ideological super-structure of male dominance and male superiority will be

---

44   Ibid., 21.
45   Ibid., 24.
46   Brownmiller, 388; Edwards, 25.
47   Edwards, 30.

undercut. Furthermore, without a revolutionary struggle against male supremacy, the fight against capitalist domination will not succeed.[48]

With this emphatic statement, Edwards pre-empted any charge that she was marginalizing or rejecting the role of feminism. The point was reinforced by the back cover of the pamphlet, which featured a portrait of STO's namesake, Sojourner Truth, alongside the long version of what is probably her most famous quote, ending in the rhetorical question "And ain't I a woman?"[49] In the context of Edwards's polemic, this question took on a second meaning in direct challenge to the "white women's movement" of the pamphlet's title.

* * *

Edwards was for a long period STO's leading theorist on women's issues, and she remembers being groomed within the group as a female intellectual. When Brownmiller's book was published, Ken Lawrence suggested to Edwards that she write a critique of it.[50] Having completed this task, she later wrote a lengthy two-part essay published in *Urgent Tasks*, entitled "Women and Modern Capitalism" that methodically laid out her analysis of patriarchy, and throughout this period she was involved in a range of political activities as part of STO and as a lawyer.[51] But Edwards was hardly the only member of STO to address women's issues during this time, either in writing or in practice. Carole Travis, Linda Phelps, Beth Henson, Elaine Zeskind, and Cathy Adolphson all published pieces about women's oppression and liberation in the pages of *Urgent Tasks*. Members of STO took on significant roles in campaigns against forced sterilization (especially in the Puerto Rican context), in defense of reproductive rights more broadly, and in support of Dessie

---

48   Ibid., 35.
49   More recent historical scholarship has disputed whether Truth actually uttered the words "ain't I a woman." See Carleton Mabee with Susan Mabee Newhouse, *Sojourner Truth: Slave, Prophet, Legend* (New York: New York University Press, 1993), 75–78.
50   Allison Edwards, interview with the author, December 13, 2008.
51   See "Women and Modern Capitalism Part One: Erosion of Material Base for Oppression," in *Urgent Tasks* #5, Summer 1979, 6–19, and "Women and Modern Capitalism Part Two: Alienation and Objectification," in *Urgent Tasks* #6, Fall 1979, 13–34.

Woods, a black woman sentenced to death for killing a white man who tried to rape her.[52] Women were in leadership positions within STO from its inception until its eventual demise. During the second half of the seventies a series of intra-organizational bodies, with names like "Women's Commission" and "Women's Wing" played an active role within the group's internal culture.

Over the course of several years, an extensive internal debate focused STO's attention on the question of women's autonomy, both within the organization and outside it. An article by Elaine Zeskind on "The Party and Autonomy for Women" was featured prominently in the first issue of *Urgent Tasks*, prefaced by a note indicating that "STO intends to break with [the] traditional model" used by most New Communist groups, which rejected substantial autonomy for women because it was supposedly "an anti-Leninist capitulation to 'petty bourgeois women's caucus ideas.'"[53] The extent to which the group did in fact distinguish itself from the "traditional model" is unclear, and no published documents ever followed up on the promise that prefaced Zeskind's article. Similarly, there was little unanimity within STO on the questions related to the nature of male supremacy, the relationship of patriarchy to capitalism, or the role of women in revolutionary struggles. No theses were ever adopted by the organization providing an official stance on any of these topics, nor did any of the unsigned editorials in *UT* address such issues. Partly as a result, outsiders were left to piece together an understanding of STO's perspective based either on their reading of STO's published materials (all signed by individuals rather than organizationally) or on individual conversations with members of the group.

Ted Allen, who had helped pioneer the analysis of white skin privilege that had always defined STO, was one such outsider, and he produced a strikingly perceptive critique of what appeared to be STO's overall position on women and revolution. In the summer of 1978, Allen sent a lengthy and often humorous letter to Noel Ignatin, his long-time comrade and friend, which, among other topics, addressed women's oppression. "I understand you to say," writes Allen, "that the oppression of women by men is not a revolutionary question because the women lack

---

52   Information on these activities comes from author interviews with Allison Edwards, Carole Travis, Carol Hayse, and Marcia LaRose, as well as various Internal Discussion Bulletins throughout the late seventies.

53   Elaine Zeskind, "The Party and Autonomy for Women," in *Urgent Tasks* #1, May 1977, 3.

the power to make a successful revolution to get rid of male supremacy."[54] "To give your argument its full justice," he continues, "you would, I presume, say that women of the oppressed classes and nations can free themselves as members of social classes and nations, but not as women; that women cannot by their own independent strength throw off male domination."[55] Further speculating on the logic of the presumed Ignatin/STO position, Allen posits that such a stance required a belief that women's liberation would come, not through an autonomous feminist struggle, but instead as an "incidental function" of successful anticapitalist and anti-imperialist revolutions.[56]

Rejecting the "invidious comparison" between women and the working class as potential agents of revolution, Allen argues in favor of the proposition that women's oppression was indeed an essential, if not necessarily "independent" revolutionary question.[57] Questioning the value of "independence" as an evaluative benchmark for revolutionary struggle, he suggests that both proletarian and feminist struggles are likely to become "dependent" on each other in important ways as they develop. "I have never been in a revolution," Allen concedes, "but from what I have heard, there comes a time when the people on *both* sides are less worried about 'independently winning' than they are about rounding up all the help they can round up to keep from getting their ass whipped."[58] Allen even invoked the key point of unity he shared with Ignatin and all of STO, suggesting that the group's emphasis on "independently winning" had the effect of "hindering the struggle against white supremacy."[59] This must have hit close to home for a group so strongly and publicly tied to the white skin privilege analysis.

---

54 Letter from Ted Allen to Noel Ignatin, 11 July 1978, 19. Reproduced in *Internal Discussion Bulletin* #4, September 1978. In author's possession. It appears that "you" here refers to STO organizationally, not merely to Ignatin alone. On page 23, Allen offers the following formulation for the contrasting positions: "I am not so ready as STO seems to be to talk about the proletariat being able to fulfill its its [sic] revolutionary task independently, while the women's struggle is helpless to make a revolution on its own."

55 Ibid., 20.

56 The line about "incidental function" comes from Ibid., 21.

57 Ibid., 23.

58 Ibid. Emphasis in original.

59 Ibid.

Allen also addresses the "incidental function" argument, offering a tentative assessment of the link between women's liberation and the reality of socialist revolution in the twentieth century. Since Ignatin was clearly aligned with the state capitalist position on the Soviet Union and other so-called socialist countries, Allen assumed STO would argue that the lack of full women's liberation in these countries was a result of the failure of their revolutions, and "that when the proletariat succeeds in its revolution, the progress of women to full equality with men will follow in consequence."[60] He counters with a probing question: "But have you ever thought of considering whether or not, and if so to what extent, the failure of the revolutionary parties to carry forward with the complete equalizing of women may have been, not just a result, but a cause of the failure of socialist revolutions?"[61]

Finally, Allen deals at length with a position that he ascribes to "some members of STO:" "that the oppression of women is not a revolutionary question because it can be solved under capitalism." Challenging this analysis as incompatible with Marxist economic analysis, he argues that strict limits existed on the ability of women to be fully incorporated into capitalist production on an equal basis with men. "Far short of the point at which women's liberation through employment as wage laborers could produce a social parity of the sexes, the trend is overtaken and reversed by the economics of the increasing cost of their general employment."[62] At the same time, Allen points to the problem of "male ego and its ideology" as "a major barrier to the development of revolutionary consciousness among men everywhere."[63] In this regard, he suggests the need for a study of male supremacy that would parallel the research done by W.E.B. Du Bois on "the relationship between white supremacy and bourgeois rule in this country."[64] Once again, Allen's deliberate reference to the shared commitment to struggling against white supremacy served to highlight the potential he ascribed to the fight against male supremacy.

The response from STO was muted. No official reply was forthcoming, either from the organization as a whole or from its Women's Commission.

---

60 Ibid., 22.
61 Ibid. Allen followed with amusing self-deprication—"Well, neither have I"—and allowed that "probably work along that line is already well advanced by women researchers and theorists of whose thinking I am in typical male ignorance." Ibid., 23.
62 Ibid., 27.
63 Ibid., 28.
64 Ibid.

In a subsequent discussion in the Chicago Branch, Ignatin clarified that the position he expressed to Allen prior to Allen's letter was "that women, as women by themselves, are incapable of making a social revolution, and thus are not 'independently revolutionary,' but certainly are capable of throwing off male domination."[65] But this begged the question of whether the "throwing off" could happen within capitalism or only as part of a broader revolution. If the former, then Allen's critique of the position held by "some members" of STO would still apply to the extent that limits existed on the ability of capitalism to accommodate women's liberation; if the latter, then Allen's rejection of the need for "independence" remained valid. Regardless, it is not clear that STO was particularly concerned to critically evaluate its own positions in light of Allen's critique. Perhaps the clearest attempt at some sort of response came in the form of Edwards' long, two-part article on "Women and Modern Capitalism."

Edwards never mentions Allen directly, but she seems to have his critique in mind when she tackles the question of capitalism's relationship to male supremacy. Drawing on the classic Marxist distinction between base and superstructure, which Allen himself had also highlighted in his letter to Ignatin, Edwards argues that the "material base" of women's oppression had been "eroded" by the development of capitalism in the twentieth century. In other words, previously important factors like the unwaged labor of women in the home and the accessibility of women as what Marx called a "reserve army of labor" that keeps all wages depressed, have increasingly been undermined by dramatic technological and sociopolitical transformations in capitalism. However, while the economic base could be reconciled to a situation in which women have substantial equality with men, there still remains the problem of the superstructure, where "male supremacy has taken on a life of its own and continues to exist as an ideology with substantial privileges and benefits (both material and nonmaterial) to men, in spite of its diminishing benefit to capitalism."[66] In a new twist on the question of being "independently revolutionary," Edwards argues that "only in a period of major social upheaval" could "entrenched ideas" like the ideology of male supremacy

---

65 This quote is from the "Chicago Branch Report: November, 1978 Discussion on Women Question," prepared by Ed Voci in April 1979, and based in part on "the recollection of" Ignatin and several others. *IDB* #10, May 1979, 11.

66 Unsigned "Introduction" attached to "Women and Modern Capitalism: Erosion of Material Base for Oppression," in *UT* #5, Fall 1979, 6.

be "open to significant challenge and change."[67] But Edwards repudiates Allen's charge of women's liberation being an "incidental function" of socialist revolution. Without speculating on the proper forms of women's autonomy within revolutionary organizations, she states flatly that "an autonomous women's movement is essential for that decisive challenge to male supremacy."[68] The end result of Edwards' piece is a coherent, if unacknowledged, response to Ted Allen.

* * *

Parallel to the question of women's autonomy, of course, was the question of the autonomy of people, organizations, and movements of color. Internally, the role of third world revolutionaries as members of STO came to a head a year and a half after the Coe Conference created the framework for their participation. In the intervening time, a handful of STO publications had addressed the issue. Hamerquist's lengthy pamphlet, *White Supremacy and the Afro-American National Question*, directly addressed the question of membership of color in groups like STO, acknowledging that the group's chosen approach, in prioritizing the health of third world movements and organizations, "creates many problems and runs counter to a normal concern for organizational viability."[69] "Who's Being Dogmatic? A Response to the Philadelphia Workers' Organizing Committee on the National Question" by Jasper Collins, published in the second issue of *Urgent Tasks*, highlighted the need for autonomy within multinational revolutionary groups via a close reading of Lenin's response to the Jewish Bund. Collins went so far as to suggest that "it is necessary for the revolutionary party to provide a great deal *more* autonomy for Third World members than Lenin proposed for the national parties in 1906."[70] While these initial attempts to theorize

---

67   Ibid., 7.

68   Ibid.

69   Don Hamerquist, *White Supremacy and the Afro-American National Question* (Chicago: STO, 1978 [1976]), 24.

70   Jasper Collins, "Who's Being Dogmatic? A Response to the Philadelphia Workers' Organizing Committee on the National Question," in *Urgent Tasks* #2, October 1977, 54. As described in Chapter Six, Collins was a pseudonym for Ken Lawrence. STO's unique interpretation of the Bund is assessed in more detail in Chapter Eight. For more background on the Bund, from a variety of perspectives, see the anthology *The Emergence of Modern Jewish Politics: Bundism and Zionism in Eastern*

the issue were important, they could not prepare STO for the actually impending challenge to its own "organizational viability."

In the fall of 1977, discussions emerged within STO around the proper framework for "third world" autonomy inside the group. Primarily, the question concerned the ability of members of color to determine or direct organizational activities that related to "their" communities and movements. The members of color and a core of supportive white members proposed that "the Third World Caucus would have autonomy after sufficient debate. This does not entail a bridling of the work of white cadre, but rather an overseeing of their work."[71] The response from the elected (and all white) leadership of STO was that this proposal would undermine the democratic principle of majority rule, to the extent that an unelected group (the Third World Caucus) could potentially overrule official decisions made either by the elected National Committee or even those made by the assembled majority of the membership at a General Membership Meeting. As a result, Ken Lawrence advocated for "moral rather than formal" authority for the Caucus in such situations: "My position at the present time is that in most instances, after a full discussion and debate, the organization ought to defer to the wishes of the Third World members—but I would not like to make this automatic."[72]

An intense debate on this question at the December 1977 GMM was variously characterized as "legitimately sharp," as "hard-hitting," or as having been "dominated by white chauvinism." The Third World Caucus and its supporters argued that "in its style, its tone and some of its implications," the debate showed a level of disrespect toward the members of color. The contradiction on the question of membership in STO implicit in the Coe Resolution had finally become concrete: in the eyes of the Caucus and its supporters, the leadership of STO believed in following the leadership of revolutionaries of color only when they functioned in separate organizations, not when they shared the same organizational space inside STO. The leadership responded that the real problem was a form of white liberalism, such that a certain percentage of STO's white membership uncritically accepted the unreasonable

---

Europe, edited by Zvi Gitelman (Pittsburgh: University of Pittsburgh Press, 2003).

71 "The Reasons for the Split in STO," 3. The phrase is a quote from "point B." of "a brief set of proposals" put forward by the Third World Caucus in advance of the General Membership Meeting in December 1977. I have not located a copy of the original set of proposals.

72 Quoted in Ibid., 5.

positions of the Third World Caucus when a more objective assessment of the situation would place priority on the health of the revolutionary movements within the oppressed nations. Formal proceedings were initiated to censure much of the elected leadership of STO for racist conduct during the debate, and after more intense discussion the votes on the motions were a mixed bag: one person was censured (though it is unclear what penalty, if any, resulted), the vote on another person ended in a tie, and two more individuals were not censured.[73]

Despite this tension, the GMM was able to unanimously approve a provisional formulation of how autonomy for members of color should function internally: "Any time the TW caucus feels that the work of the organization is mistaken it has the responsibility to call a halt to that work and for an emergency meeting of the appropriate body which could resolve the differences. Prior to that meeting the decisions of the TW caucus would prevail. After debate within the body the TW caucus would decide tactics; the organization, strategy."[74] A decision was also made to "add members of the TW caucus, selected by the caucus, to all leading bodies of the organization."[75] It is possible that this compromise solution would have merely shifted the conflict to a question of definitions—what is the dividing line between strategy and tactics, and which "appropriate body" gets to decide?—but the policy itself was never implemented. Relations between the two factions continued to sour: the Third World Caucus and its supporters felt attacked and disrespected, while the leadership continued to reject any accusations of racist behavior on its part. Given the importance STO placed on anti-imperialist solidarity work, it was inevitable that the dispute would spill over to the various national liberation movements with which STO worked, and from whom the leadership sought advice. A key part of the Coe Resolution had insisted that "every care must be exercised to insure that multinational communist groups do not function in a way that raises barriers between Third World revolutionaries and their organizations and Third World cadre in multinational organizations."[76] But since the Third World Caucus members had made deliberate decisions to join STO and *not* to join any of the nationalist groups in their own communities, the Caucus and its supporters resented efforts by STO's leadership to bring

73   For more on STO's approach to internal discipline, see Chapter Six.
74   Quoted in "The Reasons for the Split in STO," 7.
75   Ibid., 8.
76   "Third World Revolutionary Organizations and the Party Building Process." In author's possession.

in these very organizations as mediating forces. The Caucus accused the leadership of trying to poison the well with groups like the Afrikan People's Party and the Republic of New Afrika by explaining to them only one side of the dispute.

The approved resolution on autonomy also did little to address ongoing concerns within STO regarding informal hierarchy. When the leadership opposed the original autonomy proposal because the members of the Third World Caucus were not democratically elected, the Caucus and its supporters retorted that several people universally regarded as leading members of STO were not then serving in elected offices themselves. Four prominent members—Hamerquist, Ignatin, Lawrence, and Travis—had been members of (or in Lawrence's case, affiliated with) STO since its inception almost a decade earlier, and all had extensive background in the "old left" going back either to childhood or adolescence. As David Ranney argued at the time, in the eyes of some younger members, "the major basis for leadership and power in STO is tradition and experience in the old left (CP, POC) along with the presumption that this tradition and experience makes those who have it superior in matters of estimate. Those who occupy both formal and informal leadership positions on this basis believe themselves to be inherently and forever superior to others and, therefore, can never really give up the prerogatives of power to others."[77] This amounted to a critique of STO's organizational practice and its failure to live up to the unorthodox vision of democratic centralism formally embraced at the Coe Conference. One aspect of this critique was especially important to the Caucus: these prominent people inside STO had over the years developed personal relationships with leading members of various national liberation organizations, which gave them a specific base of power that was unrelated to any elective offices they might have held.

Nearly three decades later, Ranney could still maintain that among the leading members of STO "there was a profound impact of the CP on the organization that wasn't completely recognized, even by the people themselves. They had definitely made a break from Stalinism in a very profound way, but they were all kind of raised in a political culture,

---

77   Dave Ranney, "Some Notes on Faction and Factional Activity," 2. Unpublished document dated December 27, 1977. In author's possession. For more on the Provisional Organizing Committee, see Noel Ignatin, "The POC: A Personal Memoir," in *Theoretical Review* #12, 1979, 21–26. Available online at http://www.marxists.org/history/erol/1956-1960/ignatin01.htm (accessed October 31, 2011).

however, where certain things were very controlled, and they never completely let go of it…. There was a tendency of the informal leadership to circle the wagons and direct things."[78] This interpretation appears to have been a minority position within STO at the time, since in the aftermath of the conflict over autonomy, Hamerquist, Ignatin, Lawrence, and Travis were all elected to the National Committee.[79] Regardless, it was one of several sources of frustration for the Caucus and its supporters.

Another issue in the dispute was even less obvious, because it had nothing to do with questions of autonomy. Several of the most vocal supporters of the Caucus (and at least one member of the Caucus itself) were still working and organizing in factories, despite STO's decision a year and a half earlier to de-emphasize political work at the point of production. Many of the other supporters, and all members of the Caucus, were heavily involved in mass organizing work of various sorts. In this context, STO's decision at Coe to focus on "party-building" efforts, and its subsequent emphasis on developing formal relationships with other revolutionary organizations as part of those efforts, effectively alienated the members of the Caucus and many of its supporters. At the time, Ranney was working and organizing in a small factory on the south side of Chicago that produced lard. In advocating a formal split from STO, he decried the group's emphasis on maneuvering within the left in lieu of mass work, and suggested that "with our [STO's] priority on party-building we tend in practice to evaluate our work in terms of what puts STO in a better position to strengthen our tendency within the white left."[80] The organizing work many members were pursuing in industrial settings did not fit well in this new framework, especially since STO had begun to define itself in relation to other anti-imperialist groups like Prairie Fire Organizing Committee, as opposed to New Communist groups, like the October League, that continued to focus on point-of-production work. The organizational estimate regarding the "lull" further marginalized the position of factory workers and in-plant organizers like Ranney. These issues were raised in only the most oblique fashion in the surviving documents related to the split, and yet several of the people who left STO in 1978 recall their commitment to factory organizing as having been a subtext in the process.[81]

---

78   David Ranney, interview with the author, December 20, 2005.

79   "The Reasons for the Split in STO," 11.

80   David Ranney, "Position on Splitting STO" (January 9, 1978), 5. In author's possession.

81   Author interviews with Dave Ranney, John Strucker, and Jim Carrillo,

The final result was perhaps predictable: thirteen members of STO, including all four members of color, left the organization early in 1978. In the aftermath, some half-hearted efforts were made at reconciliation and at re-merging the organization, but the frustrations on both sides were too severe to be overcome immediately. Most of those who left formed a short-lived organization called the Midwest Action League (MAL), which for a year or so was involved in largely the same set of anti-imperialist solidarity efforts as STO, even as its membership remained committed to factory organizing. As late as January, 1979, both groups were credited, alongside Prairie Fire and others, with having helped publish a collection of communiqués from the Puerto Rican independence movement.[82] Several members of MAL were also involved in a range of workplace struggles, often coordinated through the Workers' Rights Center that their faction had inherited in the split from STO. This work led to the publication of the unsigned pamphlet *'There Ain't No Justice … Just Us': An Account of a Wildcat Strike*. Written by Ranney, it was a passionate first-person narrative of a struggle against management and the corrupt union at the small factory where he worked, as well as a reflection on long-standing topics of concern for the former member of STO, such as white supremacy, revolutionary organization, and industrial legality.[83] The wildcat strike was largely unsuccessful, and many of the strikers lost their jobs, but the unity inspired by the struggle was still powerful.

In many ways, this represented a return to the sorts of work that had characterized the earlier era of STO's existence, before the Coe Conference declaration of the "lull." But the return was short-lived: deindustrialization and harassment by plant management meant that Ranney himself had a hard time finding factory work after being fired; he eventually returned to his previous career as an economics professor. MAL

---

all of whom left in the split, support this assessment. Don Hamerquist agreed with this broad outline, while noting that several people still working in factories did not leave in the split.

82 See *Toward People's War For Independence and Socialism in Puerto Rico: In Defense of Armed Struggle: Documents and Communiqués from the Revolutionary Public Independence Movement and the Armed Clandestine Movement* (Chicago: STO, et. al., 1979).

83 *'There Ain't No Justice … Just Us': An Account of a Wildcat Strike* (Chicago: South Chicago Workers' Rights Center, 1978). Photographs taken by Ranney and others during the strike, some of which were featured in the pamphlet, are included on the front cover of this book.

didn't fare any better; the group was defunct perhaps a year after its founding, and the former members scattered both politically and geographically. STO continued on and even grew substantially, as will be seen, but in its remaining decade of existence it included very few if any members of color.

Chapter Five:
Iran and Cleveland:
Anti-Imperialism in Theory and Practice

One day in the mid-seventies, without putting too much advance thought into it, John Strucker dramatically altered the strategic outlook of the Sojourner Truth Organization. Strucker lived in the West Town community of Chicago, as did several other members of STO. Located on the northwest side of the city, the neighborhood was affordable, centrally located, and not too far from the Stewart-Warner plant, where several STO members worked. West Town was also, together with the adjacent neighborhoods of Logan Square and Humboldt Park, home to the largest Puerto Rican community west of New York City. As the seventies progressed, the struggle for Puerto Rican independence became a popular cause within the US left, in large part through the efforts of the Puerto Rican Socialist Party (PSP), which organized both on the island and in diaspora communities scattered throughout the northeast and midwest of the United States. But while STO had regular contact with Puerto Rican workers at Stewart-Warner and other factories, the group had never had much direct relationship with the independence movement.[1]

---

1   Noel Ignatin and Hilda Vasquez were politically engaged with the Puerto Rican community in Chicago in the late 1960s, partly through her

On this particular day, probably not long after the "Crisis" and "Balloon" splits had reduced STO to a shell of its former self, Strucker walked into the PSP office in West Town to see if there was anything he could do to help the group.[2] He spoke a little Spanish, although he didn't end up needing it because the organizer he met that day was Jose Lopez, who, like many of the most active people in the PSP's milieu, was young enough to have been raised largely in Chicago and was thus bilingual. Lopez was a teacher and a rising star in the local independence movement, although he was not a member of the PSP. Together with his older brother Oscar he had cut his teeth organizing against racism in schools, housing, and the police force. Along with several students who had been expelled from a local public high school, the brothers had helped found a community-based alternative school. Although no specific plans were made, Strucker and Lopez agreed that there was serious potential for collaboration between STO and the Puerto Rican independence movement.

Strucker later presented a synopsis of his meeting with Lopez to the other members of STO, and the eventual result was a fundamental shift in the group's approach to revolutionary strategy. The "lull" seemed to apply to the industrial workforce, but it clearly didn't reflect the prospects for revolutionary organizing in the Puerto Rican community. Here was an arena where communist politics could get a full hearing, where militant tactics were broadly accepted, and where a true mass base was at least moderately sympathetic to the arguments being put forward by the PSP and other revolutionaries. Even more encouraging was the strong connection between local organizing and resistance to the colonial plight of Puerto Rico. As an overwhelmingly white group, STO did not see itself directly participating in this struggle, but it could certainly offer significant material support during the projected downswing known as the "lull"; by this point the group had both a functioning print shop and a growing stable of lawyers within the organization, among other valuable resources. Further, it was hoped, STO could learn political and organizational lessons that might prove important once the temporary hibernation of the domestic proletariat came to an end. Thus was forged a long and fruitful, but also frequently

---

participation in the Young Lords, as discussed in Chapter One. By the mid-seventies, however, Vasquez had left STO, while Ignatin had been living and working in Gary for several years.

2   This account is based on an interview with Strucker, February 5, 2006, and was corroborated by Don Hamerquist and Jose Lopez in conversation with the author.

frustrating, relationship between STO and the Puerto Rican independence movement.

The frustrations emerged from multiple sources, including fundamental political differences between STO's unorthodox Leninism and the mixed bag of nationalism and sometimes Stalinist Marxism that characterized the independence movement. Another was the palpable tension between the group's previous priority on workplace organizing and its new emphasis on solidarity work, whether with the Puerto Rican movement or with the Republic of New Afrika and other black nationalist groupings in the US, or even further afield with the Iranian student movement (in exile) against the Shah. Years later, Noel Ignatiev remembered dragging his heels on the move toward solidarity work, while feeling unable to offer a compelling and workable alternative strategy, although in the moment he argued just as strongly as any other member for the centrality of various anti-imperialist solidarity efforts. For a cofounder of a group that had built its reputation on engagement with the domestic class struggle, the emphasis on national liberation, especially in distant locales, was almost embarrassing. "We were experts on Iran," Ignatiev recalled ruefully, "but we didn't know a damn thing about Cleveland."[3]

This contradiction was in many ways exemplary of the theory and practice of the Sojourner Truth Organization during the second half of the 1970s, especially in Chicago but elsewhere as well. The group's analysis of white supremacy and white skin privilege shifted into a framework dominated by the highly contentious "national question." The focus on factory work having been decentered by the declaration of the "lull," concrete solidarity with national liberation movements was one important way to maintain an active membership without getting sucked into a purely scholastic focus on theoretical development. As Don Hamerquist wrote in 1978, "our current approach to political work has two distinct, though related, elements. First, we put a priority on political debate on the left.… Second, we put priority on direct support to Third World revolutionary groups—particularly those functioning within the U.S."[4] In this context, the ties the group built with the Puerto Rican movement were the most substantial, so this example will be examined in some depth here.

---

3   Noel Ignatiev, author interview, January 27, 2006.
4   Don Hamerquist, "Direction," in *IDB* #1, n.d., but probably March, 1978. In author's possession.

* * *

Puerto Rico has been a colony of the United States since 1898, when it became the first territory conquered by the US military during the Spanish-American war. The independence and labor movements were already strong on the island during the last period of Spanish rule, although they frequently did not see eye to eye on the proper direction for Puerto Rican society.[5] Over the next several decades, US control resulted in a wide range of negative consequences for the Puerto Rican people: the military occupation and environmental devastation of the island of Puerto Rico; the extreme economic exploitation and racist discrimination faced by the working class, both on the island and in the diaspora; the mass sterilization of huge numbers of Puerto Rican women; and so forth. Resistance to colonialism was a constant feature of Puerto Rican life, although the political content of (and the strategic approach to) the demand for independence was always subject to debate within the movement.

Beginning in the 1930s, a section of the independence movement, under the leadership of Pedro Albizu Campos and the Nationalist Party, became more militant in its approach, leading to increased state repression as well as deliberate attempts to co-opt pro-independence sentiment. Just when Puerto Rican politicians were taking the reins of government in San Juan in the late forties, the Nationalist Party attempted an armed uprising against US domination. In the aftermath, a series of Puerto Rican revolutionaries were convicted of various crimes, and many of them were sentenced to lengthy prison terms. Foremost among these prisoners was the group that eventually came to be known as "the Five"—Oscar Collazo, Irving Flores, Lolita Lebron, Rafael Cancel Miranda, and Andres Figueroa Cordero—who were singled out for extended prison terms in part because they took armed action against the US government in Washington DC, rather than on the island.[6] This repression, along with

<hr />

5   For a comprehensive overview of Puerto Rican history in the period immediately prior to 1898, see Cesar Ayala and Rafael Bernabe, *Puerto Rico in the American Century: A History Since 1898* (Chapel Hill: University of North Carolina Press, 2007), 52–94. This book is the best overall source in English for the history of the Puerto Rican independence movement in the twentieth century.

6   Collazo had participated in the 1950 uprising for Puerto Rican independence known as the *Grito de Jayuya*, attacking the temporary home of President Truman in Washington DC. The other four prisoners had

the success of the Cuban revolution in 1959, eventually led a significant section of the Puerto Rican independence movement to embrace socialism, and in many cases Marxist-Leninism. The PSP's predecessor organization, the Movement for Independence (MPI), was the largest grouping to take this path.[7]

Meanwhile, extreme poverty and the lack of economic opportunities on the island led an increasing number of Puerto Ricans to seek work inside the United States, especially after World War Two.[8] This process had begun even before the turn of the century, when migration between Puerto Rico and both New York and Florida was not uncommon. New York became the primary point of arrival for most Puerto Ricans, but during the middle part of the twentieth century the Puerto Rican diaspora expanded to include industrial cities throughout the northeast and midwestern part of the country, in what would later be known as the rust belt. Sizeable Puerto Rican communities developed in Philadelphia, Hartford, Buffalo, and eventually Chicago as well. By the early seventies, the PSP was able to organize local chapters anywhere that Puerto Rican workers had established themselves.[9]

In Chicago, the local chapter of the PSP was well integrated into a large and vibrant Puerto Rican community that was both tight-knit and active in defense of its autonomy. As early as 1966, Puerto Ricans in West Town rioted against police brutality and discrimination in housing and employment.[10] The aftermath of the 1966 uprising helped radicalize the local Young Lords street gang, which subsequently became the Young Lords Organization and eventually the Young Lords Party, with members

---

entered the Capitol building in 1954 and fired weapons into the chamber as a demonstration against the persecution of the independence movement after Jayuya. See Ronald Fernandez, *Prisoners of Colonialism: The Struggle for Justice in Puerto Rico* (Monroe, ME: Common Courage Press, 1994), 81–94.

7   See Ayala and Bernabe, 226–227, as well as Elbaum, 74–76.

8   See Ayala and Bernabe, 194–196.

9   Andres Torres and Jose Velazquez, eds., *The Puerto Rican Movement: Voices From the Diaspora* (Philadelphia: Temple University Press, 1998), contains a number of essays focusing on the influence of the PSP and other radical organizations in various parts of the continental United States during the seventies.

10   Surprisingly little has been written about the 1966 riot. The classic description is found in Felix Padilla, *Puerto Rican Chicago* (Notre Dame, IN: Notre Dame University Press, 1987), 144–152.

in New York City and on the island itself. The influence of the Black Panther Party on the Young Lords was clear, and innovative forms of community organizing became the primary mode of political engagement for a whole generation of Puerto Rican radicals in Chicago. Protests against police brutality continued, but they were joined with actions against slumlords and demonstrations against racism in the public schools. After the decline of the Young Lords in the early seventies, many of the core organizers in Chicago were members of, or worked in the same circles as, the PSP. The milieu featured student and youth organizers, Vietnam veterans, religious activists from a variety of denominations, radical teachers and social workers, and a range of others. One context for some of this work was the National Commission on Hispanic Affairs of the Episcopal Church, which brought together progressive and radical organizers from across the country, and included people from both Puerto Rican and Chicano/Mexicano communities. As a result of these various, partially overlapping circles, many of the young Puerto Rican radicals in Chicago developed ties with like-minded activists in New York, Puerto Rico, the southwestern United States, and elsewhere.

The Puerto Rican militants in Chicago also focused special attention on the situation of the five political prisoners, who by that time had been behind bars for two decades. Around the same time, a clandestine group of Puerto Rican revolutionaries, the Armed Forces of National Liberation (FALN), began a violent campaign within the United States on behalf of Puerto Rican independence. From its very first communiqué onward, the FALN made a point of highlighting the plight of the Five and demanding their immediate release. From 1974 until 1984, the FALN carried out more than one hundred bombings against US control of Puerto Rico, primarily in New York and Chicago.[11] This newly emerging clandestine activity caused a certain amount of tension within the radical independence movement. Some sections of the Puerto Rican left in Chicago and elsewhere distanced themselves either explicitly or implicitly from the idea of armed struggle as an appropriate tactic for the time, while others proudly and publicly supported it. Quite apart from these conflicts, however, the Puerto Rican movement had, in the United States, one of the strongest communities of adherents and supporters of any national liberation struggle. Indeed, by the mid-seventies the independence movement was one of the largest and most vibrant radical movements in the western hemisphere.

---

11   For more on the FALN's bombing campaign, see Fernandez, *Prisoners of Colonialism*, 205–218.

* * *

When STO began to emphasize anti-imperialist work in solidarity with the independence movement, it not only had to navigate the complicated terrain of competing trends and strategies, it also was forced to weigh in on the knotty topic known as "the national question." Debates among Marxists over national identity and national liberation already had a long history when STO encountered the Puerto Rican community in West Town. These disputes had their origin in the efforts made by the Bolsheviks to organize for socialist revolution throughout the Russian empire, which included dozens of distinct ethnic groups spread over thousands of miles.[12] Joseph Stalin, who was of Georgian (not Russian) descent, provided the classic Marxist definition of the nation in 1913: "A nation is a historically constituted, stable community of people, formed on the basis of a common language, territory, economic life, and psychological makeup manifested in a common culture." This conception, which gained prominence when Stalin came to power, was exceptionally rigid: "it is sufficient for a single one of these characteristics to be lacking and the nation ceases to be a nation."[13] In the decades to come, the "territory" clause in particular would be the source of endless debates among Leninists as to whether a particular "people" constituted a "nation" or a "national minority" under Stalin's definition. While nations were entitled to full self-determination including political independence, Stalin maintained that national minorities were likely to assimilate into the larger population and thus were supposed to engage in struggles for equality and democratic rights rather than independence.

In the United States, the national question first surfaced during the late 1920s in relation to the Communist Party's approach to black struggles against racism, especially in the southern states. At the time, against the objections of much of the white leadership of the CPUSA, Stalin's definition (and the territory clause in particular) was used by the Soviet-led Third International as a basis for concluding that black people in the

---

12 For a basic analysis of the national question from a perspective that influenced STO's own views, see James M. Blaut, *The National Question* (London: Zed Books, 1987).

13 Josef Stalin, *Marxism and the National Question* (1913). Quoted in Jasper Collins, "Who's Being Dogmatic?," in *Urgent Tasks* #2 (October, 1977), 4. Stalin's text is available online at http://www.marxists.org/reference/archive/stalin/works/1913/03.htm (accessed December 23, 2011).

United States constituted a nation within the area known as the "black belt," running roughly from southern Virginia to Louisiana.[14] Black people living in the northeast, midwest or western US (in small but rapidly growing numbers in the late twenties) were excluded from this nation, and constituted instead a national minority. While the CPUSA had largely abandoned its emphasis on supporting black struggles by the time World War Two began, the precedent among Leninists had been set: black people constituted a nation, at least in some places. This allowed for increasing interplay between the black nationalist tradition (which up through the Marcus Garvey era had largely resisted the draw of socialism as Eurocentric) and the Leninist tradition that had been white led and dominated in the US from its creation.[15]

By the seventies, this mixture of Marxism and nationalism had produced a plethora of black revolutionary groups, including the Republic of New Afrika (RNA), the African Peoples' Socialist Party (APSP), and many others. Within the white left, debates over the national question resurged, this time with the added demographic twist that a substantial portion of the black population had left the deep south during what was known as the Great Migration, even as black communities in New York, Chicago, Los Angeles, and other urban centers were growing rapidly. Some groups, such as the October League, maintained the original CPUSA position. In OL's case this was partly due to continuity of personnel: Harry Haywood, who had been a leading CPUSA theoretician of the black belt nation, was a member of OL by the mid-seventies. Other groups, such as the so-called "anti-dogmatist, anti-revisionist" trend centered around the *Guardian* newspaper and the Philadelphia Workers' Organizing Committee (PWOC), argued that demographic shifts had ended the period of black nationhood in the US, and that the only remaining goal was to achieve full equality for black people within US society.[16] Although these debates only engaged a tiny fraction of the left

---

14   See Collins, 6, as well as Don Hamerquist, *White Supremacy and the Afro-American National Question* (Chicago: STO, 1978 [1976]), 12.

15   For an idiosyncratic but detailed take on the question of race in the early development of the CPUSA, see Harold Cruse, *Crisis of the Negro Intellectual: A Historical Analysis of the Failure of Black Leadership* (New York: New York Review Books, 2005 [1967]).

16   See Collins, "Who's Being Dogmatic?," 7. "PWOC argues that Black people do not constitute a nation anywhere within the present boundaries of the US, because the Black nation that once existed—based on 'a large Black peasantry' with the plantation economy as 'the central

(and an even smaller segment of the black population), the historical importance of black struggles led to the belief that the national question was a burning topic in need of immediate resolution.

One unifying factor among almost all the largely white groups participating in these debates was the continued and generally unthinking reliance upon Stalin's definition of the nation. STO began its analysis of the national question, in typically anti-Stalinist fashion, by rejecting his framework altogether. In its place, the group substituted an analysis developed by Lenin during the period immediately prior to the revolution of 1917. In a classic example of the almost Talmudic nature of Leninist theoretical disputation, STO engaged in a seemingly endless series of written exchanges with its debate opponents, each of which featured numerous lengthy quotations from obscure sections of Lenin's *Collected Works*.

The opening salvo in this theoretical struggle was Don Hamerquist's long pamphlet, *White Supremacy and the Afro-American National Question*, which was published as a discussion paper in 1976 and republished with a new introduction two years later. In it, Hamerquist methodically makes three main points: first, "the institution of white supremacy has played a central role in US history, specifically in the formation of the US working class." Second, it characterizes "Black people as a nation, based on the national-colonial theory of Lenin." Finally, Hamerquist attempts to "draw some implications for the strategic role and for the structure of communist organizations."[17] The first task was fairly simple: Hamerquist merely restated the by-now familiar STO narrative of US history (as described earlier in Chapter Three), emphasizing a handful of elements: slavery was capitalist; white supremacy entailed both cultural genocide and the denial of equality through the imposition of white skin privilege; Reconstruction was the pivot-point of US history; the white-led labor movement had historically abandoned black workers to the detriment of the entire working class; and, finally, the efforts of the CPUSA to support

---

unifying force in the national development of the Afro-American people'—has undergone an irreversible transformation due to geographic dispersal and a striking change in class composition. Because of these developments, says PWOC, Black people are not entitled to self-determination; the most they may legitimately strive for is 'equality' as a permanent minority within the US; movements for independence are reactionary, and must be opposed."

17 Hamerquist, *White Supremacy and the Afro-American National Question*, 2.

black liberation during the twenties and thirties, while far from perfect, did represent an important break from the otherwise racist history of the white left. This much was nothing new for anyone who had followed STO's political trajectory over the course of the seventies.

What *was* new, however, was the explicit statement that black people in the United States constitute a nation. Hamerquist argues that part of the significance of Reconstruction was that "in this span of little more than a decade, Black people developed from an oppressed color caste into an oppressed people—a nation."[18] In addition, he maintains that the demographic shifts of the previous half-century had not in any way dismantled the national identity of black people in the US. Thus, "our position is that Black people are a people—a nation—everywhere in the United States, not just in the Black Belt South."[19] Acknowledging that "most of the current Marxist-Leninist left would regard our position as heresy," he proceeds to outline the theoretical framework that STO used to justify its stance. According to Hamerquist, Stalin's 1913 definition had emerged from within "a distinct political and theoretical context," a context that ended with the outbreak of World War One in 1914, when the true character of imperialism became plain to see. As a result, "the elaboration of Lenin's conception of imperialism, and specifically of the imperialist oppression of colonial peoples, supersedes and overrides the earlier theory of the national question."

In this new analysis of the "national-colonial question," Lenin prioritized the distinction between oppressor nations and oppressed nations, and a related contrast between revolutionary and reactionary nationalism. Hamerquist argues that in this later period, Lenin never made any reference to the criteria elaborated earlier by Stalin. "To put it simply, Lenin recognized that the impact of imperialism on oppressed peoples was such that it would be a purely academic exercise to use such categories as a basis for determining anything at all. Instead, imperialist oppression and a 'national liberation movement' against it was the determinant of nationhood."[20] While this explanatory focus on oppression and resistance seems to beg the question, it is as close as Hamerquist comes to a comprehensive definition of what constitutes a nation. His bigger concern is the application of the general question to the specific case of black people in the United States. Quoting from an unfinished manuscript from 1917, Hamerquist highlights Lenin's conclusion that

---

18   Ibid., 7.

19   All further quotes in this paragraph are from ibid., 15.

20   Ibid., 17.

blacks "should be classified as an oppressed nation," and suggests that his basis for doing so had nothing to do with Stalin's criteria, but was instead based on the oppression and resistance that followed the Civil War.[21]

Having bolstered his position on nationhood for blacks, Hamerquist proceeds to attack the main alternative theory then current within the Leninist left, the idea that blacks constituted a national minority (either outside the Black Belt, or everywhere in the US, depending upon which group of Leninists was being considered) due to their failure to meet Stalin's criteria. Accordingly,

> the distinction between nation and national minority which looms so large in current debates on the various national questions in the U.S. had almost no importance to Lenin, which is exactly the status it should have for us. In the current period, this distinction has only one function. It is a mechanism to determine "scientifically" which peoples may "legitimately" struggle for self determination, and which must confine themselves to the struggle for equality. To Lenin, it would have been ludicrous to suggest that some oppressed peoples had no right to self determination.[22]

In other words, white leftists who used Stalin's analysis to determine which groups were nations and which ones were merely national minorities were not only arrogant and racist, they were anti-Leninist as well.

Hamerquist concluded his analysis with a set of strategic conclusions, mostly focusing on the need to win "a substantial section of white workers to solidarity with the struggles of oppressed peoples," since "at least a healthy minority of white workers must be involved" for revolution to be a real possibility.[23] Further, "the Black national liberation struggle is actually, not just potentially, a struggle in the interests of the entire US working class."[24] In essence, this amounted to a justification for STO's shift toward solidarity work, although it was to a certain extent in conflict with the group's move away from direct organizing work with white workers (a contradiction that Ted Allen, among others, would subsequently

---

21 V.I. Lenin, "Statistics and Sociology," (1917), quoted in Hamerquist, 14. Lenin's text is available online at http://www.marxists.org/archive/lenin/works/1917/jan/00d.htm (accessed December 23, 2011).

22 Hamerquist, 17–18.

23 Ibid., 20.

24 Ibid., 22.

challenge). If STO's solidarity work represented a microcosm of what was needed in terms of whites supporting national liberation struggles, it was never very clear how the macrocosm would come into existence.

It is worth pointing out that Hamerquist's emphasis on the black national question did not reflect an avoidance of the Puerto Rican national question. In fact, much of the theoretical framework for his analysis was credited to the pioneering work of James Blaut, himself a member of the PSP, whose essay "Are Puerto Ricans a National Minority?" was especially important. Hamerquist was clear to indicate that "the conclusions we draw about its applicability to the Black National Question are our responsibility," but it was nonetheless clear that the practical work STO was beginning to take on around the Puerto Rican situation was a powerful impetus for the theoretical analysis. In addressing the strategic implications of the theory, Hamerquist returned to the Puerto Rican case: "Specifically, class conscious socialist Puerto Ricans living in this country are not in conflict with Leninism, but in accord with it when they organize separately or as a branch of an organization centered on the island. We would extend the same argument to Black revolutionaries outside of the South."[25] Since most white leftists of whatever stripe had to acknowledge the hegemony of the island-based PSP within the Puerto Rican left in the US, this was really another way to reinforce STO's support for nationalist organizations as a legitimate alternative to the various "multinational" Leninist groups with which STO had regular contact.

* * *

Less than a year after Hamerquist's pamphlet was published, STO made its first official pronouncement on the topic, adopting fifteen "Theses on White Supremacy and the National Question" at the GMM in May of 1977. In thesis number eight, STO reiterated the view that "Black people in the US, wherever they live and work, constitute part of an oppressed nation. The fact that they do not fulfill Stalin's familiar criteria of nationhood demonstrates only that the criteria are inadequate. Nationhood evolved out of centuries of common oppression and struggle, struggle that was systematically resisted by the US ruling class and ignored (at best) by the bulk of the white working people."[26] The group

---

25   Ibid., 24.
26   "Theses on White Supremacy and the National Question," in *Urgent Tasks* #2, 3. According to the editors of *UT*, the theses "were adopted by the STO General Membership Meeting, May 15, 1977." It is also worth

maintained that the common-territory criterion should be replaced by an analysis of the ways in which the historical concentration of black population in the deep south provided the *potential* for a struggle for land and sovereignty, even though significant sections of the black nation did not live there.

A recurring dispute, both within STO and outside it, concerned the question of whether the newfound embrace of national liberation, and of the theoretical framework of the national question, represented a continuation or a repudiation of the group's initial emphasis on white skin privilege. Clearly, the majority of STO's membership considered the transition to be an advance in keeping with the organization's previous analysis: the fifth thesis is a restatement of the group's original position and the sixth and seventh theses tie this position to the newfound priority on national liberation.[27] In his discussion paper in 1976, Hamerquist had argued that STO should simply accept what had been implied all along in their theory of white supremacy. Thus,

> For a number of years, STO has argued that white revolutionaries in the US should devote their attention to the fight against white supremacy as a basis for building a principled unity between white workers and Black people. The question of whether or not Black people constituted a nation was, we argued, essentially an issue which the Black movement would resolve in struggle…. However, supporters and critics alike, have pointed out to us that our position clearly implies a definite stand on the national question. Our conception of white supremacy and the way to struggle against it rests on an understanding of the Black movement as having an intrinsically revolutionary character. Such a character could only follow from that movement being essentially a movement for national liberation, and consequently, from Black people constituting a nation. While we have never disagreed with this observation, we also have never spelled out in detail a theoretical basis for agreeing with it.[28]

---

noting that this position is exactly the opposite of the stance taken eight years earlier by Ignatin in "Without a Science…" (see Chapter Three).

27   "Theses," 1–2.

28   Hamerquist, *White Supremacy*, 14.

In other words, there was no fundamental shift in STO's politics or strategy, but only a new public attentiveness to a set of questions that had previously been answered but only internally. Certainly the romanticization of black struggles—"having an intrinsically revolutionary character"—was consistent with previous STO analysis going back at least to *The United Front Against Imperialism?*, but the terminology was strikingly different in 1976 than it had been just four years earlier. Combined with the lull, an assessment of antiracist struggle as a struggle for national liberation provided an almost *post facto* theoretical rationalization for shifting the group's practical work away from large (and mostly multiracial) factory organizing and toward solidarity work in support of black and Puerto Rican nationalist movements.

This sudden change made certain observers skeptical of STO's claim to continuity. Some people who had been largely supportive of STO previously were highly critical of the group's shift on this issue: For long-time activist Ethan Young, STO's move toward solidarity with the most militant wing of the Puerto Rican independence movement appeared to be motivated by "cynicism—since they were unable to effectively confront reformism in unions, they shifted their attention to confronting reformism in a small, marginal left coalition," the Puerto Rican Solidarity Committee.[29] Certainly, STO would have rejected this characterization, and in any event it did not invalidate the theoretical and strategic questions around the national question and armed struggle that STO was attempting to address. Nonetheless, there is a ring of truth to the ambulance-chasing aspect of Young's criticism, since STO was undeniably engaged in a process (whether cynical or merely realistic) of recalibrating its strategic outlook toward more favorable vistas in the wake of previous failures.

In a more general vein, Ignatin's long-time comrade Ted Allen wrote a lengthy letter in 1978 challenging the group's assessment of the period and of the work it had begun to prioritize. In his words, "for white radicals to limit their main efforts to support of national liberation organizations rather than also directly attacking white supremacy among white workers, is to neglect the most important support that can be given by whites to the national liberation struggles."[30] In essence, Allen was arguing that STO's declaration of the "lull" did not excuse the group's withdrawal from direct organizing in a multiracial context, whether in

---

29   Ethan Young, email to the author, October 30, 2007.
30   Letter from Ted Allen to Noel Ignatin, July 11, 1978. Reprinted in *Internal Discussion Bulletin* #4, September, 1978, 13.

factories or elsewhere. Allen's position was at the very least consistent: his criticism of STO was almost identical to the objections he leveled at the emerging anti-imperialist movement in 1969, as discussed in Chapter Three. Fittingly, STO's shift on this question coincided with its newfound willingness to collaborate with groups like the Prairie Fire Organizing Committee, which was a direct outgrowth of the movement Allen had criticized so many years earlier. Moreover, Allen's concerns were apparently shared by many within STO, although few members were willing to push the issue at the time. The Kansas City branch of STO continued to emphasize workplace organizing, although it did so in a framework of advancing anti-imperialist politics rather than prioritizing workers' autonomy. The split in STO in 1978 was partly due to disagreement with the prioritization of anti-imperialist work over workplace efforts, though even those who left the group and formed the Midwest Action League continued to participate actively in solidarity work, alongside STO and other groups.

* * *

STO's practical work in this new solidarity framework took many forms. Most importantly, the group participated for several years in an ever-shifting coalition of solidarity groups operating in support of independence, alongside other anti-imperialist groups like the Prairie Fire Organizing Committee (PFOC) and the May 19th Communist Organization.[31] Over the course of several years, these and other groups cycled through a variety of organizational forms, some of which focused on a specific issue, such as grand jury resistance, while others operated as general solidarity committees. Initially, all these groups had been involved in the broad-based Puerto Rican Solidarity Committee (PRSC), which included a range of left organizations and operated largely under the direction of the PSP. But in 1977 a Puerto Rican-led faction known as the March 1 Bloc criticized the lack of support for armed struggle within the PRSC. Jose Lopez was one of the leaders of the March 1 Bloc, and the

---

31   Both Prairie Fire and May 19th emerged from the above-ground efforts supporting the Weather Underground during the mid-seventies. May 19th resulted from a split within Prairie Fire, and Chicago was possibly the only city in the United States to house active branches of both organizations. See Berger, *Outlaws of America*, 225–243, for an overview of the activities and perspectives of PFOC and May 19th during this period.

organization he had recently helped found, the Movement for National Liberation (MLN), led the criticism of the PRSC.[32] STO, PFOC, and other groups identified with the MLN-led Bloc, and began functioning as a separate solidarity coalition, which took on several different names over the course of the next few years.

The participating groups represented a fairly narrow section of the US left, one that, despite many political disagreements, was united in its support for armed struggle as a legitimate strategy for the independence movement. In this they were opposed by most of the New Communist Movement, as well as some sections of the Puerto Rican left itself, which supported independence for Puerto Rico, but considered armed struggle to be adventurist and premature.[33] Even some radicals who had previously been drawn to STO's politics shared this concern. Ethan Young recalls the MLN as "just one of several groups to emerge to the left of PSP, but it arrived after most of the others ran out of gas, and MLN had momentum that PSP was losing, [especially] in the US. They had a youth base that had not been burned out by the faction fights that consumed Puerto Rican [revolutionaries] on the east coast. And they identified with an underground that seemed to be a portent of renewed struggle."[34]

The surge in armed activity resulted, predictably, in heightened state repression. The MLN, which began as a dual-national organization with Puerto Rican and Chicano/Mexicano membership, included many veterans of the Episcopal Church's Hispanic Commission, and it was immediately hammered with a series of subpoenas issued to its leadership by grand juries investigating the FALN. Puerto Ricans based in New York and Chicago, as well as Chicanos active in Colorado, New Mexico, and elsewhere, were granted limited immunity from prosecution in an attempt to compel them to testify regarding armed clandestine activities. Jose Lopez was among those subpoenaed, and like the others, he refused to testify. Under US law this refusal subjected those subpoenaed to a limited term of imprisonment without trial for contempt of court. Almost

---

32   It is unclear exactly when in 1977 the MLN was founded; it may not yet have formally existed at the time of the March 1 Bloc's emergence, but it was at the very least in formation at that point.

33   *Urgent Tasks* #1 (May, 1977), in author's possession, contains a "pull-out" section focused on the battles within the Puerto Rican solidarity movement, which included much of the New Communist Movement as well as the anti-imperialist left, over the legitimacy of armed struggle in the Puerto Rican context.

34   Ethan Young, email to the author, October 30, 2007.

a dozen people went to jail in 1977 and 1978 for refusing to testify in front of the grand juries.[35]

In New York, Chicago, and elsewhere, the independence movement and its supporters established Committees Against Grand Jury Repression. STO was heavily involved in the Committees, alongside PFOC and the other coalition groups. This work took several forms. One aspect was the production and distribution of literature on the issue. STO's print shop produced a large amount of agitational material supporting Puerto Rican independence generally and grand jury resistance in particular. Leaflets were produced to target specific audiences, including civil libertarians, radical trade unionists, and religious progressives. The shop also printed more sophisticated publications intended for distribution within the Puerto Rican movement itself. Most of these items were written and designed by Puerto Rican groups, especially the MLN, with STO performing typesetting and printing duties, sometimes on a volunteer basis, other times at regular rates. The print shop, by now known as C&D Printing (for Carole (Travis) and Don (Hamerquist), who formally owned and managed the presses) helped distinguish STO from the other organizations involved in solidarity work, which mostly lacked their own presses.[36] The combined allocation of material resources among the groups participating in solidarity work directly with the MLN was substantial, and greatly enhanced the latter's ability to function on a large scale in the face of government harassment.

The work around the grand jury question was largely defensive in nature, and focused heavily on legal questions within a broadly liberal framework. Since the grand juries necessarily cast a wide net in order to increase the chances that someone called to testify would actually comply rather than refuse, they routinely called as witnesses people who had little or no direct connection to any illegal activity. This made it easy for the Committees to mobilize a range of progressive and liberal organizations and individuals that did not support armed struggle but were nonetheless opposed to government harassment of seemingly benign religious and community groups. The Committees also deliberately linked the grand juries to other, more extreme forms of government repression. In

---

35 New York Committee Against Grand Jury Repression, *The Political Grand Jury: An Instrument of Repression* (n.d., but probably 1978), and "Grand Jury Chronology" (n.d., but probably 1977) leaflet in author's possession.

36 Jose Lopez, author interview, October 18, 2008, discussed the importance of STO's printshop from the perspective of the MLN.

the words of a pamphlet put out by the New York Committee, "The U.S. government, under the guise of controlling and eradicating these aggressive [militant or armed] acts, then launches a broad campaign of harassment, intimidation, grand jury imprisonment, and assassinations against ALL SECTORS of these movements."[37] STO did not perceive this work to be particularly conducive to radicalizing people around the overall issues of independence and armed struggle, but remained heavily involved in the work because of the obvious importance of winning the freedom of those jailed for contempt.[38]

* * *

A more proactive area of work concerned sterilization. In the seventies it became apparent that Puerto Rican women were being sterilized at an alarming rate of more than 30%, a process that had begun as far back as the thirties. STO and the other groups involved in the solidarity coalition saw the importance of the issue, as well as the obvious overlap with feminist concerns, and focused significant attention on it. One leaflet on the issue produced by the "Interim Committee to Build a New Solidarity Movement" (of which STO, PFOC, and other groups were members after they departed from the PRSC) described the sterilizations in Puerto Rico as part of "a program of genocide against its people."[39] In a colonial context, the high rate of sterilizations was characterized as forced or abusive, an attack on women, on the working class, and on Puerto Rican culture and identity. While the issue was distant geographically, it resonated with the large Puerto Rican community in the US, and with radical forms of feminism emerging within both black and Native American communities that had also been subject to troubling and racist attempts at "family planning."

---

37   New York Committee Against Grand Jury Repression, *The Political Grand Jury*. Present-day use of politically motivated grand juries include the "Green Scare," which targets radical environmental activists. It is worth noting that the unified resistance of the Puerto Rican and Chicano movements in the face of grand jury subpoenas contrasts sharply with the frequent willingness to testify that has marked the Green Scare. For more on the Green Scare, see Will Potter, "The Green Scare," in *Vermont Law Review* 33, no. 4 (2009), 671–687.

38   "Political Differences with the MLN" (1978), unpublished document in author's possession.

39   "Sterilization of Puerto Rican Women," n.d., but probably 1977 or 1978. In author's possession.

Practical work around the sterilization issue brought STO members into direct contact with the largely white feminist and reproductive rights movements, and provided an opportunity to challenge what the group perceived as the bourgeois and sometimes racist politics of these movements. In contrast to the mainstream feminist emphasis on access to abortion and other forms of freedom *from* reproduction, STO and others argued for an emphasis on matters of concern to women of color, including the supposedly genocidal attacks on the freedom of poor women of color *to* have children.[40] This was one aspect of STO's approach to linking struggles against white supremacy in an anti-imperialist context with the range of other social struggles that preoccupied the left as the seventies progressed. Additionally, STO's analysis of feminism was partly the result of an attempt to triangulate its perspective versus both the New Communist movement within which it had developed in the early seventies and the emerging white, anti-imperialist solidarity movement.[41]

An article by Carole Travis in the second issue of *Urgent Tasks*— "White Women and Revolutionary Strategy: STO Answers Prairie Fire: Male Supremacy is not Equivalent to White Supremacy"—focused its criticism on the most prominent organization within the latter milieu, the Prairie Fire Organizing Committee. PFOC's origins lay in the grassroots effort to distribute the clandestinely produced, book-length political statement produced of the Weather Underground Organization (WUO) in 1974: *Prairie Fire: The Politics of Revolutionary Anti-Imperialism*. The WUO encouraged the creation of "Prairie Fire Distribution Committees" (PFDCs) that would take on the task of publicizing the book, promoting discussion of the book's analysis within the various movements of the seventies, and generally raising the profile of anti-imperialist politics,

---

40   The most comprehensive scholarly study of the debates around sterilization of Puerto Rican women is Laura Briggs, *Reproducing Empire: Race, Sex, Science, and Imperialism in Puerto Rico* (Berkeley, CA: University of California Press, 2002). Briggs documents the disconnect between freedom-from and freedom-to narratives of reproduction that separated nationalist from feminist responses to sterilization, but her critique of the nationalist position is needlessly onesided and her class analysis of this tension leaves much to be desired.

41   STO's engagement with feminism and reproductive rights, in this sense, was roughly a parallel with its responses to the emerging antinuclear movement, for instance, or with the developing subculture built around punk rock and youth rebellion. See Chapter Six for more on punk rock, and Chapter Seven for more on the antinuclear movement.

all tasks that were impossible for the clandestine cadre of the WUO to undertake themselves.[42] In short order, the distribution committees had transformed themselves into "organizing committees" and unified into a fairly large, coast-to-coast group with substantial prominence within left circles. From the very start, Prairie Fire featured women in a large number of key leadership positions, and did a more thorough job than almost any other organization on the left in the seventies of incorporating feminist analysis into its overall political stance. To the extent that STO had begun to emphasize anti-imperialism and was simultaneously struggling to develop an innovative practice around women's autonomy, it was predictable that the group would feel obliged to respond to PFOC's position. This task fell to Travis, and she made the most of the opportunity.

Built around a close reading of an article entitled "Women's Oppression and Liberation" from the first issue of *Breakthrough*, PFOC's political journal, Travis's critique was thorough, and thoroughly harsh. Flatly stating that STO "disagree[s] with both their analysis and their strategy," the response challenges the historical accuracy of several PFOC claims and accuses the piece of being "loaded with confusion, imprecision and sleight of hand."[43] Travis focuses first on PFOC's analysis of women's oppression, challenging the assertion that imperialism was worsening the oppression of women *qua* women. "In fact," she argues, "capitalism tends to free women; certainly in the US today, particularly white women, are among the freest in the history of class society."[44] The crux of Travis's argument, reflected in the title of her critique, is that PFOC was wrong to "equate the questions of white and male supremacy."[45] Unfortunately it is unclear where PFOC ever argued for such an equivalence, and in retrospect the criticism comes across as something of a straw man.[46]

Travis is more compelling when she counters PFOC's strategic orientation. Quoting the *Breakthrough* article at length, she then

---

42   For more on the PFDCs and the distribution of the book, see Dan Berger, *Outlaws of America*, 207.

43   Carole Travis, "White Women and Revolutionary Strategy: STO Answers Prairie Fire: Male Supremacy is not Equivalent to White Supremacy," in *Urgent Tasks* #2, October 1977, 13.

44   Ibid, 15.

45   Ibid.

46   Doubts were raised about Travis's argument within STO at the time as well. Elaine Zeskind, "Open Letter to STO Women," in *IDB* #5, September 1978, questions "whether PFOC in fact equates white and male supremacy as clearly as Carole argued," 1.

challenges each of four key sentences regarding the essential role white women can play in revolutionary anti-imperialist struggles. She objects to the idea that "white working-class women benefit least from the privileges of white supremacy," arguing instead that the seventies have seen the creation of "a large women's movement, overwhelmingly white, with much of its work implicitly aimed at getting *more* of the privileges imperialism has to offer for women."[47] Similarly, Travis repudiates the idea that there is a "natural basis of solidarity between white and Third World women," and instead maintains that "oppressed nation women have more in common with oppressed nation men than [they do] with white women."[48] In support of this claim, Travis assesses PFOC's own version of the history of white women's organizing, contending that "the women's movement [of the sixties and seventies] was not anti-imperialist and has never been anti-imperialist."[49] Concluding with a parallel to the common left analysis of the previous decade that "youth" were the leading force for white solidarity with anti-imperialist struggles (which, tellingly, was the original position of the people who founded the Weather Underground), Travis argued convincingly against the idea that white women were specially equipped to be a "leading force" in this effort.

In the context of the struggle against mass sterilization—sometimes described as "forced sterilization" or "sterilization abuse"—STO's practical approach reflected the analysis put forward by Travis. The campaign itself necessarily foregrounded the experience of Puerto Rican women rather than white women, and the work was largely built around support for a nationalist framework for resolving the problem of sterilization via the independence of Puerto Rico, rather than through a grand alliance of feminists on the island with those in the United States. The organizational conflict implied in Travis's article did have its limits, as Prairie Fire was also actively involved in the struggle around sterilization as well. Nonetheless, the divergent attitudes regarding white feminism did reflect distinct approaches to organizing around women's issues, with STO more inclined to view Puerto Rican women as Puerto Ricans first and foremost, while PFOC, while recognizing the importance of national identity, emphasized to a greater extent their status and oppression as women.

---

47   Ibid, 17. The quote from the *Breakthrough* is on 16, and comes from p. 29 of the original article.

48   Ibid.

49   Ibid., 18.

* * *

Like many activist campaigns, the struggle against mass sterilization featured a seemingly endless series of public events, speaking tours, and rallies. The rhythm of activism around policy issues, especially those relating to a place as far away as Puerto Rico, was fundamentally different than the daily experience of the factory organizing efforts that had previously characterized STO's practice. While both forms of work highlighted the production and distribution of propaganda and agitational material, often through wheatpasting flyers or handing out newsletters, this was where the similarities ended. Point-of-production work emphasized mass organizing of—and direct action by—workers, often taking months or years to percolate before erupting into open conflict with employers or union bureaucrats. The face-to-face contact and shared experience of the job itself created an organic tie that generated a high level of camaraderie and a sense of connection between the organizer and her or his coworkers. In addition, the cycle of conflict was largely determined by the mass of workers themselves: while a handful of revolutionaries in a factory could agitate for a wildcat strike, for example, the strike of necessity required not just the support but the active participation of dozens or hundreds of coworkers.

Solidarity work could hardly have felt more different. It was something done outside of work hours, unless one happened to work for a nonprofit advocacy group, which a small number of STO members did during the second half of the seventies. It also necessarily involved developing a plan of action that could force the hand of a power structure much more distant than a foreman or a union hack—in this case the governments of Puerto Rico and the United States. This normally included one-off events, like demonstrations and rallies that were not only planned and led by small numbers of revolutionaries, but in many cases were attended largely by these same revolutionaries and their closest comrades. Since STO still had a modest presence in a number of factories (in Chicago, Kansas City, and elsewhere) during this period, attempts were regularly made to draw workers into the solidarity struggles, but these efforts only occasionally met with real success. As a result, while direct action, up to and including armed activity, was often a part of the Puerto Rican independence struggle itself, it was rarely if ever part of the daily experience of solidarity work. STO recognized these limitations, and chafed at them repeatedly during this period, but nonetheless accepted them as the price of being involved in revolutionary politics during the period of the lull.

The tensions between these two organizing models were highlighted in 1977, after STO had produced the pamphlet "Since When Has Working Been a Crime?," discussed earlier in Chapter Three. The initial response to the pamphlet from workers had been positive, and STO began discussing the prospect of distributing it door-to-door in certain neighborhoods on the far south-east side of Chicago, where the multiracial workforce of the US Steel South Works lived in the close quarters of one of the city's most diverse communities.[50] This would have marked a strategic departure from the group's earlier reliance on in-plant organizing, focusing instead on the neighborhood as a locale for struggle. Still, it maintained the direct approach of STO's earlier point-of-production efforts, and was not tied to any specific policy outcomes: instead of agitating for legal reforms around immigration, the pamphlet argued for active solidarity among workers and their families, across lines of color and citizenship. Any real-world effect from the distribution of the pamphlet would have been the result of actions by the people who received, read, and internalized the politics of the pamphlet, rather than the direct outcome of the distribution itself. And again, such results might have taken weeks, months, or even years to simmer before coming to a head in small- or large-scale conflicts with bosses, the police, or the INS.

But the door-to-door distribution was never attempted, largely because of a sudden turn of events in the Puerto Rican solidarity efforts underway over a dozen miles north and west of the South Works. Every June, the Puerto Rican community in Chicago celebrated their cultural heritage with a parade and a festival. Tensions with the police remained a constant theme for Puerto Ricans in Chicago, just as they had been before and after the 1966 rebellion.[51] On the evening of June 4, 1977, after the parade was completed and after the FALN had bombed City Hall in downtown Chicago, the festivities in Humboldt Park took a grim turn: two teenage boys, Rafael Cruz and Julio Osorio, were killed by Chicago police officers who claimed they were gang members. Almost immediately, the neighborhood erupted in violence as the community reacted against the murders. Street battles with the police raged through

---

50   Kingsley Clarke discussed the plan to distribute the pamphlet door-to-door, in several interviews. For more background on the community in South Chicago, see David Bensman's entry in the online Encyclopedia of Chicago   http://encyclopedia.chicagohistory.org/pages/1170.html (accessed January 2, 2012).

51   Tensions with the police are highlighted in Felix Padilla, *Puerto Rican Chicago*.

the night, as cop cars were torched, buildings gutted, and long-buried anger burst into the open.[52]

The MLN took the riots as solid evidence of the revolutionary subjectivity of the Puerto Rican community, and focused its efforts on politicizing and (re)focusing the popular anger that had surfaced in the riots. This activity took many forms, from direct engagement with street gangs to face-to-face organizing and leafleting the neighborhood. Everyone agreed that these sorts of direct organizing efforts within the Puerto Rican community were off-limits to the white solidarity coalition. Nonetheless, the MLN called for an emergency mobilization of the solidarity forces, and STO's leadership decided that the work in South Chicago should be put on hold in order to devote the group's full energies to what was presumed to be an emerging crisis in Humboldt Park.[53] As a result, STO members and other white radicals spent much of the next several months helping plan a series of public demonstrations and speaking events designed to galvanize public opinion in the Puerto Rican community around a revolutionary response to police brutality. As part of taking on logistical responsibilities for these events, the solidarity movement was also expected to mobilize non-Puerto Rican attendees. STO's nascent organizing efforts in South Chicago once again came into play, and Kingsley Clarke remembers bringing a young Mexican-American couple from the neighborhood up to a rally in Humboldt Park during the summer of 1977. In Clarke's recollection, the cultural differences between the two distinct Latino communities were dwarfed by the political gap experienced by the two visitors, who found themselves surrounded largely by dedicated, long-time revolutionary activists, some Puerto Rican, some Mexican-American, some white. The struggle against police brutality certainly resonated with the couple, but the broader demands for independence and socialism in Puerto Rico most likely seemed quite alien. The contrast between workplace organizing and solidarity work was reflected in the bemused faces of the young couple and, in turn, by the mild embarrassment Clarke felt for bringing them.[54]

---

52   Frederick Lowe and Derrick Blakley, "2nd Day of Humboldt Riots," *Chicago Tribune*, June 6, 1977, A1.

53   Kingsley Clarke, author interviews. Without verifying these specifics, Don Hamerquist agreed that the emergency response approach routinely characterized STO's tactical decisions during this period. Author interview, September 14, 2006.

54   Kingsley Clarke, author interview, March 19, 2010.

* * *

Puerto Rican independence was hardly the most geographically distant struggle to be echoed in the streets of Chicago during the latter part of the decade. Halfway around the world in Iran, resistance to the dictatorship of the Shah was heating up substantially after decades of quiet percolation, and the large Iranian student community in the United States did its best to promote and defend the putative revolution. Organized largely under the rubric of several competing groups commonly known as the Iranian Students Association (ISA), the student movement in exile was sizeable and quite militant, with a presence in cities across the US, including Chicago.[55] STO developed ties with the so-called "Left-ISA," and for several years emphasized support for the Iranian revolution on a level just slightly below the priority it placed on solidarity with the Puerto Rican independence movement.[56]

Iran, then as now, was a major oil producing country in the geopolitically sensitive Middle East, which naturally made it of particular foreign policy concern to the United States government. In 1953, a CIA supported coup had toppled the elected government of Mohammed Mosaddeq and installed the Shah (Mohammed Reza Shah Pahlavi) as absolute ruler of the country, a position he would hold until 1979. For a quarter of a century, all dissent was suppressed, often violently, by the Shah's secret

---

55   See Afshin Matin-Asgari, *Iranian Student Opposition to the Shah* (Costa Mesa, CA: Mazda Publishers, 2002) for an overview of the movement in Europe and the United States during the sixties and seventies.

56   The term "Left-ISA" comes from Ed Voci, "Iran Solidarity Work in Chicago," in *IDB* #7, Nov/Dec 1978, 22, which suggested sardonically that "radical Iranians have arrived in the United States without any natural immunity to frequent and sharp political splits similar to those which have plagued the US left." Voci also claimed that "no one knows for sure how many ISA's exist in the United States, or in the world for that matter," but suggested that "there appear to be three principal organizations." Decades later, Noel Ignatiev would recall that STO worked with "the smartest and the smallest" of the Iranian groups during this period. Interview with author, January 27, 2006. David Ranney questions the validity of the term "Left-ISA," and suggests that there were at least four major groupings in Chicago, including two that might plausibly have been described as "left" of the majority. Email to the author, June 2, 2010.

police, known by its Farsi acronym SAVAK.[57] At the same time, Iran's government undertook a massive modernization project, partly inspired by the ever-growing global demand for petroleum, which was lauded by the United States but also served as a cover for the disruption of traditional focal points of social struggle, especially the politicized forms of Shiite Islam. The Leninist left viewed Islam as a regressive force, and focused its efforts on toppling the regime through an array of competing parties and guerrilla organizations. STO was especially attentive to the actions and writings associated with the Organization of Iranian People's Fedayee Guerrillas (OIPFG), which was known for its Marxism and for a commitment to armed struggle as "both a strategy and a tactic."[58] The OIPFG and various other left groups operating clandestinely in Iran drew support from the range of Iranian progressives and radicals who went abroad either as political exiles or for educational purposes, or both.

Given the active support the US offered to the Shah throughout his reign, it is unsurprising that the repressive apparatus of the SAVAK was often allowed to operate freely within the United States. Similar privileges were granted to the military dictatorships of the southern cone (Argentina, Uruguay, Chile, etc.) during the same period. The most extreme example was a joint program of assassination known as "Operation Condor," which led to the murder of Orlando Letelier, a Chilean dissident killed by a car bomb in Washington, DC in 1976.[59] In the case of the Iranian student movement, the repression was less spectacular but still quite violent. Members of the ISA were regularly assaulted by groups of Iranian thugs they believed to be SAVAK agents, and the assailants were often protected by the FBI or local police when complaints were made by student radicals. In Chicago, many of the physical attacks on ISA activists took place at Central YMCA Community College, where a

---

57   For a chronology of the Shah's reign, with an emphasis on left resistance movements and their repression by the SAVAK, see Mazier Behrooz, *Rebels with a Cause: The Failure of the Left in Iran* (London and New York: I B Taurus, 2000).

58   This phrase is the subtitle of the key theoretical document produced by the OIPFG prior to the revolution, Massoud Ahmadzadeh, *Armed Struggle: Both a Strategy and a Tactic*. This book is available online at http://www.siahkal.com/english/Massoud.htm (accessed January 2, 2012).

59   For more on Operation Condor, see Jon Dinges, *The Condor Years: How Pinochet and His Allies Brought Terrorism to Three Continents* (New York: New Press, 2004).

number of them were students.[60] Central YMCA was located in the West Town neighborhood and many radical Puerto Ricans, including Carmen Valentin, later imprisoned as a member of the FALN in 1980, worked or studied there. Indeed, over the course of the seventies, the Iranian student movement and the Puerto Rican independence movement periodically engaged in various forms of mutual support.

In this context, it is worth noting that STO's connection with the Left-ISA began not in Chicago, but in Texas. In 1976, STO members Ed Voci and Lowell May went on an organizing tour through the middle of the United States in support of the five Puerto Rican nationalist prisoners. In Texas, Voci and May met members of the Left-ISA who attended a presentation about the Five, and through them gained contacts in the Iranian student movement in Chicago.[61] Over the next several years, Voci would become one of STO's key points of contact with the Iranian movement. The work he and other members of STO undertook in attempting to build a broad-based left movement in solidarity with the growing revolutionary struggle in Iran in many ways paralleled STO's work around Puerto Rican independence. The efforts of revolutionary anti-imperialists to support the Iranians were small and often isolated from the broader US left because of sectarian approaches to political differences. Much of the work involved providing legal help in the face of repression by SAVAK and the Chicago Police Department red squad. Voci was an attorney, and he often worked alongside other radical lawyers to defend ISA activists falsely accused of petty crimes. Such false accusations were a routine consequence of complaining to the police about the ongoing harassment. Nonetheless, legal avenues were vigorously pursued in an attempt to halt or diminish the attacks by those presumed to be SAVAK agents: complaints were filed with the Police Board alleging collusion with SAVAK, and criminal charges were sometimes filed against the most prominent thugs.[62]

On a less reactive level, STO worked with other radicals in Chicago to plan a series of public rallies against the Shah and in defense of the ISA and the revolution in Iran. As with the Puerto Rican work, this took the organizational form of a solidarity committee, officially known as

---

60 A chronology of attacks in Chicago is contained in the "Appendix" to a letter of complaint to the Police Board of the City of Chicago, dated March 1, 1978, included in *IDB* #7, Nov/Dec 1978.

61 Ed Voci, interview with the author, January 27, 2007.

62 Several incidents along these lines are described in "Appendix" to the letter of complaint in *IDB* #7, Nov/Dec 1978.

the Committee in Solidarity with the Revolutionary Movement in Iran, which featured a similar mixture of PFOC, May 19ᵗʰ, and other independent leftists. An internal report prepared by Voci for STO reflected frustration at the ways in which petty sectarianism within the solidarity coalition dramatically slowed its progress: "Thus, meetings (held weekly) were reduced to line by line reviews of propaganda and speeches to be delivered by committee members."[63] In other words, the organization's sincere desire to support the Iranian revolution was hampered not just by the SAVAK or by objective conditions, but also by the demands for ideological purity imposed by the Left-ISA. Leaflets were often picked apart word-by-word to ensure that all participants in the solidarity work could agree on every detail of their content. The same problem limited the options for planning rallies or for more detailed propaganda, although over the course of 1978 the Committee did manage to publish one issue of a tabloid called simply *Iran Solidarity*, as well as pamphlet entitled *Iran: Another Vietnam; ISA: Another "COINTELPRO" Target.*[64]

Partly in response to frustrations with the Committee, STO began to use *Urgent Tasks* as a forum for direct interaction with the Leninists in Iran, thus bypassing to some extent the sectarianism of the ISA milieu. The magazine repeatedly served as something of a mouthpiece for a variety of guerrilla groups, publishing their communiqués and speeches in English translation, in some cases for the first time.[65] But the engagement was not entirely uncritical: an article by Beth Henson in issue number 5 of *Urgent Tasks* presented a critical assessment of the theories of urban armed struggle then emerging from Iran and South America. Henson criticized in particular the "emphasis on practice and denigration of theory" that appeared to characterize even the more theoretical writings of the OIPFG.[66] She also expressed doubt concerning the Iranian revolutionaries' ability to prevent "the vanguard from forging too

---

63   Ed Voci, "Iran Solidarity Work in Chicago," in *IDB* #7, Nov/Dec 1978.

64   Copies of both of these documents in author's possession, courtesy of Ed Voci.

65   See, for example the speech by Ashraf Dehghani, "Armed Struggle is the Only Way," published in *UT* #8, Spring 1980, available online at http://www.sojournertruth.net/irandocs8.html (accessed January 2, 2012). The introduction to this speech notes that "it was translated for *Urgent Tasks* by comrades at Mississippi State University, Starkville, who support Ashraf Dehghani and the People's Fedayee Guerrillas."

66   Beth Henson, "Review: Armed Struggle Theories," in *UT* #5, Summer 1979, 28.

far ahead and substituting its own will for the will of the masses, forming the nucleus of a bureaucratic rather than a proletarian party."[67]

While Henson was willing to express some skepticism about the viability of the OIPFG's approach, STO as a whole was consistently unwilling to doubt the overall trajectory of the Iranian revolution, in spite of mounting evidence that it was tending toward religious fundamentalism. When the Shah fled in January 1979, a patchwork of competing groups, including the OIPFG, claimed to have played the decisive role in the victory, but over the course of the next year power was rapidly consolidated in the hands of the Ayatollah Ruhollah Khomeini. Khomeini presided over an increasingly authoritarian state structure known as the Islamic Republic, which sanctioned direct physical attacks on the OIPFG and other left groups, implemented oppressive policies against national minorities like the Kurds, and led efforts to eliminate basic civil rights for women. A number of prominent leftists were beaten and arrested, and several left organizations and newspapers were banned.[68]

Nonetheless, STO developed an analysis of the Iranian situation that compared it to the transitional period in Russia under Kerensky between the February and October revolutions of 1917. An unsigned editorial in issue number 7 of *UT* (Winter 1980) used this parallel as a pretext for defending the Khomeini regime and especially the hostage crisis then underway at the US embassy in Tehran. STO argued that the political key was "maintaining full tactical flexibility," and that "revolutionaries must rally to the defense of Khomeini's government," as the only bulwark against the risk of US intervention to restore the Shah.[69] The justification for this position was complicated, and STO maintained that "our general stance does not mean supporting Khomeini's government uncritically or unconditionally; STO supports the armed revolutionary left." The editorial did contain a fairly nuanced appreciation of the role of Islam in the Iranian revolution:

> Despite these right-wing currents there is a progressive
> side to the Islamic revival that is sweeping the Middle East
> which much of the U.S. left has failed to understand and

---

67   Ibid.

68   For more on the struggles of the Iranian left under the Islamic Republic, see Behrooz, *Rebels With A Cause*.

69   These and all other quotes in this paragraph come from "In Defense of Iran: An Editorial," in *UT* #7, Winter 1980. The editorial is dated January 5, 1980.

appreciate—largely due to its knee-jerk anticlericalism. Islam represents a third force in the region, one which is opposed to the interests of both the U.S. and the U.S.S.R. It would not have been able to make the gains which it has made if it were wholly reactionary and anachronistic. Obviously it is inadequate to the broader revolutionary current and obviously it imposes fetters on those very forces which it releases—the clearest examples are the repression of women and homosexuals and sexuality in general. But the left brings no credit on itself for its failure to understand what is positive in this Islamic movement and what is the basis of its appeal.

Unfortunately, this analysis was fatally imprecise, to the extent that it treated Islam as a "force" in general terms, rather than assessing the specific forms of Shiite fundamentalism advocated by Khomeini. As a result, the predictable support among Iranian muslims for the repression of the very groups that STO supported in Iran was, temporarily at least, beyond the organization's grasp.

STO was hardly alone in mistakenly defending Khomeini, although given the group's overall political stance it did not readily embrace its new bedfellows. According to the scholar David Greason, a number of Trotskyist organizations in the US and Europe presented similar arguments to those put forward by STO, maintaining that a careful reading of Lenin's 1920 "Draft Theses on National and Colonial Questions" required "socialists to defend Iran against imperialist attacks, while maintaining the independence of working-class or revolutionary socialist organization."[70] Greason argues convincingly that "such a reading … placed a higher value on a regime's stance towards 'imperialism' (whatever that stance's ultimate motivation—socialist, fascist or religious obscurantist) than its stance toward its own proletariat."[71] In this sense, STO's

---

70   David Greason, "Embracing Death: the Western Left and the Iranian Revolution, 1978–83," in *Economy and Society* 34, no.1, February 2005, 112. Lenin's *Theses* are available online at http://marxists.anu. edu.au/archive/lenin/works/1920/jun/05.htm (accessed January 2, 2012). Thanks to Danny Postel for first bringing the Greason article to my attention.

71   Ibid., 112–113. Contemporary radicals have attempted to address this problem in multiple ways, one of which is the "three way fight" analysis developed over the last decade with significant input from Don

defense of Khomeini stood in direct contradiction to its own longstanding critical approach to revolutions, even those claiming the mantle of socialism, most famously embodied in Noel Ignatin's 1976 pamphlet *"…no condescending saviors"*. At that point, Ignatin openly criticized the Castro regime in Cuba, despite the ongoing threat of US imperialism a mere ninety miles to the north, using the argument that "the only positive way to determine which class is wielding power in a country is to examine the decision-making process there, especially as it affects the relations of production."[72] Using this criterion, it should have been clear by the end of 1979 that the decision-making process in Iran was rapidly being placed into the hands of Khomeini and his chosen administrators, who were in no way representative of the working class. That STO chose instead to focus on the dangers of US intervention was exemplary of the one-sidedness of the group's emphasis on anti-imperialism and solidarity work during the second half of the seventies.

STO did subsequently issue an "explanatory note" to clarify its position on Iran in a way that half-heartedly criticized its previous optimism regarding the coming socialist phase of the revolution, but the group continued to maintain the overall correctness of its earlier critical defense of Khomeini.[73] Thus, "we still maintain that for the moment when it was published—and especially for US revolutionaries—our stance was correct." Nonetheless, "it is becoming increasingly evident that right-wing forces in Iran are using the confrontation with the US as a cover for attacks on the left." In the meantime, many of STO's key contacts from the Left-ISA had chosen to return to Iran, part of a mass exodus of younger radicals inspired by the 1979 revolution. By the early eighties, the Left-ISA had effectively disintegrated, and the space for real-world solidarity work was limited to the occasional rally. Unfortunately, the eventual fate of most of the returning exiles was imprisonment, death, or imposed political withdrawal and silence. Halfway across the globe,

---

Hamerquist. See the website http://threewayfight.blogspot.com/ (accessed January 2, 2012).

72   Noel Ignatin, *"…no condescending saviors"* (Chicago: STO, 1976). Ignatin did conclude that Cuba was led by "great revolutionaries, who have carried out the sharpest and most progressive struggles against imperialism anywhere in the world," so even here the precursor to the group's defense of Khomeini could be identified.

73   This term, and all other quotes in this paragraph, are from the unsigned "Explanatory Note and Introduction," in *Urgent Tasks* #9, Summer 1980, 1.

STO was largely helpless to assist its comrades and, despite many lessons learned, the group's experience with Iranian solidarity work was marked by failure on almost every level.

* * *

A much more successful venue for STO's anti-imperialist work during the late seventies was the struggle to free the five Puerto Rican nationalist prisoners who had been held since the fifties. Like the solidarity work with the Iranian left, it involved a range of groups from across the left, including New Communist groups and anti-imperialist radicals. It also enjoyed the active solidarity of revolutionary black nationalist organizations and other groups made up primarily or exclusively of people of color. As a national and international campaign, however, it did not automatically speak to the average Puerto Rican on the streets of Chicago. Thus, one primary objective of the work was to raise the consciousness of Puerto Ricans regarding the injustice of the continued imprisonment of the Five. This was accomplished largely through regular distribution of leaflets, newsletters, and stickers, as well as the predictable range of events, both public and private.

The latter category included the *charla*, a small invitation-only gathering in a home that featured both a solid meal and a presentation on the work of the campaign; there was also frequently a small-scale fundraising aspect to such an event. STO members hosted *charlas* in their homes, and the group also sponsored speaking and fundraising tours for Puerto Rican radicals, from the island or from Chicago, through places like Kansas City, Denver, or Portland, which had no Puerto Rican communities to speak of, but did have STO branches. The *charlas* and especially the tours helped raise STO's profile in the cities where it had recently expanded its presence, and they also brought the group into direct contact with revolutionary organizations based in Puerto Rico itself, especially the Liga Socialista Puertorriquena (LSP), led by Juan Antonio Corretjer. STO members and supporters were mobilized to help plan (and to attend) rallies in support of the prisoners in Chicago, New York, and elsewhere. Additionally, in a complicated, sometimes three- or four-cornered dance of mutual aid, STO made sure to lend support—often in the form of attendance at demonstrations—to struggles led by black, chicano, Asian American and Native American groups that in turn lent assistance or support to the Puerto Rican independence movement.

The campaign to "Free the Five" was eventually successful. In 1978, President Jimmy Carter ordered the release of Andres Figueroa Cordero, who was dying of cancer. A year later, the remaining four prisoners were granted clemency by Carter, whose administration—in the face of growing Puerto Rican and international anger over their continuing incarceration—calculated that they were "less a cause célèbre outside [of prison] than inside."[74] The importance of the MLN and of the Chicago branch of the solidarity movement to the overall campaign was reflected in the decision of the four former prisoners to travel to Chicago immediately upon their release, even before returning to their homes in Puerto Rico after twenty-five years in prison.[75] From an anti-imperialist perspective, this victory, along with the expanding armed struggle being waged by the FALN and other groups, was another sign of the rising power of the Puerto Rican independence movement. For some time, the MLN had maintained that the struggle was on the verge of creating a revolutionary situation that would mark the "last period of struggle against colonialism and for independence."[76]

STO did not share this assessment, and disagreed with the strategic conclusions that the MLN drew from its analysis. In a 1978 internal document outlining its "Political Differences with the MLN," STO wrote that "our fear is that exaggerated estimates of the situation in Puerto Rico will unnecessarily delay and divert essential popular education on armed struggle."[77] But of course one corollary of the belief in an imminently revolutionary scenario was the necessity of responding as urgently as possible to any emerging crisis, whether it be grand jury subpoenas or the capture of Guillermo Morales, a leading member of the FALN, in 1978.[78] In STO's view, this led to work being done "in an arbitrary

---

74 Unnamed Carter administration official quoted in "We Have Nothing to Repent," *Time*, September 24, 1979. Online here: http://www.time.com/time/magazine/article/0,9171,947395,00.html (accessed January 2, 2012).

75 Nathaniel Sheppard Jr., "Four Freed Puerto Rican Nationalists Vow to Continue Fight; Sentenced for Terrorist Acts," *New York Times*, September 11, 1979, A16.

76 "Editorial," *De Pie y En Guerra* 1, no. 1, 1978, 2. *De Pie y En Guerra* was the MLN's political journal. Copy in author's possession.

77 "Political Differences with the MLN" (1978), 2. Unpublished document in author's possession. The dating at the front of the document notes, "1978, reprinted in 1980 because essentially the same differences remain." The document is unsigned, and appears to be an official position of STO that was presented directly to the MLN.

78 Morales subsequently escaped, lived for a time in Mexico, and eventually

and erratic fashion." And each crisis resulted in a specific organizational form, usually a committee made up of representatives of the same groups that were already involved in overarching solidarity movement. As a result, argued STO, "there is a chaotic overlapping of areas of work and responsibility between various committees, organizations, and individuals. Everything is equally urgent and imperative."[79] Several former members of STO recall the frustration that resulted from this perpetual crisis: long-term projects, such as the proposed distribution of the immigration pamphlet in South Chicago, were regularly put on hold, not because they were deemed less important, but simply because everything related to Puerto Rican solidarity had to be done *right then*, while everything else could always wait.[80]

For most of the late seventies, STO kept these concerns and criticisms to itself, or shared them only in the context of closed-door meetings with the MLN or the various solidarity groupings. The risks of state repression were seen as far too high to allow for any public criticism of the MLN, PFOC, or others. Here it is important to remember the context of the times. An active armed Puerto Rican underground was detonating bombs in Chicago and New York, as well as on the island, on a semi-regular basis. Above-ground activists were routinely targeted for visits by the FBI or grand jury subpoenas. The black liberation movement had been decimated over the previous decade by dozens of assassinations and hundreds of criminal prosecutions. The release of thousands of pages of COINTELPRO documents verified long-held suspicions that the US government manipulated political differences within the left in order to disrupt the functioning of numerous radical groups. And STO was publicly and vocally supportive of the most militant tendencies within a range of openly revolutionary movements active in the United States. By the late seventies, STO itself counted as members a number of people who had served time in prison or jail, some for petty drug charges but others for acts of political violence.

In short, there was an intense awareness within the group of the likely repercussions of any public disagreements. Indeed, not only conflicts were kept private: so too were many of the activities undertaken by STO and its members.[81] This secrecy was designed to protect the

---

moved to Cuba, where he currently resides.

79   "Political Differences," 8.

80   Author interviews with Janeen Porter, Don Hamerquist, Kingsley Clarke, and others support this assessment.

81   On one level, the problem persists to this day. Many former members

independence movement and the solidarity movement from government repression, but it also had the effect of limiting the ability of the MLN, STO, and the other groups to broaden the struggle by incorporating political newcomers. Former member David Ranney suggests that "there was an internal contradiction between internal organizational transparency and democracy on the one hand, and the demands of security on the other."[82] In turn, the solidarity work that was visible to the rest of the left, not to mention to the public, was limited to the sort of isolated rallies and speaking tours that could be planned and carried out openly. The fear of government agents becoming involved in the work was hardly an unfounded paranoia, but it did reinforce the marginalization of militant anti-imperialism in an era where much of the left was looking to become involved in just this sort of activism. The occasional false accusation leveled at people who were not in fact informers only exacerbated the problem. Just as the unified exterior shown by STO and its allies papered over significant disagreements without resolving them, so too did it provide more the appearance than the reality of security from government repression.

* * *

But even while STO kept strategy and tactics, and disagreements over them, shielded from public view, the group was deliberately quite open about the politics of its solidarity work. STO was loathe to directly criticize the politics of the MLN in public, but the underlying disagreements are clear in a number of published documents aimed more directly at STO's coalition partners. In 1979, for example, the group criticized

> the confusion of unconditional support for national liberation with an uncritical identification with positions taken by the national liberation leadership or elements of it. Unconditional support involves a conscious subordination of political differences for definite political reasons. The political leadership of national liberation movements must be followed on questions concerning the form and content of the movements they head, not because this leadership is always right, but because it is the social force whose correct

---

of STO who were actively involved in the solidarity work are hesitant to discuss it in any detail.

82   David Ranney, email to the author, June 2, 2010.

and incorrect positions "matter." This has nothing to do
with any attribution of infallibility and omniscience. We
do liberation movements no favor by disguising disagreements, or, still worse, by evading questions which must be
of concern to all revolutionaries.[83]

This represented a not-so-subtle attack on the solidarity politics of
Prairie Fire and May 19th, which STO considered overly subservient to
the dictates of the MLN and other revolutionary nationalist organizations. In practice, however, STO's refusal to openly challenge liberation
movements meant that the group's public stance was for the most part
functionally identical to the one they criticized.

Internally, STO had already begun to examine this contradiction in
its engagement with anti-imperialist struggles. In 1978, Don Hamerquist identified an "obvious problem with direct support to Third World
groups. Given our view of Third World autonomy, such support entails
acceptance of strategic and tactical decisions on which STO rightly
has little voice and no vote. This cannot help but stimulate an a-criti-
cal and a-political attitude on the part of at least a section of the STO
membership."[84] Further, STO's efforts to stimulate political debate on
the left were not always well received by groups like the MLN, which,
argued Hamerquist, "regard such work as a disruption and a diversion—
as an unnecessary narrowing of the base of potential unified action, and
as a factor introducing peripheral questions into their organizations and
constituencies."[85] The subordination of the group's own longer-term
plans to the immediate needs of the Puerto Rican struggle was exemplary
of the problems that resulted from this combination of elements.

In other words, STO was divided against itself, and risked either liq-
uidating itself into the solidarity work or alienating its erstwhile allies by
pushing forward with debates that would diminish the group's capacity
for practical work. The latter scenario played on fears within STO of
being reduced to what former member Bill Lamme would later mock
as "the best debating society on the left."[86] The alternative was perhaps
even worse for a group that had always attempted to intervene directly

83   "'Unconditional Support' and 'Follow Third World Leadership': An
     Editorial," in *Urgent Tasks* #6 (Fall 1979), available online at http://
     www.sojournertruth.net/ut6editorial.html (accessed January 2, 2012).
84   Don Hamerquist, "Direction," in *IDB* #1, n.d., but spring 1978, 3.
85   Ibid.
86   Bill Lamme, interview with author, July 20, 2005.

in the working class. From this angle, the specter of the Prairie Fire Organizing Committee was (fairly or not) something of an archetype for what STO wanted to avoid. In former member Ira Churgin's recollection, PFOC and May 19th "totally unmoored themselves from the class, and we hadn't. That was what distinguished us from them."[87] But by the late seventies, STO's connection to the working class was more tenuous than ever. The belief in the lull and the progressive disengagement from factory work had created a situation where the group retained its groundbreaking analysis of the working class—dual consciousness, white skin privilege, and so on—but had less and less practical work to show for it. This of course reinforced concerns that STO was reducing itself to theoretical navel-gazing.

To break the vicious cycle, STO decided to re-examine its analysis of the lull as well as the focus it placed on solidarity work. At the General Membership Meeting in May 1979, the group overwhelmingly re-affirmed its belief that "the internal national liberation movements are the leading forces for revolution in this country at this time," and that "we are in the anti-imperialist current," but there were rumblings of a different direction.[88] The women's movement, factory organizing ("point-of-production work"), and the antinuclear movement were also highlighted as arenas of work for STO, with the latter being declared after some debate "the main area where large numbers of white people are being activated and radicalized." Intervention in all these struggles was still based on "our general plan of developing an anti-imperialist current," but with certain caveats. For example, the women's movement was not to be "organizationally subordinated" to the national liberation movement. More controversially, a majority of STO rejected the idea that the "main criteria for judging the success of our work" in point-of-production organizing should be the extent to which it contributed to building the anti-imperialist current.

This appeared to be a significant departure from the strategic outlook that characterized the "lull," and the decision was highly controversial within STO. Hamerquist argued bluntly that "the GMM took an inconsistent and mistaken position in exempting production work from the

---

87   Ira Churgin, interview with the author, December 7, 2005.

88   The quoted phrase about the "internal national liberation movements" was the first resolution voted on at the GMM, while the "anti-imperialist current" line comes from the second resolution. See "Questions and Votes from GMM," in *IDB* #11, June 1979, 3, in author's possession. All other quotes in this paragraph also come from this document.

political framework in which the rest of our work is to be developed."[89] While he advanced a series of arguments to support his claim, his main concern revolved around the practical implications of the decision. In particular, "we will regularly be faced with the necessity of choosing between the politics of production work and that of the other work," with the latter category including all the efforts broadly considered under the category "anti-imperialist." This problem, argued Hamerquist, would surface immediately, once STO began to determine "how much more resources—and which resources—will be put into this [production] work." What was needed, in his view, was a reversal of the GMM decision, so that the group's workplace organizing efforts would in fact be subordinated under the broad heading of anti-imperialist work.

Hamerquist lost in repeated procedural efforts, both at the GMM and after it, to reverse the resolution. But the dispute in the organization remained. In reality, by 1979 everyone in STO understood the problem—perpetual deference to the national liberation movements (and especially to the MLN) was retarding the organization's development, and the horizons for the group's work needed to be broadened. The question really boiled down to two competing solutions. A significant segment of STO wanted to experiment with organizing efforts that it believed would be free of the problems inherent in the anti-imperialist framework, while Hamerquist and some others believed that it was possible to redefine the meaning of "anti-imperialism" to go beyond the frustrating forms of solidarity work that had characterized STO's efforts so far. Indeed, the 1979 GMM had resolved almost unanimously that "our work in building the anti-imperialist current should not be reduced to direct support for national liberation," and that "this current must contain a variety of activities and organizational forms."[90] These areas of agreement helped paper over the substantive disagreements within STO, and in practical terms something of a compromise was reached. Thus, at the beginning of 1980 STO formally left the New Movement in Solidarity with Puerto Rican Independence, which was the then-current name for the overarching solidarity coalition.[91] Meanwhile, the workplace efforts were allowed

---

89 This and the other quotes in this paragraph come from Don Hamerquist, "Position on GMM Vote," in *IDB* #11, June, 1979, 5–6.

90 The "not reduced" quote is from resolution #4, while the "must contain" quote was the third resolution, the only one approved unanimously. *IDB* #11, June 1979, 3.

91 "Puerto Rican Fraction Report," prepared by Lee (Holstein), December 10, 1980, in author's possession, identifies the time of departure as

to develop largely unburdened by the still continuing solidarity work. This was especially true in Kansas City, where STO had always maintained a significant industrial concentration and where the Puerto Rican independence movement had no presence due to the lack of a Puerto Rican community. Over the next few years, the "production fraction" in Kansas City became actively involved in a range of efforts, including an engagement with Teamsters for a Democratic Union, a reform caucus inside the highly corrupt International Brotherhood of Teamsters.

* * *

Back in Chicago, STO's formal departure from the New Movement did not insulate it from the continuing demands of the Puerto Rican solidarity work, which intensified when another major crisis hit the independence movement. On the afternoon of April 4, 1980, eleven Puerto Rican radicals were arrested in a suburb of Chicago and charged with being members of the FALN.[92] They were captured (allegedly while casing an armored car for robbery near Northwestern University in Evanston, Illinois) after a woman called the police to report the "suspicious" presence of several young latinos in an overwhelmingly white neighborhood. Although they were heavily armed, the eleven did not resist their capture once the police arrived. When brought to the police station for processing, however, they claimed they were prisoners of war and demanded treatment according to the Geneva Conventions. None of the prisoners identified themselves as members of the FALN, and a number of them gave false names, although they were fairly quickly identified once federal authorities became involved in the investigation. The eleven prisoners were treated as a major security threat based on the previous armed activities of the FALN, and they appeared in court under armed guard. From the start, however, they refused to participate in their trials, and regularly disrupted the proceedings.

The arrests immediately reverberated throughout the militant sectors of the independence movement and the solidarity milieu. The very next day, the New Movement, of which STO was no longer a member, produced a two-sided single-sheet leaflet aimed directly at white people who could be swayed to support the armed struggle for independence. Headlined "Support and Defend the Armed Clandestine Movement!!,"

"sometime early in 1980."

92   This account is largely based on the narrative in Fernandez, *Prisoners of Colonialism*, 8.

the leaflet identified the eleven as "prisoners of the war for Puerto Rican independence," claimed that "the resistance to US colonial rule has grown to the beginning stages of people's war," and maintained that "the Puerto Rican nation is mobilizing to stop imperialist genocide."[93] The text-heavy mixture of sloganeering and analysis concluded that "we, the people of the nation that holds Puerto Rico under military domination, have a responsibility to support the combatants in the war for Puerto Rican independence and these new Puerto Rican Prisoners of War."[94] Not surprisingly, none of STO's ongoing concerns about the problems of the independence and solidarity movements were reflected in the leaflet.

Regardless, STO's immediate response to the Evanston arrests was once again to dive into the emergency response mode that had continually frustrated the group since the grand jury period two years before. Without re-joining the New Movement, STO resumed participation in "virtually the same committee structure [it] had recently left."[95] Members attended court hearings to support the prisoners, mobilized for emergency rallies, and provided direct material aid to the MLN in its efforts to build support for the prisoners. Printing services were again provided by C&D Printshop, and at least one STO member served as a legal advisor to the prisoners (although in declaring themselves to be prisoners of war they rejected all offers of formal legal counsel, and the lawyers did not impose their services). A sticker was produced for mass distribution, though most copies were provided to the MLN for distribution within the Puerto Rican community.

The frustration among STO members was palpable: according to an internal note prepared in May, 1980, by Ed Voci, the group was already "falling into the same pattern of passive, subsumed grunt work and behaving like there is nothing we can do about it."[96] By late summer, STO had again withdrawn from the formal committee structure of the solidarity work, although it continued to organize on its own around the defense of the prisoners. The reasons for the departure were both pragmatic and political. In addition to the diversion of time and energy from other efforts—such as the renewed workplace organizing initia-

---

93   The leaflet is reproduced on pages 41–42 of *IDB* #16, May 1980. The reference in the first sentence to "yesterday" indicates that the leaflet was produced on April 5.

94   Ibid, 42.

95   "Puerto Rican Fraction Report," December 10, 1980.

96   "May 20, 1980—Note to P.R. Fraction," unpublished two-page memo in author's possession.

tives—there were strategic disagreements as well. STO quietly began developing reservations about the approach to the new situation taken by the prisoners and the MLN. The internal document originally prepared in 1978, "Political Differences with the MLN," was redistributed to the membership with the explanatory note, "reprinted in 1980 because essentially the same differences remain." The assumption of broad support for armed struggle and "people's war" within the Puerto Rican community, both on the island and in the diaspora, struck STO as naïve and unsupported by the evidence.[97]

In the midst of the group's growing frustration, ten of the eleven prisoners were convicted in Illinois state court of a series of crimes, mostly conspiracy to commit armed robbery and possession of unlicensed firearms.[98] The government's strategy appeared to be to depoliticize the case by portraying the prisoners as common criminals, but when the prison sentences returned at the state level were deemed too short (only eight years for most of the prisoners, which would have potentially resulted in eligibility for parole in half that time), the federal government stepped in to try them again, this time on weightier charges, most centrally "seditious conspiracy." Sedition is the crime of organizing to overthrow the US government by force, and seditious conspiracy had long been a favorite of federal prosecutors in dealing with Puerto Rican revolutionaries, going back at least to Albizu Campos in the mid-thirties. But to bring this charge against the ten prisoners in 1980 meant implicitly acknowledging the political nature of the FALN. While not exactly a desperate move on the part of the US government, it did mark a departure from the previous efforts to cast the prisoners as simply violent thugs; now they were being portrayed as terrorists with a dangerous revolutionary

---

97   Prolonged, or "protracted" people's war is a phrase originating with Mao Tse-Tung's political military strategy in China during the thirties, and it has subsequently been adopted by a wide range of Maoist and non-Maoist revolutionary groups in places as diverse as Nicaragua, Peru, the Philippines, India, and Nepal. For more on Mao's original conception, see his long essay, "On Protracted War" (1938). Available online at http://www.marx2mao.com/Mao/PW38.html (accessed January 2, 2012).

98   The trials are described in Fernandez, *Prisoners of Colonialism*. One of the original eleven, Haydee Beltran was separated from the other prisoners almost immediately after her arrest and extradited to New York, where she was convicted separately of involvement in a specific bombing and sentenced to life imprisonment.

agenda.[99] However, the shift in government strategy did not prompt any change in the prisoners' strategy, and they continued their stance of non-collaboration with the "illegal" court of what they argued was an occupying military force. The ten continued to disrupt the court proceedings to the point where they were removed permanently from the courtroom, and replaced with large photographs visible to the jury in their absence. After a two-week trial, the jury swiftly convicted them, and they were subsequently sentenced to prison terms of up to ninety years.

In the eyes of STO, the continued refusal to mount any sort of court-room defense, even a political one, was problematic. While accepting the basic framework of the prisoner-of-war status, and while clearly acknowledging the right of the prisoners and the Puerto Rican independence organizations to determine their own strategy, STO began to push the issue. In a sharp departure from its previous refusal to publicly criticize the independence movement over questions of strategy, the unsigned editorial in issue number 11 of *Urgent Tasks* directly addressed the disagreement. "We are not convinced that the decision not to present a political defense is correct," began the key paragraph. "It seems unlikely to us that any political defense the Eleven presented would be taken by anyone to imply recognition of the legitimacy or jurisdiction of the US court structure."[100] For STO, the key issue was that "the strategy of prolonged people's war has not yet been accepted by a decisive section of the Puerto Rican people, either on the island or on the mainland." This was really a reworking of the group's longstanding concern that the key task of popular education, both among Puerto Ricans and among North Americans, was being overlooked in favor of rose-tinted proclamations of impending revolution. Thus, the problem with the prisoners' stance was that it made the mistake of "assuming the validity of the strategy and

---

99   It is worth noting that a similar quandary was raised when the seditious conspiracy charge was leveled against Albizu Campos in 1935. A Washington bureaucrat at the time criticized the government's legal strategy as one that "glorifies Albizu Campos and raises an issue that can be disguised in terms of patriotism." Quoted in Fernandez, *Prisoners of Colonialism*, 43. The original citation is to "National Archives, Washington DC. Record Group 126," and Fernandez notes that "this letter to Governor Blanton Winship is dated March 9, 1936."

100 These and all subsequent quotes in this paragraph are from "Editorial: The FALN Sedition Trials," in *Urgent Tasks* #11, Spring 1981, 17–19. Note that even though the editorial repeatedly refers to the "FALN 11," there were only ten defendants at the federal trial.

tactics of armed struggle rather than deepening the argument for them." And, of course, if the strategy of prolonged people's war had not been accepted by Puerto Ricans, then it went without saying that pronouncements regarding the impending or actual reality of people's war, as in the New Movement leaflet of April 5, were premature at best and self-defeating at worst. "In our view," concluded the editorial, "the evidence does not show that war in this sense is imminent in Puerto Rico, and it is certainly not occurring there already."

In the aftermath of this public critique, STO's approach to anti-imperialist and especially solidarity work was changed forever. The group continued to support the Puerto Rican independence movement, and collaborated occasionally over the next several years with the MLN in particular. STO could also take some small satisfaction that its critique of the prisoners' nonparticipation was incorporated after a fashion in subsequent trials. In 1983, when several more Puerto Ricans were arrested and charged with membership in the FALN, those captured identified themselves as "political prisoners" rather than "prisoners of war," and did in fact put forward a political defense quite similar to the one advocated two years earlier by STO. Nonetheless, as the eighties progressed, STO placed far greater attention on the antinuclear movement, antifascist struggles, the spontaneous potential of youth in rebellion, and other areas of work that reflected the group's growing interest in autonomous social movements. Another era in STO's existence had ended.

Chapter Six:
The Politics of Culture and the Culture of Politics in a Revolutionary Organization

On February 5, 1981, Bruce Springsteen and the E Street Band performed at the Kemper Arena in Kansas City, Missouri, as part of the group's long tour in support of their magnificent 1980 double album, *The River*.[1] Outside the venue, several members of STO, along with friends and comrades organized as the Committee Against War and Imperialism (CAWI), distributed thousands of copies of a leaflet to fans headed into the arena. The CAWI leaflet featured a classic photo of the young Springsteen, sporting a black suit and a partially buttoned white shirt with the collar out, leaning against a brick wall. Designed as an 8½ by 11 inch fold-over in booklet style with a headline in the ransom-note cut-out letters so popular in the punk-rock milieu of the

---

1   The date and venue of the Kansas City concert comes from the "Killing Floor Database of Bruce Springsteen Setlists," online at http://www. brucespringsteen.it/Showdx.htm (accessed December 19, 2011). The description of this leafleting activity comes from recollections provided by Janeen Porter, Alan Rausch, and Randy Gould, all of whom were in the Kansas City branch of STO at the time.

time, it quoted extensively from Springsteen songs like "Badlands," "Born to Run," "Racing in the Street," and of course "The River" itself: in the midst of a recession, the lyrics "I got a job working construction for the Johnstown Company/But lately there ain't been much work on account of the economy" spoke directly to the problems of working class life, and STO knew it.[2]

The CAWI leaflet took the dynamic tension in Springsteen's songs and linked it to a broader social reality. Speaking directly of contemporary problems like unemployment, police brutality, cuts in welfare, limits on abortion, Klan and neo-Nazi violence, and the threat of nuclear war, the leaflet argued that reality "contradicts the 'american dream,'" leaving people "confused, disheartened, crushed, broken and ANGRY as they chase after the illusion of having a good life."[3] Ronald Reagan, newly inaugurated as the fortieth President of the United States, represented a racist and imperialist politics that promised to make things even worse. Unfortunately, the leaflet continued, "people generally see their rotten life as a personal problem and try to solve it individually or put the blame on the wrong people. The rich and powerful in the u.s. are our real enemies, the ones making our lives miserable. This makes us angry, and we need to be more angry. We are the ones who can change all this." But this was not just a standard leftist denunciation of the laundry list of capitalist evils with an exhortation to mass resistance; it was truly aimed at fans of Springsteen and his music. "For the most part," the leaflet argued, "Springsteen is telling it like it is." Reflecting a fundamental conviction within STO that popular culture was a reflection of social struggle, it maintained that "Bruce will write and sing the songs that reflect our collective anger and our movement to make human dignity a reality for our lives. We have to FIGHT, together, for this." The leaflet ended with a brief description of CAWI, which opposed nuclear power and weapons, racist violence by fascists and the police, and "u.s. intervention in El Salvador, the Middle East, or anywhere else the u.s. wants to impose its rule." "We want," it concluded, "to help people organize themselves to REBEL against all this shit coming down. No more imperialist war! No more racist attacks!"

---

2   These lyrics, which appear in the CAWI leaflet, are from the song "The River," on the album of the same title, by Bruce Springsteen and the E Street Band (Columbia Records, 1980). The full lyrics to the song are available online at http://www.brucespringsteen.net/songs/TheRiver.html (accessed December 19, 2011).

3   All quotations in this paragraph come from the partially illegible copy of the CAWI leaflet in my possession. Capitalization is reproduced precisely for the sake of accuracy. Thanks to Vic Speedwell for providing me with this document.

While the CAWI leaflet clearly put an unorthodox and radical spin on Springsteen's music, it was not primarily opportunistic. Like much of STO's membership, a number of people in the Kansas City branch loved music—rock and roll, R&B, and punk rock in particular. For them, the chance to publicly combine the love of Springsteen's music with their passion for politics was exciting. Former Kansas City STO member Randy Gould remembers it as "one of my favorite all time leaflets."[4] Of course, this enthusiasm also reflected how rare such interventions were for the group. As an organization, STO was only intermittently attentive to cultural questions in its political work, but internally the group was hardly ascetic. Discussions on music, art, movies and television, and other cultural forms were frequent, and frequently intense. Similarly, the political aspects of the personal lives of individual STO members sometimes became the subject of organizational discussion, with both positive and negative consequences. And certainly one of the defining characteristics of the group by the late seventies was its dedication to internal political education, study, and debate. These aspects of STO's existence could be glimpsed on occasion in the group's external political work and publications, as in the example of the CAWI leaflet or the organization's well-known dialectics courses. But beyond the group's public face, an assessment of the organization's internal life is highly instructive and indeed necessary for a full picture of STO's history and legacy.

* * *

Springsteen was hardly the only musical artist to draw STO's attention. In the mid- to late seventies, the group also turned a critical and political eye to the then newly emerging genre of punk rock. Punk music had an extensive but largely submerged (pre-) history in the United States by the time it was blasted into popular consciousness with the sudden emergence of the Sex Pistols, the Clash and other British groups in 1976.[5] Punk's embrace by young people, combined with its aesthetic of rejection and extremism, guaranteed that it became fertile ground for a range of radical political perspectives, from both the right (quasi-fascist) and the left (especially Marxist and anarchist). Still, the organized left in particular had an ambivalent relationship with punk.

---

4   Randy Gould, email to the author, September 29, 2006.

5   The initial rise of punk on both sides of the Atlantic is skillfully chronicled and contextualized in Jon Savage, *England's Dreaming: Anarchy, Sex Pistols, Punk Rock and Beyond* (New York: St. Martin's Press, 1992).

While by no means devoid of people of color, the punk milieu in the US was heavily white, which turned off a significant segment of the US left, even—or especially—those segments that were themselves also lacking in diversity. Similarly, punk's aggressive attitude and sometimes antisocial lyrics did not mix well with the organized left's frequently puritanical approach to the cultural realm. This often led to a dismissal of punk rock as "a social disease" that deserved to be tossed "in the garbage heap."[6] By contrast, other left organizations, including several Trotskyist groups in the US and Great Britain, attached themselves to punk as a possible venue for recruitment among disaffected young people. Thus, for example, the Socialist Workers Party in Britain promoted "Rock Against Racism" as a way of encouraging participation in its antifascist organizing efforts.[7]

For STO, however, punk rock was more complex than either of these two extreme viewpoints could accommodate, and, in a group that prized sophisticated critical analysis, this complexity demanded research and debate. Thus, at the beginning of 1978, the group sent two members, Lee Holstein and Elaine Zeskind, on a three week tour of California and the southwest "to investigate the punk scene."[8] This trip immediately resulted in an article by Zeskind, which after more than a year of "informal debates about punk among Sojourner Truth Organization members" was finally published in *Urgent Tasks* in 1979, along with an interview she conducted with Tony Kinman, himself a political radical as well as the bass player and lead singer for the San Francisco punk band the Dils. Zeskind's article, entitled "Punk Rock: Music in Search of a Movement," is as much an examination of Marxist theories of art and aesthetics under capitalism as it is an analysis of punk rock in particular. The article was clearly aimed at people on the left with little to no experience of punk music or culture, as evidenced by the detailed (and humorous) explanation of pogo dancing: "an asexual 'dance' consisting of shoving or pulling the person next to you while simultaneously jumping up and down on

---

6   This view is attributed to Tim Patterson, a cultural critic for *The Guardian* newspaper, by Elaine Zeskind, "Punk Rock: Music in Search of a Movement," in *Urgent Tasks* #5, Summer 1979, 1. For more on socialist realism, see C. Vaughn James, *Soviet Socialist Realism: Origins and Theory* (New York: St. Martin's Press, 1973).

7   For more on Rock Against Racism, see Paul Gilroy, *'There Ain't No Black in the Union Jack': The Cultural Politics of Race and Nation* (Chicago: University of Chicago Press, 1991 [1987]), 114–152.

8   Lee Churgin (Holstein), interview with the author, December 7, 2005.

every beat, and, preferably, having something handy to throw towards the stage."[9]

Zeskind's article repudiates the left tendency to judge punk, preferring instead to contextualize and understand it. She begins with a series of questions about the politics of punk—"Is punk decadent and fascist, or revolutionary? Is it a Madison Avenue hype-job, or a revolt against the record and radio industries? Is it art or is it noise?" Committed to complexity, she rejects the binaries and instead maintains, "It is all those things."[10] The defining characteristics of early punk, according to Zeskind, were its lack of commercial appeal as music and its refusal to lyrically glorify love and dancing. The fact that punk lyrics sometimes tended toward political topics, as with the Clash for example, made it possible to consider the punk milieu something like a movement in embryo. Zeskind's article adopts a view of the complicated relationship between movement and culture derived largely from the work of C.L.R. James, who was a significant and growing influence within STO at the time. James repeatedly suggested that the specific forms of cultural production that most thoroughly capture the popular imagination, whether in literature, film, music, or sports, are reflective of the level of consciousness and struggle in the society in question. In the cultural context of 1950, James argued "it is in the serious study of, above all, Charles Chaplin, Dick Tracy, Gasoline Alley, James Cagney, Edward G. Robinson, Rita Hayworth, Humphrey Bogart … that you find the clearest ideological expression of the sentiments and deepest feelings of the American people and a great window into the future of America and the modern world."[11] STO took

---

9   Zeskind, "Punk Rock," 1.

10   Ibid.

11   C.L.R. James, *American Civilization*, edited and introduced by Anna Grimshaw and Keith Hart (Cambridge, MA: Blackwell, 1993), 119. While *American Civilization* reflects the clearest statement by James of his approach to popular culture, it was not published until 1993, meaning that it could not have been the direct source of STO's interpretation. Ken Lawrence suggests that for STO the key text was actually *Modern Politics*, which was published in the US in 1973 and does contain an assessment of early popular filmmaking, including Charlie Chaplin and D.W. Griffith. C.L.R. James, *Modern Politics* (Detroit: Bewick Editions, 1973) 134–137. Also, according to Lawrence, the idea of culture as reflective of the level of consciousness and struggle "was also a key aspect of nearly every lecture that [James] and George Rawick gave in the US." Lawrence, email to the author, December 19, 2011.

this analysis to heart, applying it both to punk rock and (in the CAWI leaflet) to Springsteen.[12] Thus, in Zeskind's formulation of the theme, "the level of class struggle has been in a period of lull. Therefore the prospects for progressive developments in the realm of culture catching hold and polarizing masses of people becomes necessarily limited."[13] This was especially true compared to the sixties, when the relative strength of mass movements meant that "culture was often an effective weapon in revolutionaries' arsenals."[14] As the CAWI leaflet would argue three years later about Springsteen, Zeskind suggests that the potential inherent in punk rock could only fully emerge from within an upsurge of social struggle.

Still, there were some immediate possibilities. In Zeskind's view, the vibrant intensity of early punk culture was reflective of age-old spontaneous tendencies toward popular resistance. In discussing fans' anger at security guards and bouncers at a Ramones concert, she notes parenthetically that "sometimes people stand up before they know precisely why or for what. If they didn't, revolutionaries would have gone out of business long ago."[15] Zeskind also criticizes a common left approach to culture that was indebted (whether consciously or not) to Soviet-style socialist realism. She mocks "the idea that we [the organized left] are going to produce the working-class culture singlehandedly, and preferably in the folk or blues modes."[16] Indeed, the US left in the seventies, often under the leadership of a generation of radicals who had come of age in the civil rights era of the late fifties and early sixties, featured a combination of rising cultural puritanism and fetishized romanticization of what was perceived to be true or authentic working-class culture.[17] In terms of music, this often meant a rehashing of Pete Seeger stylings or an opportunistic devotion to whatever was popular in a given organizing context. This last attitude had characterized some of STO's initial

---

12   Contemporary musical analysis along strikingly similar lines can be found on the website known as the "Democracy and Hip-Hop Project," which explicitly identifies both James and STO as influences. http://democracyandhiphop.blogspot.com (accessed December 27, 2011).

13   Zeskind, "Punk Rock," 2.

14   Ibid. Zeskind does note the dual character of cultural efforts in the sixties, pointing out that they "were partly responsible for diverting the movement into the dead ends of the counterculture."

15   Ibid., 5.

16   Ibid., 4.

17   For more on this problematic combination, see Max Elbaum, *Revolution in the Air*, 170–171.

interventions in workplace settings, as discussed earlier in Chapter Two, but by the mid-seventies the group had begun to appreciate the autonomous complexity of the cultural realm, even as much of the rest of the left took increasingly rigid positions on cultural questions. As Tony Kinman put it in his interview, "they [the organized left] don't want to hear about it [punk]. All they want is their folk song records, or like the Berkeley Women's [Music] Collective singing songs of feminist struggle in this country. They just seem really closed-minded to what we're doing."[18]

In this context, it was easy for many STO members to relate to Kinman's confusion in the face of the organized left's willingness to believe mainstream stereotypes of punk as "irresponsible, violent, [and] sexist." In his words, "the left in this country has been victims of that same sort of thinking. And they turn around and do it to us. And I can't see why, why they want to."[19] Zeskind's piece suggests that this dismissive attitude on the part of the left was a small part of what she believed was the coming suppression of punk music. While punk was in fact eventually recuperated by the musical mainstream, her view was at the time supported by considerable evidence, including police raids on many punk clubs and the refusal of major record labels to sign additional punk bands after Warner Brothers' debacle with the Sex Pistols (who broke up shortly after signing with the label). Regardless, Zeskind points out, "it is a bit ludicrous to debate … whether [punk bands] should be *allowed* (!) to play at left events which do not attract the masses anyway."[20] The article ends with a call to "criticize the immediate and blanket condemnation of punk by most of the left," which Zeskind identifies as "another example of the knee-jerk, self-righteous responses [the left] brings not only to cultural questions but political questions generally."[21] Without demanding that all her comrades start listening to punk rock, Zeskind's

---

18   "Interview: The Dills" [sic], in *Urgent Tasks* #5, Summer 1979, 39. The text of the interview and Zeskind's article consistently spelled the band's name—the Dils—correctly, but the headline of the interview added an extra "l". For more on the general category of "women's music," of which the Berkeley Women's Music Collective was exemplary, see Cynthia M. Lont, "Between Rock and a Hard Place: A Model of Subcultural Persistence and Women's Music" (PhD diss., University of Iowa, 1984).

19   Ibid.

20   Zeskind, "Punk Rock," 37.

21   Ibid.

article encouraged them to take it seriously as a cultural—and thus political—phenomenon.

* * *

One reason STO took such questions seriously had little to do with politics as it was traditionally construed: the members of the group had real and full human lives beyond their political work. It is too easy to think of the revolutionary cadre of the seventies as what one STO sympathizer called "the 100% political person" who ate, breathed, and slept revolution.[22] In reality, every leftist of this or any other era necessarily participated in the culture of the times, from when they were children all the way through adulthood. Like the rest of the world, people in STO listened to music, on record or in concert, not primarily to assess its organizing potential but because they enjoyed it. As former member Lee Churgin remembers it, culture and "especially music was really important for a lot of people [in STO].… We did a lot of dancing too. Dancing and going to listen to music."[23] The group was diverse enough that there was no narrow subcultural unity, however. Instead, according to former member and sometime musician Bill Lamme, culture broadly and music in particular "was the uniting element between certain subgroups. You know, there would be the rocking group, the dance partying-oriented, or whatever. To me it never degenerated to the level of cliques or competing groups. But I think that the group was not strongly culturally united, you know around sex, drugs, and rock'n'roll, or around Beethoven, Bach, and Brahms. It was too diverse, and there was no attempt to try to bring that into the group."[24] The organization claimed several other musicians as members, including an accomplished classical violinist, and classical, jazz, and folk music all had followings in STO. Similarly, some members held particular interests in fine art, in sports, or in film.

Still, in the memories of many STO veterans, such musical and cultural interests were tolerated within the group, but they were not always fostered. Former member Hal Adams, himself a fan of baseball and

---

22   Paula Rubio, "More on Kids and Politics," in *Continuation of Special Supplement to IDB #16, May/June, 1980*, 27, in author's possession. Rubio's husband Phil was a member of STO at the time. I am grateful to Alexander Van Zandt Akin at Bolerium Books in San Franscisco for facilitating my access to this document.

23   Lee Churgin (Holstein), interview with the author, December 7, 2005.

24   Bill Lamme, interview with the author, July 20, 2005.

classical music, later came to believe "that was one of the weaknesses of the program. We didn't have much cultural life, to tell you the truth. The meetings were … there was no singing, or dancing, or entertainment."[25] In 1980, Phil Rubio lamented this as the price of STO's intense pursuit of political education during the lull: "Now I'm proud of the intellectual strides we've made in the past two years—but now we're so academic—what happened to our culture—the skits at the GMM, playing the 'Internationale' on the harmonica. Having fun?"[26] In some ways, the intensity of the political work itself substituted for any sort of common cultural framework, even while it necessarily limited the opportunities for having fun within the group.

This scenario was common on the left in the seventies. As the writer and veteran of the era Max Elbaum put it, "if one word had to be chosen to characterize the culture of the New Communist Movement, that word would be *intense*."[27] In many cases, this resulted in solid and lasting friendships. Adams, for example, later indicated that "my best friends are from that period of my life; it's not like we didn't have personal relationships."[28] Given the high expectations placed on people, in terms of organizing, writing, and other political activity, it is not surprising that many cultural pursuits were sometimes informally mocked within the group, only to be pursued surreptitiously. STO never developed any official critique of professional sports, for example, but Adams remembered feeling like he had to be a "closeted [Detroit] Tigers fan."[29] In retrospect, he said, "I share an interest in sports with a lot of different people I knew then, but we didn't share that thing then."[30] Thus, the cultural bonds formed by members of STO, even if they were overshadowed by the often all-consuming nature of participation in a revolutionary organization, in many cases proved to be more lasting

---

25 Hal Adams, interview with the author, August 4, 2005.
26 Phil Rubio, "More on Kids and Politics," 31.
27 Elbaum, *Revolution in the Air*, 163.
28 Hal Adams, author interview, August 4, 2005. In this regard, it is worth noting that of the nearly three-dozen former members I either interviewed or corresponded with in researching this book, I contacted the vast majority of them as a result of personal friendships they have maintained with other former members I was already in contact with. (At the same time, I only interviewed a tiny fraction of the total membership of the group over the course of its existence.)
29 Ibid.
30 Ibid.

than the ideological commitments that formally determined membership in the group.

At the same time, some members of STO did feel ostracized for their cultural preferences. Ken Lawrence, for instance, was critical of "spectator music" and advanced a political argument for "folk music and hootenannies and so on. You know, the singing movement of SNCC that I came out of."[31] This was partly an age gap, since most of STO's members by the late seventies were younger than Lawrence and had been teenagers during or after the end of the sixties. For them, just as for Tony Kinman, folk music was a historical relic that did not speak to their cultural reality. As a result, Lawrence believes that popular music—"spectator music"—was in fact "part of the cohesion of the group but it was definitely alienating to me."[32] For Lawrence, and certainly for others as well, this only reinforced the overriding importance of political affinity in keeping the group together. As former member Lowell May recalls, "What I liked about STO was that there was an explicit renunciation" of shared (sub-)culture as the basis for organization, "with especially Don [Hamerquist] and Carole [Travis] insisting that it must be the political commitment and not the personal affinity that anchored a revolutionary group. Not that we didn't develop multiple layers of cultural affinity—that's why many of us are still close today—but the affinity grew out of the politics and not vice versa."[33]

* * *

While Lawrence may have felt isolated culturally within STO, he certainly contributed to the group's awareness of the political importance of cultural questions. In issue number four of *Urgent Tasks* (Summer 1978), he published a long and wide-ranging article addressing a very different aspect of culture than contemporary music. In "Behind Tutankhamen's Treasures: A Marxist Appreciation," Lawrence takes the same Jamesian understanding of culture that Zeskind would subsequently use to assess punk rock, and applies it to review the incredibly popular exhibit of Egyptian archeological artifacts then traveling the United States as the *Treasures of Tutankhamen*.[34] Focusing squarely on "the ambiguities,

31   Ken Lawrence, interview with the author, August 24, 2006.
32   Ibid.
33   Lowell May, email interview with the author, May 16, 2006.
34   It should be remembered that Lawrence had known James long before joining STO, and had introduced James to Noel Ignatin shortly before

complexities, and contradictory features which merit a close look," Lawrence's review runs the gamut. It assesses, among other things: the choice of items in the exhibit itself; the aesthetics of the book-length catalog of the exhibit, which became a *New York Times* bestseller; the marketing of and mainstream media response to the exhibit; the politics of archeology as a discipline; the submerged history of class struggle in ancient Egypt; the geopolitical context of the then-current vogue for Egyptian artifacts; and the somewhat unexpected popular enthusiasm for all things related to King Tut.[35] Lawrence even makes time to toss in a gratuitous swipe at punk, connecting it to the garishly over-the-top approach to color photography that characterized the marketing of "Treasures of Tutankhamen:" "Flashing strobe-lit dayglo posters and punkrock music are logical outgrowths of a culture based on this sort of hard-sell."[36]

Lawrence begins with a straightforward explanation of the Jamesian approach to cultural questions: "because popular culture is a reflection of the status of the mass imagination—albeit shaped and distorted by the dominant ideas of the rulers of society—measurable *changes* in the cultural interests and activities of large numbers of ordinary people can provide an important index to the development of a worldview which has not yet emerged as mass consciousness."[37] For Lawrence, the mass appeal—and massive appeal, with more than eight million people viewing the exhibit in several cities over the course of two-and-a-half years—of the Tutankhamen exhibit reflected subtle changes in the working-class view of race relations, and "the degree to which the fierce grasp of racism on the white masses is being eroded."[38] More than this, the show's

---

the formation of STO. Thus, Lawrence (along with Ignatin) was largely responsible for bringing into STO the Jamesian influence that can be seen in Zeskind's article, the CAWI leaflet, and other STO analyses of cultural questions.

35 The quote is from Ken Lawrence, "Beyond Tutankhamen's Treasures: A Marxist Appreciation," in *Urgent Tasks* #4, Summer 1978, 2. Interestingly, one of the only reference points left out of Lawrence's article—Steve Martin's April 1978 performance of the song "King Tut" on *Saturday Night Live*, subsequently released as a single that surged up the Billboard charts—has had perhaps the longest cultural legacy of anything related to the exhibit. The video can still be viewed in several locations on the Internet.

36 Ibid., 37.

37 Ibid., 1.

38 Ibid., 2.

popularity demonstrated a widespread "feeling that there is more universal significance in the African civilization of 3,000 years ago than in the
mass culture of North America today."[39] The promoters of the exhibit,
argues Lawrence, had no real awareness of the political undercurrents of
their own efforts. "The bourgeois crisis," he explains, "is expressed in its
'art for art's sake' awe of the objects."[40] At the same time, "vulgar Marxists" were wrong to assume that corporate sponsorship of the exhibit,
from Exxon in particular, guaranteed some correlation between reactionary politics in the present and reactionary art of the past. As Lawrence
astutely points out, "the bourgeoisie's taste in art is not limited to its
most backward manifestations. It fears the revolutionary present, not the
revolutionary past."[41]

But this blind spot created an unexpected opening for potentially
radical perspectives to percolate among the millions who viewed the exhibit, and the millions more who experienced its spectacle through the
catalog or other media coverage. The sheer longevity of ancient Egyptian
culture, lasting as it did for three millennia, "suggests a harmony between
people and their environment which has never been matched."[42] "This,"
argues Lawrence, "is the magnetic force that draws millions to the long
lines waiting to see *Treasures of Tutankhamen*. The fact that they do not
understand or articulate their quest in this way should come as no surprise given the torrent of propaganda standing in the way of a full com-
prehension, and the shortcomings of the exhibit itself."[43] Having already
pointed to the complicated historical relationship between the undeniably black Kushite civilization in what is now Sudan and the Egyptian
civilization that had been historically portrayed as "white," Lawrence
concluded his review by pointing to the future:

> If we learn well, we will someday admire the accomplish-
> ments of [the Kushites] as today we esteem the Egyptians.
> At that point we will permanently part company with the
> bourgeoisie in matters of culture. By adding a coat of *white*-
> wash, the ruling class has found a way to absorb, or co-opt,
> Egyptian civilization as an acceptable ancestor to its own,
> thus predating the Greeks who were long credited with

39   Ibid., 4.
40   Ibid.
41   Ibid.
42   Ibid., 42.
43   Ibid.

being the originators of all that is good in the bourgeois social order. But I don't think they can grant the same status to undeniably Black Africans without calling into question their most basic, white supremacist assumptions. Nonetheless, the welcome the masses have shown to *Treasures of Tutankhamen* has taken them a long step in that direction.[44]

In retrospect, Lawrence was probably wrong to believe that acknowledging the historical importance of black African antiquity would lead directly to a rejection of white supremacy. Still, his detailed assessment of the interlocking questions of culture and science, history and art, race and class, publicly illustrated—at least to readers of *Urgent Tasks*—the best aspects of STO's approach to cultural questions and the "personal" realm of human life.[45]

* * *

The worst aspects of this approach, by contrast, were often hidden from public view. Like many left organizations of the era, STO used a range of internal mechanisms to deal with conflict and bad behavior within the group, and these methods were largely kept secret. A number of organizations in both the anti-imperialist and New Communist milieus utilized the "criticism/self-criticism" approach popularized by Maoism. "Crit/self-crit," as it was sometimes known, featured intense efforts to scrutinize the emotional weaknesses of problem-causing members in a small group setting as part of a process of individual transformation that "was seen as an integral, if subordinate part of social transformation," according to Max Elbaum.[46] This method utilized sessions that were rela-

44 Ibid., 43.
45 C.L.R. James himself apparently agreed. In September 1978, he sent a letter to STO saying he was "astonished and delighted at the high quality" of the issue that contained Lawrence's article, which also contained an exchange on the politics of the French Marxist philosopher Louis Althusser, as well as a piece by Ignatin on fascism (see Chapter Eight). Writing from Washington, DC, James explained that he was "teaching a class on socialism and communism and the essays in this journal are the best I can think of for the work of a semester." The letter is the first item in the *IDB* #7, Nov/Dec. 1978.
46 Max Elbaum, *Revolution in the Air*, 165. The origins of "criticism/self-criticism" in Mao's writings can be gleaned from Chapter 27 of the

tively ad hoc in their format, but which often used popular understandings of psychology to promote the changes in worldview and behavior needed for a full rehabilitation of the member accused of wrongdoing.

STO also made use of criticism/self-criticism, but for its own internal discipline, the group relied much more heavily on a method derived more or less directly from the original Communist Party of the United States: investigations and hearings for members charged with a range of offenses, including, in particular, political errors like racism or sexism. This approach went back decades. In 1931, the CPUSA staged a semipublic trial of a Finnish immigrant and Party member named August Yokinin on the charge of white chauvinism. More commonly, such proceedings took place behind closed doors.[47] By 1935, the Party was utilizing a fairly elaborate set of procedures and norms to govern the filing and investigation of charges: "Charges made by one member against another, as a rule, should be made in writing," noted the *CPUSA Manual on Organization* published in that year, which further maintained that "Every accused member has the right to a hearing before any disciplinary action can be taken against him. The main thing in the examination is to establish the essential facts in each case and to give an opportunity to the accused member to present his side with his witnesses and documents."[48]

STO modified this procedure only modestly, despite the intervening decades, a fact that may have been influenced by the extensive background in and around the CPUSA of many leading members of the group. This sort of system was used repeatedly throughout STO's existence to deal with a wide variety of problematic situations. The investigation of the charges was

---

famous *Quotations from Mao Tse-Tung* (Peking: Peking Foreign Languages Press, 1966), which circulated widely within the US left during the sixties and seventies. Available online at http://www.marxists.org/reference/archive/mao/works/red-book/ch27.htm (accessed January 2, 2012).

47   The Yokinin proceedings are described in some detail in Mark Naison, *Communists in Harlem During the Depression* (Urbana, IL: University of Illinois Press, 1983). The trial was conducted in public as part of the CP's organizing efforts among blacks in Harlem and elsewhere. Thanks to Gregor Baszak for suggesting Naison's book to me.

48   Both quotations from J. Peters, *The Communist Party: A Manual on Organization* (New York: Workers' Library Publishers, 1935), chapter five "Rules and Methods for Disciplinary Cases." Available online at http://www.marxists.org/history/usa/parties/cpusa/1935/07/organisers-manual/index.htm (accessed January 2, 2012).

normally assigned to a small team of STO members, who then interviewed the accuser and the accused, as well as any witnesses (these interviews were sometimes recorded), and subsequently issued a report on the investigation that included recommendations on how to resolve the charges, including proposed sanctions against the member charged with wrongdoing. Finally, the membership was asked to vote on both the guilt of the accused and on the sanctions. One high-profile example was the vote on censure of several leading members for racist behavior at the GMM in 1977, prior to the split in the organization, as described in Chapter Four. This situation was unusual in that the charges related to activity that took place in view of the vast majority of the membership, and even more unusual because it was resolved more or less immediately by a vote of the assembled members, during the GMM itself.

Somewhat more common were charges of sexist behavior, termed "male chauvinism" or even "male supremacy," filed by women in STO against male members, often as a result of actions that took place either in private or in a small group setting. Problems along these lines happened frequently enough that the group established specific rules to govern certain situations. For instance, by the late seventies it was formal policy that "when a member of STO who's involved in a monogamous sexual relationship breaks that form, they are obligated to inform their partner."[49] When charges relating to sexist behavior were filed, they were often assigned directly to the Women's Commission, which then had responsibility for impaneling the investigative team and subsequently for coordinating a vote of the women in STO (sometimes referred to as the "Women's Wing") on the guilt of the accused. While common enough to prompt rules like the one governing monogamy, problems of sexist behavior were still relatively rare, and when they emerged there was often some haggling over exactly how to proceed. In one case, for example, the Central Committee regarded the vote of the Women's Wing on the guilt of the accused to be final, but argued that all members—including men—should weigh in on proposed disciplinary measures or sanctions. This latter topic was eventually subject to a "signed referendum vote" of all members conducted by mail.[50]

---

49   The policy as quoted is described in Cathy Adolphson, Janeen Creamer, Lee Holstein, Carol Loretz, and Carole Travis, "Fighting Male Supremacy: A Contribution," in *Special Supplement to IDB #16*, May, 1980, 19. Once again, I am grateful to Alexander Van Zandt Akin at Bolerium Books in San Franscisco for facilitating my access to these documents.

50   "NC Agenda" (n.d., but c. January 1981), 7. Again, thanks to Alexander

While the process for such investigations was generally accepted within STO, concerns were sometimes raised about their adequacy in dealing with certain problematic situations. In 1980, the majority of the Women's Commission issued a statement arguing that "formal grievance procedures do nothing more but diffuse appropriate and righteous anger."[51] Lee Holstein, who was not at that point a member of the Commission, pursued this issue, comparing the process to the grievance procedure used under many union contracts: "It is certainly true that waiting to express strong feelings tends to dissipate them. The contractual grievance procedure in the factory is an excellent example of this. When someone waits, their immediate anger 'cools off' and the whole incident prompting the anger takes on a different dimension. It sometimes becomes embarrassing after the fact, even when the anger was completely justified. Details of the time become insignificant and frequently appear silly out of context of the situation."[52] Given STO's lengthy collective experience in point-of-production work, it is somewhat remarkable that criticisms based on this parallel had not emerged earlier in the group's decade of existence.

* * *

Holstein did not propose a precise solution to this dilemma, but her analysis emerged in the aftermath of a major challenge to the group's traditional reliance on charges and investigations. In early 1980, STO's *Internal Discussion Bulletin* contained an unusual item: an anonymous, one-page, typed letter, signed "Phantom Pheminists," which listed several instances of behavior by men in STO that the authors regarded as sexist.[53] For example, "To the man who told a sister one thing he really liked about her is that she won't rat on him for making insulting, male

---

Van Zandt Akin at Bolerium Books in San Francisco.

51   Allison Edwards and Linda Phelps, "Women's Commission Response to CC (Majority Statement)," in *Special Supplement to IDB #16*, May 1980, 5.

52   Lee Holstein, "Some Questions and Comments on Procedure," in *Special Supplement to IDB #16*, May, 1980, 29.

53   All quotes in this paragraph come from the untitled letter, hereafter referred to as "Phantom Pheminists letter," in *Special Supplement to IDB #16*, May 1980. This was apparently the second publication of the letter, with the first having taken place in the supplement to an *IDB* in February.

supremacist little remarks to her, YOU'RE WRONG. She's no scab. WE TALK—WE ALL TALK." Mocking their own organization's analysis of the nature of the period in the US, the letter maintained that "a pig is a pig is a pig—in periods of revolutionary upsurge *and* in periods of temporary lull." The letter ended with a call to continue the conversation it started: "Phantom Pheminists invite additions and comments."

Comments were certainly forthcoming. The Central Committee, as well as numerous individual members of STO, compared the unsigned nature of the Phantom Pheminists letter to the use of anonymous mailings as part of COINTELPRO operations. Ken Lawrence, for instance, maintained that "the document struck me as a classic example of a well-known COINTELPRO technique—anonymous communications that attempt to exploit real or imagined grievances, especially personal ones." Lawrence offered a range of examples from the publicly released government papers documenting the disruption of the left, and attached copies of several pages of the Final Report prepared by the Church Commission in 1976.[54] He deliberately highlighted FBI attempts to destroy Don Hamerquist's first marriage in the mid-sixties, when both he and his wife were members of the CPUSA. Lawrence was particularly concerned about the risk of broad distribution of the letter, which would have allowed its "use against STO by the women's movement, with which we already have difficulties due to genuine political differences." Not surprisingly, Lawrence defended STO's standard practice of filing charges, and even proposed that the authors of the Phantom Pheminists letter "should be severely disciplined, perhaps expelled" for having violated the "proper approach." In closing, he argued that "no legitimate political aim can be accomplished within a revolutionary organization anonymously."

Anonymity did not last. Allison Edwards, herself a member of the Women's Commission, soon took responsibility as the primary author of the Phantom Pheminists letter, and proceeded to defend it from the criticisms leveled by Lawrence and others. On the question of anonymity and COINTELPRO, Edwards and Linda Phelps (also a member of the Commission) drew an important distinction: "the issue is not one of an anonymous *action*, but of unnamed targets. To our knowledge, there is no parallel in the COINTELPRO scheme you refer to. Quite the reverse. Leaving off the name of the target protects his identity and gives him a

---

54   The full Church Commission report can be viewed online at http://www.icdc.com/~paulwolf/cointelpro/churchfinalreportIIIa.htm (accessed January 2, 2012).

chance to clean up his act."[55] But they also defended another aspect of this approach: "the 'anonymous target' method has a political purpose as well. When it comes to male supremacy, WE WANT NO MAN TO FEEL SAFE." Edwards and Phelps also suggested that the initial replies to the letter had, perhaps deliberately, misdirected the organizational discussion away from problems of sexism in the group and toward the danger of police activity. More centrally, they defended the anonymity of the letter on another basis. Much as Holstein linked STO's standard procedure to the union grievance process, Edwards and Phelps compared the filing of charges *inside* STO with the pursuit of criminal charges by women in and through the legal system. "As in cases of rape," they argued, "reporting and being investigated is frequently more demeaning to the woman than to the man." By comparison, the Phantom Pheminists letter was a relative success, to the extent that it prompted a continuing—and not demeaning—discussion.

But not all women in STO, nor even all members of the Women's Commission, agreed with the position Edwards and Phelps put forward. Cathy Adolphson, the third member of the Commission, issued her own statement on the letter, supporting the linkage to COINTELPRO and defending the charges and investigation method on the basis that "without it there is no democracy."[56] Adolphson also signed a joint statement, along with four other women in STO, which challenged the Phantom Pheminists letter more directly. Describing it as "embarrassing," the five women argued that "the content of the letter certainly does not reflect our position on what constitutes male supremacy."[57] Presaging some of the intense debates that would emerge among feminists over the coming years, they staked out a fundamentally pro-sex position as women, which they contrasted with the examples of supposedly sexist acts from

---

55   All quotes in this paragraph come from Edwards and Phelps, "Women's Commission Response to CC (Majority Statement)," 4–5.

56   Cathy Adolphson, "Minority Statement of Women's Commission," in *Special Supplement to IDB #16*, May 1980, 7. Lee Holstein subsequently highlighted this key value: "Oppression implies resistance. Resistance takes many forms. The form required in a communist organization has to be democratic." Holstein, "Democracy, Marxism and Male Supremacy," in *Special Supplement to IDB #16*, May 1980, 24.

57   All further quotes in this and the immediately following paragraphs are from Cathy Adolphson, Janeen Creamer, Lee Holstein, Carol Loretz, and Carole Travis, "Fighting Male Supremacy: A Contribution," in *Special Supplement to IDB #16*, May, 1980, 19.

the letter: "Eliminating the behavior described in several of the [letter's] examples limits sexuality in a way which we oppose."[58] These examples mostly described fairly direct pick-up lines uttered by men in STO— "variety is the spice of life," "you're attractive enough to try for," and others—and the five women laid out alternative readings of each, interpretations that emphasized the "sensible and healthy" aspect of open and direct discussion of sexual attraction. "As long as they are not violating the terms of their 'primary relationship' or being unclear or unprincipled in some other respects," they argued, men should be just as free as women to initiate romantic encounters. "Attacks on sexuality," they maintained, "particularly heterosexuality, are not appropriate methods of raising and attacking male supremacy."

The five women acknowledged that there appeared to be disagreement among the women members of STO as to what constituted sexist behavior. "Not all sexual advances," they pointed out, "are offensive to all women even though the line may have been crossed for some." Reflecting on the interplay between freedom and responsibility at an individual level, they argued that "the choices exist among men and women to say 'yes' or 'no' to an advance or to challenge an offensive advance." The alternative, which they believed to be implied in the Phantom Pheminist letter, was "routine organizational prying into these areas," which they worried could lead down a slippery slope toward "a Stalinist operation whereby every action of every individual in every instance is judged correct or incorrect." To avoid this sort of worst-case scenario, the five

---

58   The so-called "feminist sex wars" had only just erupted when this debate took place within STO. Within a few years, the conflict over questions of pornography, sadomasochism, and other aspects of sexuality would consume wide swaths of the (white) feminist movement in North America. The perspective advanced in "Fighting Male Supremacy" echoes arguments advanced by Ellen Willis in her 1979 essay, "Feminism, Morality, and Pornography," originally published in the *Village Voice* and later expanded in *Beginning to See the Light: Pieces of a Decade* (New York: Alfred A. Knopf, 1981), 219–227. It also in some ways presages the theoretical elaboration of pro-sex feminism in Gayle Rubin's seminal essay "Thinking Sex: Notes for a Radical Theory of the Politics of Sexuality," in Carol Vance, ed., *Pleasure and Danger* (New York: Routledge, Kegan, and Paul, 1984). A useful compendium of critical perspectives produced in the midst of the debates was the special section of the feminist journal *Signs* in 1984 on "The Feminist Sexuality Debates" (10, no. 1, August, 1984, 102–135).

women suggested that "STO's priority on the development of critical Marxists properly interrelates with an internal practice of combating male supremacy." The trick was to "develop strong women thinkers and actors" within the group, which could best be accomplished by skill-sharing in more abstract areas like "debate, argumentation and political discussion" as well more practical endeavors like "printing, mimeographing and layout."

Lee Holstein elaborated on the theoretical question of freedom and responsibility under oppression in a subsequent contribution to the ongoing dialogue. Here, she focused on "the dual character of victims/oppressed people," where on the one hand victims are "victimized … killed, destroyed, harmed … dominated," while at the same time "some form or level of desire to resist dominance, to *not* be a victim, is involved."[59] "In the duality of the oppressed," she continued, "the oppressed/victim, believing she is a victim, will behave like a victim. When she behaves like a human she is breaking her oppression/victimization. So the oppressed is both victimized and resisting victimization. The former aspect is a fact and it is what the latter aspect destroys." STO's deepening commitment to autonomy as a concept (see Chapter Eight) was reflected in Holstein's analysis of the "difficult but necessary … qualitative change from a self-view which is externally imposed and internally reified—the view of oneself as inferior—to the realization and activation of one's real self-potential."[60] At this point, Holstein had wandered somewhat far afield, but her examination of the philosophical complexities of responding to sexism on individual and collective levels was certainly in keeping with the original call in the Phantom Pheminists letter for "additions and comments." To bring things back to a more practical level, Holstein

---

59   All quotes in this paragraph from Holstein, "Democracy, Marxism, and Male Supremacy," 26. Similar arguments regarding agency among the oppressed were taken up by the feminist (and especially lesbian) philosophy milieu during the eighties and nineties. See, for example, Maria Lugones, "Structure/Anti-Structure and Agency Under Oppression," in *The Journal of Philosophy* 87, no. 10, (October, 1990), 500–507, which advances a position similar to Holstein's but frames it in *anti*-Marxist terms.

60   A parallel argument was advanced by Holstein that same year in a more public setting: in *UT* #9 (Summer 1980) she published an article entitled "Working Class Self-Activity," which focused on the contradictions of class rather than on those of sex oppression. See Chapter Eight for more on this question.

concluded her rumination with a set of next steps, which emphasized the need for the women of STO to come to some basic agreement on "what is male supremacy" and on how to respond to it, both collectively and individually, within the organization.

For their part, Edwards and Phelps eventually came to have second thoughts about the anonymous nature of the original letter, though the rapidly mounting pile of thoughtful responses to the controversy around the letter spoke for itself. On the question of sexuality, however, they held firm. "We do not believe," they wrote in early May, "that sexuality can be easily separated from the fact that women and men are not equal in this society."[61] After examining in detail the effects of pervasive power differentials on romantic and sexual encounters between men and women, they concluded that the pro-sex position staked out by five of their comrades was naïve. In embracing the open attitudes about sex that emerged from the sixties, they had forgotten that "underneath the 'guilt' about sex that we [women] discarded are needs for self-protection in an unequal situation." This position was strikingly similar to the argument put forward by Andrea Dworkin, especially in her seminal work *Pornography: Men Possessing Women*, published the following year. Dworkin consistently maintained, contrary to extensive interpretation to the contrary, that she was not against sex *per se*, but rather against the exercise of male power over women, which was often *disguised* as sexuality.[62]

Given the historical failure of women to resist male supremacy effectively on an individual basis, Edwards and Phelps believed that what was needed inside STO in particular was a change in the "atmosphere" of the organization. The current atmosphere was one where, as Edwards put it, STO's women's meetings "were like regular left meetings, only without men."[63] Edwards and Phelps wanted the Women's Wing to become "a militant and highly conscious milieu in which women combat male chauvinism, both individually and collectively, and, most importantly,

---

61 Except as noted, all quotes in this paragraph are from Alison Edwards and Linda Phelps, "In Defense of Feminism: A Response to 'Fighting Male Supremacy,'" in *Continuation of the Special Supplement to IDB #16*, May/June 1980, 1–5.

62 Andrea Dworkin, *Pornography: Men Possessing Women* (New York: Putnam, 1981).

63 Alison Edwards, "Some of the Events Behind the Phantom Pheminist(s) Action," in *Continuation of Special Supplement to IDB #16*, May/June, 1980, 13.

one in which women support and encourage each other."[64] While this suggestion was certainly compatible with the approach taken by Holstein and others, it was clear that the rather fundamental disagreements about the nature of male supremacy, especially in regards to sexual and romantic relationships, were likely to continue. Looking back, Janeen Porter argues that these disagreements were at least partially related to the differences in class and educational background among the female members of STO: women with more extensive formal education, who were sometimes denigrated by other members as "bourgeois" or "middle class," tended to identify with the women's liberation movement in some form (although they routinely rejected bourgeois biases within the movement), while those from more stereotypically proletarian backgrounds, often with less formal education viewed the women's liberation movement as less central and more alien.[65]

* * *

Apart from—but clearly related to—the question of sexism in the organization, the other major issue raised as a result of the Phantom Pheminist letter related to children and the attitude within STO toward parenting. This was a question that had come up periodically throughout the group's prior decade of existence. Marcia Rothenberg, who was a member of the group during its early years, recalls having felt marginalized within STO because she and her husband Mel were the only members at the time with young children. She remembers pushing for more family-oriented events within the group, but in her view the culture of the organization was not pro-family. In fact, echoing Phil Rubio's assessment in 1980, she believes that in the early seventies there was no real culture to STO at all; certainly there was "no laughing together" during their time in the organization.[66] While other members of the group during this and later periods would certainly disagree, the Rothenbergs were not alone in their discontent, and throughout most of the decade, only a few STO members were parents.

But by 1980, things had changed. According to Lance Hill's estimate at the time, "over one fourth of the people in STO have children. Some still live with them, some don't."[67] One side effect of the Phantom Pheminist

---

64   Edwards and Phelps, "In Defense of Feminism," 5.

65   Janeen Porter (Creamer), interview with author, September 14, 2006.

66   Marcia and Mel Rothenberg, interview with author, October 12, 2006.

67   All quotes in this paragraph from Lance Hill, "Comments on the

letter was a new discussion regarding the appropriateness of active parenthood for revolutionary cadre and the extent to which child-rearing interfered with the necessary work of a group like STO. The question arose because some of the examples from the letter related to insensitive comments by men in STO directed at a single mother. Other examples were tied to a member of STO who was perceived by some as resisting (or shirking) the responsibilities that came with fatherhood, in the name of pursuing explicitly political work. The resulting discussion was illuminating, even if it failed to resolve the key questions. Hill began by suggesting that while young children could indeed be a "hindrance to political work," they should not be "viewed as a special case." Romantic relationships, for example, "are no more indispensable to human life than children," and "STO has had much more trouble with love relationships hampering work than with children," yet no one was suggesting that all members become celibate. There was, by contrast, an undercurrent (without any explicit advocacy) that children were a "bourgeois" "self-indulgence," and this suggestion irritated Hill, as a revolutionary and as a father.[68]

Other members of STO extended the argument even further. Phil Rubio denounced the "double standards—people who begged off meetings or political work for 'personal business' (like rock concerts or hair dressers) were excused, but if the conflict involved a commitment made to a *child*, that was a *different* story."[69] Edwards strongly repudiated the idea that an active parent could be nothing more than a "movement sympathizer. The only way such a charge can be justified is by mistaking the most immediate, narrow, and short-range needs of STO for the needs of the movement generally, thereby creating a measure of one's political worth solely on the basis of how much that person produces at any given moment."[70] As Paula Rubio pointed out, "children do grow up—and

---

Phantom Pheminists Papers," in *Continuation of Special Supplement to IDB #16*, May/June, 1980, 9–12.

68   It has proven remarkably difficult to find written documentation of explicit political opposition to parenting by revolutionaries, although it clearly was a perspective that held some sway both within STO and in other corners of the left. The relatively one-sided nature of my coverage of this question should therefore be viewed less as an unthinking reflection of my own biases (though those are in fact with the pro-parenting faction) and more as an unfortunate byproduct of a lopsided debate where the other side failed to defend itself.

69   Phil Rubio, "More on Kids and Politics," 31.

70   Edwards, "Some of the Events," 21.

incredibly fast. I look at the years of being a parent as only a period of my life, and I intend to be as good a parent as I can during that time."[71] In this sense, the negative attitudes about child-rearing that were emerging in STO may have been reflective of the emergency response mode of activity that characterized much of the group's anti-imperialist period. If, as the MLN proclaimed in the title of one of its pamphlets, *The Time Is Now*, then the time for things like parenting was clearly "later."[72] By 1980, most STO members had long since become frustrated with the perpetual crisis mentality that dominated the various solidarity committees the organization participated in, but this did not necessarily prevent people from unconsciously importing the same approach into other areas of work, especially when children were involved.

In this context, Paula Rubio considered the logical consequence of this line of thinking: "My conclusion over the years has been that STO is an organization for people without children—or for those with children who wish to put themselves through unbelievable shit because of them."[73] This helped explain why she never joined the organization, but her husband Phil, who was a member, was not much more optimistic. The family had moved to Denver, but he remembered their days in Kansas City, where "for a long time there was the expectation that you inform the branch (or at least the EC [Executive Committee]) before you had a child, regardless of whether your spouse was in STO. Otherwise, it was 'unfair' to expect other cadre to help do childcare when they had no say in its procreation!"[74] Experiences like this led him to conclude that "overall, people's treatment in STO of families has been pretty dismal." Still, he had no interest in leaving the group. At the very least, he argued, "it is not bourgeois to want to have kids and still be a revolutionary." In fact, he maintained some hope that their children might turn out to be communists as well, although after identifying himself as a red-diaper baby, he wondered, "Will STO have any?" Regretfully, he answered, "I doubt it—not at the present rate."[75]

---

71   Paula Rubio, "More on Kids and Politics," 27.

72   Movimiento de Liberación Nacional, *The Time is Now! A Discussion Bulletin* (n.d., but c. 1978).

73   Paula Rubio, "More on Kids and Politics," 26.

74   This and all subsequent quotes in this paragraph are from Phil Rubio, "More on Kids and Politics," 29–32.

75   My limited encounters with the grown children of former STO members suggest that Rubio was largely correct, if by "red-diaper baby" he meant children of radicals who grow up to be radicals themselves.

Several participants in the discussion advanced arguments for parenthood as a positive factor in STO's continuing work. Phil Rubio, for instance, suggested that the range of new experiences involved in child-rearing "puts you in touch that much more with that aspect of working people's lives that occupies so much of their time and energy."[76] Similarly, Hill maintained that "children are a source of human enrichment and enhance my ability to work politically."[77] Several people pointed out that the rigors of parenthood routinely force people to become *more* organized and *more* efficient, in addition to bringing joy to their lives and thus boosting their enthusiasm for political work. In this vein, Phil Rubio bolstered his analysis of the problem by arguing that "Kids are a constant reminder that you're not here forever—if you want to leave something besides a bibliography when you go." Drawing on no less an authority than one of the recently released five Puerto Rican Nationalist prisoners, he concluded, "That theme was stressed by Rafael [Cancel] Miranda when he spoke to a room of 400 people, mostly Chicanos, here this winter. You could barely hear him with his quiet voice over the din of the kids running around. One little Chicana ran in front of him. He grabbed her and said, '*This* is what it's all about. *This* is what we're fighting for.'" Rubio rested his case by chastening his comrades: "And don't let's forget it."[78]

It is frankly unclear whether Rubio's story, or for that matter any of the other polemics put forward in the aftermath of the Phantom Pheminists letter, had any lasting impact on STO's internal culture. Certainly the organization did not collapse, a fate that befell more than a few revolutionary groups that went through similar internal conflicts during the same period.[79] Over the coming years, STO would continue both its external political work, including extensive efforts around reproductive rights for women, and its internal emphasis on the development of what

76   Phil Rubio, "More on Kids and Politics," 31.

77   Hill, "Comments," 11.

78   Phil Rubio, "More on Kids and Politics," 32.

79   See Elbaum, *Revolution in the Air*, 255–258, which describes the collapse of the CP(ML) and, more pertinently, the Organizing Committee for an Ideological Center (OCIC), which was led by STO's old antagonist, the Philadelphia Workers' Organizing Committee. The OCIC fell apart as a result of an internal Campaign Against White Chauvinism, which in superficial ways paralleled STO's conflicts during the exact same period over male chauvinism. By comparison to the OCIC debacle, the Phantom Pheminists controversy was a model of civil discourse.

Holstein called "critical Marxists."[80] But this is not to say that all was well within the group after several months of internal struggle. In mid-May, one member of STO expressed "a sense of futility in this entire effort. The bulk of the organization," she continued, "responded so defensively to Phantom Pheminist that the question of male supremacy in the organization and positive methods to deal with it were nearly forgotten."[81] This may well have been true, but at the same time, the whole experience was also reflective of the strain the group routinely found itself under as the mass upsurges of the sixties receded ever further in the past.

* * *

In retrospect, the controversy stoked by the publication of the Phantom Pheminist letter seems like something of a tempest in a teapot. Several members actively involved claim not to recall much about the events a quarter-century later, despite the apparent intensity of the written documents that were exchanged at the time.[82] Certainly the dispute did not keep STO from engaging in practical work in the outside world: during the six months that the controversy raged, the group provided extensive emergency support to the Puerto Rican independence movement after the capture of the eleven prisoners in Evanston that April (see Chapter Five). The group also produced two issues of *Urgent Tasks*, as well as the second edition of *Workplace Papers*, which was its largest and most well-designed publication to date and was part of the ongoing attempt to revive the point-of-production work that had characterized STO's early years. Still, morale within the organization was not at a high point, between frustration over the solidarity work and the difficulties of re-engaging with factory organizing in the era of deindustrialization. Looking back, Noel Ignatiev argues that the difference between 1970 and 1980 was not that there were no internal problems around sexism or similar issues when STO was founded, but that the group's organizing successes—and the overall context of popular upsurge—in the early years helped mitigate some of the stress that exacerbated the conflicts a decade later.[83]

---

80   Holstein, "Democracy, Marxism, and Male Supremacy," 24.

81   Cherie A., "Is STO Really Serious About Fighting Male Supremacy?," in *Continuation of Special Supplement to IDB #16*, May/June, 1980, 37.

82   Author's interviews with Alison Edwards, Carole Travis, Lee Churgin (Holstein), and Janeen Porter (Creamer) support this assessment.

83   Noel Ignatiev, telephone conversation with the author, July 16, 2005.

Even in the moment, some members of STO attempted to contextualize the situation. Lance Hill pointed out that "the Soviet Union has occupied Afghanistan, Carter is on the brink of military action in Iran, the FALN has been dealt a serious blow, and we in STO are talking about offensive sexist remarks and broken marriages. Our troubles seem somewhat trivial when held up to the light of History's volatile march."[84] But Hill still found real significance in the controversy, even if the lesson he took from it was different from the one Ignatiev would draw twenty-five years later. "We can grow," argued Hill, "at the point at which we stop bemoaning these problems as typical of a lull, and begin to accept them as part of our tasks.... We have to eliminate the notion that these dynamic problems are a nuisance to the real work of the organization. They *are* part of our real work." The priority on organizational growth was one shared generally by the membership, which was increasingly coming to grips with the disparity between the extensive amount of work to be done in a host of arenas and the limited capacity of a small revolutionary organization to accomplish the needed tasks. This experience was by no means limited to STO, as discussions of organizational "regroupment" began to proliferate within all factions of the far left.[85] In STO, at precisely the moment of the Phantom Pheminist controversy, this took the form of a short-lived courtship with Workers' Power (WP), a nominally Trotskyist organization formed from a split in the International Socialists.[86] Nothing came of the discussions, and WP eventually helped found the group Solidarity in the mid-eighties.

Again, part of the context for these sorts of discussions, and for the issues Hill was raising in terms of the Phantom Pheminists letter, had to do with the sheer quantity of work to be done. As a cadre organization, and in keeping with many other groups across the far left, STO tended to demand an enormous amount of time and effort from its membership. At the time of the letter, for instance, the Kansas City branch was thought of as one of the *least* heavily burdened branches, in large part because of its distance from major centers like Chicago, where the demands of the anti-imperialist work were greater. Nonetheless, the same month the Phantom Pheminists letter was originally published, the Kansas City branch began to utilize a chart to record the responsibilities of

---

84 All quotes in this paragraph are from Hill, "Comments," 9–12.

85 For more on regroupment efforts, see Elbaum, *Revolution in the Air*, 258–266.

86 See Don Hamerquist, "Proposal to Workers' Power," in *Internal Discussion Bulletin* #16, May, 1980, 2.

individual members. Janeen Creamer's workload, for instance, consisted of five areas: Teamsters for a Democratic Union (TDU), anti-imperialist work, women's issues, STO responsibilities, and "ad-hoc" or short-term work.[87] For TDU, she was responsible (together with three other members of the branch) for typing, layout, and distribution of an agitational newsletter; for writing an article on health and safety issues; and for "organizing women and wives, including car haulers in Lawrence [Kansas]." Her responsibilities for anti-imperialist work included the creation of a slide show and the task of "contacting people." On women's issues, she was expected to participate in STO women's meetings and to call about deportation hearings for Iranian feminists. The "ad-hoc" work related to an impending speaking tour in Missouri and Kansas by members of an Irish radical group that had developed ties with STO. Finally, her STO responsibilities included being on the National Committee and being the national coordinator for relations with the South African Military Refugee Aid Fund, a group of antiracist and anti-imperialist deserters from the South African Army, which at the time was developing a political relationship with STO. The other members of the Kansas City branch had similar workloads. In this context, it is easy to see both how such a small group could accomplish so much, and why organizational growth would be a major priority. And, it is important to remember, Creamer's list of responsibilities did not include one hugely significant emphasis for STO—the continuing tasks of political study, education, and debate that were shared by all members of the group, whatever their other organizational and political tasks.

* * *

If there was one single factor that drew people to STO during the second half of the seventies, it was the group's intellectual culture. Not only was it rigorous and demanding, it also avoided the typical pitfalls of most far-left groups of the era, which had a rigid, or at least very clearly defined, set of political positions that new members were expected to learn and adhere to without challenging them. While it is important to avoid caricature when comparing STO to groups like the Revolutionary Communist Party or the Communist Party (Marxist-Leninist), the subjective experience of those who joined STO cannot be ignored. Hal Adams,

---

87   The following information comes from a typed chart labeled "K.C. Assignments" attached to the "Decisional Minutes, January 6, 1980 [K.C.] Branch Meeting," in *IDB* #15, February, 1980, 50.

for instance, later recalled encountering the group in the mid-seventies and being "taken with the quality of the discussion, the serious nature of things, the complexity—it was like nothing I'd ever been affiliated with before on the left. I joined shortly after that."[88] For Bill Lamme, the appeal as a potential member was the way in which competing views were allowed to contend openly with each other inside the group:

> I was particularly attracted to the fact that there was a significant number of very strong intellects with good positions in the group. It was not a single-leader type group, you know, where everybody else is kind of carrying out the [orders] from a very narrow central committee. Debate was so wide ranging, and I had had enough exposure to that early on, that I thought, this is cool. This is cool, because I don't have to say anything I don't think, you know, I'm not obligated to mouth somebody else's position. And what's more, some of these people are quite brilliant, and I can probably learn a lot in this group. And the fact that there's more than one brilliant person, that means I'm not just going to eat what one person is shooting out there because there's nothing else. In fact, there's a lot of ideas contending. I think that is part of STO's greatness, as great as it ever was: the fact that it had some really outstanding revolutionary thinkers who were able to butt heads in a very constructive way.[89]

And it wasn't simply the leadership of the organization that modeled this approach. As Ira Churgin puts it, "I don't think there was any anti-intellectualism at any level. Nobody thought that it was bad to be smart, or that that interfered with work."[90]

Still, the situation was never perfect. Many members had long complained about the dominating presence of a handful of intellectual "heavies," who frequently monopolized political debate, whether intentionally or not. Hamerquist, Ignatin, and (after he joined the group around 1976) Lawrence were most frequently identified in this category, and all three of them were well aware of the problem. By the mid-seventies, they and the rest of the organization determined that something needed to be done.

---

88   Hal Adams, interview with the author, August 4, 2005.
89   Bill Lamme, interview with the author, July 20, 2005.
90   Ira Churgin, interview with the author, December 7, 2005.

While STO, like most other left groups of the era, had long prioritized collective study of key political texts, the group took this emphasis to a new level. Around 1977, Ken Lawrence was initially assigned the task of developing an intensive political education course on dialectics. The explicit goal was to avoid approaching students as empty vessels waiting to be filled with knowledge. At the same time, there was no pretence that all participants had the same level of understanding. Instead, the idea was to train STO members, especially newer ones, in the methods of critical thinking that were essential to the work of theorizing and implementing revolutionary politics.

Taking its cue from the Bolshevik study of Hegel and dialectics, the curriculum began by quoting Lenin's observation that "People for the most part (99 percent of the bourgeoisie, 98 percent of the liquidators, about 60–70 percent of the Bolsheviks) don't know how to *think*, they only *learn the words by heart*."[91] Of course there were clear limits on what could be accomplished in a single course of study, but the immediate objective for students was to gain "a *functional* ability to use Marxism. This is quite different from the usual introductory course which intends to convince the newcomer of the value of Marxism and to familiarize her/him with its terms and scope, but on the whole to leave the important decisions to the more advanced."[92] Toward this end, participants in the course were encouraged to continue their study, both individually

---

91   V.I. Lenin, letter to Inessa Armand, December 1913, in *Collected Works*, Vol 35, 131, emphasis Lenin's. Quoted in "How to Think: A Guide to the Study of Dialectical Materialism," in *Urgent Tasks* #7, Winter 1980. In Lenin's usage, "liquidators" referred to a faction of the Russian Social Democratic Labor Party in the period after 1908 that believed the clandestine apparatus of the Party should be dismantled ("liquidated") because the opportunities for legal and above-ground organizing had expanded. In Lenin's view this was a significant right-wing deviation from the proper approach to revolutionary struggle. Lenin's letter is available online at http://www.marxists.org/archive/lenin/works/1913/dec/00ia2.htm (accessed January 2, 2012); "How to Think," available online at http://www.sojournertruth.net/htt.html (accessed January 2, 2012). The curriculum went through many revisions, based on the feedback received after each implementation. Thus, the *UT* version is somewhat arbitrary, since both earlier and later versions differed somewhat from this one.

92   This and subsequent quotes in this paragraph are from the introduction to the *UT* version of "How to Think."

and collectively, and to judge their own progress in the realm of social struggle rather than abstract knowledge. The dialectics course was intended to be "armament, preparation for battle. The test of that will be in our political practice."

Part of what made the dialectics course unique was its combination of length and intensity. By the time the curriculum was published in *Urgent Tasks* in 1980, it contained nine distinct parts, which were generally taught more or less continuously over a fairly short time-frame. Hal Adams recalled years afterward that "people had to go for a week, five days or seven days or something, and it was all day long. Other people had to cover for your political work, you had to take your vacation time to go, and it would be in some rural setting. The materials were distributed ahead of time, and you were expected to read them. There were study questions and you would go over them."[93] The sections covered topics like "Base and Superstructure in Motion," "How Revolutionaries are Made," and "The Marxist Method." Extensive readings from Marx, Engels, and Lenin were interspersed with selections from a wide range of other thinkers and writers, both historical and contemporary: Hegel, Luxemburg, Gramsci, Lukacs, Mark Twain, C.L.R. James, W.E.B. Du Bois, George Rawick, among many others. STO itself was represented by short pieces from both Ken Lawrence and Noel Ignatin.

A standard course had perhaps a dozen total participants, with roughly four "teachers" and eight "students." This allowed both for the competing views among the instructors that Bill Lamme appreciated and for individualized attention for each new participant. While the eventual goal was to level the intellectual playing field inside STO, the dialectics course deliberately reflected the reality of uneven development within the group. According to Adams, for each session,

> there would be one of the leaders who would be in charge
> of organizing the discussion, and people were encouraged
> to talk. They made a big thing that it wasn't just a circle
> discussion, because a lot of what was going on in the left at
> that point was open circle discussion and no matter what
> anybody said, it was accepted as equal. And this wasn't that,
> because there was stuff that was hard to understand…. So
> that there was a role for a teacher to play in the thing.[94]

---

93   Hal Adams, interview with the author, August 4, 2005.
94   Ibid.

The introduction to the *Urgent Tasks* version of the curriculum high-lights this role with an example. In the first session, after reading selections from Marx and Engels, students were to be asked about "the fundamental contradiction of modern capitalism."[95] After rejecting two competing views on this question, STO's official perspective is put forward as follows:

> According to Marx, the social contradiction which can only be resolved by revolution is that between the forces of production and the relations of production.... Forces of production includes both capital and labor, while relations of production includes capitalists and workers. Thus the proletariat is an essential of both sides of the antagonism— on one side as the creator of use value, on the other as wage laborer. The contradiction is therefore internal and essential to the working class itself, and cannot be resolved externally. STO's political line—in particular our understanding of the role of white skin privilege—is based on this recognition of the conflict internal to the proletariat.[96]

For those more familiar with STO, this was also a theoretical restatement of the analysis of dual consciousness that had been central to the group's political theory from the very beginning. The problem was that this interpretation of capitalism's contradictions would not spontaneously emerge within a traditional study group, because most participants (that is, most newer members of STO at that point) "are experienced leftists who have assimilated the various distortions of Marxism which constitute the conventional wisdom."[97] As a result, the presence of more advanced revolutionary thinkers was essential to the success of the course. Still, this distinction was always treated somewhat gingerly: references to "teachers" and "students" routinely came in scare quotes, and teachers were expected to continue learning themselves, even while they guided the study of the other participants.

In this context, one innovative aspect of the dialectics courses was STO's decision to have students from one course become instructors the next time. This contributed to the education of the new instructors, and reflected the organizational goal of raising the overall level of intellectual

95   "How to Think," in *UT* #7, Winter 1980.
96   Ibid.
97   Ibid.

skill within the group. Over time, the courses became one of the signature components of STO's approach to politics, and word of them spread within the broader left. For a few years, the courses were even viewed as something of a recruitment tool, attracting people like Bill Lamme, who remembers being "a sucker for an intellectual approach."[98] After two years of largely internal use, the curriculum was published in *Urgent Tasks*, and subsequent courses often included sympathetic nonmembers as participants and even instructors.[99] Lamme recalls that around this time, not yet a member but having already attended one course as a student, "I got recruited to [teach] some of the other dialectics classes, and in the process of that they said, well, if you're going to be doing these dialectics classes, then it sure would be nice if you were a member of STO when you go around to these other places."[100] In the end, STO's dialectics courses took on a modest life of their own, and managed to far outlast the organization that initiated them; in the last decade, several versions of the course have been offered in multiple cities across the US, with the help of a handful of former STO members. Certainly the course changed the self-understanding of many of the participants. Former member Carol Hayse credits Lawrence in particular with having insisted that he could "make theoreticians out of all of you." Although she initially refused to believe it was possible, she acknowledges that, in fact, "that son-of-a-bitch made a theoretician out of me!"[101] And she was certainly not the only one.

* * *

While the dialectics course became the most widely known manifestation of STO's internal intellectual culture, it was hardly the only one. By the late seventies, the group had a standing educational committee, which was responsible for coordinating a variety of efforts. Other multi-session courses were developed, covering topics like political economy, the national question, or the theory of "crisis" that developed within STO at the end of the decade. Shorter courses, often called "line educationals," were designed to bring new members up to speed with the basic

---

98 Bill Lamme, interview with the author, July 20, 2005.
99 The report by the Education Coordinator in *IDB* #21, January 1981, predicted that "between Aug. '80–Aug. '81 at least 50 non STO people who share some of our political perspective and who we have a clear interest in helping to develop theoretically will have taken the class."
100 Bill Lamme, interview with the author, July 20, 2005.
101 Carol Hayse, telephone interview with the author, September 6, 2006.

politics of the group. Occasionally, the organization sponsored larger educational conferences, which were intended to showcase STO's politics in a framework that also allowed sympathetic groups and individuals to explore areas of agreement and disagreement. One such conference was held in November 1978, focusing on three main topics: the basis of bourgeois hegemony, the nature of the Soviet Union, and the potentials and limitations of national liberation struggles. Approximately sixty people were invited, including representatives of several anti-imperialist groups.[102] STO's overall assessment of the educational conference was positive. An internal evaluation afterwards indicated that "most people felt that the conference was a success in terms of our periphery—virtually everyone loved it, and some people were probably recruited from it."[103]

One exception to the love-fest related to perhaps the most high-profile participant in the conference. In a nod to the growing Jamesian influence inside STO, Grace Lee Boggs was invited to present as part of the bourgeois hegemony panel. After years of close collaboration, including co-authorship of several key documents, Boggs had split from James over questions of political orientation in the early sixties. Nonetheless, she still retained much of the general approach that distinguished James and his circle. Boggs's participation in the conference was subsequently described as "a disaster," because she "made any sort of discussion impossible."[104] Apparently the sense of frustration was mutual, as Boggs quickly began circulating a written criticism of STO attached to the text of her speech. The group, she wrote, upheld labor struggles as the only road to revolution and "showed little appreciation of the way that striking white workers have time and again turned on blacks."[105] Given STO's longstanding emphasis on this very problem, it is hard to imagine what aspects of the group's participation in the conference gave rise to this criticism. It was also seemingly contradicted by Boggs's simultaneous critique of the solidarity politics that characterized STO's anti-imperialist period. Thus, to the extent that she was correct in criticizing the group for

---

102 Descriptions of the conference can be found in the National Committee Minutes for September 16, 1978 (planning notes), in *IDB* #6, October 1978, and NC Minutes for December 9, 1978 (evaluations), in *IDB* #8, December 1978.

103 NC Minutes, December 9, 1978.

104 Ibid.

105 Boggs's comments were copied into the *IDB* #8, December 1978, with the following explanation: "Grace Boggs is circulating the speech she gave at the STO Educational Conference. The two notes below are appended to her speech and give her impressions of STO."

seeing themselves "only in the role of supporters, defenders and critics of the struggles of others, people in other countries and the oppressed in this country," her accusation of a white blind spot in the group's politics seems misguided.[106] Indeed, for STO, the opposite problem—the romanticizing of black and national liberation struggles—was far more pervasive in 1978.

More believable, though still uncharitable, was Boggs's critique of STO on questions of feminism. She was "surprised and disturbed by the absence of any sign at the STO conference that female or male comrades had been influenced by the women's movement."[107] "Female comrades," she continued, "said little and when they spoke did so hesitatingly, as if seeking male approval."[108] The group took this latter criticism quite seriously, and the internal evaluation of the conference included significant discussion of the low level of participation from STO members, "especially from women but also from men."[109] This was viewed as a particular manifestation of the general need for intellectual development that the dialectics courses were meant to address.

The remainder of Boggs's criticisms, however, gained less of a hearing inside the group. Thus, for instance, her rejection of a basic theoretical tenet of Marxism—"we cannot understand the revolutionary age we are living in as long as we look at the history of humanity in terms of class struggle and economic development"—was diametrically opposed to STO's emphasis on just these aspects of historical materialism.[110] More valid in retrospect, but only slightly less incomprehensible to STO at the time, was her critique of the group's continued reliance on the textual analysis of key writers in the Marxist canon: "[STO's] attempts to fit contemporary Russia, China and the Third World revolutions into quotations from Marx, Engels and Lenin reminded me of Ptolemy's continual creation of new epicycles in the heavens to account for phenomena that could not be fitted into the theory of the sun revolving around the earth."[111] In the end, despite STO's growing attachment to C.L.R. James, their brief interaction with his former cothinker was anything but fruitful.

* * *

---

106 Ibid.
107 Ibid.
108 Ibid.
109 NC Minutes, December 9, 1978.
110 Boggs's comments, *IDB* #8, December 1978.
111 Ibid.

STO's internal political education process was punctuated by events like the 1978 conference, but the backbone of its continuing efforts was really the group's *Internal Discussion Bulletin*. Publication of the *IDB* began immediately after the split in the group at the beginning of 1978, and nearly three dozen issues (many running over a hundred pages) were produced over the next six years. Certainly, internal debate had taken place in the eight years prior to the creation of the *IDB*, but it had always been somewhat haphazard. As a well-organized and fairly regular publication, the *IDB* rapidly became the primary venue for ongoing political debates inside the organization, featuring polemics on an astonishingly broad range of topics, from the nature of the period to the purpose of revolutionary organization. Most issues also contained minutes and reports from meetings of various internal bodies, such as local branches, working groups or "fractions," and especially the National Committee, which was expected to guide political discussion within the group. Copies of leaflets and speeches authored by members were routinely included, as were written criticisms of STO's politics and activities by outside groups and individuals. Reviews of movies, television shows, and books, both by STO members and reprinted from other left publications, appeared regularly. Finally, most issues contained a number of "clippings," from both the mainstream media and the movement press, on a host of current topics.

Despite the serious business of revolution, the *IDB* periodically featured humorous content as well. The most frequent contributor along these lines was Ed Voci, who submitted a recurring column entitled "Light Stuff from a Lightweight." The title was a mocking reference to the problem of intellectual "heavies" within the group. Voci's contributions deliberately mimicked the style of newspaper gossip columns, mixing (often dark) political humor with news briefs and the occasional inside joke. In the run-up to Reagan's triumph in the 1980 election, one entry read, "What is it that Ted Kennedy has and Jimmy Carter wants? A dead brother," while another read simply, "A Kansas City member is said to have made quite an impression at the opening of the Crosscurrents Cultural Center in Chicago."[112] Humor also surfaced in many of the clippings that appeared in the *IDB*. One classic example was "Peter Rabbit and the *Grundrisse*," which had previously been published in the journal *Theoretical Review* and was inserted without comment in the *IDB*. A spoof of the then-burgeoning academic trend toward Marxist literary criticism, the article was an amusing send-up

112 Ed Voci, "Light Stuff…," in *IDB* #19, October 1980.

of "the political economy of the cabbage patch."[113] Predictably, most of the *IDB*'s attempts at humor played off of political topics, especially in gentle mockery of the intellectual pretensions that dominated the rest of the bulletins.

It quickly became clear that the *IDB* was a useful tool in drawing sympathizers and fellow travelers of the group into its ongoing political dialogue, but this presented certain risks in terms of exposing too much internal discussion to the scrutiny of nonmembers, even those who were fairly close comrades. Thus, in 1979, STO decided to split the contents of each issue into a "regular" section, simply titled the *Internal Discussion Bulletin*, and a restricted section, normally titled either the "Special Supplement" or the "Secret Supplement" to each issue. These supplements were often labeled "For Members Only," in order to indicate the sensitive nature of the contents, relative to the more broadly aimed items in the regular sections.[114] The items relating to the Phantom Pheminists controversy, for instance, were all distributed via two "Special Supplements," and part of Ken Lawrence's anger regarding the initial letter related to the fact that it had been submitted for inclusion in the regular section, where nonmembers would have had access to it. (The long-time editor of the *IDB*, Ira Churgin, decided to publish it, but only in the members-only section.) Although even the Supplements were readily accessible to nonmembers (spouses, for instance), the security issues were certainly real in a world where—as noted earlier—government repression efforts frequently exploited internal disagreements.

Similar concerns grounded one other peculiar instance of security culture developed during STO's anti-imperialist period. When Ken Lawrence joined STO in the mid-seventies, he did so effectively as a "secret member." While he was well known to all members of the group (and many people in competing groups) as a high-profile and quite active figure in leadership, he was for several years routinely referred to in written documents as "Jasper Collins." The original Collins was a deserter from

---

113 Rosa and Charley Parkin, "Peter Rabbit and the *Grundrisse*," in *Theoretical Review*, #17 July/August 1980, reprinted in *IDB* #21, January, 1981. The article was originally published in 1974 in the *European Journal of Sociology*, and was reprinted by *Theoretical Review*.

114 It is worth noting that this distinction is still taken seriously by many former members, none of whom was willing to grant me access to the supplements, even though several of them were willing to share the regular sections. The few issues in my possession came through Alexander Van Zandt Akin and Bolerium Books in San Francisco.

the Confederate Army during the Civil War who became a leading participant in what has been described as the "Free State of Jones," a small region in southern Mississippi that was a haven for anti-secessionist and pro-Union dissidents, including a number of interracial families.[115] Lawrence lived ninety miles north of Jones County in Jackson, Mississippi, and was involved in a range of antiracist organizing efforts. When he joined STO there was apparently a general agreement between himself and the leadership of the group that his ongoing work in Mississippi might be compromised by public association with an avowedly Leninist organization with a defined strategic orientation toward revolutionary struggle.[116] As a result, Lawrence used the name Jasper Collins when writing about topics with immediate strategic implications, such as the introduction to Don Hamerquist's long pamphlet on *White Supremacy and the Afro-American National Question*, but used his own name for documents of a more theoretical or historical nature, such as his review of *Treasures of Tutankhamen* or his pamphlet *Marx on American Slavery*.[117] In almost all internal documents up through at least 1981 or so, he was referred to as Jasper Collins, or simply by the initials "J.C."

* * *

One possible reason for Lawrence's eventual abandonment of his pseudonym was the changing nature of STO's self-understanding as the eighties began. The group that had been so strongly identified with Leninist party-building efforts just a few years earlier was now beginning to conceive of itself more clearly in terms of the autonomist politics then emerging in several European countries. Paradoxically, this shift meant that the group began to consider giving greater weight to its own political work than had been the case at the height of the anti-imperialist period. At the same time, as the various episodes in this chapter have highlighted, the organization was being pulled in divergent directions—simultaneously emphasizing the development of

---

115 For more on Collins and Jones County, see Victoria E. Bynum, *Free State of Jones: Mississippi's Longest Civil War* (Chapel Hill: University of North Carolina Press, 2001).

116 Ken Lawrence, interview with the author, August 24, 2006.

117 Some members of STO found this distinction to be vague and arbitrary, and found Lawrence's use of the pseudonym to be unnecessary, if not pretentious. Kingsley Clarke expressed this position in an author interview, April, 2006.

theory and direct intervention in a range of new social movements. As the Reagan Revolution got into full swing, STO continued to struggle with the politics of culture and the culture of politics, but it did so against a backdrop radically different from the one that had been present at the group's founding eleven years earlier.

Part Three:
The River is Dry

Is a dream a lie if it don't come true

Or is it something worse?

Bruce Springsteen, "The River"

Chapter Seven: Building a Tendency, but How?

On October 10, 1980, nearly one thousand people arrived in Pittsburgh for the National Labor Conference for Safe Energy and Full Employment. They had two objectives in mind: to build ties between organized labor and the then-burgeoning environmental movement, and to shore up union power in the face of deindustrialization. Alan Rausch, one of STO's most active antinuclear activists, was officially there in his capacity as a rank-and-file trade unionist working at an Oscar Mayer factory in Chicago. He had helped draft a resolution expressing solidarity with Native American struggles for self-determination. The resolution noted the long history of US government disregard for treaties signed with sovereign Indian nations, opposed both the extraction of fissile material and the dumping of nuclear waste on reservation land, and concluded by declaring that the conference "supports the rights of Native people to self-determination."[1]

In reality, Rausch's participation in the conference had a dual purpose. As rank-and-file militant, he was part of STO's attempt to re-establish a workplace presence, as had been approved at the General Membership Meeting the year before. At the same time, he was also centrally involved in the group's engagement with the antinuclear movement. The key goal

---

1   "A Resolution in Support of International Indian Solidarity Day," October 12, 1980, reprinted in *IDB* #21, January 1981, 46. The resolution was signed by more than a dozen labor union and Native activists.

of this latter project was to help coalesce a revolutionary tendency within the movement that could combat the reformist approaches that pervaded antinuclear struggles. The resolution on Native self-determination was exemplary of this effort, though predictably STO's objective was not passing the resolution but initiating debate regarding the relationship between Native, environmental, and labor questions. This would open space for Rausch and others to advance a vision of anti-imperialist politics that might attract other participants in the conference. "My concern," Rausch subsequently reported to other STO members, "was not that it would not be heard but that it would get adopted without any debate or understanding. This is in fact what happened. The chair ... said this was a resolution that everyone would have to support and it went through with a round of applause."[2] For Rausch and for STO generally, this sort of death by acclamation was excruciating. But it also represented a failure on their part, since the resolution as submitted clearly did not draw sharp enough lines of political demarcation to cause any real disagreement over its content among conference attendees.

Far beyond this small example, the attempt to cohere a tendency defined most of STO's work during the last period of its existence. The group worked to advance its politics both within so-called "mass" movements, like the antinuclear movement, and within more narrowly defined "left" formations. The organization's analysis of what the tendency meant politically, and its ideas about who belonged (or should belong) in the tendency, changed dramatically over the course of a few years, but the underlying assumption remained the same: that STO was far too small to accomplish by itself the work it saw as necessary to bring about a revolutionary situation. Tendency building required both practical work—active participation in the daily operations of various social movements—and theoretical work—the promotion of ideological and strategic debate within these same movements. As the eighties progressed, a contradiction surfaced within STO between these two aspects of tendency building, which along with a parallel tension between "mass" and "left" approaches, contributed to the final decline of the organization.

STO's emphasis on tendency building originated in the sequence of solidarity coalitions that characterized much of the group's anti-imperialist phase in the second half of the seventies. In 1978, Don Hamerquist had summarized one major aspect of STO's activity: "We put a priority on political debate on the left. Our intention is to begin the process

2   Alan Rausch, "Fall Foliage and Fossil Fools," in *IDB* #21, January 1981, 42.

of developing a political tendency which shares what we think is a viable revolutionary perspective in the US."[3] Despite the group's ongoing frustrations with solidarity work, it continued to define this tendency as anti-imperialist. The unifying political positions of the tendency were expected to be three-fold: a belief that "the internal national liberation movements are the leading forces for revolution in this country," a conviction that "the white working class has a dual and contradictory character," and an understanding that "our responsibility is to develop revolutionary proletarian internationalism through directly confronting white supremacy."[4] By 1979, however, the group was agreed that the best avenues for tendency building were not to be found in a focus on solidarity campaigns, but in "the development of revolutionary potentials in all areas of work."[5] Along with the women's movement and workplace organizing, the newest venue for STO's attempt to coalesce a tendency was the struggle against nuclear power.

* * *

The move toward STO involvement in the antinuclear movement actually began in 1978, when members of the Denver branch accepted an invitation to attend a meeting of the Mobilization for Survival chapter in Boulder, Colorado.[6] This connection quickly blossomed into a series of collaborations, including a workshop on "imperialism in relation to the nukes issue," as well as a short-notice demonstration against the sale of a reactor to the Philippines, then a dictatorial client state of the US.[7] The protest was notable, in part, for the active participation of the Chicano/Mexicano-led Colorado Committee Against Repression (El Comite), which STO had supported for several years. After the march was

---

3   Don Hamerquist, "Direction," in *IDB* #1, Spring 1978.

4   Quotes are from the document "Questions and Votes from the GMM," in *IDB* #11, June 1979, 3.

5   Ibid.

6   Phil Rubio, "Report on Work with the Anti-Nuke Movement in Denver," in *IDB* #7, Jan/Feb 1979, 18. Mobilization for Survival (often shorthanded as "the Mobe") was a nationwide anti-war organization founded in the mid-seventies.

7   Ibid, 18–19. Yok-Shiu F. Lee and Alvin Y. So, eds., *Asia's Environmental Movements: Comparative Perspectives* (Armonk, NY: M. E. Sharpe, 1999) details the struggle against nuclear power in the Philippines during the seventies and eighties.

over, some antinuclear activists participated in a previously scheduled El Comite action. The Denver branch of STO pushed for alliances between movements, rather than what it perceived as the liberal approach of "build[ing] Third World constituencies, workers constituencies, and so forth."[8]

Eventually, STO members and close comrades in Denver helped initiate a group called the Committee Against Nuclear Imperialism.[9] As the name makes clear, STO's earliest forays into antinuclear work were conceived as a way to expand the audience for the group's version of anti-imperialist politics among the antinuclear movement's milieu of predominantly white activists, many of whom were in the midst of profound individual and collective processes of radicalization. The whole cycle of nuclear production, from the "front end" (uranium extraction) to the "back end" (waste disposal), was cast as tightly linked to US imperialist interests. Thus, uranium and plutonium mining activities largely took place on Native land in the southwestern part of the country, which added environmental devastation and radioactive contamination to the long history of genocide against American Indians. Nuclear reactors in the US (and the health and environmental risks that came with them) were normally placed in low-income rural communities that had been historically marginalized under capitalism. Worse still, nuclear plants in the developing world were being used to help prop up allies of the US government in countries like the Philippines, Iran, South Africa, Israel, and elsewhere.[10] Similarly, STO argued that the presence of nuclear fuel in these countries was intended to suggest that the threat of nuclear weapons for use against national liberation movements was not far behind. Finally, the difficulty inherent in "disposal" of nuclear waste (really, its isolation and containment for hundreds of thousands of years) was one of the main mobilizing points for mainstream antinuclear activists, and here again STO noted the white supremacist implications of

---

8   Ibid., 14.

9   The name is used in the introduction to the interview with Ken Lawrence described below.

10   See Phil Rubio, "Crossroads for the Anti-Nuclear Movement," in *UT* #10, Fall 1980, which points out that the Iranian revolution halted construction of four nuclear plants that had been planned (with support from the US) by the Shah. Available online at http://sojournertruth.net/antinuke.html (accessed January 9, 2012). Of course, the subsequent pursuit of nuclear capability by the Islamic Republic has now been the focal point of conflict between Iran and the US for more than a decade.

locating temporary and so-called "permanent" storage facilities in low-income communities of color.

Early in 1979, shortly before the Three Mile Island incident brought the antinuclear movement to national prominence, the Denver branch of STO proposed that the organization as a whole place priority on involvement in the antinuclear movement. Phil Rubio, one of STO's earliest and most committed antinuclear organizers, argued that, while the work in Colorado was proceeding, "for an intervention to be really effective, it should be national in scope."[11] Since increasing numbers of white people were being drawn to the movement, Rubio believed that "we can recruit from the anti-nuke movement to our [anti-imperialist] tendency."[12] Seen from this angle, the problems of the movement—largely "middle-class" demographics, anticommunist liberalism, an unexamined commitment to consensus process and pacifism, among others—presented a potentially valuable opportunity for STO to highlight its political analysis, its strategic approach, and its fundamentally revolutionary outlook.

Rubio's perspective was not immediately embraced within STO. The whiteness of the movement was problematic, as was its failure to "prefigure worker control of the production process."[13] An STO member in San Francisco, where antinuclear struggles were escalating rapidly, argued in March of 1979 that "work in the anti-nuke movement, when evaluated against other possibilities, does not have great potential for advancing our politics."[14] The same member drew a distinction between "the *issue* of nuclear power and the *movement* to oppose nukes," and maintained that questions of environmental concern were most likely to be addressed in struggle "outside of the so-called ecology movement of which the anti-nuke movement is a part."[15] Given limited resources, this position held that it was better to emphasize STO's long-standing priority on support for national liberation struggles that could raise environmental questions directly in an anti-imperialist context, or alternately to re-invigorate the group's point-of-production efforts with a special attentiveness to struggles around workplace environmental issues.

Such an assessment might well have been shared by a majority of STO's membership at the beginning of 1979, but by the time the group's

---

11　Rubio, "Report on Work," 22.

12　Ibid.

13　RJ, "On Anti-Nuke Work," in *IDB #9*, March 1979, 6.

14　Ibid.

15　Ibid.

General Membership Meeting took place in early May of that year, the whole landscape had changed. On March 28, one of the two units at the Three Mile Island Nuclear Generating Station outside of Harrisburg, PA, suffered a partial core meltdown.[16] Although the actual health and environmental effects of the accident remained disputed for years, one undeniable and immediate result of the incident was a dramatically heightened global awareness of the dangers posed by nuclear power plants. Suddenly, previously planned antinuclear demonstrations began to draw exponentially larger crowds than expected. In this context, STO quickly realized that a window was opening in which Rubio's approach might bear fruit. Although there was still skepticism in the organization, the GMM approved a resolution stating that "the anti-nuclear movement is the main area where large numbers of white people are being activated and radicalized."[17] A parallel resolution indicated overwhelming support for the proposition that "the main criteria for judging the success of our work" in the antinuclear movement "will be our success at building the anti-imperialist current."[18] The Denver position had won, and for the next few years, STO maintained an active engagement with antinuclear struggles not only in Colorado but also in Chicago, the East Coast, and places as far afield as Mississippi.

There, in the spring of 1979, Ken Lawrence attempted to implement STO's approach to tendency building in the antinuclear movement. To do so, he helped plan a rally against a nuclear plant then under construction in Port Gibson, alongside the Mississippi River.[19] The protest was

---

16   The most comprehensive account of the Three Mile Island incident is a semi-official history produced by and for the US Nuclear Regulatory Commission. J. Samuel Walker, *Three Mile Island: A Nuclear Crisis in Historical Perspective* (Berkeley, CA: University of California Press, 2004). The intensity of the public response was augmented by the release of the popular Hollywood thriller *The China Syndrome* less than two weeks prior to the meltdown.

17   "Questions and Votes from the GMM," in *IDB* #11, June 1979, 3.

18   Ibid.

19   Most of the information and all quotes unless otherwise noted for this and the subsequent paragraphs comes from "The Anti-Nuclear Movement in Mississippi: Interview with an Activist," in *UT* #6, Fall 1979. Ken Lawrence was the activist in question, and at this point he was still a "secret member" of STO, so his membership is not discussed. Email from Lawrence to the author, February 23, 2011, provided additional context and details. For more background on the history of anti-racist

planned to coincide with an international day of action against nuclear power on June 2. Earlier demonstrations against nuclear power in the state, as elsewhere in the US, had been attended almost exclusively by white activists, an issue that Lawrence and others had raised as a problem. But Claiborne County, of which Port Gibson was the county seat, was overwhelmingly black, and the planning committee immediately saw the pitfalls of staging another all-white rally, especially at a time when Ku Klux Klan activity was resurging across the South. Partly in response, some antinuclear activists argued against staging any sort of rally in Port Gibson, claiming that the heavily black population might actually favor the plant because of the jobs it would provide.

Lawrence and others turned this argument on its head, suggesting first that "there probably was opposition in the community, and nobody had really bothered to check enough to find it and help organize it," but alternately arguing that if there really was support for the plant among locals then the educational aspect of a rally was all the more important. Furthermore, the chief of security for the nuclear plant was a notorious former police chief in the state capital of Jackson, and was widely known for tolerating police brutality, especially against African Americans. This provided an opportunity to "raise concretely the issue of the threat to civil liberties that is posed by the nuclear industry." These arguments proved persuasive, and the rally went forward as planned. The organizers got in touch with local leaders of the NAACP in Port Gibson, and with a local black politician who was opposed to the nuclear plant, and helped spread word of the demonstration within the community. Just as important was an agreement with the United League, a regional black organization focused on anti-Klan and other antiracist struggles. The League had planned a rally for the same day in Lexington, Mississippi, 120 miles northeast of Port Gibson. Since the antinuclear demonstration was timed to coincide with the international day of action, the United League agreed to change the date of their own rally so that League members would be able to attend the Port Gibson event. In exchange, Lawrence and other antinuclear activists attended the demonstration in Lexington later in the month, which helped build ties across the movements. As in Denver the year before, the model was mutual support between movements.

When the antinuclear rally took place, a majority of the attendees were still white activists from other parts of the state, but perhaps a

struggle in Claiborne County Mississippi, see Emilye Crosby, *A Little Taste of Freedom: The Black Freedom Struggle in Claiborne County, Mississippi* (Chapel Hill, NC: University of North Carolina Press, 2005).

quarter of the participants were local residents, mostly black. In contrast to earlier demonstrations that took place at the gates of various nuclear facilities (and thus out of public view, given the rural locations normally assigned to the plants), this one was held outside the county courthouse in the center of Port Gibson. The demonstration itself was standard fare: a range of musicians and speakers, including the local politician, environmental activists, and Lawrence himself, who spoke about "the political repression related to nuclear power and about Mississippi Power and Light's racist and reactionary political record." Perhaps the most unusual contribution was a speech written by a political prisoner who was a key member of the Republic of New Afrika, which was read to the crowd. Afterward, many people traveled by car to the reactor site itself, where they released helium balloons that had notes attached to them "indicating to anyone who finds one of them downwind that the path of the balloon would be the path of radiation in the event of an accident." While STO's subsequent involvement in antinuclear work in the South was limited (the organization had only three active members in the entire territory that had once been the Confederacy), the Port Gibson rally was repeatedly offered as something of a model for the antinuclear movement. An interview with Lawrence was published in *Urgent Tasks*, and later reprinted in a movement magazine called *No Nukes Left!*

* * *

The more that STO participated in the antinuclear movement, the more the group's core ideas gained a hearing among other activists, but it was always an uphill struggle. In the run-up to a major national demonstration in 1980, for instance, STO and its allies attempted to replicate the anti-nuclear-anti-Klan mutual support that figured prominently in the Port Gibson protest the prior year. However, at a January meeting of the Coalition for a Non-Nuclear World (the sponsor of the rally), a proposal to endorse a hastily called but important national anti-Klan rally in Greensboro, North Carolina the next weekend was voted down because the Coordinating Committee representatives from various regions of the country claimed "they would have to talk it over in their regions."[20]

---

20   John [Garvey], "Some Notes on the Coordinating Committee Meeting in Washington—January 25–26," in *IDB* #16, May 1980, 14. Garvey was a close comrade of STO living in New York City, and actively involved in a group called People Against White Supremacy (PAWS). For more on Greensboro, see Chapter Eight.

For some representatives, this may genuinely have been nothing more than a commitment to the often frustrating form of consensus-style direct democracy so popular within the antinuclear movement. At least as important, however, was a common belief that such endorsements risked watering down the antinuke message and alienating less politically sophisticated participants in the movement. Rubio had previously predicted "a debate between those who favor making the connections between the anti-nuke struggle and the overall fight against imperialism, and those who want to remain an 'untainted' single-issue pressure group," and the vote on the Greensboro rally endorsement seemed to indicate that the latter tendency still held the balance of power.[21] This was even more clear when the same meeting voted against adding an antiracist slogan (offered by a black-led community group from Harlem that had become actively involved in the antinuclear movement) to the publicized list of chants and slogans officially endorsed for the rally.[22]

A much-cited example of the implicit racism of the antinuclear movement was the disparate responses to the Three Mile Island incident in April 1979 and the somewhat larger spill four months later at Churchrock, New Mexico. Three Mile Island received extensive media coverage, while Churchrock was quickly forgotten. This contrast was reflected within the movement itself, where "TMI" was a recognizable acronym for years to come, "but the international wave of protest … was not duplicated even when the damage was greater" in New Mexico.[23] For STO, the reason was obvious: Three Mile Island forced the evacuation of a largely white suburban community, while the Churchrock spill contaminated land inhabited almost exclusively by Navajo Indians. In the words of Phil Rubio, "the anti-nuclear movement must consider the prevalence of racism and chauvinism not merely in society at large, but within its own ranks."[24]

The implications of Native American participation in particular for the antinuclear movement (and vice versa) were important to STO, as indicated by the resolution Rausch helped bring to the Pittsburgh conference. According to Rausch, the group prioritized a focus on Native struggles within the antinuclear movement "because of the potential these struggles have. Their antifederalist nature and the struggle for land, the militance that is present and will be necessary to prevent genocide,

---

21   Rubio, "Report on Work," 13.
22   Carol Hayse, "Yet Another Nuke Report," in *IDB* #16, May 1980, 18.
23   Rubio, "Crossroads," 3.
24   Ibid., 2–3.

and the totality of oppression that nuclear capital visits on them because of their sitting on top of energy resources," all played a role.[25] While STO's focus in terms of domestic anti-imperialist efforts during the latter part of the seventies had always been on black and Puerto Rican struggles, the same period had witnessed the continuing militancy of the American Indian Movement (AIM) and other groups.

Among the groups aligned with AIM was the Black Hills Alliance (BHA), a multiracial but Indian-led organization founded in 1979 to oppose uranium mining in the Black Hills of South Dakota.[26] The BHA had branches and supporters throughout the Midwest by 1980, and STO was initially enthusiastic about working with the group, which it viewed as a likely pillar of an anti-imperialist current within the antinuclear movement. Nonetheless, the difficulties of working with the BHA quickly became reminiscent of STO's experiences with the MLN, and some members began to view it as yet another example of the limits of "falling into solidarity-only work."[27] By 1981, STO retained an emphasis on the implications of nuclear production for Native societies, but it no longer had direct ties to any Indian-led organizing effort against nuclear power.

Another aspect of the anti-imperialist, tendency-building approach utilized by STO was a special attentiveness to international questions. The promotion by the Denver branch of a demonstration focusing on the Philippines was just the beginning of a trend in the group's work. Nuclear power and weapons were also an issue in Puerto Rico, and STO's connections to the independence movement in the US and on the island itself offered the opportunity to highlight the connections between the two movements. South Africa and Namibia presented a similar scenario: construction of the only nuclear power facility in Africa was initiated in South Africa in 1976, and was heavily supported by the US government in spite of the continuing horrors of the apartheid regime. That same year, the South African colonial government in Namibia (also called

---

25   Alan Rausch, "A Response," in *IDB* #21, January 1981, 21.

26   For background on the Black Hills Alliance, see Zoltán Grossman, *Unlikely Alliances: Treaty Conflict and Environmental Cooperation Between Native American and Rural White Communities* (PhD diss., Geography, University of Wisconsin, Madison, 2002). The relevant excerpt is available on his website at http://academic.evergreen.edu/g/grossmaz/bha. html (accessed January 9, 2012). Grossman was a close comrade of STO during the early eighties, but it is not clear that he shared their somewhat critical perspective on the BHA.

27   Hayse, "Yet Another Nuke Report," in *IDB* #16, 19.

South West Africa) opened the Rossing Uranium Mine, which subsequently became one of the largest open pit uranium mines in the world. Rossing was owned by an international consortium of mining companies, with significant investment from the Iranian state under the Shah.[28]

STO's attention was drawn to this combination of imperialist forces partly because of the ties it had recently developed with a small cohort of activist refugees from both Namibia and South Africa. The South African Military Refugee Aid Fund (SAMRAF) was established in New York City in 1978 to support draft resistance and desertion by South African soldiers. Along with a sister organization in London, SAMRAF attempted to apply a version of the white skin privilege theory to the very different conditions facing South Africa, and was naturally interested in STO as one of the theory's leading proponents in the United States.[29] STO collaborated with SAMRAF on a variety of projects over the next several years, and utilized this connection to help build an anti-imperialist tendency within the antinuclear movement. SAMRAF also viewed the nuclear question as important, since it was a key link in the relationship between the Apartheid regime and the US government. In a 1981 newsletter, SAMRAF explained that "we participate in the mass movements i.e. anti-nuke, anti-draft and anti-Klan movements. These are important areas to make the connections between South Africa and the US and expose American/South African collaboration."[30]

Working closely with SAMRAF in New York was the United Nations delegation of the South West African People's Organization (SWAPO), which was engaged in an armed struggle against the South African occupation of Namibia, and had gained official representation at the UN in the sixties. As early as 1979, SWAPO's permanent observer at the

---

28   Information on the Iranian involvement comes from the official Rio Tinto website for the mine, http://www.rossing.com/history.htm (accessed January 9, 2012).

29   For more on SAMRAF's interpretation of the white skin privilege theory in a South African context, see "Refusniks Down South" (2006), the recollections of founding member Mike Morgan, an ex-soldier from South Africa and later a member of STO, available online at http://www.smokebox.net/archives/what/morgan1206.html (accessed January 9, 2012).

30   "SAMRAF: Who We Are," in *SAMRAF News & Notes* #3, August/September 1981, 7. Available online at http://kora.matrix.msu.edu/files/50/304/32-130-FE2-84-GMH%20SAMRAF%20AugSept81.pdf (accessed January 9, 2012).

UN wrote the preface to one of SAMRAF's first publications, and the two groups participated jointly in a coast-to-coast US speaking tour in the fall of 1980, with a number of the events coordinated by members of STO.[31] The nuclear question was not the primary order of business, but the tour did present an opportunity to build ties between otherwise disparate movements. In particular, the universal hatred for Apartheid on the US left meant that STO was able to draw parallels to South Africa and Namibia around questions of imperialism and domestic racism that would have been far less clear and far more controversial for many antinuclear activists had they been raised in the context of a speaking tour by Puerto Rican militants, for instance.

* * *

Parallel to its critique of the racial politics (and the demographics) of antinuclear struggles, STO also focused attention on the class basis of the movement. It was clear from the outset that the antinuclear milieu represented at best a cross-class alliance. In addition to being white, the typical antinuclear activist was reasonably well-off financially, and would have been classified (though not by STO, which in general rejected the terminology) as "middle class."[32] The demographic issue was problematic

---

31   *The Right to Say No to a Crime Against Humanity: A Report on the Militarization of South Africa and the Right of Conscientious Objection* (Brooklyn, NY: SAMRAF, 1979), available online at http://kora.matrix.msu.edu/files/50/304/32-130-505-84-african_activist_archive-a0b2q2-a_12419.pdf (accessed January 9, 2012). Predictably, the booklet was printed at STO's in-house printshop, C&D Press. (See Chapter Four for more on C&D.) For more on the joint speaking tour, see untitled SAMRAF letter with a schedule of the tour, listing STO members as contact people in multiple cities, available online at http://kora.matrix.msu.edu/files/50/304/32-130-779-84-african_activist_archive-a0b6d0-a_12419.pdf (accessed January 9, 2012).

32   For STO, "middle class" had two distinct and opposed meanings. The first, derived directly from Marx and Engels in the *Communist Manifesto*, was essentially a time-specific term designed to describe the bourgeoisie while it was still in the process of becoming the ruling class. The other, according to Ken Lawrence, is "a bourgeois huckster's propaganda term, to undercut the clear meaning of working class. What they intend is to define class based on consumption rather than production, and define class values by material aspirations. Thus to Obama,

enough, but the problem extended more deeply into the consciousness of the participants. As one STO member argued, the antinuclear movement "reflects [the] disdain the bourgeoisie has for white workers."[33] As the movement gained strength after Three Mile Island, this contradiction became even more pronounced. A rally at the Rocky Flats nuclear facility in Colorado in July of 1979, sponsored by pronuclear power forces, was attended by large numbers of unionized white workers who saw nuclear production as a protection against unemployment in an uneven economy.[34] One of the speakers was Peter Brennan, a longtime labor leader in the building trades who had opposed affirmative action and served at Secretary of Labor under President Nixon. Brennan was infamous on the left for organizing New York City construction workers in support of the Vietnam War in 1970, including the so-called "Hard Hat Riot" of May 8, in which trades workers physically attacked students at a memorial outside New York's City Hall commemorating the students killed at Kent State University four days prior.

For STO, the spectacle of white workers supporting the nuclear industry only reinforced the original impetus behind the critique of white skin privilege that had marked the organization from its inception. At the same time, however, the group's collaboration with even more privileged sectors of the class who were mobilizing inside the antinuclear movement did not immediately result in a productive challenge to the consciousness of pronuclear workers. One key factor here was STO's stated position that "large numbers of white people are being activated and radicalized" in the movement.[35] While undoubtedly true, this assessment flattened the class aspects of the question. The same month STO adopted its stance, the Boston-based Midnight Notes Collective published a critical analysis of the class composition of the antinuclear movement, based heavily upon its own members' participation in the Clamshell Alliance in New England. *Strange Victories: The Anti-Nuclear Movement in the US and Europe* contained a number of dubious assertions and

---

unionized workers are 'middle class,' the opposite of the Marxist view." Email to the author, January 9, 2012. Thus, for STO, neither usage was productive, the former obsolete, the latter deceptive.

33   "Minutes from the Anti-Nuke Meeting, March 2, 1980," in *IDB* #16, May 1980, 12.

34   See Rubio "Crossroads."

35   "Questions and Votes from GMM," in *IDB* #11, June 1979, 3. Note that this resolution was among the most controversial at the Meeting, and passed only by four votes.

reflected an analysis that STO no doubt found insufficiently committed to anti-imperialism, but it did a skillful job of assessing the origins of the movement in the back-to-the-land migration of urban radicals to rural areas that took place in the late sixties and early seventies. Viewing the antinuclear movement from an anticapitalist perspective, *Strange Victories* expressed concern that "capital can play the anti-nuke movement against the poor and vice versa. For example the energy companies and the state (the government) can blame the anti-nuclear movement for the higher electric bills."[36]

Perhaps sensing this problem but sidestepping the class composition issue, STO began to promote an analysis in which the nuclear question was only one component of a comprehensive approach to energy issues. Many other forces within the movement also recognized the implications of developing an energy framework, and they actively promoted a range of energy "alternatives," from so-called "clean coal" to solar power. Along with other left groups involved in the movement, STO took the opportunity to bring not just an anti-imperialist but also an anticapitalist sensibility into play. The arguments for coal, for instance, were quite popular with a section of the mainstream labor movement, including most prominently the United Mine Workers (UMW). The UMW advocated for coal at conferences like the one Rausch attended in Pittsburgh, on the basis that coal production would provide labor-intensive (if dangerous) employment opportunities far more plentiful than the highly technical and even more dangerous work involved in capital-intensive uranium extraction and refinement.[37] In these debates, STO aligned itself with the environmental advocates who put the lie to the supposedly safe aspects of coal production and usage. At the same time, however, the group attempted to apply its critique of labor unions in order to win rank-and-file workers to their perspective. The overt collaboration between the UMW leadership and the (nonnuclear) mining industry, in advocating for coal as an "alternative" to nuclear power, represented a classic example of

---

36   Midnight Notes Collective, *Strange Victories: The Anti-Nuclear Movement in the US and Europe* (Boston and New York: Midnight Notes, 1979), 4. Available online at: http://www.midnightnotes.org/pdf-strangvic0.pdf (accessed January 9, 2012). The claim that coal was "an abundant energy source which could be made safe with available technology" (5) is representative of some of the more tenuous assertions in the pamphlet. For more on the Clamshell Alliance, see below.

37   This resulted in the pun in Rausch's report on the conference, "Fossil Fools."

STO's long-standing claim that "the general function of trade unions is … the containment of [class struggle] within the framework of capital."[38] However, the group was unable to successfully resuscitate its workplace efforts in the midst of deindustrialization, and this analysis produced few meaningful results in terms of rank-and-file organizing.

Solar power, by contrast, was generally less appealing to labor unions and more seductive to antinuclear activists because of its perceived environmental benefits relative to nuclear, coal, and other nonrenewable energy sources. Many activists went so far as to argue that solar represented a viable nonrevolutionary path beyond capitalism, using the classic line "they can't buy the sun." STO and others took pains to point out that many major corporations, including Mobil, Boeing, and especially General Electric, which also produced nuclear power plants, spent the latter part of the seventies acquiring patents specifically relating to solar energy. The problem with "can't buy the sun" arguments, of course, was that companies like GE didn't want to purchase sunlight itself, they wanted to own the electricity that could be produced from sunlight via emerging technologies. In 1980, Rubio offered a dystopian vision of this possible future for "alternative" energy production: "Under present social conditions, Filipinos could slave in a factory making heliostats for solar power plants for low wages, and walk home at night to their huts by the new school [that was] built for foreign technicians' children, [complete with] solar panels. Nothing is 'gentle' in the hands of the imperialists."[39]

The issue of class composition, however, went far beyond the energy question, and even beyond the environmental movement. New social movements generally, from the women's movement to student struggles and beyond, did not resemble either the multiracial, class-based, point-of-production struggles that characterized STO's early years or the largely proletarian national liberation movements that the group focused on

38 Don Hamerquist, "Trade Unions/Independent Organizations," in *Workplace Papers*, 1980 edition [1973], 38.

39 Rubio, "Crossroads," 4. For a somewhat different analysis of the relationship between environmental questions and social questions of exploitation and oppression, it is worth investigating the range of written work produced under the rubric of Social Ecology, especially the writings of Murray Bookchin. For an overview relative to social movements including the anti-nuclear movement of the late seventies and early eighties, see Brian Tokar, "On Bookchin's Social Ecology and its Contributions to Social Movements," in *Capitalism, Nature, Socialism* 19, no. 1, March 2008, 51–66.

supporting during the second half of the seventies.[40] As the new decade dawned, STO was unable to resolve this contradiction between its desire to influence the radicalization of "large numbers of white people" and its belief in the decisive role of the working class. One factor here may have been the subtle influence within the group of versions of anti-imperialism (and the white skin privilege theory) that automatically identified "whiteness" with bourgeois class status and viewed the category of "Third World people" as synonymous with "the working class." From such a perspective, the goal of any engagement with white people could only be winning moral and material support for the revolutionary efforts of people of color. As STO progressively distanced itself from the vulgar sort of anti-imperialism that characterized some of its prior solidarity efforts, the class-composition issue drifted onto the terrain of the group's mostly stillborn efforts to recreate its workplace concentration. In this context, however, the general lack of involvement in the antinuclear movement by traditional sectors of the working class—of any race or nationality—remained troubling. Some other revolutionary tendencies within the movement were better positioned than STO to deal with this reality. Many anarchists, for instance, adopted the "post-scarcity" analysis of Murray Bookchin as a rationalization for accepting the skewed class composition of the movement.[41] Such an approach, which decentered the traditional proletariat from its pivotal position in revolutionary struggles, was unacceptable to STO, and the group's participation in antinuclear struggles remained perpetually ambiguous in relation to the movement's class demographics.

* * *

---

40   Marta Fuentes and Andre Gunder Frank analyze the class composition of new social movements in a global context in "Ten Theses on Social Movements," in *World Development* 17, no. 2 (1989), 179–191.

41   Bookchin's analysis of class structure and his utopian vision of anarchist communism were highly influential among the numerically strong anarchist segments of many anti-nuclear groups, beginning with the Clamshell Alliance, of which Bookchin himself was a member. For an early summation of his analysis, see his "Listen, Marxist!" and the other essays in his book *Post-Scarcity Anarchism* (Montreal: Black Rose Books, 1986 [1971]). For more on the anarchist influence within the Clamshell Alliance and other anti-nuclear groups, see Barbara Epstein, *Political Protest and Cultural Revolution: Nonviolent Direct Action in the 1970s and 1980s* (Berkeley, CA: University of California Press, 1991).

Distinct from the ideology or composition of the antinuclear movement, another of its features was viewed by STO as an appealing opportunity for tendency building: its long-standing commitment to direct
action, up to and including illegal activity designed to slow down or
disrupt the completion of nuclear facilities. The foundational experience
of the antinuclear movement was the attempt, largely coordinated under
the rubric of the Clamshell Alliance, to utilize nonviolent direct action
to stop the construction of the Seabrook Nuclear Plant on the Atlantic
coast of New Hampshire.[42] Drawing indirectly on the legacy of the early
civil rights movement and more directly on nonviolence training provided by radical Quakers, the Alliance organized a series of ever-larger
occupations of the Seabrook property. These takeovers were designed to
be archetypal symbolic forms of civil disobedience. No clandestine activities were involved, and the planning was entirely open and transparent. First 18, then 180, then more than 1,400 protesters were arrested
over the course of three brief occupations between August 1976 and May
1977. This math was the deliberate result of a "power of ten" approach,
with which the Alliance hoped to dramatize the expanding power of
mass resistance.[43]

Numerous antinuclear groups across the country modeled themselves on the Alliance over the next several years, emphasizing mass
direct action, an organizational model based on affinity groups and
consensus-based decision making, and extensive nonviolence training
for all participants. Some even adopted names inspired by the Alliance,
highlighting local aquatic life forms that would be endangered by specific nuclear plants—the Oystershell Alliance and Catfish Alliance near
the Gulf of Mexico, or the Abalone Alliance in California, for instance.
Another common naming convention, the "Action Group," emphasized
the movement's commitment to militant direct action. Communication
among the various organizations was extensive, facilitated in part by previous shared experiences of older members in the antiwar and student
movements of the late sixties. Just as important by 1980 was the ability
and willingness of younger activists to travel, sometimes thousands of
miles, to participate in previously scheduled mass actions.[44] In short, a
broad culture of mass illegality was spontaneously developing inside the

---

42 For a detailed overview of the Clamshell Alliance and its relationship to
    questions of non-violence, see Epstein, *Political Protest*, 58–91.

43 See Epstein, *Political Protest,* 65.

44 Epstein offers multiple examples of this kind of cross-country travel,
    itself in some ways a legacy of the movements of the sixties.

antinuclear movement. Given its own background in supporting wildcat strikes, armed struggle, and other forms of extra-legal activity over the previous decade, it was no surprise that STO found the movement exciting and full of potential.

But this potential was limited, in STO's view, because of the antinuclear movement's traditional commitment to a rather strict vision of nonviolence. In fact, the Clamshell Alliance collapsed in part due to an extended conflict over whether it was "violent" or "nonviolent" to cut the fence around the Seabrook plant in order to facilitate an occupation.[45] The issue was actually two-fold: first, did property damage constitute violence? And second, was fence-cutting likely to "provoke" violence by the police? Similar quandaries vexed antinuclear activists from coast to coast, once media coverage of the Seabrook occupations eliminated any element of surprise for the direct-action wing of the movement. For the most part, leading antinuclear organizers were fully committed to the civil disobedience model, where activists allowed themselves to be arrested and hoped to utilize their detention and prosecution as a sort of moral high ground, in much the same way that they believed the early civil rights movement in the South had done a quarter-century earlier. In this context, the question of fence-cutting was really about which sorts of "arrestable" actions were acceptable, and which were not. There was a moral issue involved, but also a question of symbolism and a desire to attract broad-based public support for the movement.

For STO members who had spent the previous several years vocally supporting bombings carried out by Puerto Rican revolutionaries, it was no doubt perplexing to witness a movement so torn over the acceptability of petty property damage. Nonetheless, the group viewed such debates within the movement as an opening to develop the tendency by advancing a radically different analysis of violence and nonviolence. This perspective was put forward inside the movement itself, in debates about specific actions and campaigns, but also in a more public way in Phil Rubio's 1980 essay "Crossroads for the Anti-Nuclear Movement," which addressed the ideology of pacifism and nonviolence at length. Rubio begins his analysis with a basic statement of fact, then quickly escalates:

> It is difficult to argue the whole question of non-violence
> in the anti-nuke movement. Like many other things, it
> has not been open to debate, but taken as a "given." Social
> movements past and present have used non-violence as one

---

45   See Epstein, *Political Protest,* 70–76.

tactic among many. But in the anti-nuke movement there
is a strong commitment to ideological pacifism. The fact
that this tendency survived the civil rights and anti-war era
of the '60s, and the brutal repression that came down on
certain segments of those movements, particularly the Black
movement, is a tribute to the flexibility of capital in dealing
with white dissent, especially its "loyal opposition" in the
liberal/left community.[46]

The linkage between nonviolence and white loyalty to capitalism
almost certainly infuriated the relatively small number of committed
pacifist revolutionaries involved in the antinuclear movement, but the
connection was defensible. Everyone in the movement knew that it was
divided between people who had a reformist agenda and those who
thought in revolutionary terms. Of course, this distinction did not map
cleanly onto the question of violence. But the hegemony of the reformists—though under constant challenge from the left wing of the movement—was undeniably part of the source of the movement's devotion to
nonviolence.

Rubio's critique of pacifism comes from two directions: first, he criticizes the historical origins of modern political pacifism in the theory
and practice of Mohandas Gandhi, after which he turns his sights on
the selective historical record advanced by contemporary pacifists in the
United States. Gandhi was a key influence in the vision of nonviolence
propounded within the antinuclear movement, but Rubio points out
that his theory was built around a concept of self-sacrifice and noble
suffering that was unlikely to spark fundamental change or appeal to the
most oppressed sectors of any society.[47] He quotes a radical minister from
Britain, Colin Morris, to the effect that "… the wretched of the earth do
not go in for passive resistance. It is no novelty for them to suffer without retaliation."[48] Rubio does acknowledge that "both Gandhi and King

---

46 Rubio, "Crossroads," 5.

47 On the importance of Gandhi to the anti-nuclear movement, see Ep-
    stein, *Political Protest*, 270–271 and 30–31, which describes the various
    liberal and radical interpretations of Gandhi's theory that developed in
    the US during the fifties and sixties.

48 Rubio, "Crossroads," 37. The original citation is to Dr. Colin Morris,
    Unyoung, Uncolored, Unpoor (Nashville, TN: Abingdon Press, 1969),
    92–93. Ellipses are Rubio's, who also corrects Morris's mis-application
    of the term "passive resistance" to Gandhi, but argues that "despite

were able to attract poor people, who were willing to be non-violent for a while, for a reason."[49] But he connects the question of violence to STO's long-standing analysis of dual consciousness, which

> exists in conflict in all people at the same time: the one, that tends to be subordinate, blaming itself for its oppressed condition, accepting it, and usually falling prey to religious ideas ("love thine enemy," "turn the other cheek," etc.). The other, the side that desires passionately to master its own fate and, in Fanon's words "embody history in his own person," is willing to do anything to turn the tables on its oppressor, to force him to stop forever.[50]

In this analysis, the unwillingness of the antinuclear movement to discuss the question of violence was a virtual guarantee of failure and irrelevance. Rubio bolsters his critique of nonviolence theory by challenging a then-popular text called *The Power of the People: Active Non-Violence in the United States*, published in 1977 with collaboration from a range of pacifist groups.[51] The book offered a history of North American movements for social change, emphasizing their nonviolent aspects. In Rubio's view, the book also distorted the historical record by ignoring parts that did not fit their narrative. In describing the struggle to end the Vietnam War, for instance, the authors failed to mention the protracted *military* struggle of the Vietnamese people against the occupying French and US forces. Similarly, the depiction of the black freedom movement during the sixties focused on the demise of the Student Non-Violent Coordinating Committee after its move toward black power, while Rubio emphasizes the subsequent rise of a range of militant black organizations that rejected nonviolence, most prominently the Black Panther Party. The popularity of the book as a primer for younger activists with less direct familiarity with the movements of the sixties was troubling for Rubio, and in his estimation added to the movement's demographic shortcomings while simultaneously misdirecting the discussion of strategy and tactics.

Morris's inaccuracy in terminology, he is correct in substance."
49   Ibid.
50   Ibid., 38.
51   Robert Cooney and Helen Michalowski, eds. *The Power of the People: Active Non-Violence in the United States* (Culver City, CA: Peace Press, 1977).

One reflection of the conflict between reformists and revolutionaries in the antinuclear movement was disagreement over the strategic function of direct action. The original escalating occupations model pioneered by the Clamshell Alliance was implicitly built on an assessment of the symbolic power of mass arrests, drawing inspiration from the perceived legacy of Gandhi and Martin Luther King. But as the movement took off, newer participants increasingly arrived with a belief in the power of occupation to actually physically prevent construction or to shut down nuclear plants. Movement historian Barbara Epstein, in discussing the movement against California's Diablo Canyon reactor, suggests that "probably most people in the Abalone [Alliance] never thought very clearly about what they meant by direct action. They knew that the blockade [of Diablo Canyon] itself was not likely to cause PG&E to close down the plant, but they were unwilling to adopt the cynical view that the blockade was simply a way of catching media attention."[52] For STO, given its conviction that revolutionary consciousness comes in large part from action, direct action to physically stop construction of nuclear plants was a necessary component of shifting the antinuclear movement away from pacifist reformism and toward a revolutionary anticapitalist and anti-imperialist outlook.

* * *

As STO's frustrations with national liberation solidarity work finally became insurmountable, a related shift was developing within the group's approach to tendency building inside the antinuclear movement. The group's antinuclear working group acknowledged the problem in the spring of 1980. Alan Rausch expressed concern that "our main and almost sole emphasis has been solidarity work," especially with the Black Hills Alliance, the Puerto Rican independence movement, and the South African and Namibian struggles.[53] Without jettisoning its commitment to anti-imperialism, the organization began

---

52   Epstein, *Political Protest*, 122. Epstein references an unpublished paper by Marcy Darnovsky as the source of some of this analysis; Darnovsky was herself a co-editor of *No Nukes Left!* in 1980, alongside (among many others) STO's Alan Rausch. It is also worth noting that Epstein's analysis incorporates a vision of nonviolent revolution that would have been rejected by Rubio and the rest of STO.

53   "Minutes from the Anti-Nuke Meeting, March 2, 1980," in *IDB* #16, May 1980,12.

to use the language of "left" or "revolutionary" approaches to the nuclear question. This allowed STO to reach out to a somewhat broader range of potential allies. As Carol Hayse argued at the time, "*confining* our work and understanding to anti-imperialist solidarity work had been a problem, and … what we are aiming at is broader. We want to do a whole range of stuff around confronting various tactics in the [movement] or lack of them, confronting bourgeois electoralism, single-issueism, domestic racism, etc. Hence the terminological change" from anti-imperialist to revolutionary.[54] The result was a deliberate shift toward working more directly with other like-minded radicals in the movement as opposed to pushing a specific anti-imperialist line. Viewed from a different angle, it represented a subtle but unmistakable change in how STO approached the tendency it hoped to build: where once the obvious participants were Prairie Fire and other anti-imperialists who could be recruited to *join* the antinuclear movement, now they might just as easily be social-ecology-style anarchists, less-than-orthodox Trotskyists, or radical feminists, all of whom were to be found already *within* the movement. At the same time, this broadening of horizons sewed the seeds of confusion within STO about the nature of the tendency-building project, as shall be seen shortly.

The most immediate outcome of this shift in perspective was STO's participation in the production of the first issue of the magazine *No Nukes Left!* (NNL!) in the summer of 1980. Put together by an unlikely assortment of antinuclear activists from all parts of the country, *NNL!* covered a wide range of topics, including racism's relationship to nuclear power, questions of nonviolence in the movement, and criticisms of electoral and legislative approaches to antinuclear struggles, among others. The interview with Ken Lawrence that had run the year before in *Urgent Tasks* was reprinted, alongside an interview with a key activist from the Harlem Fight Back! group that had led the attempt to add an antiracist slogan to the national rally that May. An official position paper from the Black Hills Alliance was included, along with a number of reports from the militant direct action wing of the movement. Alan Rausch collaborated on the production of the magazine, alongside social ecologists, native activists, and others. It was widely distributed within the antinuclear movement, but as an effort to cohere a "left" tendency inside the movement it did not really bear fruit, and the promised second issue never materialized.

---

54   Carol Hayse, "Yet Another Nuke Report, 3–80," in *IDB* #16, 18. Emphasis in original.

Nonetheless, STO's move to engage the left wing of the movement did produce some limited results, especially organizationally. A number of younger activists either joined STO or became close comrades around this time, and some of them arrived through direct experience with the group's participation in the antinuclear movement. Leslie Byster, for instance, recalls being pursued by STO when she was an activist in Madison, Wisconsin, focusing on antinuclear and pro-Native American struggles: "They actually came up and recruited me, rather than my seeking them out. Because the work I was doing, they saw it as valuable."[55] On a cultural level, STO's openness to developing subcultures, like punk rock, was encouraging to a newer generation of antinuclear activists whose touchstones were more likely to be the Clash than Woody Guthrie or even Jimi Hendrix. Further, the shift in emphasis from "anti-imperialist" to "left" was not limited to STO's participation in the antinuclear movement. By the beginning of 1982, an unsigned editorial in *Urgent Tasks* reflected on the group's efforts over the years to promote "a distinct tendency. Initially, we defined this tendency as 'anti-imperialist,' but our attempts to define it further and to consolidate it organizationally convinced us that it could not be developed out of those groups which labeled their politics as anti-imperialist."[56] The title of the editorial offered the newly preferred nomenclature, strikingly reminiscent of Hayse's comments on the group's tendency-building efforts in the antinuclear movement two years prior: "A Revolutionary Left."

Just as STO began to alter its understanding of the tendency it hoped to build, the antinuclear movement as a whole began a profound shift of its own. In the mid-seventies, when the movement against nuclear power was beginning the period of its greatest growth, the threat of nuclear war was relatively distant. As a result, according to Epstein,

> to the founders of the Clamshell, nuclear weapons seemed too large and too abstract to be a promising basis for building a mass movement. Nuclear power, on the other hand, was concrete and local. Unlike nuclear weapons, which threaten everyone more or less equally, nuclear power plants pose special dangers for those living near them. Furthermore, victories seemed more easily attainable in the arena

---

55   Leslie Byster, interview with author, September 16, 2006.
56   "A Revolutionary Left," in *Urgent Tasks* #13, Spring 1982, 41.

of nuclear power. It is easier to halt the construction of a
particular plant than to take on the arms race.[57]

The election of Ronald Reagan as president in November of 1980,
alongside the rise of Margaret Thatcher in Britain and the increasingly
militarized and bellicose character of the Soviet Union under Brezhnev,
rapidly changed the calculus. Suddenly the issue of nuclear power was
overshadowed by the immediate question of nuclear weapons, as millions
of people worldwide became convinced that nuclear war was imminent.

As Rausch recalls it years later, "If we use books as a guide, we went
from *No Nukes* (1980) to *Protest and Survive* (late 1980)."[58] The former
was a militant but reformist guide to the antinuclear movement produced by veterans of the Clamshell Alliance, while the latter was a call for
nuclear disarmament from the prominent British radical historian E.P.
Thompson. Thompson's contribution was not so much in demonstrating
the importance of the issue, but rather in offering an optimistic take on
the possibilities of a mass movement that could successfully resist the arms
race. A number of the left forces previously active against nuclear power,
including STO, quickly pivoted toward the question of nuclear weapons.

In many ways, this transition was a return to more familiar terrain
for STO. Disarmament discussions naturally led to questions of non-
nuclear military activity, especially the Reagan administration's rapidly
escalating attacks on national liberation movements in Central America.
In fact, the first major left demonstration of the Reagan era was a 60,000
person rally in Washington, DC against US intervention in El Salvador,
Nicaragua, and Guatemala, known as the People's Anti-War Mobilization (PAM). Despite STO's frustration with its previous involvement in
anti-imperialist solidarity efforts, the group participated actively in the
movement, initiating a National Anti-War Fraction (NAWF) to coordinate efforts throughout the organization. The NAWF's initial emphasis
was on helping plan the PAM, which was the brainchild of the small and
sectarian Worker's World Party but had drawn involvement from a wide
range of progressive and left groups. Viewing the demonstration itself
as a success, the organizers followed up with a call for an "All-People's
Congress" (APC), to be held in Detroit the following October. Fraction members, especially in Kansas City and Chicago, remained active
in the build-up to the APC. Gone for the most part were the anarchists,
environmentalists, and pacifists who had dominated antinuclear work,

---

57   Epstein, *Political Protest*, 82.
58   Alan Rausch, email to author, February 1, 2011.

replaced with a cast of characters more reminiscent of the group's earlier work in the Leninist and anti-imperialist milieus.

* * *

Organizing around PAM and the APC also revealed some developing tensions within STO that in some ways were reminiscent of prior splits in the group's history. The bulk of STO's leg-work in advance of the APC was taken on by the group's National Anti-War Fraction, but when people arrived in Detroit, more senior members of the organization took over the primary responsibility for networking with potential allies at the conference. This led to criticism from the Fraction that "there are STO members and STO members. Some people are leaders and the rest of us are something else."[59] Part of the problem had to do with the persistence of informal hierarchies and the geographic dispersal of the group, but the conflict was also reflective of the limitations of STO's shifting approach to tendency building. Coalescing a tendency in this milieu came to be perceived more as a form of "left" work than as a way of engaging in "mass" struggles. In this context, networking was almost a goal in itself, and was often aided by the personal connections older members had built up over the decades. The fact that the APC was a conference in search of a campaign—the only real decisions to come out of it related to a national day of "resistance" against Reagan's agenda—did not help matters.

The criticism of STO's informal hierarchy by the NAWF in the fall of 1981 was part of a torrent of conflict around poor communication and lines of authority within the organization. Two Kansas City-based members of the Fraction, Carol Loretz and Randy Gould, eventually resigned from the role of "national coordinator" they had shared with one member based in Chicago. They enumerated their frustrations with STO's internal functioning in a series of reports and letters over the spring and summer of 1982. Similar criticisms emerged from members based in Portland and Seattle around the same time. One recurring concern was that STO's Central Committee (CC), made up entirely of Chicago-based leading members of the group, functioned as a proxy for the informal hierarchy that persisted in the group. The by-then notorious inability of the CC to communicate its decisions to the rest of the organization only

---

59   Randy Gould, "Criticism of STO's Functioning," in *IDB* #25, December 1981, 66.

made things worse.[60] Loretz and Gould, in particular, chafed at the ways in which their attempts to take initiative within the antiwar milieu were constrained, and sometimes overruled, by people (on the CC) who were not themselves actively involved in antiwar organizing.[61] Underlying this criticism was a belief that some members of the CC and/or the informal leadership were more interested in the bureaucratic work of running STO and coalescing a left tendency than they were in engaging in direct political activity. While the dysfunction on the CC served as evidence against the latter claim, it was undeniably the case by the early eighties that the organization overall was floundering in its efforts to influence broader social movements like the antiwar movement.

In fact, STO routinely made strategic decisions that could be seen as undermining its own organizational viability, all based on the assumption that cadre organizations (like STO itself) were less important to the revolutionary process than were mass organizations. The decision to prioritize tendency building over and against the group's previous emphasis on party building was reflective of this organizational modesty. As Hamerquist argued at the end of 1979, "we are not premising our work as an organization on what is most likely to make STO grow or what would make our individual activity more satisfying, but what has strategic centrality for the revolution.… The work which arguably would do the most to build STO is not the strategically central work."[62] Even as the group focused more and more heavily on tendency building in the early eighties, the emphasis was increasingly on facilitating the success of mass movements rather than on the growth or even the organizational stability of STO itself.

Ironically, the continuing issues around poor communication and unclear lines of authority were perceived by many in the leadership of the group as a reflection of "a lack of understanding of the nature and importance of our organization, and consequently of the importance of our growth and development for the development of a revolutionary

---

60   The Central Committee itself acknowledged this problem more than once. For instance, in the summer of 1982, a position paper (drafted by Ignatin) began by noting that "the CC has for some time been functioning poorly." In *Special Supplement to IDB*, August 1982, 55.

61   Gould has reiterated these criticisms in correspondence and interviews with the author.

62   Don Hamerquist, "Anti-Imperialist Tendency & Production Concentration," in *IDB* #13, November 1979, 6.

movement in this country."[63] Early in 1981, STO's Central Committee attempted to address the "sense of malaise and drift" that was causing real concern among the membership by reflecting on the group's position within the broader trends of the post-sixties left. Part of the problem, the Committee argued, was the failure of many members to take initiative in areas of political work where the leadership of STO was not providing clear direction. Of course, this simply reversed the blame assigned by those who believed their attempts to take initiative were stifled by the demands of the leadership to micromanage all areas of political work.

A more evenhanded, and strikingly prescient, response to STO's internal crisis was presented by long-time leading member Carole Travis. In 1981, she argued that the group had long been too small, but that this problem had actually borne fruit in a way: "As a result of our over-extended hard work for many years in many areas, we have finally earned a well deserved good name."[64] But to capitalize on this opportunity, STO desperately needed to grow. Failure to do so would ensure that the group would fail to meet its increasing commitments to various social movements, and "our opportunities will hang us rather than enable us to extend our influence."[65] Travis went so far as to offer a sort of doomsday scenario based on what she perceived as a perpetually unexamined problem of limited size:

> The continued long-term smallness of the group has led necessarily to a questioning of the form of continued political existence. It is not expressed openly anywhere in the form of responsibly tackling these questions, but rather expresses itself by individualism, periodic depression, elements of cynicism, interpersonal tensions, small group interpersonal dynamics, the operation of male chauvinism and male

---

63 Central Committee and Bureau of Organization, "On Organization," in *IDB* #21, January 1981, 2. The "Bureau of Organization," to which there are no other references in the STO documents at my disposal, may have been a humorous reference to the Organization Bureau (Orgburo), a key committee used by Stalin in his consolidation of power within the Communist Party of the Soviet Union during the early twenties. See Leonard Schapiro, *The Communist Party of the Soviet Union* (New York: Vintage Books, 1964), 240–241.

64 Carole Travis, "On Recruiting," in Secret Supplement to *IDB* #24, September 1981, 37.

65 Ibid.

> supremacy, all to some extent exacerbated by the inevitable
> gross dissatisfaction of operating on a level which is doomed
> to failure without expansion. It is not healthy, intelligent,
> rational or useful. STO must grow or transform or we may
> dissolve, fragment or explode.[66]

In the event, the group failed to grow and within two years it had fragmented, only to subsequently dissolve fully. Several of the items on Travis's list—cynicism, interpersonal tensions, and more—manifested themselves in the process.

In the midst of this internal crisis, STO's approach to antiwar organizing became more scattershot as the decade progressed, although the tendency-building concept still appeared to provide a solid foundation. The group devoted significant attention to the Second Special Session on Disarmament held at the United Nations in New York City in June of 1982, where the planning for a massive antiwar rally in Central Park revealed issues of racism in the movement eerily reminiscent of those that emerged during the run-up to the 1980 demonstration against nuclear power described earlier. STO simultaneously became more engaged in campaigns against US military intervention in Central America, often carried out in local coalitions like Kansas City's Committee Against War and Imperialism, or in the local branches of national formations like the Committee In Solidarity with the People of El Salvador. The NAWF produced a broadsheet intended for mass distribution, entitled *Battlecry*, although only one issue was published before the recurrent problems of bad communication derailed subsequent numbers.

The overall situation called to mind the concept of the "get rich quick scheme," which had been used inside STO for several years as a shorthand critique of this sort of scrambling effort to find viable avenues for work.[67] In some ways, the entire history of STO was a continuing attempt to identify sites of potential revolutionary rupture and to intervene productively in those areas. The original approach had been

---

66 Ibid., 38.

67 Don Hamerquist used the term as far back as 1979, in response to early estimates that SAMRAF was a viable alternative to the group's previous focus on the Puerto Rican independence movement. "National Committee Notes," in *IDB* #10, April 1979, 10. Years later, Noel Ignatiev used the term to describe most of STO's political activity after the end of its initial workplace era in 1974. Interview with the author, January 2006.

industrial concentration in the context of the independent labor activity of the late sixties and early seventies. When the upsurge faltered, STO began a continuing search for the next big thing—party building, anti-imperialist solidarity, intellectual development, tendency building, reproductive rights, and the carrousel of antinuclear, antiwar, and antifascist struggles. All were carefully thought through, debated inside the group, and approached with a fairly clear strategic orientation toward developing their revolutionary potentials. But the increasingly rapid shifts led to heightened confusion and frustration among members of the group, especially when the contentious decision to re-establish the original emphasis on workplace organizing failed to produce any real gains, either for the group or for the workers they interacted with (for more on this see Chapter Eight). The cultural and political tidal wave later known as the Reagan Revolution added to the internal difficulties and further dampened morale. As the decade advanced, two inadvertently competing notions of STO's future would develop, one focusing on the theoretical and practical development of a left tendency, the other prioritizing direct action and mass illegality. At least initially, the momentum of the former placed tendency building front and center.

* * *

Having long-since abandoned the original vision of a tendency populated by groups like the Prairie Fire Organizing Committee, STO further refined its ideas on a "revolutionary left" tendency. In particular, the group became more concerned about "rightward drift" within not only the antiwar milieu but in a range of progressive movements. Especially in light of Reagan's election, many veterans of the movements of the seventies began to focus on electoral campaigns and other reformist approaches to struggle. In a speech given at the end of 1981, STO member Maryon Gray noted that "STO feels that at this time it is important to counter this drift to the right by coalescing a revolutionary left tendency within the communist movement. We think that such a tendency exists but generally in the form of small isolated groups or individuals."[68] To the extent that the tendency did exist, the group believed that five key points defined its political basis for unity. Not surprisingly, these

---

68   Maryon Gray, "Current Debates Within STO: Speech given in the Twin Cities, Dec. 12, 1981," in *Urgent Tasks* #13, Spring 1982, 10. Gray specifies "the rightward drift of the left" in the context of both the women's movement and the antiwar movement.

included an analysis of white supremacy that foregrounded white skin privilege, an awareness of the low ebb of popular movements that characterized the era, a rejection of "order" and "legality" as norms for the struggle, an acknowledgement of the leading role in struggle played by women, and a conviction that "socialism (communism) grows out of and embodies the creative self-emancipation of the working class."[69] The group's earlier insistence on anti-imperialism remained visible only in a reference to the importance of "autonomous movements of nationally oppressed peoples."[70]

To advance the development of the tendency, STO began to promote the idea of a conference that could bring the isolated component parts of the tendency together face to face. At the same time, the group began publishing the *Tendency Newsletter*, a roughly produced magazine containing a mixture of reprinted reports on local activity and analysis of national efforts like PAM, the APC, and the Central Park demonstration. While clearly reflective of STO's influence, it did manage to include regular submissions from other groups and from independent leftists. Of course, the tendency-building effort was not limited to just these two projects. Noel Ignatin, by then one of the leading proponents within the STO of the tendency concept, suggested that "in all work, it is necessary to demonstrate that [the] tendency is a living idea, not an abstraction."[71]

Nonetheless, despite talk of a conference and the appearance of the *Newsletter*, there was little common understanding within STO about what the tendency was, or how to develop it. Some in the group viewed the tendency as a sort of membership organization that various grassroots groups could join, not unlike a version of PAM with better politics.[72] This view was seemingly bolstered by the inclusion of the five "Points of Agreement" in most issues of the *Newsletter*. But a committee established to guide internal activity around the tendency described as "erroneous"

---

69   The five points were reprinted repeatedly, but appeared for the first time in the editorial in *Tendency Newsletter* #1 (n.d., but c. January 1982), 6–7.

70   Ibid.

71   "Summary of Tendency Discussion—National Committee Meeting, Chicago, September 17, 18, 19, 1982," in *IDB* #29, December 1982, 18.

72   For example, Carol Loretz drafted a document entitled "Why CAWI Should Join the Tendency," which appeared in *IDB* #25, December 1981, 42.

the idea of recruitment and formal membership.[73] Ignatin, meanwhile argued that the tendency itself should not be viewed as a membership organization, but that the outcome of successful tendency building might include a form of "regroupment" in which STO proper would cease to exist. Thus, he hoped that the group would "undertake this initiative with a view toward emerging from the process as part of a larger organization."[74] Quite apart from any organizational patriotism that might have led members to oppose Ignatin's stated goal, his conception of the tendency was also seen by some members to prioritize discussion at the expense of action. By the early eighties, STO was known on the far left as much for its Dialectics Course as for its work in mass movements, and many people in the group were concerned that the approach to tendency as networking and regroupment was likely to exacerbate this dubious reputation.

This fear dovetailed with one side of a debate then emerging within STO regarding the relative importance of "left work" and "mass work." Much of the group's involvement in the antinuclear movement, as well as subsequent participation in local and regional antiwar organizing, as well as parallel work around women's issues and reproductive rights, was conceived of as engagement with mass movements.[75] By contrast, the *Newsletter* was identified from the beginning as part of an attempt to build a tendency among self-identified revolutionaries who were already at least somewhat familiar with STO's politics and history.[76] In this context, there was a disconnect between the group's stated vision for the tendency and its primary tendency-building activities. Discussions of the tendency within STO routinely "emphasized joint action potential over line/theoretical agreement. The test of the tendency is its ability to act together in a fight."[77] Nonetheless, the most tangible steps

73   "Tendency Discussion, March 1982 NC," in *Notes from the March 1982 National Committee Meeting* (a "For Members Only" supplement to the *IDB*).

74   Noel Ignatin, "On the 'Tendency,'" in *IDB* #28, September 1982, 7.

75   Bill Lamme, "On the Left/Mass Discussion in Anti-War Work," in *IDB* #28, September 1982, 62–63.

76   The brief introduction to the first issue of the *Newsletter*, for example, indicates that "this [newsletter] will not be publicly distributed," *Newsletter* #1 (n.d., but c. January 1982), 2.

77   "Tendency Discussion, March 1982 NC," *Notes from the March 1982 National Committee Meeting* (a "For Members Only" supplement to the *IDB*).

the group took toward the development of the tendency highlighted more theoretical aspects of the process. For instance, while most of the material that appeared in the *Newsletter* reflected on a range of actions, campaigns, and projects that amounted to mass work, it was clear that the reflections themselves were a form of left work. In addition, the time involved in producing and distributing the *Newsletter* was substantial, and in the context of concerns about the relative priority of discussion over action, it only exacerbated fears that STO was being progressively transformed into what Bill Lamme would later call "the best debating society on the left."[78]

In an attempt to head off this possibility, Lamme and other members of STO worked to ensure that the proposed conference would be attended not by armchair radicals but by "activists interested in theoretical questions," and that the conference materials would "attempt to make a connection between theory and practice."[79] By the time the conference actually took place in 1983, the idea behind it was already several years old. Originally conceived as a sort of summit between STO and one or more other small revolutionary groups (with an eye to possible organizational merger or regroupment), the concept gradually changed in ways that paralleled the group's shifting approach to tendency building. Drawing on connections made through STO's involvement in the antinuclear and antiwar movements of the preceding years, a conference planning committee was established that featured a variety of far-left groups, all smaller in size than STO, but most of them involved in the various struggles of the time. Indeed, in an attempt to bridge the left/mass divide, the invitation to the conference began by emphasizing "the failure of left-initiated attempts to generate mass activity throughout the past decade."[80]

Regardless of the activist credentials of the participants, the conference was squarely focused on a series of more analytical and theoretical questions. The invitation targeted a range of activists who rejected both Stalinism and Social Democracy, and summarized the overall theme of the conference as "New Trends in Capital and the Implications for State and Society."[81] Questions of joint activity were deferred because "such

---

78   Bill Lamme, interview with the author, July 20, 2005.

79   "Summary of Tendency Discussion—National Committee Meeting, Chicago, September 17, 18, 19, 1982," in *IDB* #29, December 1982, 19.

80   "Invitation Letter, October 28, 1982," in *IDB* #29, December 1982, 9.

81   Ibid, 10.

a discussion is best undertaken after we have explored our immediate context."[82]

At the same time, the topics under discussion were so broad that the conference itself could only serve as a beginning of needed debate, with the clear hope that continuing the conversation afterward would also help build the tendency. In the end, a depressingly telling title was chosen for the conference itself: "No Easy Answers Left."

The conference was attended by approximately 120 people from all parts of the United States, as well as a handful from overseas.[83] Structured around a series of plenary panels, the conference aimed to focus discussion around key topics while still scheduling time for small group conversations. Written versions of several speeches were circulated in advance of the conference, which was especially helpful in a number of situations where scheduled speakers were not able to be present for a variety of reasons. Still, according to at least one evaluation, "plenary discussions were frequently difficult and frustrating."[84] This was due in part to lax facilitation that allowed conversations to wander, and in part to the hazy line between sharp debate and sectarianism. Many participants appeared to consider the conference as a whole to be a failure, largely as a result of the intensity of disagreement and the difficulty of connecting the conference discussions to any forms of joint activity. Leslie Byster, for example, remembers it as "a black hole" that sucked in enormous efforts without producing much of anything.[85] At least one project did emerge from the proceedings, however: an antiwar speaking and organizing tour of Europe that took place late in 1983, targeting both active-duty military personnel and European activists.[86] Nonetheless, the conference was really the last hurrah for the wing of STO that advocated a strong focus on theoretical issues, organizational regroupment, and left tendency building. In the aftermath, power within the group shifted sharply toward a faction that emphasized direct action, mass activity, and a radical break with the limitations of the organization's previous orientation.

---

82   Bill Lamme, "Conference Evaluation," in *Discussion Bulletin* #32, June 1983, 21.

83   Mailing list of conference attendees, in author's possession.

84   Bill Lamme, "Conference Evaluation," in *Discussion Bulletin* #32, June 1983, 22.

85   Leslie Byster, interview with the author, September 16, 2006.

86   Bill Lamme, "Conference Evaluation," in *Discussion Bulletin* #32, June 1983, 23. See also the disarmament newsletter prepared for the tour, "About Face," October 1983.

* * *

In the years preceding the conference, Don Hamerquist had been among the most prominent theoreticians in STO. He was assigned the responsibility to present the group's semi-official position paper on the nature of the period. His final draft was a two-dozen-page, single-spaced treatise, full of careful analysis of what he argued was a "secular crisis" in the functioning of capitalism. While the content of the paper itself was reflective of STO's ongoing discussions and might have made a major contribution to the *No Easy Answers Left* conference, Hamerquist did not make it to New York to present his findings.[87] Instead, while driving east from Chicago with a trunk full of propaganda, discussion papers, and other written material he had helped produce at C&D Printshop, the front axle of his car snapped in two. While no one was seriously injured in the accident, the car was a total wreck. Janeen Porter was traveling in the vehicle at the time, and recalls that the trunk flew open and a substantial portion of the printed matter scattered across the Pennsylvania Turnpike. Neither Porter nor Hamerquist has forgotten the sight of the State Trooper who, having verified the safety of the car's occupants, spent half an hour running up and down the highway retrieving the papers that littered the ground.

Porter in particular had been skeptical of the value of the conference, and was dismayed by what she perceived as STO's focus on discussion at the expense of direct action. For her, the accident was a blessing in disguise, since she didn't have to attend a conference she expected to be a failure. It was also something of a metaphor for the end of an era in the group's existence. Never again would STO focus the same level of energy on tendency building from a standpoint of theory rather than practice. And Hamerquist would join Porter as a leading member of the faction that pushed the group toward its final phase.

---

87   The description of events in this paragraph comes from interviews with Janeen Porter and Don Hamerquist, September 14, 2006. The basic outline was initially provided by Bill Lamme, interview with the author, July 20, 2005.

Chapter Eight: Autonomy in STO: From Dialectics to Diabolics

Chicago, which remained the geographic and political center of STO throughout the group's existence, was never more in the political spotlight than during the mayoral election in the winter and spring of 1983. The city had a lengthy history of highly corrupt politics, with the local Democratic Party maintaining tight, one-party control over the apparatus of government; this arrangement was commonly shorthanded as "the machine." Richard J. Daley had been the mayor for twenty-one years at the time of his death in 1976, by which time he had successfully consolidated all operations of the machine under his direct control.[1] City services, government employment opportunities, and other prizes were doled out to neighborhoods in proportion to the support Daley and his allies received at election time, with one major exception. African Americans constituted roughly 40 percent of the population but were marginal to both the economic and the political mechanisms of power in the city. Chicago also had long been extremely segregated along racial lines, and Daley's administration institutionalized the sort of quality-of-life disparities that made the city the target of Martin Luther King's short-lived northern campaign in 1966.[2] Everything from garbage collection and

---

1   For more on the first Mayor Daley, see Adam Cohen and Elizabeth Taylor, *American Pharaoh: Mayor Richard J. Daley—His Battle for Chicago and the Nation* (New York: Back Bay, 2001).

2   Taylor Branch, *At Canaan's Edge: America in the King Years, 1965–1968*

building inspection to infrastructure and public schooling were of lower quality in black neighborhoods than in white neighborhoods. In short, the machine exemplified STO's idea of white skin privilege, even after Daley's death forced a necessary reorganization of control.

In this context, the sudden rise of Harold Washington in 1983 was shocking. Washington had been a successful black politician on the south side of Chicago, serving as both a state representative and a US congressman, but he had never run for any elected office in a district that was not overwhelmingly African American. Once he began his campaign for mayor, he received overwhelming support from the black community, but only token interest in white and latino neighborhoods. The two other candidates in the Democratic Party primary on February 22, incumbent Jane Byrne and newcomer Richard M. Daley, the son of the deceased former mayor, were both white and represented rival factions of the machine. As the contest heated up, the white left—both locally and across the country—began to pay attention to the racial dynamics, and overwhelmingly supported Washington. In many ways, the Washington campaign was a precursor to radical support for Jesse Jackson's "rainbow coalition" campaign for president the following year.[3]

But there were exceptions to this left enthusiasm for Washington. The Movement for National Liberation (MLN), which had always maintained an abstentionist approach to US electoral politics, resisted efforts to mobilize the Puerto Rican community in support of any of the three candidates, and did not make any exception for Washington based on his race or his political platform.[4] A mayoral debate was scheduled to take place on January 31 at Roberto Clemente High School, in the largely Puerto Rican neighborhood of Humboldt Park, and the MLN decided to picket the event in protest. Shortly before the debate, STO was invited to join the MLN's demonstration. After a brief discussion, the Chicago branch decided to participate on the condition that it could distribute its own leaflet, aimed at progressives who were considering voting for

---

(New York: Simon and Schuster, 2006), 235–241 and 500–522, describes the racial aspects of the Chicago machine as well as King's attempts to organize in the North.

3   This connection is made directly in Max Elbaum, *Revolution in the Air*, 275–281.

4   One factor here may have been that while the Puerto Rican Socialist Party was in serious decline at that point, the remnants of the Party in Chicago were actively supporting Washington's candidacy. Jose Lopez, interview with the author, October 18, 2008.

Washington. The distribution of this leaflet caused a minor shit-storm on the far left in Chicago, as well as a major crisis inside an already weakened STO.

The leaflet itself was a text-heavy document, addressed "To Activists Who Think That Working for Harold Washington Is a Way to Build a Movement for Social Change."[5] It began with a sharp dismissal of those backing Byrne and Daley, noting that "support for either of them obviously means support for the traditional, racist, anti-popular politics that have prevailed in Chicago for decades." From there, the leaflet took two approaches. First, it argued that Washington's platform was politically indefensible because it was largely identical to that of his competitors, especially on issues of racism. "In fact," the leaflet crowed, "we challenge anyone to delete the names of the various speakers and then determine, from the text of the debates, which speaker is which!" This was clearly an exaggeration, although Washington's campaign did tack somewhat to the right politically in a (largely futile) effort to gain white support. Second, and more compellingly, the leaflet complained that Washington was running a very traditional electoral campaign that accepted support from grassroots and left forces without engaging in "genuine dialogue with any sector of the community." It compared the 1960s campaigns of Mississippi Freedom Democratic Party congressional candidate Fannie Lou Hamer, "who ran on a program determined by open forums and discussions at the grassroots," with the more recent and less encouraging experiences of cities like Newark, Detroit, and Atlanta, each of which elected "a representative of old-line official politics who happens personally to be a member of an oppressed racial group."[6] While the positive reference to Hamer evaded the question of generalized anti-electoralism that the MLN foregrounded, STO's leaflet represented a firm criticism of Washington from the left.

The leafleting action drew immediate negative response from people both inside and outside STO. Three main issues emerged from the barrage of criticism. First, in the eyes of many, the leaflet failed to acknowledge the antiracist content of (white) support for Washington. Steve Whitman, a local white antiracist activist with strong ties to STO, mocked the group's inattentiveness to the racial question by suggesting

---

5   The leaflet is reproduced in *IDB* #31, April 1983, 61. All quotes in this paragraph come from the leaflet.

6   For more on Fannie Lou Hamer, see Chana Kai Lee, *For Freedom's Sake: The Life of Fannie Lou Hamer* (Urbana, IL: University of Illinois Press, 1999).

it change its name: "perhaps the 'Jane Byrne Organization' would work better as a name indicative of their politics."[7] STO member Bill Lamme criticized the leaflet for focusing solely on Washington's stated positions instead of looking at the bigger picture of popular attitudes. Ira Churgin, also a member of STO, argued forcefully that "in Chicago today when a white person wears a Washington button, or displays a poster … it means, and is taken to mean, just one thing—that person is opposed to racism."[8] This dynamic became even more clear after Washington won the primary, and almost all sectors of the white-led Democratic Party machine suddenly switched allegiance to back the previously marginal candidate of the Republican Party, Bernard Epton, whose main redeeming feature was his whiteness.

Second, the decision to distribute the leaflet in the Puerto Rican community was widely criticized, largely because of STO's all-white demographic makeup. Churgin put it bluntly: "it was stupid for a white group to go into a Puerto Rican neighborhood to leaflet white progressives about a Black candidate."[9] One prominent Puerto Rican activist not in the MLN wrote an angry letter denouncing STO for disrupting the efforts she and others were making to use the Washington campaign to "open discussions about racism between Blacks and Latinos, and how we need to unite and organize because in our unity lies our strength."[10] A major part of the problem was the vaguely defined target audience of STO's leaflet. While Churgin and others inside STO clearly believed it was aimed at white leftists, the leaflet itself only mentions "activists." Many Puerto Ricans and African Americans fitting that description were no doubt present at Clemente High School when the leaflet was distributed and could easily have perceived the leaflet as having been aimed at them. Of course, STO was only at the debate as a result of a request from the MLN, but Lamme noted that "using the MLN invitation to shield ourselves from such criticism is failing to take responsibility for our own actions."[11] As an alternative, he pointed out, "we could easily have found a Washington-only event in a white neighborhood within a week's time."[12]

---

7   Steve Whitman, "Dear Zulma" letter CC'd to STO and reprinted in *IDB* #31, 77.

8   Ira Churgin, "STO and Washington," in *IDB* #31, 63.

9   Ibid., 63.

10   Zulma Ortiz Berria, letter to Bill Lamme, in *IDB* #31, 62.

11   Bill Lamme, "On the Washington Leaflet," in *IDB* #31, 66.

12   Ibid.

The third main criticism of the leaflet had to do with its revolutionary tenor. While a majority of STO's local members clearly agreed that progressive support for the Washington campaign was part of the rightward drift of the US left, there was internal disagreement on how to respond. Churgin accused his own organization of "Sparticist behavior," referring to the small and hyper-sectarian Trotskyist group the Sparticist League, insofar as STO was "sabotage[ing] the work of other progressives because we disagree with it or think we know better."[13] This criticism no doubt stung, but it was inconsistent, considering Churgin's own participation in STO's long history of presenting a critical left challenge to a range of progressive organizations, from labor unions to women's rights organizations to the MLN itself. Janeen Porter flipped this issue on its head, arguing that white leftists who supported Washington "use anti-racism to cover up their bad politics."[14] Churgin was on more solid ground when he suggested that "our effort was not really designed to raise the issue or encourage debate, but was our attempt to go on the record and keep our revolutionary credentials clean."[15] Certainly, as Lamme and others pointed out, STO had failed to address the significance of the Washington campaign until less than a month before the primary. This was especially ironic for an organization that prided itself on emphasizing attentiveness to black struggles, given that Washington's campaign was the largest upsurge of organized political activity in the city's black community in more than a dozen years.

In the face of all this criticism, the Chicago branch of STO spent significant time reviewing its actions and reformulating its position. Things were complicated by the fact that one leading local member of STO, Marilyn Katz, not only supported the Washington campaign, but was actually employed as its media director. Katz had been a founding member of STO more than a decade before, had quit the group shortly after when she moved to Los Angeles, and had subsequently moved back to Chicago, rejoining STO around 1980. By 1983, she was on the group's Central Committee and had a leading role in the group's relationship to both the reproductive rights movement and to anti-Klan and antifascist struggles. After accepting the job with the Washington campaign, she became less attentive to her organizational duties, and eventually took a leave of absence from STO. She finally left the group for good when

---

13   Churgin, "STO and Washington," 63.

14   "STO National Committee Minutes, February 13, 1983—Harold Washington Campaign," in *IDB #*31, 41–42.

15   Churgin, "STO and Washington," 63.

it became clear that her enthusiasm for the campaign was not shared by most members.[16] No one else in STO had a strongly pro-Washington position, though many—including most members from the Pacific Northwest—felt that his election would be basically beneficial to the regrowth of black struggles in Chicago and across the country. Years later, Bill Lamme remembers the appeal of supporting Washington as having been the excitement of potentially "winning," despite the problematic content of the victory. In his words, the thing "that can always distract us from pursuing revolutionary activity is to get involved in a liberal thing that is attractive partly because it has a lot more people in it. And in this case it was more attractive because it looked like it could win, and in fact did."[17]

Indeed, Washington surprised many by winning the Democratic primary, having successfully split the machine vote between Byrne and Daley. The focus then shifted to the general election, where he faced a surprisingly stiff challenge from Epton, who was backed publicly or privately by the entire machine. Washington had pledged to replace the white police chief, which led many white cops to support Epton, reinforcing perceptions of the police department as racist. The small but growing fascist movement in Chicago encouraged white resistance to Washington, but did not embrace Epton because he was Jewish. In this potentially explosive environment, the Chicago branch of STO decided to distribute a leaflet telling white voters not to support Epton, because "a vote for Epton will be a clear signal to Blacks that white people stand on the side of maintaining business as usual."[18] Still, the leaflet did not encourage people to vote for Washington, because "no politician, including Washington, is going to stop business as usual for the banks and corporations. To do that would require breaking the law. And politicians, including Washington, uphold the law."[19]

The question of legality was in some ways the central issue for many in STO. After the primary, the majority of the Chicago branch adopted a formal position on the campaign, which noted that "the movement for Washington is not autonomous in any meaningful sense... certainly not from the state....It is not militant, not based on mass active

---

16   The leave of absence is noted in the letter from Marilyn Katz to "Dear National Council Members," in *IDB* #31, 59. Her subsequent departure from the organization was described by Bill Lamme, interview with the author, July 20, 2005.

17   Bill Lamme, interview with the author, July 20, 2005.

18   "Thinking of Voting for Epton?" leaflet, in *IDB* #31, 73.

19   Ibid.

participation, not anti-capitalist or even anti-corporate, and certainly not class conscious. Its premises are parliamentary legality, 'good government,' interest group politics and class collaboration."[20] STO's view stood in stark contrast to the perspective of many other leftists, who saw Washington as the product of a resurgent and autonomous black movement.[21] Nonetheless, as the concept of autonomy grew in importance inside STO during the early eighties, the group focused more clearly on the differences between reform and revolution within social struggles. Illegality and violence were in the air at the time, despite, or possibly because of, the rise of Reagan and the New Right. Beyond the direct action tactics of the antinuclear and antiwar movements, mass—and seemingly spontaneous—uprisings dotted the landscape. Miami, Florida, in 1980, and Brixton, near London, England in 1981, experienced riots aimed squarely at racist police. Germany, Denmark, the Netherlands, Switzerland, and other parts of western Europe were home to a growing autonomist movement for which squatting and street fights with cops were both commonplace activities.[22] Poland was still under martial law as the Soviet client state attempted to suppress one of the most vibrant autonomous working-class movements on the planet, *Solidarność*. All these experiences, among many others, contributed to the maturation of STO's understanding of autonomy, but its origins stretched back more than a decade, and were internal to the group as well as external.

* * *

---

20   "Adopted Stance," in *IDB #*31, 72.

21   A decade earlier, STO had published as a pamphlet a speech given by Richard Hatcher, the black mayor of Gary, Indiana. In 1983, Hatcher was still mayor, and Gary was not the hotbed of revolution STO had hoped it would become. It is possible that the bitterness of this experience influenced the group's negative response to Washington. Richard Hatcher, "…And We Shall Take With Us the Best…," (Chicago: STO, c. 1972), pamphlet in author's possession.

22   For more on Miami, see Bruce Porter and Marvin Dunn, *The Miami Riot of 1980: Crossing the Bounds* (Lexington MA: Lexington Books, 1984); on Brixton, see *We Want to Riot Not to Work: The 1981 Brixton Uprisings* (London: Riot Not to Work Collective, 1982); for continental Europe's autonomist movement, see George Katsiaficas, *The Subversion of Politics: European Autonomous Social Movements and the Decolonization of Everyday Life* (Atlantic Highlands, NJ: Humanities Press, 1997).

On some level, the concept of autonomy had been a defining part of STO's political theory since the group's inception at the end of the sixties. The idea of dual consciousness that the group laid out as early as 1971, in *Toward a Revolutionary Party*, implied a process whereby, through struggles in the workplace, the proletarian side of workers' consciousness becomes progressively more autonomous from the previously hegemonic bourgeois aspect. Gramsci himself had described the worker's individual process of developing class consciousness as one "whose elementary and primitive phase is to be found in the sense of being 'different' and 'apart,' in an instinctive feeling of independence, and which progresses to the level of real possession of a single and coherent conception of the world."[23] For STO, the purpose of existing as a revolutionary group (and eventually, it long hoped, as a revolutionary party) was "to discover and articulate" the independent instinct that Gramsci had noted.[24] In particular, "the party must assume some responsibility for the translation of individual resentment and resistance into collective action."[25] While this initial understanding of the party's leadership role mitigated somewhat against STO's later embrace of the full meaning of autonomy, it nonetheless indicated the group's developing analysis of the concept that would eventually characterize its approach to struggle.

An extended quotation from *Toward a Revolutionary Party* can help shed light on the complexity of the strategic conception that flowed from STO's understanding of dual consciousness. After criticizing a range of alternative party building efforts, from the Communist Party USA, the Socialist Workers Party, and the Revolutionary Union, among others, STO lays out the fundamental basis for its own approach:

> In our view, the primary role of the party in the mass movement is to discover and articulate the patterns of thought, action, and organization which embody the potential of workers to make a revolution. These patterns are manifested, embryonically, in the course of every genuine struggle. The characteristic content of mass struggle provides the only possible social basis for integrating the experiences of masses of workers into a coherent revolutionary ideology and culture. The real work of the party involves linking these

---

23   Antonio Gramsci, "The Study of Philosophy," in *The Prison Notebooks*, 333.

24   *TARP*, 26.

25   Ibid.

fragmentary autonomous elements and socializing them into a new culture of struggle. This means that the party must emphasize and develop those forms of struggle which show workers the possibility of relying on their own collective solidarity and strength, not on capitalist legality and bureaucratic procedures; it must emphasize these programs which lay the basis for the unification of the working class. Particularly important in this regard are concrete challenges to the institution and ideology of white supremacy. Our perspective aims at the development of an anti-capitalist dual power as the engine for the transformation of the mass reform struggle into a mass revolutionary movement. This dual power constitutes a revolutionary social bloc that exists within the framework of capitalism without ever acquiescing in the legitimacy or the permanence of the social order. The development of such a revolutionary social bloc determines our conception of the nature and role of the party.[26]

Here we find most of the key elements of STO's eventual "mature" position on autonomy: the idea that autonomy is implicit—if "fragmentary"—in "every genuine struggle," the notion that autonomy is not static but develops in the course of social conflict, the importance of a "revolutionary social bloc" that positions itself within but against the "framework of capitalism." The only missing aspect, the need for autonomy from self-proclaimed leadership, is implied in the criticism of other party-building models that formed the basis for the group's positive conception.[27] In short, working-class autonomy was part and parcel of STO's revolutionary strategy from its earliest phase of existence.

Just as STO's analysis of workers' dual consciousness drew upon and concretized a belief in the autonomy of the class, so the group's understanding of white supremacy and white skin privilege was always informed by an almost religious faith in black autonomy. Thus, Noel Ignatin, in his Portland speech from 1972, later published as "Black Worker, White Worker," explains that "by Black struggle I mean the autonomous Black movement. I do not mean any particular organization, although a number of organizations are part of it." Indeed, Ignatin

---

26 Ibid., 26–27.

27 The same aspect is also implicit later in the pamphlet in the criticism of "communist leadership" of the Flint Sit-Down Strike of 1936–1937. Ibid., 35.

was good enough to furnish one of the earliest working definitions of autonomy produced by STO, again in the specific context of black autonomy. By autonomous black movement, he writes, "I am referring to the tendency on the part of large numbers of Black people, especially workers, to find ways of acting together independent of white control and white approval, and to decide their course of action based simply on what they feel is good for Black people, not what serves some so-called larger movement."[28] In Ignatin's definition, the complexities and ambiguities of the concept of autonomy come into clearer view. To be autonomous is to proclaim (or to struggle for) independence not only from capital or the state, but also from a range of self-identified leaders, representatives or comrades. In the case Ignatin describes, the list could potentially be quite lengthy: white-led labor unions, multiracial revolutionary parties, integrated civil rights organizations, not to mention bosses, landlords, social workers, school boards, various regulatory agencies, other government bureaucracies, and of course the police. Putting to one side the questions of corruption and racism, many of the listed entities would sincerely claim to be working in the best interests of the black community. For the "Black struggle" to identify itself as autonomous from some or all of these forces is a rejection of the idea that anyone else knows more than they do about how to change the world.

A parallel vision of autonomy, though less romantic, animated STO's approach to women's issues and gay and lesbian struggles throughout the late seventies. As has been clear, the group generally respected and encouraged the independent action of women against male supremacy. Still, it was always willing to criticize feminists who took bad political stances, especially on questions relating to white supremacy, regardless of any abstract claim the women's movement might have had to its own autonomy from mixed-gender organizations like STO. Similarly, in its limited interventions into the arena of gay and lesbian liberation, the organization viewed autonomous efforts as an important form of resistance against oppression, but not as something above criticism. Thus, Alan Rausch, in his lengthy 1978 essay on the subject, "In Partial Payment: Class Struggle, Sexuality, and the Gay Movement," depicts the history of the fraught relationship between Marxism and homosexuality in terms far more sympathetic to gays and lesbians than to the left. At the same time, he rejects any notion that "gay liberation is by nature

---

28   Noel Ignatin, "Black Worker, White Worker" (1972), reprinted in *Workplace Papers*, 1980, 25.

revolutionary," preferring to describe it as a "democratic rights struggle."[29] While Rausch's essay sounds stilted to contemporary ears in many places, it reflected a relatively advanced position among Leninists at the time. However, the disparity between its critical treatment of gay and lesbian struggles and the kid-gloves approach taken with black and national liberation movements reflected the subordinate position autonomy still had in STO's politics in the latter part of the seventies.

Around the same time, as STO began to emphasize the national question as a framework for resisting white supremacy, the group started to draw on additional external sources to defend its growing emphasis on autonomy. Don Hamerquist's 1976 pamphlet *White Supremacy and the Afro-American National Question* contains a highly unorthodox take on what had been a fairly standard Leninist parable: the story of the Jewish Bund. The Bund participated actively in the founding of the Russian Social Democratic Labor Party (RSDLP, the forerunner of the Communist Party of the Soviet Union) in 1898, and had maintained a general autonomy "in matters generally concerning the Jewish proletariat."[30] But in 1903 the Party Congress voted overwhelmingly to reject this autonomy, and the Bund split from the RSDLP.[31] Throughout the seventies, this story was routinely used by self-described multiracial revolutionary organizations as an argument *against* national or racial autonomy, but Hamerquist turns the argument on its head. He notes that Lenin had actually argued for the readmission of the Bund three years later in 1906, despite the fact that the Bund leadership was politically much closer to the Menshevik faction of the Party, which Lenin consistently opposed. "Thus," argues Hamerquist,

> if anything, the unique features of the Bund would have
> dictated against concessions in the direction of autonomy
> for it within the RSDLP, but the Bolshevik position was for

---

29   Alan Rausch, "In Partial Payment: Class Struggle, Sexuality, and the Gay Movement," in *UT* #7, Winter 1980, 11. This essay was subsequently republished as a pamphlet in 1981, with an introductory note that indicates it was originally written in 1978. "Queer," "transgender," and other more contemporary terms do not appear in Rausch's piece (other than in a negative reference to "queer-baiting"), and are thus avoided here as well.

30   Leonard Schapiro, *The Communist Party of the Soviet Union* (New York: Vintage Books, 1964), 30.

31   Schapiro tallies the vote as 41 to 5, with 5 abstentions. Ibid., 50.

substantial autonomy. Isn't it obvious, then, that in situations where the national character of a people is much more evident than with Russian Jews (i.e. North American Black people or Puerto Ricans living in the U.S.), and where the level of consciousness and organization among the working class in these national groups is well advanced over that of white working people, the precedent of the Bolshevik attitude towards the Bund would certainly entail a large degree of autonomy and rights to separate organizations within the party?[32]

Despite Hamerquist's enthusiasm, however, subsequent advocacy within STO for the concept of autonomy, whether for national/racial groupings, for women, for youth, or for the whole working class, rarely made use of this particular line of argument. This was perhaps in part the result of an ironic twist in the group's trajectory, the split of 1978.

Little more than a year after raising the Bund in defense of autonomy, STO began the awkward discussions on third world autonomy within the group that led to the split in which the last remaining members of color left the organization. In practice, this represented the precise inversion of Hamerquist's analysis of the Bund. One key complication of STO's analysis of autonomy as a concept was that it was applied largely to movements and to organizations rather than to individuals. The majority position in the 1978 schism effectively held that autonomy was necessarily a social phenomenon to which individuals must be subordinated. Thus, the handful of black and latino revolutionaries who chose to join STO in the mid-seventies were criticized for having placed their individual preferences (for the sort of anti-Stalinist political conceptions that distinguished STO from most of the revolutionary nationalist organizations of the era) above the needs of "their" communities. Of course, as the splitting faction was quick to point out, such an assessment neatly mirrored the condescension that Ignatin had forcefully rejected only a few years earlier in his Portland speech, as if the white leadership of STO knew better than the members of color what those needs were and how best to meet them.

---

32   Don Hamerquist, *White Supremacy and the Afro-American National Question*, 23. Schapiro notes that while Lenin and Stalin both voted for the Bund's re-admission, "many other Bolsheviks voted against it." Schapiro, *The Community Party*, 74.

* * *

Another major external source for STO's ideas on autonomy was likely responsible for the refusal to see autonomy in individual terms—the impact of the European autonomists, especially in Italy, during the seventies. As was discussed in Chapter Two, the Hot Autumn of 1969 was one of the foundational influences on STO's initial approach to organizing. Over the course of the following decade, the Italian movement went through a maze of ups and downs, producing a range of organizational forms and theoretical insights, always foregrounding the concept of autonomy. Interestingly, the Italians were themselves heavily influenced by the same upsurge of black radicalism in the United States that inspired STO. Thus, Potere Operaio (PO), the Italian organization that most closely resembled the early STO, argued as early as 1967 that "Black Power means therefore the autonomous revolutionary organization of Blacks."[33] Like STO, PO was "anti-parliamentarian, contemptuous of work within the unions, committed to an insurrectionalist perspective," and like STO it went into crisis as the labor militancy of the early seventies receded.[34] While STO was able to reconstitute itself on the terrain of anti-imperialist solidarity in the middle part of the decade, PO passed from the scene and was organizationally replaced by a plethora of smaller groups, collectively referred to as *Autonomia*. This trend participated actively in workplace, student, and community struggles, always pushing for militant direct action and resisting the attempts of labor unions, political parties, or anyone else to direct their activity.

As the decade progressed, autonomist ideas migrated northward in Europe, so that by 1980 there were self-described autonomist movements active in Switzerland, the Netherlands, Denmark, and especially in Germany, where they took the name *Autonomen*. The influence of the Italian movement was also felt in Britain, where the group Big Flame fully embraced autonomy as a political framework and followed a trajectory quite similar to that of STO, from workplace organizing, through third world solidarity, to engagement with new social movements in the early eighties.[35] Meanwhile, the major thinkers of the Italian milieu, in-

---

33   Potere Operaio Veneto-Emiliano, "La lotta dei Vietcong ci insegna che la rivoluzione e possibile," in *Potere Operaio* #1, 1967. Quoted in Steve Wright, *Storming Heaven: Class Composition and Struggle in Italian Autonomist Marxism*, (London: Pluto Press, 2002), 132.

34   Steve Wright, *Storming Heaven*, 131.

35   The website http://bigflameuk.wordpress.com/ (accessed January 10,

cluding Sergio Bologna, Ferruccio Gambino, Mariarossa Dalla Costa, and above all Antonio Negri, produced a stunning array of written output, all aimed at developing the theoretical underpinnings for the concept of working-class autonomy. Quantifying and timing the impact of this body of work on STO is difficult, since translations of most Italian autonomist writings did not begin to appear in English until the end of the seventies.[36] There had been some individual points of contact earlier in the decade, with Noel Ignatin and Don Hamerquist, in particular, maintaining communication with Gambino and others at various points in time.

By the end of the decade, STO had initiated the first in a series of delegated visits to Europe, where meetings were held in various countries to help develop an international tendency built around anti-imperialism and autonomy as guiding principles. Along with the Italians, the participants included Big Flame, the Irish group Revolutionary Struggle, and others. An international journal was planned, though it apparently was never published in English. This international tendency, like the US-based efforts described in Chapter Seven, was amorphous, although at some point around 1980 Noel Ignatin attempted to define "who 'we' is." His definition spoke directly to questions of autonomy, drawing heavily on the rhetoric of *Toward a Revolutionary Party*, by then nearly a decade old:

> The task of the Marxist organization [is] not to "lead the masses" according to some scheme of our own, but to seek out and discover those elements of the spontaneous struggle which are autonomous and subversive of official society, and weld them together in a revolutionary social bloc. This task, which is more easily accomplished in times of general upsurge but which cannot be left for those times alone, has two aspects: 1) the positive one, of linking the autonomous elements together organizationally, intervening to transform them from spontaneous to conscious, and drawing a clear line between these elements and the institutions and practices—trade unions, parliamentarianism, etc.—which

---

2012) provides an impressive collection of original documents and contemporary reflections on Big Flame.

36   The Red Notes Collective in England began to produce translations as early as 1976, but it is not clear when and to what extent these were available in the United States.

mediate them; and 2) the negative aspect, of counterposing these subversive elements to the ordinary "loyal" patterns of behavior, which are also spontaneously generated.[37]

One notable feature of the European autonomist trend was its implicit assumption that autonomy was a social phenomenon. Drawing on this tradition, the contemporary radical writer George Katsiaficas suggests that "autonomy has a variety of meanings. Western philosophy since Kant has used the term to refer to the independence of individual subjectivity, but as I use the term … autonomy refers mainly to collective relationships, not individual ones."[38] This usage has roots in Marx's *Grundrisse*, which begins with a broadside against the "illusion" of the atomized individual. For Marx, then, "the socially determined production of individuals constitutes the starting point" of all economic and social theory.[39] The *Grundrisse* was a supremely important text for the Italian autonomists, and for STO, in part because it rearticulated the humanism implicit in the so-called "early Marx" of the 1844 Manuscripts, emphasizing the concept of alienation. For the autonomists, alienation was the flipside of autonomy, and both were fundamentally social rather than individual experiences.

---

37 Noel Ignatin, "Who 'We' Is" (nd, but c. 1980), unpublished manuscript in author's possession. Thanks to Steve Wright for providing me a copy of this document, which was initially distributed among the members of Big Flame.

38 Katsiaficas, *Subversion of Politics*, 6. A very different radical vision of autonomy is presented by the philosopher Sarah Lucia Hoagland, who shares with Katsiaficas and others a critique of Kantian individualism, but attempts to resolve the contradiction between the individual and social aspects of autonomy by coining the term "autokoenony," from the Greek words for "self" and "community." In her terms, "an autokoenonous being is one who is aware of her self as one among others within a community that forms her ground of be-ing, one who makes her decisions in consideration of her limitations as well as in consideration of the agendas and perceptions of others. She does not merge with others, nor does she estrange herself; she *interacts* with others in situations." Sarah Lucia Hoagland, *Lesbian Ethics: Toward New Value* (Palo Alto, CA: Institute of Lesbian Studies, 1988), 145.

39 Karl Marx, *Grundrisse*, translated by David McLellan, quoted in McLellan, ed. *Karl Marx: Selected Writings* (New York: Oxford University Press, 1977), 345.

Another element of the Italian autonomist tradition in particular was also imported into STO as it began its own autonomist turn: a millenarian anticipation of massive and fundamental social upheaval on the horizon. As the group began to reconsider its declaration of "the lull" at the end of the seventies, some members of STO introduced the concept of a "secular crisis" in capital, based again on certain passages in the *Grundrisse* that discussed the possible breakdown in the law of value that had always served as the bedrock of capitalism. Marxism has traditionally posited that the value of any commodity is a direct result of the labor put into its production. Hamerquist, in particular, was especially fond of the following provocative assertion from Marx, which seemed to suggest an impending change in the traditional formula:

> The theft of alien labour time, on which the present wealth is based, appears a miserable foundation in the face of this new one, created by large scale industry itself. As soon as labour in the direct form has ceased to be the great wellspring of wealth, labour time ceases to be its measure, and hence exchange value must cease to be the measure of use value.... With that, production based on exchange value breaks down, and the direct material production process is stripped of the form of penury and antithesis.[40]

In other words, to the extent that capitalism becomes increasingly dependent on technology, actual living workers and their labor become less and less central to the process of production.

In typically dialectical fashion, this prospect implied a contradictory set of outcomes. By the early eighties, Hamerquist had come to view this prospect through a dark lens, speculating about possibilities of genocide (to reduce the supply of superfluous workers) and impending barbarity or fascism, should the revolutionary left fail to transform itself into mass insurgent opposition to capitalism.[41] On the other hand, the crisis

---

40   Marx, *Grundrisse*, translated by Martin Nicolaus (New York: Penguin, 1973), 705–706. (This translation differs from McLellan, and was the preferred version in use by STO in the early eighties.)

41   Hamerquist's unpublished essay simply titled "Rewrite #3" from 1983, quotes the relevant passage from the *Grundrisse* and discusses the bleak possibilities that presented themselves in the absence of a revitalized anti-capitalist left. In author's possession. This is the speech that Hamerquist was to have given as a keynote at the *No Easy Answers Left*

in the law of value could also be seen to herald the coming of a communist society, such that, for Marx, the prospect of machines displacing human labor carried with it an opening for "the artistic, scientific, etc. development of the individuals in the time set free" from work.[42] Here, again, was STO's understanding of the fundamental contradiction of Marxism, between the means or "forces" of production (technology, machines) and the mode or "social relations" of production (the slavery of the wage vs. the autonomy of the proletariat). Capitalism reflected one view of each side in this contradiction, while communism crystallizes an opposite view. Thus, in Marx's phrasing, "Forces of production and social relations—two different sides of the development of the social individual—appear to capital as mere means, and are merely means for it to produce on its limited foundation. In fact, however, they are the material conditions to blow this foundation sky-high."[43] This, in short, was the secular crisis of capitalism.

Like Hamerquist and some other members of STO, the wing of the Italian autonomists led by Negri believed that the crisis in the law of value was actually playing out in the economic restructuring of the seventies, alongside the apparent rise in autonomous resistance to capital among broad sectors of the population. Thus, according to Steve Wright, a leading historian of the Italian movement, "while he continued to reject traditional Marxist conceptions of crisis, Negri's own framework became no less catastrophic."[44] For Negri, the catastrophe was to be welcomed. Indeed, in 1977 he made the grandiose claim that "we are here; we are uncrushable; and we are in the majority."[45] While STO never approached this level of delusional optimism, there was a decidedly rosy aspect to the

---

conference in New York City.

42 Marx, *Grundrisse* (Nicolaus translation), 706. A similarly optimistic take on the shift toward technology can be found in the sixties writings of the anarchist Murray Bookchin, especially his 1968 essay "Post-Scarcity Anarchism," in *Post-Scarcity Anarchism* (Montreal: Black Rose Books, 1986 [1971]),55–76.

43 Ibid.

44 Steve Wright, *Storming Heaven*, 173.

45 Antonio Negri, "Capitalist Domination and Working Class Sabotage" (1977), as quoted in Steve Wright, *Storming Heaven*, 173. Wright maintains that this pamphlet "went on to become a best seller." At the very least, it was popular within STO during the early eighties, with Janeen Creamer in particular utilizing it on several occasions in polemics within the organization.

group's view of the crisis, Hamerquist's fears of genocide notwithstanding. At the very least, it was commonplace to assert the need to maximize the opportunities that were sure to emerge in the coming years. This tendency was especially prominent in discussions of production work and antifascist organizing. It built upon the perceived upsurge of mass illegality in hotspots from Miami and Brixton to Gdansk and Berlin. Hindsight makes clear the substantial misestimate built into this line of thinking, but the dialectical approach to crisis was a hallmark of STO's theory of autonomy as the eighties progressed.

* * *

In many ways, the emergence of the dialectics course grounded STO's discussion of autonomy in a broader and deeper framework than had previously been the case. Instead of limiting the question to issues of race and nation, the group began something of a return to the broad defense of working-class autonomy that had characterized *Toward a Revolutionary Party*. This did not entail a rejection of the insights gained over the intervening years, but rather their re-articulation into novel discussions of class. A valuable marker in that process was Lee Holstein's essay, "Working Class Self-Activity: A Response to Kim Moody," in the Summer 1980 issue of *Urgent Tasks*. Moody was a prominent member of the International Socialists, a key Trotskyist group of the era, who had written a lengthy set of articles in 1979 on the Marxist theory of revolution. But Moody and his articles appear mainly as a foil for Holstein's efforts to articulate a theoretical analysis of autonomy tied directly to STO's longstanding critique of trade unions. "Working class self-activity is working class autonomy—autonomy from capitalism," argues Holstein.[46] Her problem with advocates of trade union reform efforts, such as Moody, is that they "mush together the reform and revolutionary aspects of resistance and insurgency, treating forms of resistance and insurgency which are confined within the framework of capitalism in the same way as those which break out of that framework."[47] For Holstein, by contrast, "self-activity is not just resisting and attacking, but resisting and attacking in a way that undermines capitalist power, destabilizes its institutional framework, and foreshadows and demonstrates, in the form and content of

---

46   Lee Holstein, "Working Class Self-Activity: A Response to Kim Moody," in *UT* #9, Summer 1980, 13.

47   Ibid., 12.

the current struggles, the potential of the workers to be rulers."[48] On a practical level, she maintains, this conception necessitates a "break with the trade union structures," while on a more theoretical level it requires a careful attentiveness to "the working class in its humanness."[49]

Much of the textual support on which Holstein's essay draws is taken more or less directly from the dialectics course. She notes Marx's distinction between the "class-in-itself" and the "class-for-itself," and quotes extensively from Gramsci's discourse on consciousness in the *Prison Notebooks*. She highlights STO's conviction that the essential contradiction in capitalism is that between the means of production and the mode of production, utilizing citations from various key texts by Marx. At the same time, Holstein makes use not only of her recent reading, but also of her own personal experiences over many years working in factories, in particular when she uses a lengthy and thoughtful reflection on the contradictions of a hypothetical worker in a piece-rate shop to show how all workers, not just those who conform to left stereotypes of advanced or militant proletarians, express "both revolutionary and non-revolutionary elements."[50] While her specific reading of Moody's piece comes across now as nitpicky, her holistic analysis of self-activity as autonomy was pivotal as STO entered the eighties.

One practical form taken by this reframing of autonomy in terms of class was the abortive attempt to reinvigorate STO's workplace organizing efforts. This effort had been approved at the General Membership Meeting in 1979, but stalled repeatedly for a number of reasons. Deindustrialization was making it harder for members to obtain work in factories, especially in the heavy industries (steel, auto, etc.) that had been STO's previous areas of concentration. However, even where a number of members were involved in production work, as in Kansas City, there were problems. The union reform efforts the group had long disparaged were showing some limited signs of immediate success, which made it more difficult for STO's critique of unions to gain a hearing among workers. This was especially true among those workers most inclined toward organizing in the shop, since they were drawn to the prospect of victory that reform movements like Teamsters for a Democratic Union (TDU) represented. STO members in Kansas City and elsewhere carried on an uneasy relationship with TDU for a period of time at the turn of the decade, but in this effort they always faced resistance within STO

_____

48   Ibid.
49   Ibid., 18–19.
50   Ibid., 17.

as well as within TDU, which was one of the International Socialists' (IS) key targets for organizing.[51] Eventually, it became clear that work with TDU was unlikely to produce the sort of growing radicalization of workers that STO believed was both desirable and increasingly possible.

Over the course of 1981, another attempt was made to kick-start the "Production Fraction," as it was known. The new proposal called for the creation of a general workers' organization, as opposed to the sort of site-specific factory committees that had been the hallmark of STO's original workplace efforts. Kansas City branch member and factory worker Janeen Creamer wanted the group "to build a city-wide, multi-national, class-conscious, hell-raising, ass-kicking group of working-class people who view themselves as organizers."[52] The proposal was to cohere a core of insurgent workers who could advance a solidly revolutionary response to the economic crisis that dominated STO's estimate of the period. A key veteran of the early years and a longtime auto worker, Carole Travis, pointed to the needed tactical shift: "Our old methods of shop floor work are not now relevant. Building shop floor organization reflective of particular plant or department grievances cannot be at the heart of our organizing now. Those techniques incorrectly emphasize struggles which are neither central nor winnable as isolated struggles."[53] Instead, Travis and others wanted to establish a more proletarian version of the various social movements that had taken up so much of STO's time since the late seventies. Most activities of such a group would happen outside the workplace, either through demonstrations or through small-scale militant direct actions. As an example, Travis suggested a focus on the problems of the economic crisis, especially the rise of far-right and Klan forces among unemployed and underemployed white workers, as well as some predictable foreign policy issues.

For Creamer and for Travis, as for others, the key aspect of any such organization was its autonomy, not only from capitalism but from STO itself. Travis warned that "our work should not degenerate into pressuring or manipulating people. Activity and projects of the group as a whole,

51   Geoff Bailey, "1960s Radicals Turn to Party Building," in *International Socialist Review* #53 (May/June, 2007) describes the role played by the IS in the development of TDU.

52   Janeen Creamer, "Proposal for a Citywide Workers' Group," in *IDB* #19, October 1980, 28.

53   Carole Travis, "Some Thoughts on Proletarian Organization," in *IDB* #23A, June 1981, 13.

once it becomes a whole, must be determined by it."[54] But the heightened emphasis on autonomy drew some complaints from inside STO, even before the proposal could be initiated. Lowell May, for instance, argued that "we're expecting to organize advanced workers without the benefit of a sufficient anti-imperialist/anti-white supremacist context. What will produce the revolutionary consciousness (as opposed to militant oppressor nation worker consciousness)? Not us. Even without the commitment to autonomy, we couldn't do it."[55] May's phrasing suggests he thought the group's interest in autonomy was a burden, but mostly he was interested in highlighting its one-sidedness in the absence of a resurgent black radicalism, inside or outside the ever-shrinking factories. In any event, the proposal, as with so many of STO's initiatives during its declining years, came to naught. While individual members of STO continued to work in factory settings throughout the rest of the group's existence, it would never again mount a meaningful campaign that focused squarely on efforts to organize the working class.

* * *

STO's failure to reinvigorate its production work was also reflective of a recurrent element of STO's commitment to autonomy: a form of organizational self-deprecation. Because it was an overwhelmingly (at times, exclusively) white organization, the group's early realization of its own potentially antagonistic role relative to the black liberation movement was permanently humbling. It was precisely this respect for black autonomy that led the group to decide in its early years against the recruitment of close comrades such as the black communist Macee Halk.[56] The issue went beyond just race relations, however, and broached the question of working-class autonomy. For the most part, the group was always loathe to recruit as new members militants (of whatever color) encountered in the context of mass struggle, whether on the shop floor or in the antinuclear movement. When the group's internal crisis began in the early eighties, as described in Chapter Seven, the membership focused on both practical questions—poor communication between the Central Committee and the branches, for instance—and more theoretical issues—the tension between left and mass work, for example. Many of these factors

---

54 Ibid., 14.

55 Lowell May, "Class Organizing Comments," in Secret Supplement to *IDB* #24, September 1981, 35.

56 For more on Halk, see Chapter Three.

no doubt contributed to the growing organizational frustrations, but what is striking in the group's surfeit of otherwise thoughtful reflections and proposals is the total absence of any reference to STO's growing attachment to autonomy. Certainly, the idea of autonomy as formulated by STO and others was an important counterweight to the tendency toward authoritarianism that had plagued the Marxist tradition in all its many variants. But for a group whose cohesion had always been framed by a Leninist commitment to building a true revolutionary party, the shift toward autonomy certainly exacerbated the problems of organizational drift.

These contradictions were on full display in a paper written by Noel Ignatin at the beginning of 1983. In "For Autonomism," Ignatin drew an important distinction between the broad trend within black radicalism toward "autonomism," defined as "the general tendency which regards an independent black movement as a strategic principle," and black nationalism as a narrower trend toward creation of an independent nation-state.[57] Though STO had long prioritized support for revolutionary nationalism, it was clear by the early eighties that a majority of the group's membership had fundamental political differences with the dominant tendencies within the black nationalist milieu. In that sense, Ignatin's paper pointed to a real shift in STO's political strategy as a result of the growing importance of autonomy within the group. At the same time, the paper represented something of a throwback to the early seventies, when STO pamphlets like *The United Front Against Imperialism?* flirted with a fully romanticized vision of the black freedom struggle. In the new era, however, Ignatin—no doubt reflecting on the frustrations of working with the Puerto Rican independence movement—was suggesting that revolutionary nationalism was potentially a barrier to autonomy rather than its standard-bearer. This was yet another sign of the ways in which the growing pull of autonomy was shattering previously undisputed components of STO's analysis. But again, "For Autonomism" limited itself to addressing the implications of autonomy for the black movement, and failed to address the ways in which a commitment to autonomy was changing STO itself.

* * *

Autonomy as a concept did not only apply to the political left, and over time STO came to view the threat of fascism through a lens of

---

57   Noel Ignatin, "For Autonomism," in *IDB* #30, February, 1983, 3.

autonomy as well. For a number of years, the group's unified approach to fascism provided a counterweight to the mounting frustrations of tendency building. Fascism presented both a theoretical challenge and a physical danger to committed revolutionaries at the turn of the eighties, especially in the deep South, where the Klan was well organized and highly violent. Certainly the most chilling example was the massacre of five members of the newly minted Communist Workers Party (CWP, formerly the Workers' Voice Organization, a Maoist outgrowth of the New Communist Movement) by Klansmen and neo-Nazis in Greensboro, North Carolina on December 3, 1979.[58] While STO was harshly critical of the politics of the CWP, including its analysis of fascism as a transparent tool of the capitalist system, it recognized certain common risks resulting from the emphasis on direct action-oriented antifascist organizing that characterized both groups despite their divergent trajectories.

Much of the US left at the end of the seventies rejected this emphasis, arguing that the danger of fascism was exaggerated and that antifascism was a distraction from more essential work around labor struggles or race relations.[59] Indeed, STO itself had long held an almost identical position. In 1976, the group had published a discussion paper (originally written in 1974) by Don Hamerquist entitled "Fascism in the U.S.?" Written as an intervention in debates around the role and strategy of the National Lawyers Guild, Hamerquist's piece presented a fairly straightforward argument with implications well beyond the practice of leftwing attorneys. The essay begins with an acceptance of the common Marxist assumption that fascism represents "the course of desperation for the ruling class, a course only taken in the event of the failure of the bourgeois democratic forms of rule which have worked in this country since its beginnings."[60] While STO was later to challenge this premise in favor of emphasizing the autonomous potential of fascist movements,

---

58   For more on Greensboro, see Elizabeth Wheaton, *Codename Greenkil: The 1979 Greensboro Killings* (Athens, GA: University of Georgia Press, 2009 [1987]) as well as the analytical memoir written by a survivor of the massacre, Signe Waller, *Love and Revolution: A Political Memoir: People's History of the Greensboro Massacre, Its Setting and Aftermath* (Lanham, MD: Rowman and Littlefield Publishers, 2002).

59   Noel Ignatin presented multiple examples of this phenomenon within the seventies left in "Fascism: Some Common Misconceptions," in *UT* #4, Summer 1978.

60   Don Hamerquist, "Fascism in the U.S.?" (Chicago: STO, 1976 [1974]), 2.

Hamerquist was more focused on proving that capitalism in the US was unlikely to embrace fascism anytime soon. If fascism represented a last-ditch response to a rising tide of left revolutionary sentiment, then the unmistakable decline of the radical movements that had rocked the country during the late sixties was all the evidence required to support Hamerquist's argument.

The analysis went deeper, and (unsurprisingly) related back directly to STO's theory of white supremacy and white skin privilege. In this regard, Hamerquist counters the "imminent fascism" thesis by pointing to the ways in which white supremacy was woven into the very fabric of "bourgeois democracy." The repressive terror associated with fascism, he argues, has long been characteristic of the daily life of people of color in the United States, especially in their dealings with the police and state bureaucracies. Nonetheless, "despite the fascistic aspects of the oppression of Third World people, in fact, national oppression and its manifestation in the institution of white supremacy are essential and defining features of US capitalist—that is, of WHITE SUPREMACIST bourgeois democratic rule, the only "democracy" which has ever existed in this country with the exception of a brief period in the South following the Civil War."[61] What is more, "to a large degree, bourgeois democracy in this country is a white privilege."[62] After briefly restating STO's long-standing perspective on the role of white skin privilege in dividing the working class, Hamerquist returns to the question of fascism. "So long as the bulk of the white working class sees its interests mainly in terms of skin color, not class position, the likelihood of fascist rule being extended to the society as a whole is minimal."[63] With the status quo functioning successfully, there was no incentive for the ruling class to pursue fascism as a policy option.

Hamerquist concludes his polemic with an assessment of the strategic implications of the competing analyses of fascism. Those who argue that fascism is imminent, he maintains, are really looking for a way to avoid the hard work of challenging white supremacy within the white working class. In this scenario, "the approach to white workers is not to attempt to win them to a stand of class solidarity with oppressed peoples, but to convince them that they are next on the list."[64] It was no surprise to those familiar with STO's politics that Hamerquist rejected this strategy as an

---

61   Ibid., 5.
62   Ibid., 6.
63   Ibid.
64   Ibid.

inherently doomed attempt at shortcutting the hard work of defeating white supremacy within the working class. At the time (1974), this was consistent with STO's emphasis on direct organizing at the point of production. As the decade progressed and the group focused its efforts on anti-imperialist solidarity, the specific critique of the "imminent fascism" theory was subsumed in a more general political shift. The real-world result for STO was a general failure to engage in explicit antifascist organizing efforts for most of the seventies, until shortly before the Greensboro massacre.

The gradual move toward a conceptual emphasis on autonomy led STO to reconsider its approach to fascism and antifascism, a process that was accelerated by the difficulty (and, to a lesser extent, danger) experienced by Ken Lawrence in Mississippi as he attempted to develop and maintain connections with a range of black and other radical groups that faced sustained harassment by a newly resurgent Ku Klux Klan. In some ways, Noel Ignatin began the theoretical shift with an important article published in *Urgent Tasks* in 1978, entitled "Fascism: Some Common Misconceptions." In it, Ignatin challenges many standard left assumptions about fascism, most prominently the famous definition put forward by the Thirteenth Plenum of the Executive Committee of the Comintern in 1933: "Fascism is the open terrorist dictatorship of the most reactionary, most chauvinistic and most imperialist elements of finance capital."[65] By contrast, argues Ignatin, fascism must be understood to have its own dynamic, quite apart from the supposed desire of some sections of capital to establish dictatorial control over society. Thus, "it is necessary to recognize the relative autonomy of the fascist movement in relation to all classes, as an important feature that distinguishes it from other rightwing governments."[66] Ignatin goes on to offer a set of hypothetical examples designed to demonstrate the *potential* (if not actual) autonomy of fascism as a political movement in periods prior to a seizure of power.

Around the same time, Ken Lawrence and many other southern revolutionaries were receiving threats of physical violence from various Klan factions across the region. While this experience prompted many of the targeted radicals to identify the Klan as a proxy for state repression on the model of COINTELPRO, Lawrence took another tack. He focused on the growing interaction between the uniquely "American" Klan milieu

---

65   Quoted in Ignatin, "Fascism: Some Common Misconceptions," in *UT* #4, Summer 1978, 27.

66   Ibid., 29.

and the previously distinct tradition of European-influenced fascism. In this context, the fact that Klan and neo-Nazi groups had themselves been the targets of COINTELPRO operations was indicative of their *actual* autonomy from the state, at least at the level of the federal government.[67] Similar conclusions were drawn by other STO members based on local experiences in Kansas City and Chicago, and rather quickly the organization had developed a coherent and rather unorthodox analysis of fascism. As Lawrence put it, "we have correctly identified the distinguishing characteristics of fascism as its autonomous, mass, plebian qualities; its 'revolutionary' vision; and its own brand of 'internationalism,' or at least super-nationalism."[68]

For STO, the obvious parallel to divisions on the far right were those on the far left, especially the contrast between revolution and reform that informed the group's response to the Harold Washington campaign. A similar tension manifested in right-wing contexts like the anti-abortion movement, between those who focused on legislative efforts and those who emphasized illegal activities like bombing clinics. This assessment influenced a growing belief inside STO that the main danger of fascism was that its radicalism and militancy was gaining it adherents in precisely the place that STO had long prioritized: the white working class. Lawrence again framed the group's changing view: "the question arose as to whether we are in competition with the fascists for the same constituency. On reflection I would say the entire discussion was pretty naïve, because the answer is a resounding yes on every level, but the fact that this answer wasn't instantly obvious is not so much a failure to grasp our political aims as it is a failure to understand the strength of the Klan/Nazi ideology."[69] The biggest outcome of this realization was the major investment STO put into antifascist work during the early eighties. The group was heavily involved in building two different nationwide anti-Klan organizations, the National Anti-Klan Network (NAKN) and a group with the rather unwieldy name People United Against Government Repression and the Klan and Nazi Coalition. On a local level STO members were active in a range of antifascist efforts, including direct action responses to Klan and neo-Nazi rallies.

Still, the situation was complicated: in the aftermath of the Greensboro massacre, for instance, it became clear that there was substantial

---

67   Ken Lawrence, "Fighting the New Ku Klux Klan/Nazi Threat," in *IDB* Special Issue, April 1981, 11–14.

68   Ibid., 1–2. Lawrence explicitly acknowledges the importance of Ignatin's 1978 piece in this regard.

69   Ibid., 6.

interaction between law enforcement and the Klan and neo-Nazi groups. This realization invariably raised the question of how to interact with the government in the process of organizing against the fascists. For some in the burgeoning antifascist movement, the obvious response was to reject any alliance with the state because of the two-faced role police were known to play. STO broadly encouraged this perspective, not least because of its fear that the fascists might successfully portray the antifascists as hopelessly reformist and compromised by their dependence on the state. Still, even within STO there were debates on how to address this question. In 1981, for instance, a dispute emerged in Kansas City over two competing slogans for use in antifascist work: "smash the Klan" and "ban the Klan." The former was perceived as opposing "any call for any reliance on the state in the struggle against the Klan."[70] According to Randy Gould, "the danger of the 'Ban the Klan' approach is that it does not allow Blacks or working people to build their own organizations for their own struggles under their own control, and more that it implies that the State can take care of the Klan for us, will take care of the Klan for us, can and will be fair and anti-racist. Of course we know that this is not the case at all. It is dangerous to spread such an illusion."[71] Regardless, others in STO argued that it was harmfully sectarian to forcefully exclude the "ban the Klan" approach. Certainly, the NAKN was open to "ban the Klan" strategies, and STO was actively involved in what Lawrence identified as "the largest and potentially most influential of the various anti-fascist coalitions."[72] But Gould and others questioned the political value of such national work, emphasizing instead local direct action-based efforts, where it was often easier to convince people to adopt more militant stances based on goodwill accumulated over years of joint work.

Issues such as these were the subject of extensive debate inside STO, leading to the approval of a set of "Theses on Fascism" at the General Membership Meeting in 1981. Subsequently published in *Urgent Tasks*, the theses focus primarily on the character of the fascist movement, and only secondarily on the question of antifascist organizing. Thesis number three locates the basis of the emerging fascist threat in the ongoing economic crisis (whether "secular" or "cyclical"), while thesis number four cautions that

---

70   Randy Gould, "Smash the Klan," in Secret Supplement to *IDB* #24, September 1981, 55.

71   Ibid., 55–56.

72   Lawrence, "Fighting," 17.

To understand fascism as growing out of the crises endemic to capitalism is not to say that it is a simple tool of the capitalist class. One important element in fascism is its autonomous character, expressed in a mass movement among sectors of the population who have been dislocated by the capitalist crisis and alienated from the traditional institutions of conciliation and repression. Fascism contains an anti-capitalist 'revolutionary' side that is not reducible to simple demagogy.[73]

Yet STO was careful to reiterate that this autonomy only represented one aspect of fascism. In an accompanying "Note on the Theses," Ignatin pointed to the simultaneous continuity and discontinuity between fascism and traditional conservative forces in the US. As he put it, "from conservatism to fascism there is both a continuum and a break, and it is necessary to keep both in mind."[74]

The theses argue for a reformulation of the classic Leninist idea of the "United Front" as the key strategic concept in antifascist organizing. Thesis number eight defines the United Front as "a defensive posture aimed at achieving an alliance for the sole purpose of stopping the fascist advance."[75] While the United Front would necessarily be broad, STO hoped to build a pole within it that could

criticize certain incorrect approaches which currently hold sway. Foremost among these are: first, the view that it is possible to defeat fascism through reliance on liberal, constitutional sectors of the bourgeoisie and their representatives in the popular movement; second, the view that holds fascism and the bourgeois state to be identical, therefore overlooking the autonomous character of the fascist movement which is an important source of its dangerous potential.[76]

---

73   "Theses on Fascism," in *UT* #12. Available online at http://sojourner-truth.net/thesesonfascism.html (accessed January 10, 2012).

74   Noel Ignatin, "Comment on the Theses," in *UT* #12. Available online at http://sojournertruth.net/thesesonfascism.html (accessed January 10, 2012).

75   "Theses on Fascism," in *UT* #12.

76   Ibid.

This amounted to a specific application of the group's tendency-building approach, with the tendency defined by reference to its revolutionary opposition to both fascism and the liberal, capitalist state. Just as the fascists struggled to maintain their autonomy from the conservative mainstream, so must the antifascist milieu.

The theses managed to paper over at least one set of disagreements within STO around fascism: the question of anti-Semitism. Thesis number seven emphasized the centrality of anti-Semitism to the developing fascist threat, but Ignatin's "Comment" argued that "To the extent that fascism establishes its independence from the bourgeoisie as a whole, to that extent it is likely that anti-Semitism will diminish in importance within the fascist program."[77] The next issue of *Urgent Tasks* published an exchange on this topic between Ignatin and Lenny Zeskind, a long-time STO member from Kansas City and a leading figure in the group's antifascist efforts. Zeskind accepted STO's position on the increasing autonomy of fascism, but argued strenuously that this independence was actually likely to *increase* the prominence of anti-Semitism within the fascist program. Thus, he maintained, "the Nazis' anti-capitalism, like everything else, is a function of their racialism. In this case the racialism means anti-Semitism. My logical inference is that the Nazis' revolutionary anti-capitalism stems from their anti-Semitism. Noel argues that the reverse is true, that the greater the anti-capitalism the less the anti-Semitism."[78] Ignatin responded that fascist autonomy from capital "eliminate[s] the need for a mythical ruling class to substitute for the real one as a target for their attacks."[79]

From the outside, this may have appeared similar to many other amicable theoretical disputes in STO's long history, but internally the stakes rapidly escalated. In part because of the devastating war in Lebanon, the debate quickly expanded to include not only the question of anti-Semitism but also the issue of the ongoing conflict in Israel/Palestine.[80] STO had never taken an official stance on the question, but many members had long maintained the longstanding Leninist approach of advocating a single state, whether conceived of as "bi-national" or simply "secular." Several members of the Kansas City branch challenged the necessity of

---

77 Ignatin, "Comment."

78 Lenny Zeskind, letter to *UT*, in *UT*#13, Fall/Winter 1982, 36.

79 "Ignatin replies," in *UT*#13, 37.

80 This narrative is synthesized from several letters in *IDB* #30, February, 1983, and #31, April 1983, as well as interviews with Randy Gould, Ira and Lee Churgin, and others.

this position, and forced a debate at the group's National Committee meeting in September 1982, followed by a losing vote on the question of accepting a two-state solution. The meeting became quite heated, and Kansas City branch member Randy Gould accused the leadership of the group of adopting a "smash or be smashed" attitude. Certainly the animosity was not simply the result of a political disagreement, since it came as the culmination of several years of frustration on the part of the Kansas City branch regarding lines of communication and authority (as described in Chapter Seven). The final result was an acrimonious split, with Zeskind, Gould, and the remainder of the Kansas City branch leaving STO to form a short-lived antifascist collective.

* * *

In one of its final activities in the fall of 1982, the Kansas City branch produced a single issue of a magazine called *Special Sedition*, which was distributed largely within the white punk rock scene in that city. Designed in the style of a punk-rock fanzine with overlapping text and images cut and pasted on top of each other, the front cover features images of guns, knives, and other weapons. Prominent images inside depict police officers as targets for shooting practice, while the text includes lyrics from the Clash, reprints of photos and headlines from the mainstream media depicting protesters fighting police in Europe, and two long, unsigned original pieces. The first addresses the relationship between punk rock and youth rebellion, while the second is an impressionistic fictional take on a rebellious white teenager named "Filthy McNasty." Both essays discuss violence against the police, with the first piece concluding, "Basically the idea is this: Go beyond a rebellious personal style, and make it really PUNK. Do the pogo stick on the racist KC cops, who are among the most bloodthirsty in the country. Take over the streets from the Plaza bozos, take what we need to survive and be happy, and when the cops try to stop us, burn down their stations, just like they do in England. Like the Clash says: LET'S GO CRAZY!!!!!"[81] The endorsement of righteous violence against the police is perhaps the dominant theme of the entire magazine, although the embrace of autonomous youth rebellion in all its forms runs a close second.

Special Sedition was a departure for STO, and a controversial one inside the organization. Even though the group had long supported violence and even military action by oppressed groups such as the Puerto

---

81   *Special Sedition*, November 1982, 5. In author's possession.

Rican clandestine movement, this was the first time that STO had openly published anything that could reasonably be described as a direct incitement to violence. The Northwest branch of STO, based in Portland
and Seattle, strongly criticized the content of the magazine, denouncing
it as "a call for random violence against the police and others."[82] They advanced two different arguments against the publication. First, they feared
police harassment and repression of STO members as a result of the
magazine's public support for antipolice violence. Without rejecting illegality as such, they argued that "illegal activities demand clandestinity,
and clandestinity has its own set of rules, and they are inflexible."[83] Second, they rejected the potentially antisocial attitude conveyed by *Special
Sedition*. "We are aware," they wrote, "that many of today's working class
but workless youth are seriously alienated from mainstream society.…
Our task is to try to harness the alienated energy and turn it toward more
useful channels of change."[84]

Thus began a minor but instructive debate within STO over the concept of autonomy, this time in the context of youth, and especially white,
working-class youth. Many members of STO responded negatively to
both aspects of the argument made by the Northwest branch. Ken Lawrence focused his attention on the question of violence, and in particular
on the question of whether *Special Sedition* amounted to "adventurism."
Drawing on the example of the broad public support for antipolice violence in Northern Ireland, he tied his answer to a speculative estimate of
the future prospects of youth revolt and its ability to cross racial lines: "if
we hope someday for white people to join the radical insurgent movements in the US with some recognized legitimacy, it is only likely to
happen when oppressed people have some reason to view a sector of
whites as revolutionary in the way they are, part of which would entail
the use of similar forms of revolutionary struggle, both spontaneous and
planned, increasingly organized, self-conscious and massive."[85] Lawrence
also made it clear that he did not think it was problematic for STO to

---

82   Letter from Frank Giese "for the NW branch" November 16, 1982, in
      Secret Supplement to *IDB* #29, December 1982, 1.

83   Ibid.

84   Ibid.

85   Ken Lawrence, "Questions for the NC Debate on *Special Sedition*,"
      in *IDB* #31, 9. In defining "adventurist," Lawrence utilized the term
      "Custeristic," coined in 1969 by Fred Hampton, then Chair of the Illi-
      nois Black Panther Party, to criticize the Days of Rage coordinated that
      fall by the Weatherman faction of SDS.

endorse illegal activity in which its own members would not engage, again using the Irish example of Sinn Fein's public support for the IRA's illegal activities.

Others in STO were less concerned with the question of violence than with the concept of youth autonomy. Ted Whitney, himself a younger member of STO, forcefully rejected the Northwest's "harness the energy" approach, noting that "this phrase has terrible implications as an organizing principle if it is applied to youth, the working class, or a movement. It violates STO's position on self-activity and autonomy. It unfortunately sounds so much like the left I have come to hate, a left that thinks of itself as the eventual leadership and conscience of the movement."[86] This concern was shared by many others in STO, which by this point was solidly attached to an expansive version of the idea of autonomy. While recognizing the possibility that white youth violence could manifest in antisocial and even fascist forms, Whitney and others maintained that "a left which is too conservative may end up losing potential comrades to the growing fascist movement."[87] In an antifascist context, then, the problem was not the danger of supporting youth rebellion, but rather the danger of *not* supporting it, of appearing to be too loyal to the status quo.

In some ways, the publication of *Special Sedition* marked the beginning of STO's final phase of existence, one marked less by theoretical sophistication than by an intense commitment to militant direct action in a range of venues. As former member Bill Lamme comments, "this was not the period of dialectics workshops, this was post-dialectics and into diabolics."[88] He explains the transition as a sort of self-criticism of STO's complicity in the impotence of radical movements:

> We're essentially playing the game by the rules that the ruling class wants, that is, that we don't support the state, but our forms of protest are not threatening to the state. The movement presents no challenge to the state, only rhetorically, and its actions belie that. So, the last period for me was the period in which we attempted to do things, mass forms of illegal activity. You know, petty forms of property destruction, cut a lock or glue a lock, paint a wall at a demonstration, block the street, or interfere with what's

---

86   Ted Whitney, "Dear Comrades of the NW Branch," letter in *IDB* #31, 31.

87   Ibid.

88   Bill Lamme, interview with the author, July 20, 2005.

going on, and then not wait to get arrested, to run away and live to fight again, that sort of attitude. To just take a little feistier position in terms of our action and direct action. Direct action was not something new to STO, but the practicing of it had been limited.[89]

Even though he had been centrally involved in the preparations for the *No Easy Answers Left* conference, Lamme himself heartily embraced what appeared to some other veteran members of the group to be a 180 degree turn from what STO had previously represented. "I could certainly understand how somebody could say that that wasn't STO because, as I said at the beginning, part of the thing that attracted me to STO was its intellectual rigor, and that period did not have that…. So, I think people left as the group changed … [but] to me, it was logical, the argument to do what we did at that point."[90]

Of course, the group did not entirely abandon a commitment to theory, but its most distinctive theorizing during this period was concerned with revolutionary strategy. One major example was the strategy of refusal, borrowed from the writings of Antonio Negri, who by the early eighties was a political prisoner in Italy. Janeen Creamer and others in the group were especially interested in Negri's 1977 essay "Working Class Sabotage and Capitalist Domination," which they believed offered a workable approach to revolution. Creamer argued that "refusal is also an approach of confrontation—confrontation with all capitalist alternatives among sectors of the working class."[91] In STO's hands, this strategy consolidated itself into the promotion of mass, public illegality as a way to break out of the constraints of reformism. Major direct actions against the US military, defense contractors, and other targets became the order of the day. This represented in some ways the practical implementation of the millenarian view of capitalism's secular crisis described earlier, and it was part and parcel of the declining fortunes of STO. For every member who was enthusiastic for the strategy of refusal, there were others who left demoralized or confused at the left's ever-worsening disarray.

* * *

---

89   Ibid.
90   Ibid.
91   Janeen Porter, "On Negri," in *Discussion Bulletin*, December 1983, 132.

By 1983, STO was in full organizational freefall. Having already lost the Kansas City branch, the group quickly shed its members in the Pacific Northwest, largely as a result of frustration at the handling of the Kansas City split, as well as disagreement with the majority sentiment in Chicago around *Special Sedition* and the limitations of the Harold Washington campaign. Others left as well, including longtime members like Noel Ignatin and Alan Rausch. Some newer members, recruited in the context of STO's involvement with antinuclear and antiwar organizing, departed out of a growing skepticism of Leninism, a process that was unintentionally abetted by the group's embrace of autonomy. (At least one person, former member Kingsley Clarke, rejoined the group during this period, but this was certainly the exception to the rule.) The shrinkage snowballed, and by September it was clear that only a handful of members outside of Chicago were still active in the organization. As a result, "it was decided to dissolve the NC [National Committee] and henceforth to have membership meetings."[92] Even though the group's *Discussion Bulletin* for December of 1983 was one of the largest ever at 165 pages, replete with draft theses on topics like white supremacy and the Middle East, it was to be STO's last gasp as far as publications were concerned. (*Urgent Tasks* had published its final issue a year before, in late 1982.)

While the sudden organizational silence may have given the impression of a group fading away, veterans of the final phase see it differently. Lamme, for instance, argues that

> the left was also in the process of ending its run … by the mid-eighties, there were still groups out there, but it had lost a lot of its dynamic. There were still very committed people there, but not as many; the numbers had fallen. And I think partly, that impelled STO to go one way or the other. It was very hard to hold a middle ground in the politics that we represented. So in a way, we, those of us who were left at the end, were actually going out with a bang. We were saying, "If we're going to do it, we're going to give a little shock to the wing of the movement that we're most a part of, in the form of this direct action, and see if we can light a spark. And part of the reason the movement is declining is because it's never been serious enough, never

---

92   "Organization/Membership," in *Discussion Bulletin*, December 1983, 109.

really challenged the system in ways that people can identify with and do themselves, and so forth.[93]

Seen from this perspective, the turn toward direct action represented a final stab at resuscitating the dying remnants of the movements of the seventies that had always been STO's milieu. As the final phase unfolded, STO existed in a form that contemporary radicals (especially anarchists) would immediately recognize as an affinity group: no more than a dozen members who, having developed a high degree of trust in each other through shared experience, worked together in the context of larger protests to push the envelope of business as usual.

In this final stage, STO's biggest contribution was a series of actions outside the Rock Island Arsenal in 1984 and 1985. The Arsenal, located on an island in the Mississippi River between Illinois and Iowa some 170 miles west of Chicago, was the US military's largest plant for the production of conventional weapons. In the mid-eighties, many of the machine guns and howitzer cannons manufactured on Rock Island were destined for US client states in El Salvador, Guatemala, Israel, Lebanon, and other imperialist hot spots. This made it a natural site of protest for those opposed to US military involvement in Central America and the Middle East. In fact, a small number of faith-based activists had held regular prayer services on the island, but outside the gates of the Arsenal itself, for several years. At the same time, STO had utilized its longstanding contacts within the anti-intervention movement, going back to the People's Anti-War Mobilization in 1981, to participate in building a small activist core in Chicago known as the Disarm Now Action Group, sometimes shortened to Disarm Now. Early in 1984, Disarm Now worked to galvanize dozens of organizations and hundreds of individuals in support of a militant protest outside the Arsenal that June. According to Janeen Porter and others, the first Rock Island protest was the result of a dream she had one night, in which a carefully orchestrated direct action shut down the Arsenal. Three bridges linked the island to the surrounding cities of Davenport, Moline, and Rock Island (collectively known, along with Bettendorf, as the Quad Cities), and the plan was to block traffic across the bridges.

The action was organized in a manner that carefully balanced the need to maximize media exposure with an attentiveness to secrecy in planning; spokespeople (including STO member Bill Lamme) routinely announced their objective was to shut down the plant, but they refused

---

93   Bill Lamme, interview with the author, July 20, 2005.

to specify the methods to be used. In yet another nod to the idea of autonomy, the participating groups were encouraged to devise their own action plans, produce their own leaflets and placards, and generally engage in what a later generation of activists came to know as "diversity of tactics."[94] In a subsequent evaluation of the day's events, a member of Disarm Now pointed to the "contradiction in organizing" for the shutdown, between wanting to encourage militant creative tactics and needing a critical mass of participants for the action to be successful: "the invaluable aspect of this action that would have been lost in resolving the contradiction by compromise in either direction is the exposure of a large number of participants to autonomous direct action."[95]

Outreach for the day of action was extensive. Both movement and mainstream media outlets across the country covered the impending showdown. Activist spokespeople like Lamme deliberately crafted their media comments as a moral appeal to the 9,000 civilian employees of the Arsenal. Contrasting the evident prosperity on the island with the shrinking farm equipment factories in the rapidly deindustrializing Quad Cities, Lamme said, "We're not telling [Arsenal employees] to quit work. We're not threatening them. We just want them to think about the end result of their work and realize they aren't just some cog in a wheel.… There is job stability for weapons makers while people who make implements for food production are out of work."[96] Even in its final phase, STO incorporated an appeal to working-class autonomy into its activities.

Direct appeals for support and participation were also made to working-class people in the Quad Cities. According to one report, "several distinct leaflets were written, one called 'Hungry? Eat your 105MM Howitzer' for unemployed workers and workers in the agricultural

94   For a sympathetic analysis of the emergence of "diversity of tactics" in the context of the movement against capitalist globalization from the Seattle protests of 1999 to the Québec City demonstrations of 2011, see Chris Hurl, "Anti-Globalization and 'Diversity of Tactics'," in *Upping the Anti-* Number 1 (2005). Available online at http://uppingtheanti.org/journal/article/01-anti-globalization-and-diversity-of-tactics/ (accessed January 10, 2012).

95   Mike Haywood, "The Siege of the Arsenal: Project Disarm's Direct Action at the Army's Rock Island," unpublished manuscript in author's possession (n.d., but c. 1984, 3).

96   Quoted in "Arsenal protest aims for 1-day shutdown," *Chicago Tribune*, May 29, 1984, N4.

implements plants in the Quad Cities."[97] Kingsley Clarke distinctly re-members distributing this leaflet to people waiting in lines at welfare offices in Davenport.[98] Another key target audience was disaffected and especially punk-rock-oriented young people. When the Clash toured the US that spring, they played in Davenport and encouraged their fans to attend "a party on June 4th to push all the tanks into the river."[99] Concert-goers there and at other Midwestern punk shows that spring received a leaflet that described the planned demonstration and joked about "the Disruption, a new street dance."[100]

The US Military responded to the impending protest by dramatically enhancing security procedures. New chainlink fencing and concertina wire were installed on the island, and guard posts were built on all ap-proaching bridges. A new commander was appointed, and one of his first actions was to prohibit the long-standing prayer vigils and seal off previously open parts of the military base.[101] In a telling sign of military anxiety, three hundred specially trained military police were redeployed from Georgia and Kansas to reinforce the Arsenal's ranks. Local police forces in each of the surrounding cities spent heavily on riot gear and other new equipment as the siege-like atmosphere filtered out from the island. Quad Cities activists claimed they were under police surveillance as the day of the protest approached.

Finally, in the early morning of Monday, June 4, several hundred protesters converged on the Quad Cities. Because of the autonomous affinity group design of the demonstration, there was a wide range of protest activity, all of it militant while remaining nonviolent. People used street repair barricades and detour signs to divert traffic as it ap-proached the bridges. Others performed educational skits for workers and others stuck in traffic. Kingsley Clarke recalls that "there were five hundred or so people in Rock Island, ranging from people who wanted to do what I call pranks, like dressing up in clown uniforms, people who chained themselves to various stable objects, people who just ran wild in the streets, and of course STO took pride in its slightly more militaristic, planned approach."[102] In the end, close to two hundred protestors were

_____

97   Haywood, "The Siege of the Arsenal," 5.

98   Kingsley Clarke, interview with the author, April 2, 2006.

99   Quoted in Haywood, "The Siege of the Arsenal," 5.

100 Ibid.

101 See "Arsenal protest aims for 1-day shutdown," *Chicago Tribune*, May 29, 1984, N4.

102 Kingsley Clarke, interview with the author, April 2, 2006.

arrested over several hours, but the bridges and the Arsenal remained open. Organizers from Disarm Now nonetheless claimed victory for having severely disrupted the normal operations of the plant.

Inside STO and Disarm Now, discussions began almost immediately about staging a second attempt. A small protest with no arrests took place that September, but Rock Island "Two" did not take place until October 21, 1985. This time, the organizers actively encouraged a more militant approach to shutting down the Arsenal. While still welcoming traditional civil disobedience, one leaflet designed to recruit participants allowed people to check a box labeled "I want to mess up the Arsenal, get away, and do it again."[103] This approach led to the withdrawal of several groups that had participated in the first action, and the total number of participants was perhaps three hundred instead of the five to six hundred that showed the prior year. Clarke remembers that the second attempt was "a smaller effort in every way, and an attempt to be more precise."[104] Local police put their own spin on the difference, with a Rock Island Police Sergeant claiming that "this year, they were more hostile and violent."[105] Activists used railroad ties, car tires, and other objects to stop traffic approaching the bridges. Others pushed junked automobiles into the roadways and then chained themselves inside. Some demonstrators clashed directly with police, and several injuries were reported. Once again, the bridges and the Arsenal remained open for business, but this time protesters claimed "we at least slowed Arsenal production momentarily."[106] The official response denied this, claiming that "98 percent" of employees arrived on time to work.[107] While the outcome was still far short of the stated goal of shutting down access to the island, many participants believed it was more effective than the first attempt. Nonetheless, in the aftermath the organizing groups splintered further over the question of proper tactics. In a context where neither attempt had achieved its stated objective of shutting down the plant, and where Reagan's warmongering seemed more popular than ever, demoralization began to set in. After 1985, no further attempts were made to shut down the Arsenal.

---

103   Disarm Now Action Group leaflet in author's possession, n.d., but c. 1985.

104   Clarke, interview with the author, April 2, 2006.

105   Quoted in "85 Seized in Demonstration at Arsenal," *Chicago Tribune*, Tuesday October 22, 1985, 3A.

106   Quoted in "117 Arrested in Arsenal Clash," *Moline Daily Dispatch*, Monday October 21, 1985, 1A.

107   Ibid.

The two Rock Island demonstrations were part of a series of militant direct actions in which STO was actively involved during the mid-eighties. Others targeted the major defense contractor Northrop, the Great Lakes Naval Base in the north suburbs of Chicago, as well as companies that were using strike-breaking scab labor, including Greyhound Bus Company. Each of these protests arguably enhanced the skills and experience of a number of activists and raised public awareness on a range of causes, but they did not force immediate, substantial changes on the part of the targeted entities. Without concrete victories, it was difficult to sustain the energy required to plan and execute actions that included a substantial risk of arrest. Nonetheless, the direct-action wing of the anti-intervention movement remained strong in the Midwest throughout the decade, and many of the veterans of the Rock Island demonstrations were involved for years to come.

* * *

In the end, STO's bang really did become a whimper, however. Participation in direct-action protests continued, but eventually the organizational framework simply stopped functioning. No former member can pinpoint precisely when in the mid-eighties the Sojourner Truth Organization ceased to exist. The remaining members were getting older, so the physical exertion and risk aspects of the direct-action model were relatively more demanding. Meanwhile, dozens if not hundreds of former members had moved on in their lives, some still working in factories or offices, others returning to school or to professional careers they had earlier abandoned in favor of revolutionary struggle. Almost without exception, they remained politically on the left, although a great number made their personal peace with the persistence of capitalism and ceased to identify as revolutionaries. STO was hardly alone in its terminal decline: it was preceded in death by the Communist Party (Marxist-Leninist), the May 19th Communist Organization, the Philadelphia Workers' Organizing Committee, and literally dozens of other sometime competitors on the far left. And while the various broader social movements continued to ebb and flow, the revolutionary aspects of many of them were increasingly eclipsed by the pull of reform and social democracy. The mid-eighties was a very difficult time to survive politically on the outer fringes of the US left.

At a certain point, possibly in 1986, someone still in the group received a notice from the US Postal Service that they needed to pay their annual bill for maintaining STO's mailing address. For at least fifteen years, the Sojourner Truth Organization had been associated in its print-ed material with P.O. Box 8493, Chicago IL 60680. But when the pub-lishing side of things stopped, the remaining members apparently forgot about the P.O. Box. As Bill Lamme remembers it, laughing while he tells the story, "And at one point, I forget how I got it, but all of a sudden I got the responsibility to go check the mailbox. The mailbox hadn't been checked in something like a year.... I went and picked up the junk, and I think I renewed the thing for another year, but I don't think I ever went back and checked it."[108] So ended the Sojourner Truth Organization, more than a decade and a half after it sprang to life at the end of 1969.

---

108 Bill Lamme, interview with the author, July 20, 2005.

Conclusion:
Reading STO Politically

I had been working on this book for two years when our son Nico was born in 2007. With our daughter Sofia not yet two years old, my wife and I desperately needed a double stroller. Craigslist led us to a wealthy family, not far from us in Chicago, who were willing to part with one for a remarkably low price. I went to their house to complete the purchase and immediately realized that they lived in the gated community that sits on the former site of the Stewart-Warner factory, which had been the focal point of so much of STO's early workplace organizing. Noel Ignatiev had previously remarked to me how it was the epitome of STO's failure that deindustrialization had replaced a vibrant nexus of proletarian activity with a thoroughly contemporary example of bourgeois hegemony.[1] Needless to say, when I gently quizzed the sellers, they had no inkling of what had preceded them, other than some vague knowledge that there had once been some sort of factory there.

The history of STO is fundamentally a tragic tale. The revolution for which the group ceaselessly agitated not only never came, but was arguably further away after its fifteen-plus years of effort.[2] The same is true, of course, regarding the overall arc of the revolutionary left in the

---

1   Noel Ignatiev, interview with the author, July 16, 2005.
2   Such a statement is not intended to endorse a linear approach to revolution; upsurges of mass activity often emerge very quickly, or in largely unanticipated circumstances. This was the case with the Occupy movement in 2011. Still, the apparent prospects for such an upsurge in 1986 looked so much less promising than had been the case in 1969 that this assessment seems justified.

United States over the past century and half. But the purpose of history is neither to bemoan failure nor to offer rose-tinted platitudes; as the young Marx famously remarked, "the philosophers have only *interpreted* the world, in various ways; the point is to *change* it."[3] With that in mind, a continuing debate among former members of STO is instructive: some veterans of the group attribute the organization's collapse to shifting objective conditions as the upheaval of the sixties was replaced by the seemingly irreversible trend toward deindustrialization and the coming of the Reagan Revolution in the seventies and eighties. Other former members view STO's demise as first and foremost a failure of will, arguing that a sufficiently determined revolutionary core could have adapted to the changing circumstances. Both arguments have merit, and they are hardly incompatible.

Part of the problem in assessing the legacy of STO is the undeniable fact that the contemporary context is dramatically different than it was during the era of STO's rise and fall, and deindustrialization is only the tip of this iceberg of changing objective conditions. In the quarter-century since the group finally gave up the ghost, the world has been profoundly transformed—economically, technologically, culturally, and ideologically. Deindustrialization was revealed to be part of a broader process sometimes known as neoliberalism or "globalization from above." Capital, which had long been transnational, has become increasingly unmoored from individual nation-states, even those long considered superpowers. The Soviet Union collapsed in 1991, and both Russia and China are now central nodes in an integrated system of global capitalism. (Arguably, this shift—especially regarding China—was predictable based on the theory of state capitalism that was popular within STO after 1976.) The US, meanwhile, has been substantially displaced from the pivotal position at the center of global capital that it held for several decades after the end of World War Two. At the same time, the rise of new technologies like cell phones and the Internet has permanently altered the speed of communication and the accessibility of information on a local, national, and global scale. The demographics of the US population have also been reconfigured, with new immigrants from Latin America (especially Mexico) moving ahead of not only Puerto Ricans but also African Americans to become the second largest racial grouping after whites. Global warming represents a deepening of the ecological crisis whose contours were only sketchily mapped in the mid-eighties. On an

---

3   Karl Marx, "Concerning Feuerbach" (1845), in Marx, *Early Writings* (New York: Vintage Books, 1975), 423.

ideological level, the attacks of September 11, 2001 symbolize a new reality where the most visible challenge to capitalist hegemony emerges from the right rather than the left.

Simultaneously, the forms of resistance that featured prominently in STO's era have largely been swept from the field. Cities like Chicago and Kansas City now retain few of the massive factories that employed tens of thousands of demographically diverse proletarians, which for several years the group thought of as the hot house within which revolutionary movements would develop. The revolutionary nationalist currents that STO spent many years supporting have fared even worse. Whether in South Africa, El Salvador, or the Puerto Rican community in Chicago, they have been thoroughly recuperated and incorporated into the functioning of global capitalism. New formations, from the EZLN in Mexico to the antifascist current represented by Anti-Racist Action in the US and Canada, have developed in ways that challenge traditional notions of revolutionary struggle. The arc of the so-called antiglobalization movement between the Seattle protests of 1999 and the Genoa demonstrations just prior to September 11, 2001, represented one possible future for radicalism, but in more recent years the touchstones for the left have been (variously, depending upon one's perspective) the Bolivarian revolution in Venezuela, the Maoist movement in Nepal, the Arab Spring phenomenon, and, closest to home and most recently, the Occupy movement.

All these changes demand adjustments when attempting to implement the best insights of STO in the present day. To do so is consistent with STO's own approach. Even though a number of former members acknowledge, for example, that the group did not recognize deindustrialization for what it really was until very late in the process, it is nonetheless true that STO was consistently attentive to the changing objective conditions within which it operated. Ironically, there has been something of a tendency (among the tiny number of contemporary leftists who have any knowledge of the group) to approach STO with what might be called a "Civil War Reenactment" mentality. The group's semi-famous dialectics course represents one example: during the several year period—roughly 1978 to 1983—when STO organized intensive dialectics courses, the curriculum was frequently revised, sometimes in substantial ways. But when the course was resuscitated around 2008 by a collection of former members and people associated with the group Bring the Ruckus, the curriculum was lifted more or less whole cloth from the version published in *Urgent Tasks* in 1980, despite major shifts not only in objective conditions but also in left theory over the intervening decades. Certainly, the new courses should be welcomed, and they have proven useful to many revolutionary activists across the country who have participated over the past few years. Nonetheless, for contemporary radicals to fully appreciate the legacy of STO, they must reconcile themselves to the incredible changes the world has seen since the group's demise.

At the same time, it is hard to avoid the conclusion that STO was plagued by certain internal subjective flaws that could and should have been corrected, but never were. Since such mistakes are at least capable of being addressed by contemporary radicals, and especially since a number of them continue to beset a range of left projects in the new millennium, the bulk of this chapter will be devoted to this part of STO's legacy. Of course, many of the group's problems were simultaneously the flip-side of some of its greatest contributions to subsequent left projects, and this dialectical relationship between error and insight must be kept in mind. The list of possible "lessons learned" is quite lengthy, but in general it can be consolidated into four categories. The first, regarding the fundamental changes in external context over the past quarter century, has already been addressed, if only briefly. The others, each of which deserves extended consideration, can be labeled "theory," "strategy," and "organization." To a certain extent, these categories and the lessons that they contain have relatively little to do with the specific work undertaken by STO in the factories, communities, and social movements of the seventies and eighties. It would not in general be useful, for example, simply to translate forward in time the specific approaches to organizing in the steel mills that were essential to STO's efforts in 1972. Instead, I have attempted to generalize lessons that can be applied in varying ways to the broad range of contemporary radical efforts, including work around the situation of immigrants, police brutality and the prison industrial complex, and certainly the Occupy movement that emerged in the fall of 2011, among many, many more.

* * *

STO has been remembered, to the extent it has been remembered at all, first and foremost for its contributions to revolutionary theory. The group's main innovations were in the areas of white skin privilege, dual consciousness, autonomy, and the overall intellectual development of the left. Each of these holds real value for radicals today, though each also contains serious problems that can be traced to their development within STO. White skin privilege represents by far the broadest diffusion of ideas associated with STO, having been adopted in one form or another by a strikingly wide range of activists, intellectuals, faith-based groups, and even politicians.[4] On one level this is evidence of the accuracy of the term in describing the daily reality of white supremacy in the US, but on another level it indicates the limits of the theory as an organizing principle. STO was by no means the only group of its era to adopt a white skin privilege analysis, but Noel Ignatin was one of its most important theorists (alongside Ted Allen), and the organization overall was one of the most consistently vocal sites of advocacy for the idea within the US left. Its degeneration into a form of liberal guilt-tripping therefore cannot be laid solely at the feet of STO, but the group must bear some of the responsibility for this all-too-common manifestation of the theory.[5] At the same time, in the years since his departure from STO Ignatiev himself has put incredible effort into combating this version of the white skin privilege theory, advancing instead the idea that "treason to whiteness

---

4   The most famous example here is former Senator Bill Bradley, who referred directly to white skin privilege in a presidential debate in Harlem with then-Vice President Al Gore during the Democratic Primaries of 2000. Bradley answered a question about race and the criminal justice system by saying, "That requires a president who is strong and willing to lead on the central question of race in our country today. And that means sometimes telling white Americans what they don't want to hear. And I, therefore, don't do it with any kind of pointed finger. But take the issue of white skin privilege… When I was a rookie in the NBA, I got a lot of offers to do television and commercials, to do advertisements. And why did I get those? White skin privilege. I wasn't the best player on the team, but I didn't take those because I thought that was not the right thing to do and that they were—should have gone to my African American teammates. We have to explain white privilege." Transcript of the Democratic Presidential Candidates Debate at Harlem's Apollo Theater, February 21, 2000. Available online at http://transcripts.cnn.com/TRANSCRIPTS/0002/21/se.04.html   (accessed January 12, 2012).

5   For a more nuanced take on the twists and turns of privilege-based models of oppression, see my 2007 talk, "The White Skin Privilege Concept: From Margin to Center of Revolutionary Politics," given at the *Renewing the Anarchist Tradition Conference* that November. Available online at   http://sojournertruth.blogsome.com/2007/11/09/the-white-skin-privilege-concept-from-margin-to-center-of-revolutionary-politics/ (accessed January 12, 2012).

is loyalty to humanity."[6] The journal *Race Traitor*, which he co-edited, represented a clear counterweight to liberal interpretations, although it regularly succumbed to a sort of atomized approach that called upon individual white people to abandon their whiteness, as if such privileges were affirmatively chosen rather than granted by outside forces.

As I write, we are living through the tenure of the United States' first black president, so it is also worth contemplating the future of white supremacy. STO was correct in identifying whiteness as a division within the working class that prevented unified action against capitalism in the US, but it is entirely possible that sections of an increasingly globalized capitalist class will willingly jettison traditional forms of white supremacy, much as they are quickly relieving themselves of most vulgar versions of homophobia.[7] Any such process will of course be uneven, and subject to repeated reversals of direction. Just as obviously, white supremacy has developed into an independent ideology with a strong foothold among whites in all class strata, such that it no longer lives or dies depending solely upon its value to the continued functioning of capitalism. Fascist movements will probably become more enamored of whiteness to the extent that capital retreats from it. But the traditional idea of privileges granted by capital and the state may come to mean less and less as the new century progresses. To that extent, the value of STO's most widely appreciated contribution to political theory may decline precipitously in the coming years.

If white skin privilege is STO's most utilized theoretical construct, the idea of dual consciousness has certainly been its most under-applied

---

6   This slogan appeared on the cover of each issue of the journal *Race Traitor*. Selections from the first several issues were collected in Noel Ignatiev and John Garvey, eds., *Race Traitor* (New York: Routledge, 1996).

7   Much of California's corporate elite, including both Apple and Google, opposed the 2008 ballot initiative known as Proposition Eight, which prohibited gay marriage. See the full page ad, headlined "Silicon Valley Leaders Urge You to Stand for Equality," which ran in the *San Jose Mercury News*, October 31, 2008, available online at http://techcrunch.com/2008/10/30/silicon-valley-stands-united-against-prop-8/ (accessed January 12, 2012). Similarly, sixty-eight Fortune 500 corporations submitted an amicus brief to the US Supreme Court in 2003 in support of the University of Michigan's affirmative action admissions policies. See the list "Amicus Curiae Briefs on Behalf of the University of Michigan" on the Association of American Colleges and Universities website, available online at http://www.aacu.org/About/amicuscuriae.cfm (accessed January 12, 2012).

innovation. This is unfortunate, because the notion that individual working people reflect the contradictions of capitalism, and that these contradictions can come to a head in the course of collective struggle, is a profoundly reassuring prospect for any contemporary radical attempting to reconcile the continuing reality of bourgeois hegemony with the hope for a revolution organized from the bottom up. Without it, one is doomed either to a naïvely optimistic view of the revolutionary vanguard or to a needlessly pessimistic belief in delusional false consciousness as the roadblock to social change. Each of these alternatives removes masses of people from their central role in revolutionary struggle, a pride of place that STO was always determined to maintain. And yet, many versions of contemporary revolutionary theory lack any clear idea of what "class" is, let alone a sophisticated treatment of class consciousness and its development. Present-day and future radicals have much to learn from close readings of *Toward a Revolutionary Party*, Ignatin's "Black Worker, White Worker," and Lee Holstein's "Working Class Self-Activity: A Reply to Kim Moody," among many other pieces associated with STO that address the question of dual consciousness. The only real downside here is that dual consciousness always remained a largely theoretical insight, one whose real-world application by STO was too often tied to a particular concept of autonomy that had built-in limitations.

Autonomy, like white skin privilege, is rather broadly incorporated into the radical theories of the new century. Similarly, it has also been utilized in ways that contrast sharply with its development in STO. Once again, however, this has at least something to do with the fact that autonomy as a concept was never the exclusive property of STO. Indeed, it represents one of the main bridges between the legacy of STO and my own political tradition of contemporary revolutionary anarchism, with "libertarian communism" as the point of overlap. The novel application of autonomy to communities of color, youth, and other strata of the working class, was one of the most valuable insights generated by the group. By the same token, autonomy was one of the seeds of STO's own destruction, insofar as it led some members to neglect the organizational needs of their own group. In the intervening years, this sort of negligence has become far more extreme. As Kevin McDonnell, a veteran of the English revolutionary group Big Flame, argues, some contemporary advocates of autonomy maintain that

> the revolution cannot be predicted. It is the sum of all the diverse struggles underway against the current order. These need to stay outside of any form of institution unless they

become tainted. They cannot be organized. Any talk of a
strategy is about some people doing the thinking for other
people. Whatever the differences which existed in Big
Flame, I assume that everyone would distance themselves
from autonomism in its purest form.[8]

Presumably the same is true for veterans of STO, despite the internal
confusion sown by the concept's expanding popularity among the membership during its final years.

Above and beyond its own theoretical preoccupations, STO was committed to the development of revolutionary theory and the production
of what Gramsci called organic intellectuals, both inside and outside the
organization.[9] The dialectics course was the most obvious manifestation
of this aspect of STO's theoretical legacy, but the implications run far
deeper. It could be argued that STO was in fact led by organic intellectuals, in light of the ways in which many of the group's leading members
personally distanced themselves from the academy. None of STO's three
major theorists—Don Hamerquist, Noel Ignatiev, and Ken Lawrence—
held a college degree while a member of the group, although Ignatiev
did obtain a Ph.D. after leaving it.[10] It is true that the "second tier" of
intellectuals (the range of members who contributed in varying ways
to developing theory within the group but were not major theorists) in
STO featured a number of attorneys and some people who had received
advanced degrees before joining the group, as well as a number who, like
Ignatiev, returned to school and obtained advanced degrees after leaving STO. Regardless, the question has less to do with the composition
of the group itself, and more to do with the broadmindedness of the
organization's approach to theory. STO was unusual among left groups
of its era in having three distinct and often competing theoretical lead-

---

8   Kevin McDonnell, "Big Flame's Legacy: What is of Value and What
     Isn't" (2010), published on the Big Flame web archive, available online
     at http://bigflameuk.wordpress.com/2010/01/18/opinions-about-big-
     flame-no-5-kevin-mcdonnell/ (accessed January 12, 2012).

9   This commitment contrasts sharply with the general distaste for theory
     in the otherwise comparable British group Big Flame. See Kevin Mc-
     Donnell, "Big Flame's Legacy."

10   Interestingly, Ignatiev was admitted to graduate school in the mid-
     eighties without ever having completed his undergraduate degree,
     having dropped out of college some two decades earlier to pursue revo-
     lutionary organizing in a factory context.

ers, as Ignatin, Hamerquist, and Lawrence routinely disagreed with each other on major issues. Additionally, each of them was frequently challenged by newer members who had their own theoretical insights. This process accelerated as the dialectics courses produced a new generation of communist theoretician-activists. As the eighties progressed, however, STO was riven with conflict between those who wanted to go deeper into theoretical questions (whether relating to Jamesian autonomy or to a *Grundrisse*-influenced analysis of the nature of the period) and those who demanded a higher priority be placed on enacting their theoretical conclusions—however provisional—in revolutionary practice.

Parallel to this internal conflict was a contradiction around the group's publicly proclaimed and idiosyncratic pantheon of theoretical influences. Marx and Lenin were certainly standards, but Antonio Gramsci, W.E.B. Du Bois, and C.L.R. James were anything but commonplace touchstones among the revolutionary left at the time. (The fact that each of these latter three subsequently became the subject of minor trends in academic study bears observation, but does not invalidate the innovativeness of STO's early promotion of their work.) The group made use of ideas from both Maoism and Trotskyism, even while it eschewed both labels. Similarly, STO's extensive publication record in terms of pamphlets, discussion papers, *Urgent Tasks*, and the *Internal Discussion Bulletin*, much of which is now available on the Internet at the STO web archive, was reflective of its commitment to developing new theory.

One longstanding problem with this continuing project, however, was the group's persistent determination to frame its ideas within the confines of Leninism. Of course, this was a proudly unorthodox Leninism, focused largely on the Lenin of *State and Revolution* rather than on more commonly referenced texts like *Left Wing Communism, an Infantile Disorder*. Nonetheless, it took a seemingly endless series of contortions—both of STO's ideas and of Lenin's—to maintain the notion of a shared lineage traceable to the Russian experience but independent of later deviations, be they Stalinist, Trotskyist, Maoist, or Eurocommunist. All three of the intellectual "heavies," as they were known, were well versed in the arcane sport of quoting obscure sections of the complete works of Lenin, as well as the equivalent collection from Marx and Engels. To take just one example, Ignatin suggested in 1980 that, while it was possible that Lenin's position on rejecting dual unionism was wrong (he even included a self-deprecating "gasp!" to indicate just how unusual such a conclusion would have been in the milieu within which STO operated), his own position was "that Lenin is universally misinterpreted."[11] Hamerquist and Lawrence were at least as willing to advance similarly contrarian arguments, whether they referred to the question of the autonomy of the Bund (see Chapter Eight) or to the validity of Stalin's four criteria for nationhood (see Chapter Five). Despite occasional protests that being Leninists was less important than being correct, it is difficult to read much of STO's theoretical output without confronting a standard sort of appeal to authority that sounds dated and sectarian to contemporary ears. While Lenin remains an incredibly rich source for theoretical insights into revolutionary struggle, the idea that any emerging revolutionary formation in the new millennium is obligated to uphold some allegiance to Lenin*ism* seems completely beside the point.

* * *

Connecting all of STO's diverse experiences was a sort of real-world revolutionary pragmatism that did not always track with its seemingly unshakeable theoretical commitments. While this tension opened the door to criticisms of the group's practical work as needlessly eclectic, there are actually any number of themes that connect a wide range of activities undertaken over the better part of two decades. Most of these have less to do with theory than they do with revolutionary strategy. Questions of mass action and illegality, of internationalism and anti-imperialism, of antifascism, feminism, popular culture, and the central role of class struggle, all present themselves when considering the contemporary value of STO.

The group's long-standing emphasis on mass action and illegality was directly connected to the notion that proletarian consciousness emerges in the context of struggle, and especially direct action. There was an almost mystical aspect to this analysis, with more than a touch of Fanon's ecstatic embrace of the transformative qualities of revolutionary violence.[12] For STO, however, the key was not necessarily violence (though the group always rejected pacifism) but rather the need to move beyond the confines of bourgeois legality. The mystical element was also related to a millenarian outlook that was perpetually anticipating the next (and

---

11   Noel Ignatin, "Preface," in *Workplace Papers* (Chicago: STO, 1980), i.

12   For Fanon's views on violence as the purveyor of "positive and creative qualities" (93) among the oppressed, see *The Wretched of the Earth* (New York: Grove Press, 1963), 35–106.

possibly, hopefully, *final*) upsurge, whether in the factories or emerging from within new social movements. Even during the period of the "lull" the group was convinced that mass struggles would return; it was only a question of when. On the one hand, this approach led many of the group's most enthusiastic members to burn out and leave in disillusionment when the hoped-for moment of upsurge continued to be put off. At the same time, it was precisely this constant attentiveness to new motion that allowed STO to engage at the earliest stages with the antinuclear movement, for example. The trick for contemporary radicals, of course, is to balance these two aspects, to avoid burnout without missing the boat when mass movements emerge (as they often do) suddenly and in unexpected places.[13] The revolutionary left's recent interaction with the Occupy movement presents a relevant case study. Some radicals immediately dismissed Occupy Wall Street as a liberal or populist manifestation of the sense of entitlement of bourgeois youth, while others latched on in order to aggressively push their specific organizational line. Still, there were some who quickly recognized the organic prospects for militant, anticapitalist organizing inherent in the movement. This latter tendency (including a number of organizations and individuals across the US who drew direct inspiration from the legacy of STO, not to mention a few former members) successfully involved itself in some of the most exciting aspects of the Occupy phenomenon, such as the Oakland General Strike of October 2011.

Considered more directly, the issue of illegality also has profound implications for revolutionary strategy. STO was highly aware of the ways in which public discussions of illegality were guaranteed to draw the attention of the repressive apparatus of the state and of private capitalist entities. The group spent significant time researching and analyzing the contours of both forms of repression, while scrupulously trying to avoid any direct entanglements with either. One of the small handful of STO-related documents to have been recently republished is Ken Lawrence's pamphlet *The New State Repression*, which challenged many common (then and still) left assumptions about police activity in the post-COIN-TELPRO era.[14] Echoing STO's general analysis, Lawrence argued that

---

13   A contemporary theoretical framework for this process can be found in the work of the French radical philosopher Alain Badiou, who encourages being "porous" to fundamental changes in the social terrain, the most extreme of which he calls "the event." See Alain Badiou, *Metapolitics* (London and New York: Verso, 2005).

14   Ken Lawrence, *The New State Repression* (Portland, OR: Tarantula, 2006

the legalistic defense of constitutional protections and civil liberties (so common on the left since the sixties) in fact undermined radical insurgencies instead of bolstering them. The same confusion around these issues that plagued the left in 1985 is ubiquitous today, and contemporary radical formations have much to learn from STO's attentiveness to illegality and repression.

Another aspect here was the deliberate decision to prioritize "mass" and "class" over "party," focusing on the decisive role masses of people would play in any revolutionary upsurge. This approach became more pronounced over time, basically in tandem with the group's growing attachment to autonomy and the eventual pyrrhic victory of the "mass" side in the debate over mass vs. left work (see Chapter Seven). There is incredible value today in this set of insights, especially when compared to the still-lingering legacy of what Max Elbaum has called the sect-building approach, which placed self-described vanguard parties at the center of all struggle.[15] When contemporary movements like the Arab Spring or Occupy show the ability to emerge almost without warning, it is essential to have a framework that allows for a critical analysis of the shortcomings of such developments, while still recognizing the central importance of the movements themselves. This was the approach taken, for instance, by a loose network of STO-inspired groups and individuals who participated actively in Occupy across the US. Critical reflections from a range of revolutionary perspectives were collected in the pamphlet *Hella Occupy!*, produced in December of 2011.[16]

One common manifestation of the support for mass action is the uncritical perspective that has sometimes been called "movementism," essentially the belief that social movements are entirely self-directing and that there is no value (or even negative value) in attempting to critically intervene within them as conscious revolutionaries. This viewpoint is in large part a result of a proper rejection of the sect-building model, but it bends the stick too far in the opposite direction. While STO consistently rejected this sort of approach and always emphasized the need to interact critically with any social struggle, it is not hard to see the line that leads from certain STO positions to movementism. The creation of what has

---

 [1985]). STO did not publish the original edition of the pamphlet (as it did not publish anything after 1983), but Lawrence did much of the research for it while still a member of STO.

15 See Elbaum, *Revolution in the Air*, 323–325.

16 *Hella Occupy!* pamphlet, available online at http://bringtheruckus. org/?q=node/167 (accessed January 12, 2012).

been termed the "nonprofit industrial complex" has also been part of the problem to the extent that NGOs routinely impose limits on forms of struggle and in particular the demand for legality.[17] One contemporary response to this problem has been the idea of the "intermediate level," advanced most clearly by S. Nappalos and the group Miami Autonomy and Solidarity.[18] Briefly, the argument is that between the small revolutionary organization and any mass movement there will always be a stratum of advanced or militant participants in the latter. For a revolutionary group to participate successfully within broader movements it is essential to build formations that can incorporate this intermediate level and allow both revolutionaries and the masses to learn from each other in ways that can advance the struggle. Nonetheless, even though this insight is fully compatible with STO's legacy, it does not resolve the deeper difficulty of attempting to develop revolutionary momentum in an era where mass movements of any sort are few and far between, the sudden rise of Occupy notwithstanding. This was partly the cause of the decline of STO itself, as the movements that emerged from the sixties receded and the organization became something of a fish out of water. Unfortunately, it is not clear that STO's strategic perspective on the importance of mass struggles provides any clear lessons that can solve this continuing problem. STO was always better at creating a pole within already existing movements than it was at catalyzing new ones.

The absence of social struggle is nowhere more stark than in the milieu of anti-imperialism and revolutionary nationalism, which in the second half of the seventies provided STO with a needed anchor in its efforts to develop a strategic orientation. Certainly, nationalism is just as important a force in the world today as it was in 1976, but the liberatory aspect of third world nationalism that was so attractive to STO has been replaced in almost every instance with a willful procapitalist stance that is in some cases frighteningly xenophobic.[19] In this context, it would

---

17   The classic work on the non-profit industrial complex is INCITE! Women of Color Against Violence, eds., *The Revolution Will Not Be Funded: Beyond the Non-Profit Industrial Complex* (Cambridge, MA: South End Press, 2007).

18   See S. Nappalos, "Defining Practice: The Intermediate Level of Organization and Struggle" (2010). Available online at http://anarkismo.net/article/16350 (accessed January 12, 2012).

19   It is certainly subject to debate whether the liberatory aspect was ever real, or if real, ever dominant, even in the seventies. Some nuanced insight on this question can be found in Alfredo M. Bonanno, *Anarchism*

be the height of foolishness to simply cut and paste specific strategic approaches from STO's anti-imperialist solidarity phase into the present day. For some former members, this awareness means much of the group's work after 1975 was a waste, but that conclusion is too harsh. It is possible to view this era of STO's work as a necessary error, one which produced a slew of lessons, many of them negative. For instance, while it was quite willing to criticize other anti-imperialist organizations (especially Prairie Fire and May 19th) for subordinating themselves to the organizational or ideological outlook of various revolutionary nationalist groups, in practice STO all too often did the exact same thing, specifically in relation to the MLN (see Chapter Five). In this regard, the internationalism promoted by the EZLN in Chiapas since 1994 has only reinforced the idea that solidarity must be an interplay between parties that acknowledge both their differences and their areas of agreement, leading to an honest form of mutual support.[20] Retaining an awareness of the reality of unequal footing and relative privileges for first world participants in this sort of interaction does not have to mean accepting a one-way relationship.

Whatever the limits of revolutionary nationalism then or now, there is real value in the broadly internationalist outlook that STO developed over the course of the seventies. The idea that revolution must be global now seems fairly commonplace, but for STO this went beyond simply an analysis of the international situation. As an organization, it expended considerable effort and material resources to build direct ties with radicals in or from Europe, southern Africa, Iran, and Latin America. This involved funding international travel, organizing speaking tours for visiting revolutionaries, offering translation services and assistance with publishing, and developing communication networks and collaborative projects across multiple borders. None of these efforts were uncritical. STO offered direct and public criticism of both the Puerto Rican and Iranian revolutionary movements while simultaneously working actively in support of them, and it also criticized various tendencies within the European movements with which it was closest. Importantly, it did all this in a time before the Internet began to facilitate instantaneous contact

---

    and the National Liberation Struggle (London: Elephant Editions, 1990 [1976]).

20   The literature on this topic is extensive but uneven. One place to begin is Thomas Olesen, "Globalizing the Zapatistas: From Third World Solidarity to Global Solidarity?," in *Third World Quarterly* 25 no. 1, (2004), 255–267.

across the planet. One of the many unfortunate side effects for contemporary radicals of the new information technology is the way in which email and other forms of communication have substantially *replaced* face-to-face international relationships. Things like international travel and speaking tours should be more frequent and more extensive today, since they are so much easier to coordinate now than they were thirty years ago. But the reality is arguably the opposite. The expansion and increasing sophistication of the repressive apparatus at the level of the nation-state and on a global scale, especially since 2001, has changed the terms of the game, making travel harder in many situations, especially for radicals from the global south. But in cases where international travel is still a real possibility it must be pursued by today's radicals.[21]

Beyond simply logistical aspects, there is also a political lesson here: STO sought out groups in other countries that held political stances fairly close to its own, but it did not for the most part apply any sort of strict litmus test, either around labels (anti-imperialist, Leninist, etc.) or around a lengthy checklist of necessary positions. In some ways, this is comparable to the fairly broad-minded approach taken by the loose network of groups affiliated with the Anarkismo website (www.anarkismo.net). Anarkismo emerged in part from a post-Seattle era effort known as the International Libertarian Solidarity Network, which attempted to connect likeminded anarchist groups from around the world through fundraising campaigns and solidarity initiatives supporting anti-authoritarian militants in Africa and Latin America. Anarkismo includes a range of diverse organizations under the banner of class-struggle anarchism and has recently taken initial steps toward advancing the "real world" interaction of the organizations involved. At the same time, participating groups are expected to identify strongly with the anarchist label and tradition. This seems unnecessarily limiting in at least some cases, and it is narrower than the approach taken by STO, which was concerned far less about the historical lineages (Maoist, Trotskyist, feminist, libertarian, etc.) of the groups it worked with, and far more about their actual politics and practice.

---

21   An example of the potential difficulties in international travel due to government repression is provided by the experience of the European anarchist writer and activist Gabriel Kuhn, who appears to be on the US Government's "No Fly List" and was forced to cancel a speaking tour of North America in early 2010. See Matthew Rothschild, "European Anarchist Has to Cancel Trip to US," *The Progressive*, February 19, 2010. Available online at http://www.progressive.org/mc021910.html (accessed January 12, 2012).

A more direct legacy of STO's strategic outlook can be found in the realm of antifascism. The group's attentiveness to the autonomous and revolutionary potential built into the far right, as well as the resulting need to operate as antifascists at a clear distance from the state and capitalism, was quite innovative at the time. This analysis, as well as a commitment to militant, direct action against fascist attempts to organize, has been widely taken up within the broad activist trend known in the United States and Canada as Anti-Racist Action (ARA). ARA groups coast to coast have, over the course of the past two decades, built their reputations around a no-platform-for-fascists approach that has repeatedly led to physical confrontation, as well as a no-reliance-on-the-state attitude that has sometimes resulted in government repression.[22] The incorporation of STO's views on fascist autonomy has been far more uneven, though in recent years the small current known as "Three Way Fight," best represented by the website of the same name, has helped expand the audience for the notion that fascism is not reducible to being the most brutal face of capitalism.[23] This trend emerged largely from the experiences of ARA veterans who, in 2001, participated in the development, publication, and distribution of a book on antifascism cowritten by Don Hamerquist.[24]

If there are many positive lessons to be learned from STO's approach to fascism, the results are much more ambivalent in terms of the group's response to a far more progressive movement: feminism. Throughout its existence, STO had an uneasy relationship with the women's liberation movement in its many permutations. On the one hand, the group was heavily involved at different points in supporting various feminist projects, ranging from women's caucuses at factories and hospitals to

---

22   The best historical and political analysis of ARA remains Rory McGowan, "Claim No Easy Victories," in *Northeastern Anarchist* #7 (2003), available online at http://anarkismo.net/article/327 (accessed January 12, 2012).

23   See the website http://threewayfight.blogspot.com for a range of content produced under this rubric (accessed January 12, 2012).

24   See Don Hamerquist, J. Sakai, et. al., *Confronting Fascism: Discussion Documents for a Militant Movement* (Chicago and Montreal: Arsenal, ARA, Kersplebedeb, 2002). A different approach to anti-fascism directly descended from STO can be found in the writings of former member Leonard Zeskind, especially in *Blood and Politics: the History of the White Nationalist Movement from the Margins to the Mainstream* (New York: Farrar, Strauss and Giroux, 2009).

the Reproductive Rights National Network. Some members joined STO with a background in the women's movement, and they and others actively incorporated its methods and insights into their work as part of STO. Throughout most of its existence, the group maintained a Women's Commission (or similarly titled formation) to ensure that male supremacy did not dominate its internal operations (see Chapter Six). Women were found in formal leadership positions from beginning to end of the organization's existence. All these things are important to note, as a reminder that STO was not fundamentally defined by any sort of crude antifeminist politics.

Nonetheless, STO did routinely treat the women's movement with suspicion and distrust, largely due to a broad-brush belief that feminism was white and bourgeois in character. At times this attitude produced a refusal to engage with the women's movement's insights, as when the organization effectively gave a collective shrug to the suggestion that members incorporate the notion that "the personal is political" into their political work.[25] In other situations, the result was public criticism: Allison Edwards challenged the theoretical underpinnings of radical feminism in a two-part article on capitalism and male supremacy in *Urgent Tasks*, while Carole Travis used the same forum to attack what she saw as the uncritical embrace of feminism by the Prairie Fire Organizing Committee. Internally, the group was perpetually unable to agree on the appropriate level of autonomy for women in the organization, despite repeated attempts to resolve the question. When interpersonal dynamics around sexuality and parenthood became a major source of conflict within STO at the turn of the eighties (see Chapter Six), the group was ill-equipped to deal with them in part because it had never internalized the personal-political connection.[26] A substantial number of heterosexual couples were members of STO at different points, and in almost every instance of divorce the woman left the group before the man did. There is of course no guarantee that a more successful engagement with feminism would have avoided any

---

25   Two nuanced and thoughtful contributions to the *IDB* by Linda Phelps, "Notes for a Discussion of the Personal as Political," in *IDB* #15, February 1980, 37–38, and "More on 'Process,' or, How I Never Give Up," in *IDB* #17, June 1980, 46, produced little to no response from the rest of the organization.

26   By contrast, Big Flame was fully engaged with the feminist milieu in Great Britain throughout much of its existence. See Kevin McDonnell, "Big Flame's Legacy."

of these problems, and any such alternative would have produced its own set of problems. But contemporary radical groups would do well to note the difficulties that arose as a result of STO's approach. To some extent this has already happened, at least within the wings of anarchism and Marxism that have actively integrated a feminist analysis into both organizational structures and strategic orientations.

While the group may never have fully understood the extent to which the personal is political, it definitely acknowledged the political implications of popular culture. STO utilized the analysis of culture—as a reflection of the state of struggle—that had been pioneered by C.L.R. James, and applied it skillfully to various musical genres, as well as to high art. Unfortunately, it never managed to accomplish the same task in relation to sports, food, or a range of other cultural forms. Nonetheless, the group's refusal to adopt the classic left instrumentalist approach, largely descended from Soviet-inspired socialist realism, was refreshing. Two indirect outgrowths of the legacy of STO reflect the best impulses of this Jamesian attitude. On and off over the last decade, the Democracy and Hip-Hop Project (DHHP), a website initiated by the founders of the STO web archive, has published critical writing on the whole range of hip-hop music and culture, always incorporating the same thoughtfulness that STO members had applied to punk rock or Bruce Springsteen decades before.[27] In contrast to many other left responses to hip-hop, the DHHP never used the political content of lyrics as the central metric by which to measure the political impact of the music. Instead, it viewed new trends in hip-hop as a reflection of the dialectical process through which an entire culture was developing. Whether the object of study is music or sports, art or television, emerging radical formations would benefit from adopting a similar stance.

In a slightly different vein, Hal Adams, an educator and a former member of STO, founded two publications over the course of the nineties that combined the Jamesian analysis of working-class culture with the Gramscian belief in organic intellectuals. Every issue was filled with the writings of people who are trained by society *not* to think of themselves as writers—factory workers, single parents, students in GED or ESL programs, and so forth. Each set of poems and stories was crafted in a series of gatherings over the course of weeks or months, with peer editing and response at the core of the process. While not a traditionally political project, the writing group concept reflected Adams's firm commitment

---

27   For examples, see http://democracyandhiphop.blogspot.com (accessed January 12, 2012).

to Gramsci's assertion that "every man [sic] is a philosopher."[28] When his first attempt, the *Journal of Ordinary Thought*, was progressively incorporated into the world of liberal foundations and nonprofits, Adams quit and founded a more grassroots alternative, *Realconditions*, to carry on the idea. The mission statement for the latter offers a rather straightforward explanation of the politics behind it: "Because only the collective efforts of ordinary people can make a better world, we are particularly interested in the creative expressions and unique understandings of those who have been relegated to the margins of society, including the poor, the oppressed, immigrants, and those who risk their privileges to join them. Their stories are found in these magazines."[29] Similar projects could definitely be initiated by contemporary groupings hoping to carry on the legacy of STO.

Every activity, project, and strategic direction undertaken by STO was informed by its commitment to class struggle. This was the obvious guiding principle that led to the group's early work around factory organizing (see Chapter Two), but in equally important (if sometimes obscure) ways, it was the motivating factor for its intervention in venues—like the antinuclear movement—that at first glance appeared to be nothing more than cross-class alliances. The point was never to obscure forms of oppression that did not map neatly onto questions of class, but rather to better understand and resist all of them from within a holistic perspective. The whole purpose of developing the analysis of white skin privilege was to pave the way for collective action by "a class which is coming alive."[30] Repeated engagements with the women's movement were motivated by a desire to strengthen the participation of working-class women as part of the struggle of the class overall. The group's dialectical approach to revolution was built around the notion that dual consciousness among working people (including its manifestations in racism and sexism) was a reflection of the grand contradiction between the forces of production and the relations of production. Whatever the value of these ideas in the abstract, Noel Ignatiev has linked STO's demise to a perpetual failure to speak in practice to the breadth and depth

---

28   This phrase recurs in Gramsci's *Prison Notebooks*, notably on pages 9, 323, 344, and elsewhere.

29   This mission statement is available in every issue of *Realconditions* and online at http://www.prairiegroup.org/communityprojects/communitywritingproject.html (accessed January 12, 2012).

30   STO, *The United Front Against Imperialism?* (Chicago: STO, 1972).

of the lives and dreams of any appreciable section of the working class.[31]

Nonetheless, at least STO made an effort. Since the group's demise, precious few revolutionary organizations have carried on this sort of basic understanding of class struggle. Far too often, the only options put forward have been either a fundamentally liberal version of identity politics that views white skin privilege as just one in the litany of social problems, along with a form of oppression known as "classism"; or a vulgar reductionist worldview where any struggle that doesn't look like mechanical notions of class struggle is irrelevant, or worse, a distraction from what really matters. Certainly there have been exceptions, many of them coming from the tradition of radical women of color. A fairly recent example is the approach known as intersectionality, which argues that oppression can best be understood as an interlocking matrix of elements, including race, class, and gender hierarchies.[32] This model is compelling as a description of the reality of oppression, although little attention is paid to those situations where multiple forms of oppression are not mutually reinforcing, but instead actually interfere with each other.[33] Further, intersectionality provides no clear guidance in terms of

---

31   Noel Ignatiev, interview with the author, January 27, 2006.

32   For a classic collection of theoretical interventions from radical women of color, see Cherríe Moraga and Gloria Anzaldúa, eds., *This Bridge Called My Back: Writings by Radical Women of Color* (New York: Kitchen Table, Women of Color Press, 1983). The key foundational texts of intersectionality theory include Patricia Hill Collins, *Black Feminist Thought: Knowledge, Consciousness and the Politics of Empowerment* (New York: Routledge, 2009 [2000/1990]) and Kimberlé W. Crenshaw, "Mapping the Margins: Intersectionality, Identity Politics, and Violence Against Women of Color," *Stanford Law Review* 43, no. 6 (1991), 1241–1299.

33   For example, it is not clear how an intersectional analysis helps us analyze the decision of the government of Malawi in 2010 to imprison two gay men who staged a public wedding ceremony in a country where homosexuality is illegal. This amounted to a form of oppression, but one that was justified in terms of resisting the likewise very real oppression of Western imperialism that is maintained, in part, through foreign aid that was under threat of being withheld until the men were pardoned by the president of Malawi. At the same time, the otherwise laudable defense of gay rights by the US State Department in this context was in part an exercise in maintaining hegemonic control over the global south. While advocates of intersectionality are certainly

plotting revolutionary strategy, since neither the agent nor the processes of struggle are specified. In this situation, there is definitely room for contemporary radicals to draw on STO's legacy and make a sophisticated understanding of class struggle the backbone of a flesh and blood strategy of resistance against all forms of oppression.

Whether despite or because of its bedrock faith in the centrality of the proletariat, the overall trajectory of STO's strategy was undeniably toward failure. This is true in multiple senses. First, it is clear that each of the areas of work successively prioritized by the group failed to maintain itself. It was never able to overcome the limits it encountered in factory organizing, or in anti-imperialist solidarity, or in engaging with other social movements. The tendency toward millenarianism and burnout was on some level symptomatic of repeated failures to agree upon and implement a strategic direction that could last longer than a couple years. Kevin McDonnell, a veteran of Big Flame, has suggested that there may be a natural life-span for small radical groups, in the range of ten to fifteen years.[34] If so, STO might have actually been rather old when it finally dissolved. But as Ignatiev has suggested, in order to overcome this sort of "natural" limitation a revolutionary group must successfully reflect and articulate the experiences and aspirations of at least a sector of the working class. Thus, the early IWW, for example, thrived to the extent that it successfully spoke to the lived reality of unskilled new immigrant laborers and other groups that built it into the most vibrant radical group of its era. STO was no more able to accomplish this task than were competitor groups like the October League or Prairie Fire, and simply having better politics did not keep it from meeting the same fate as the others. In this sense, the essential job of new generations of revolutionaries may be to identify a sector of the class within which and through which to develop new forms of organization and struggle. Where is the twenty-first century equivalent of the Petrograd of 1917 or Barcelona in 1936 or Gwangju in 1980? While STO's achievements can offer certain

---

aware of the complex contradictions involved in a situation like this, it is not clear how intersectionality accounts for them in a way that is different than other reasonably sophisticated narratives of oppression. For details on the Malawi case, see James Butty, "Malawi Government Pleased With Homosexual Couple Conviction," *Voice of America* website, May 18, 2010. Available on the internet at http://www.voanews.com/english/news/africa/Butty-Malawi-Gay-Verdict-React-Thotho-19may10-94221744.html (accessed December 5, 2011).

34   Kevin McDonnell, "The Legacy of Big Flame."

lessons peripheral to this task, it is at least as important to learn what is *not* to be done by looking carefully at what STO actually did.

* * *

Finally, there are a number of organizational questions raised by the history of STO. On some level, STO was always struggling to reinvent itself. In fifteen-plus years, it never utilized the standard left approach of developing a constitution or bylaws, and this fact created repeated opportunities to tweak its structural model, for better and for worse. It is possible this approach was modeled on the early history of the Russian Social Democratic Labor Party, which did not have formal membership rolls or a set of bylaws for the first period of its existence. While the concept of local branches was a standard import from the history of the CPUSA, STO never put much effort into determining internal lines of authority or communication. As it grew to be a larger organization in the late seventies with members from coast to coast, the lack of a clear structure fed into the growing frustrations felt by many members, especially those in Kansas City and the Pacific Northwest (see Chapters Seven and Eight).

One persistent problem facilitated by this relatively lax attitude toward structure was informal hierarchy. This manifested in what many members called "the heavies," who were the universally acknowledged intellectual leading lights of the group—Hamerquist, Ignatin, and Lawrence. (For a period of time, Carole Travis had roughly the same level of prestige and power inside the organization, though she was for the most part not an active theoretician.) All were somewhat older than most other members, and they each had years of left experience prior to the founding of STO, including time spent in various "old left" organizations. Some former members have suggested it was precisely this experience, and the attendant early exposure to Stalinist method, that produced the worst forms of manipulation that went along with the informal hierarchy (see Chapter Four). The leadership this grouping provided the organization was undeniably valuable on many levels, but many members at many different moments in time chafed at it. The group's formal decision-making structure after 1975—an elected National Committee and semiregular General Membership Meetings—did not eliminate the problem, and often the worst conflicts occurred when one or more of the heavies were *not* on the NC, but continued to use their left contacts and rhetorical skills to retain a disproportionate influence on STO's activity. Ignatin and Hamerquist developed some theoretical insights into the need for a highly democratic version of democratic centralism, but in reality they, along with Lawrence and occasionally Travis, were regularly identified as roadblocks to democracy rather than its enforcers.

The overall history of the left has made it clear that there is no magic bullet that can prevent informal hierarchies from asserting themselves, though STO seemed at times perversely interested in actively cultivating them. The most significant intellectual effort the group made in the opposite direction was to institute the dialectics course for the membership. Beginning in 1978, Lawrence, Ignatin, and Hamerquist put significant effort into designing a course that could create something resembling a level intellectual playing field inside the organization. While the effort was never fully successful, it did raise the overall level of theoretical discussion within the group over several years. The idea of using political education as a means to teach a method or approach ("How to Think"), rather than as a way of conveying a correct ideological line, retains significant value in the present day. In practical terms, contemporary groups would be better served by acknowledging and institutionalizing leadership based on organizing and intellectual experience, while deliberately establishing precise limits on this power and developing other measures designed to broaden and deepen the available pool of leaders over time.

Perhaps STO's biggest failure in organizational terms was its failure to grow. It is doubtful the group ever had more than a hundred members at any given time, even around 1980 when it had a physical presence in a dozen states across the country.[35] It is tantalizing to imagine an organization of two thousand or more people armed with STO's politics, but as discussed in Chapter Eight the group repeatedly sabotaged itself such that there was never really any clear path for it to grow to that scale. In part, this had to do with the fact that STO was always identified more in terms of what it was *not*—Stalinist, Maoist, Trotskyist, anarchist, reformist, antitheory, opportunist, and so forth—and only secondarily in terms of what it *was*. The laxness in terms of structure contributed here, as did the group's consistent lack of clarity around the organizational implications of the concept of autonomy. STO and its members took inconsistent stances as to whether growth itself was a key to success or a counterproductive attack on autonomy. But the largest piece of this puzzle was that STO itself was never sure, in demographic terms at least,

---

35   Illinois, Iowa, Missouri, Kansas, Louisiana, Mississippi, New York, Pennsylvania, California, Oregon, Washington, and Colorado.

what it *was*. Was it an all-white group? Was it multiracial?[36] Was it a group of workers? A cross-class organization of communist militants?

It is shocking to realize that a group with such a developed theory of white supremacy was unable to apply that theory inside its own organization in a productive way, but that is effectively what happened to STO. The founding members of the group included two women of color, and the initial vision (linked directly to the choice of the name Sojourner Truth) was to build a multiracial revolutionary organization (see Chapter One). The decision to focus on organizing in large factories with mixed populations of workers was born of a similar vision for a broadly diverse workers' movement. At the same time, one of the founding insights of STO emphasized the ways in which white supremacy necessitated a respect for the autonomous organizing efforts of people of color. STO from the beginning operated under a largely unexamined assumption of being a "white" group, and refused to actively recruit radicals of color, even those who closely shared its political stance (see Chapter Three). Once the group took its anti-imperialist turn, this commitment became even more emphatic, as revolutionaries of color were more or less directed to join revolutionary nationalist groupings in "their" communities. The contradiction left deep scars on STO as an organization, especially during and after the split of 1978 when the entire Third World Caucus left the group, along with many white supporters (see Chapter Four). In the aftermath, STO was always identified as a "white" group.

It is tempting to imagine STO as a fully multiracial group, but it is important to remember that to have developed in such a direction would have required a fundamentally different approach to autonomy as a concept. That is, STO generally saw autonomy as something manifested exclusively by the separate organization of people of color. The alternative would have been to view autonomy as both an individual and a social experience, one that could exist in either nationalist or multiracial groupings. In this case, STO's longstanding awareness of white skin privilege would have presented at least a partial bulwark against what has been called "premature universalism."[37] Instead, STO's self-understanding as

---

36   This term has clear shortcomings, especially from a perspective that aims eventually to move beyond racial categories, but there is no better alternative phrasing.

37   I credit my brother Peter with introducing this term to me. It helpfully calls to mind the earlier concept of "premature anti-fascism," while focusing squarely on the need to differentiate the shared experience of life under capitalism.

a largely, and eventually entirely, white group dovetailed with its belief from the mid-seventies on that other groups (especially revolutionary nationalist organizations) would be far more important to any revolutionary process than STO would ever be. The popularity inside STO in the late seventies of a vulgar version of anti-imperialism also contributed to the problem. Subsequently, as the group moved away from solidarity efforts in the eighties, the attempt to develop a revolutionary tendency (see Chapter Seven) reinforced the idea that STO was organizationally unimportant. All these elements combined to create a feedback loop of perpetual failure to grow.

Comparable confusions arose in terms of the class composition of the group, with an effort, especially in the early seventies, to "proletarianize" the membership (see Chapter Two), alongside a desire to avoid patronizing the "real" workers with whom the group had developed relationships. Here again, the result was a contradictory response to the question of class, one which carried forward into the group's interaction with the antinuclear movement at the end of the decade (see Chapter Seven). In these two areas, then, the STO veterans who argue that the group fell victim to a failure of will are on fairly solid ground, at least in terms of demographic questions relating to race and class. For a new generation of revolutionaries, the importance of reaching a viable critical mass must be combined with an awareness of just how difficult it will be—not just logistically but first and foremost politically—to achieve this critical mass. What is the value of a revolutionary organization? How important is the designation of participants in such organizations as "cadre," and what does the latter term mean in terms of responsibilities and expectations for members? STO's early insights into the "party" are surely worth examining. The group emphasized, among other points, the priority of common action over strict adherence to a precise theoretical line, the need for a highly democratic internal culture of debate, and the responsibility of the party to "articulate and organize popular aspirations in a framework of class struggle," rather than to provide top-down leadership and direction to the masses.[38] A useful point of comparison in this context is the rather different historical tradition within Latin American anarchism known as *especifismo*, which similarly defends the importance of "specifically revolutionary organizations" that can pursue a policy of "social insertion" in broader social movements.[39] Of course,

---

38   The quote is from Don Hamerquist, "Discussion Points on the Party and Revolutionary Strategy," in *Collective Works* #3 (June 1975), 8–9.

39   Relatively little literature exists in English on *especifismo*. Perhaps the

there are competing traditions, including those that would draw more on the legacy of STO's later tendency-building efforts (see Chapter Seven). The jury is still out on the relative merits of these various approaches, but in the interim, STO's difficult experiences with organizational self-perpetuation are worthy of careful review.

＊ ＊ ＊

What to make of STO in the final analysis? Noel Ignatiev once described the group to me as "an organization of revolutionaries that tried to think."[40] On one level this may seem one-sided, insofar as it focuses on the "thinking" rather than "doing" aspect of the process. But perhaps we should think of revolutionaries as those who actually attempt to make revolution rather than simply those who profess its value in the abstract. Seen from this angle, the seventies left was peppered with organizations that tried to make revolution, and it was the attempt to reflect critically on that process that made STO unusual. John Garvey, a close comrade of STO for many years, argues that, in spite of many flaws, "STO remains the single most remarkable political organization of its era."[41] Hopefully this book at the very least has adequately demonstrated what made it remarkable, both for better and for worse. On the other hand, Mario Tronti, a veteran of the Italian autonomist Marxist current that so influenced STO, reflected on his own milieu by claiming that it produced "many flowers, little fruit."[42] This seems in some ways a helpful metaphor for understanding STO, if we think of "flowers" as valuable insights and "fruit" as lasting practical outcomes. No matter how remarkable STO might have been, today's radicals are largely tasked with reinventing the wheel of revolutionary struggle, as have so many earlier generations.

---

best resource is a small collection of documents available online as a Google Doc. See the blog *Machete 408*, at http://machete408.word-press.com/2009/02/21/reader-on-especifismo/ (accessed January 12, 2012).

40   Noel Ignatiev, interview with the author, July 16, 2005.
41   John Garvey, interview with the author, April 21, 2011.
42   Quoted in Steve Wright, *Storming Heaven*, 225. Wright argues this description of the Italian movement was inaccurate, and it is worth noting that, by the time Tronti wrote those words in 1978, he had long since become a critic of *operaismo* and *autonomia* from the right, as a member of the mainstream Italian Communist Party.

At the same time, the list of groups and projects on the revolutionary left that have featured former members of STO is extensive: the Love and Rage Revolutionary Anarchist Federation, *Race Traitor*, Anti-Racist Action, the Industrial Workers of the World, and Bring the Ruckus, among many others. Other small groups with no membership overlap nonetheless take significant inspiration from STO, including Unity and Struggle, Advance the Struggle, the Black Orchid Collective, the First of May Anarchist Alliance, Miami Autonomy and Solidarity, and the Kasama Project, again among a long list of others. That none of these has so far proven capable of catalyzing or inspiring insurgent mass movements in the twenty-first century is no crime, though it must be considered a failure. Like STO's overall failure, this tragedy is the result of both objective and subjective conditions. If the continuing legacy of the Sojourner Truth Organization is of any value, it will be seen in the future successes that overcome past failures.

Bibliography

Ahmadzadeh, Massoud. *Armed Struggle: Both a Strategy and a Tactic.* Accessed February 21, 2012. http://www.siahkal.com/english/Massoud.htm.

Al, Evi, Gary, Hilda, Jim C., Marsha, Mel, Mike, Pauline. "The Crisis in STO." Unpublished paper in author's possession (n.d., but fall 1973).

Al, Evie, Gary, Hilda, Jim C., Marcia, Mel, Mike, Pauline. "The Role of a Proletarian Party in the Development of Mass Socialist Consciousness." Unpublished paper in author's possession (n.d, but fall 1973).

Allen, Ted. "White Supremacy in US History" (1973), in *Understanding and Fighting White Supremacy.* Chicago: STO, 1976.

Allen, Ted. "Can White ~~Workers~~ Radicals Be Radicalized?" *New Marxist Forum: A Journal of Debate and Theory for Marxist-Leninists* 1 (January 1973).

Allen, Theodore William. *Class Struggle and the Origin of Racial Slavery: The Invention of the White Race.* Somerville, MA: New England Free Press, 1976.

Allen, Theodore W. *The Invention of the White Race.* New York: Verso, 1994. Two volumes.

Aronowitz, Stanley. *False Promises: The Shaping of American Working Class Consciousness.* New York: McGraw-Hill, 1973.

"Arsenal protest aims for 1-day shutdown." *Chicago Tribune*, May 29, 1984, N4.

Ayala, Cesar, and Rafael Bernabe. *Puerto Rico in the American Century: A History Since 1898.* Chapel Hill, NC: University of North Carolina Press, 2007.

Badiou, Alain. *Metapolitics.* London and New York: Verso, 2005.

Bailey, Geoff. "1960s Radicals Turn to Party Building." *International Socialist Review* 53 (May–June, 2007).

Barber, David. "'A Fucking White Revolutionary Mass Movement' and Other Fables of Whiteness." *Race Traitor*, 12 (Spring 2001).

Barber, David. *A Hard Rain Fell: SDS and Why It Failed.* Jackson, MS: University Press of Mississippi, 2008.

Behrooz, Mazier. *Rebels with a Cause: The Failure of the Left in Iran.* London and New York: I B Taurus, 2000.

Bensman, David. "South Chicago." *Encyclopedia of Chicago.* Accessed February 21, 2012. http://encyclopedia.chicagohistory.org/pages/1170.html.

Berger, Dan. *Outlaws of America: The Weather Underground and the Politics of Solidarity*. Oakland, CA: AK Press, 2006.

[Big Flame.] "Report on the Sojourner Truth Group in Chicago." Unpublished paper in author's possession (n.d, but probably early 1974).

Blaut, James M. *The National Question*. London: Zed Books, 1987.

Bonanno, Alfredo M. *Anarchism and the National Liberation Struggle*. London: Elephant Editions, 1990 [1976].

Bookchin, Murray. *Post-Scarcity Anarchism*. Montreal: Black Rose Books, 1986 [1971].

Bookchin, Murray. *The Third Revolution, Volume Three*. London: Continuum, 2004.

Booth, Heather, Evi Goldfield, and Sue Munaker. *Toward a Radical Movement*. Somerville, MA: New England Free Press, 1968.

Boyd, James. "Nixon's Southern Strategy: 'It's All in the Charts.'" *New York Times*, May 17, 1970.

Branch, Taylor. *At Canaan's Edge: America in the King Years, 1965–1968*. New York: Simon and Schuster, 2006.

Bread and Roses: a Paper by and for Working Women 1, no. 1. (n.d., but late 1970).

Breakout! 1, no. 4. December 11, 1973.

Brenner, Aaron, Robert Brenner, and Cal Winslow, eds. *Rebel Rank and File: Labor Militancy and Revolt from Below During the Long 1970s*. New York: Verso, 2010.

Briggs, Laura. *Reproducing Empire: Race, Sex, Science, and Imperialism in Puerto Rico*. Berkeley, CA: University of California Press, 2002.

Brownmiller, Susan. *Against Our Will: Men, Women and Rape*. New York: Simon and Schuster, 1975.

Buhle, Paul. *Marxism in the United States: Remapping the History of the American Left*. New York: Verso, 1991 [1987].

Buhle, Paul, and Nicole Schulman, eds. *Wobblies! A Graphic History of the Industrial Workers of the World*. New York: Verso, 2005.

Bynum, Victoria E. *Free State of Jones: Mississippi's Longest Civil War*. Chapel Hill, NC: University of North Carolina Press, 2001.

Carson, Clayborne. *In Struggle: SNCC and the Black Awakening of the 1960s*. Cambridge, MA: Harvard University Press, 1995 [1981].

Carter, David. *Stonewall: The Riots that Sparked the Gay Revolution*. New York: St. Martins Griffin, 2005.

Castoriadis, Cornelius. *The Imaginary Institution of Society*. Cambridge, MA: MIT Press, 1987.

Cleaver, Harry. *Reading Capital Politically*. San Francisco: AK Press, 2000 [1979].

Cohen, Adam, and Elizabeth Taylor. *American Pharaoh: Mayor Richard J. Daley—His Battle for Chicago and the Nation*. New York: Back Bay, 2001.

Cohen, G. A. *Karl Marx's Theory of History: A Defence*. Princeton, NJ: Princeton University Press, 2000 [1978].

Collective Works. Various issues, 1974–1976.

Collins, Patricia Hill. *Black Feminist Thought: Knowledge, Consciousness and the Politics of Empowerment*. New York: Routledge, 2009 [2000/1990].

Cooney, Robert, and Helen Michalowski, eds. *The Power of the People: Active Non-Violence in the United States*. Culver City, CA: Peace Press, 1977.

Cortright, David. *Soldiers in Revolt: GI Resistance During the Vietnam War*. Chicago: Haymarket Books, 2005 [1975].

Coyle, Laurie, Gail Hershatter, and Emily Honig. *Women at Farah: An Unfinished Story*. El Paso: Reforma, 1979.

Crenshaw, Kimberlé W. "Mapping the Margins: Intersectionality, Identity Politics, and Violence Against Women of Color." *Stanford Law Review* 43, no. 6 (1991): 1241–1299.

Crosby, Emilye. *A Little Taste of Freedom: The Black Freedom Struggle in Claiborne County, Mississippi*. Chapel Hill, NC: University of North Carolina Press, 2005.

Cruse, Harold. *Crisis of the Negro Intellectual: A Historical Analysis of the Failure of Black Leadership*. New York: New York Review Books, 2005 [1967].

Cunningham, David. *There's Something Happening Here: The New Left, the Klan, and FBI Counterintelligence*. Berkeley, CA: University of California Press, 2004.

Davidson, Carl. "Toward Institutional Resistance." *New Left Notes*, November 13, 1967.

"Democratic Centralism." *Marxist Encyclopedia*. Accessed February 12, 2012. http://www.marxists.org/glossary.

Dinges, Jon. *The Condor Years: How Pinochet and His Allies Brought Terrorism to Three Continents*. New York: New Press, 2004.

Du Bois, W. E. B. *Black Reconstruction in America, 1860–1880*. New York: The Free Press, 1998 [1935].

Du Bois, W. E. B. *The Souls of Black Folk*. New York: Signet Classic, 1995 [1903].

Duberman, Martin. *Stonewall*. New York: Dutton, 1993.

Dworkin, Andrea. *Pornography: Men Possessing Women*. New York: Putnam, 1981.

Echols, Alice. *Daring to Be Bad: Radical Feminism in America, 1967–1975*. Minneapolis: University of Minnestoa Press, 1989.

"Editorial." *De Pie y En Guerra* 1, no. 1 (1978).

Edwards, Allison. *Rape, Racism and the White Women's Movement: An Answer to Susan Brownmiller*. Chicago: STO, 1976.

"85 Seized in Demonstration at Arsenal." *Chicago Tribune*, Tuesday October 22, 1985, 3A.

Elbaum, Max. *Revolution in the Air: Sixties Radicals Turn to Marx, Che and Mao*. London: Verso, 2002.

Epstein, Barbara. *Political Protest and Cultural Revolution: Nonviolent Direct Action in the 1970s and 1980s*. Berkeley, CA: University of California Press, 1991.

Fanon, Frantz. *The Wretched of the Earth*. New York: Grove Press, 1963.

Ferguson, Ann, Ilene Philipson, Irene Diamond and Lee Quinby, and Carole S. Vance and Ann Barr Snitow. "The Feminist Sexuality Debates." *Signs: Journal of Women in Culture and Society* 10, no. 1 (August, 1984): 106–135.

Fields, A. Belden. *Trotskyism and Maoism: Theory and Practice in France and the United States*. New York: Autonomedia, 1988.

Final Report of the Select Committee to Study Governmental Operations with Respect to Intelligence Activities, United States Senate. April 23, 1976.

Fernandez, Lilia. *Latina/o Migration and Community Formation in Postwar Chicago: Mexicans, Puerto Ricans, Gender, and Politics, 1945–1975*. PhD Diss., University of California, San Diego, 2005.

Fernandez, Ronald. *Prisoners of Colonialism: The Struggle for Justice in Puerto Rico*. Monroe, ME: Common Courage Press, 1994.

Fuentes, Marta, and Andre Gunder Frank. "Ten Theses on Social Movements." *World Development* 17, no. 2 (1989): 179–191.

Gadamer, Hans-Georg. *Truth and Method*. London and New York: Continuum, 2004 [1975].

The General Strike for Industrial Freedom. Chicago: IWW, 1946.

Georgakas, Dan, and Marvin Surkin. *Detroit: I Do Mind Dying: A Study in Urban Revolution (Updated Edition)*. Boston: South End Press, 1998 [1975].

George S. "Critique of the Paper Entitled 'The Crisis in STO.'" Unpublished paper in author's possession (n. d., but fall 1973).

Gilroy, Paul. *"There Ain't No Black in the Union Jack:" The Cultural Politics of Race and Nation*. Chicago: University of Chicago Press, 1991 [1987].

Gitelman, Zvi, ed. *The Emergence of Modern Jewish Politics: Bundism and Zionism in Eastern Europe*. Pittsburgh: University of Pittsburgh Press, 2003.

Goldner, Loren. "Introduction to the Johnson-Forest Tendency and Background to 'Facing Reality.'" (2002). Accessed Feb 12, 2012. http://home.earthlink.net/~lrgoldner/johnson.html

Gombin, Richard. *The Radical Tradition: A Study in Revolutionary Thought*. New York: St. Martin's Press, 1979.

Goodman, James. *Stories of Scottsboro*. New York: Pantheon, 1994.

Gordon, Linda. *Woman's Body, Woman's Right*. New York: Penguin, 1990 [1976].

Gramsci, Antonio. *Prison Notebooks*. New York: International Publishers, 1991.

Gramsci, Antonio. *Selections From Political Writings, 1921–1926*. Minneapolis: University of Minnesota Press, 1990.

Gramsci, Antonio. "Soviets in Italy." *New Left Review* 51 (September–October, 1968): 28–58.

Greason, David. "Embracing Death: The Western Left and the Iranian Revolution, 1978–83." *Economy and Society* 34, no. 1 (February 2005).

Grossman, Zoltán. "Unlikely Alliances: Treaty Conflict and Environmental Co-operation Between Native American and Rural White Communities." PhD diss., Geography, University of Wisconsin, Madison, 2002.

Haas, Jeffrey. *The Assassination of Fred Hampton: How the FBI and the Chicago Police Murdered a Black Panther*. Chicago: Lawrence Hill Books/Chicago Review Press, 2010.

Hamerquist, Don. "Discussion Points on the Party and Revolutionary Strategy." *Collective Works* 3 (June 1975): 8–9.

Hamerquist, Don. "Reflections on Organizing" (1970), in *Workplace Papers*. Chicago: STO, 1980.

Hamerquist, Don. "Lenin, Leninism, and Some Leftovers." (2009). Accessed February 12, 2012. http://sketchythoughts.blogspot.com/2009/09/lenin-leninism-and-some-leftovers.html.

Hamerquist, Don. "Trade Unions/Independent Organizations" (1973), in *Workplace Papers*. Chicago: STO,1980.

Hamerquist, Don. *White Supremacy and the Afro-American National Question*. Chicago: STO, 1978 [1976].

Hamerquist, Don, and Noel Ignatin. "A Call to Organize," in *Workplace Papers*. Chicago: STO, 1980.

Hamerquist, Don, J. Sakai, and Mark Salotte. *Confronting Fascism: Discussion Documents for a Militant Movement*. Chicago and Montreal: Arsenal, ARA, Kersplebedeb, 2002.

Hatcher, Richard. "And We Shall Take With Us the Best." Chicago: STO, 1972.

Hella Occupy! 2011 pamphlet. Accessed February 12, 2012. http://bringtheruck-us.org/?q=node/167

Henson, Beth. Selection from Untitled Memoir. n.d.

Hinton, William. *The Turning Point: An Essay on the Cultural Revolution*. New York: Monthly Review Press, 1972.

Hoagland, Sarah Lucia. *Lesbian Ethics: Toward New Value*. Palo Alto, CA: Institute of Lesbian Studies, 1988.

Hochberg, Arthur. "U of Chicago Students Seize Building, Protest Woman's Firing." *New Left Notes*, February 5, 1969.

Hoyles, Andree. "The Occupation of Factories in France: May 1968," in *Trade Union Register*, edited by Ken Coates, Tony Topham, and Michael Barrett Brown. London: Merlin Press, 1969.

Hurl, Chris. "Anti-Globalization and 'Diversity of Tactics.'" *Upping the Anti-* 1 (2005).

Ignatiev, Noel. *How the Irish Became White*. New York: Routledge, 1995.

Ignatiev, Noel and John Garvey, eds. *Race Traitor*. New York: Routledge, 1996.

Ignatin, Noel. *"…no condescending saviors."* Chicago: STO, 1976.

Ignatin, Noel. "Preface," in *Workplace Papers*. Chicago: STO, 1980.

Ignatin, Noel. "Outline History of STO." Unpublished manuscript in author's possession (1980).

Ignatin, Noel. "Introduction to 'The White Blindspot.'" *New Marxist Forum: A Journal of Debate and Theory for Marxist-Leninists* 1 (January 1973).

Ignatin, Noel. "Learn the Lessons of US History." *New Left Notes*, March 25, 1968.

Ignatin, Noel. "Without a Science of Navigation We Cannot Sail in Stormy Seas, or, Sooner or Later One of Us Must Know," in *The Debate Within SDS: RYM II vs. Weatherman*. Detroit: Radical Education Project, 1969.

Ignatin, Noel. "Black Workers, White Workers," *Radical America* 8, no. 4 (July–August 1974): 41–60.

Ignatin, Noel. "The POC: A Personal Memoir," *Theoretical Review* 12 (1979).

Ignatin, Noel, and Ted Allen. "The White Blindspot" (1967), in *Understanding and Fighting White Supremacy: A Collection*. Chicago: STO, 1976.

INCITE! Women of Color Against Violence, eds. *The Revolution Will Not Be Funded: Beyond the Non-Profit Industrial Complex*. Cambridge, MA: South End Press, 2007.

International Workingmen's Association. "General Rules." (1864).

Jackson, Peter, and Edward Montgomery. "Layoffs, Discharges and Youth Unemployment," in *The Black Youth Employment Crisis*, edited by Richard B. Freeman and Harry J. Holzer. Chicago: University of Chicago Press, 1986.

Jacobs, Harold, ed. *Weatherman*. Berkeley, CA: Ramparts Press, 1970.

Jacoby, Russell. "Stalinism and China." *Radical America* 10, no. 3 (May–June 1976): 7–24.

Jaggar, Allison. *Feminist Politics and Human Nature*. Totowa, NJ: Rowman and Littlefield, 1988 [1983].

James, C.L.R. "The Revolutionary Answer to the Negro Problem in the USA" (1948), in *CLR James on the "Negro Question,"* edited by Scott McLemee. Jackson, MS: The University Press of Mississippi, 1996.

James, C.L.R. (with Raya Dunayavskaya and Grace Lee). *State Capitalism and World Revolution*. Chicago: Charles H. Kerr, 1986 [1950].

James, C.L.R. *American Civilization*. Edited and introduced by Anna Grimshaw and Keith Hart. Cambridge, MA: Blackwell, 1993.

James, C.L.R. *Modern Politics*. Detroit: Bewick Editions, 1973.

James, C. Vaughn. *Soviet Socialist Realism: Origins and Theory*. New York: St. Martin's Press, 1973.

Jones, Beverly, and Judith Brown. *Toward a Female Liberation Movement*. Somerville, MA: New England Free Press, 1968.

Joseph, Peniel E. *Waiting 'Til the Midnight Hour: A Narrative History of Black Power in America*. New York: Henry Holt and Company, 2006.

Kathy and Lynn. "Organizing in an Electrical Plant in Chicago," in *Collective Works* 1, no. 1 (October 1974): 11–20.

Kathy W. "A Lesson in What Democratic Centralism Is Not, or How a Representative-Democratic Exec Did Not Work in a Revolutionary Organization." Unpublished paper in author's possession (n.d., but circa November 1973).

Katsiaficas, George. *The Subversion of Politics: European Autonomous Social Movements and the Decolonization of Everyday Life*. Atlantic Highlands, NJ: Humanities Press, 1997.

Kelley, Robin DG, and Betsy Esch. "Black Like Mao: Red China and Black Revolution." *Souls: A Critical Journal of Black Politics, Culture and Society* 1, no. 4 (1999): 6–41.

Kempton, Murray. *The Briar Patch: The Trial of the Panther 21*. Cambridge, MA: Da Capo Press, 1997 [1973].

Kersten, Andrew E. *A. Phillip Randolph: A Life in the Vanguard*. Lanham, MD: Rowman and Littlefield, 2007.

Kifner, John. "28 Year Old Snapshots Are Still Vivid, and Still Violent." *New York Times*, August 26, 1996.

Kornbluh, Joyce, ed. *Rebel Voices: An IWW Anthology*. Chicago: Charles H. Kerr, 1998.

Lawrence, Ken. *The New State Repression*. Portland, OR: Tarantula, 2006 [1985].

Lee, Chana Kai. *For Freedom's Sake: The Life of Fannie Lou Hamer*. Urbana, IL: University of Illinois Press, 1999.

Lee, Yok-Shiu F., and Alvin Y. So, eds. *Asia's Environmental Movements: Comparative Perspectives*. Armonk, NY: M. E. Sharpe, 1999.

Lenin, V.I. *On the So-Called Market Question* (1893). Accessed September 15, 2011. www.marxists.org/archive/lenin/works/1893/market/06.htm.

Lenin, V.I. "The Urgent Tasks of Our Movement" (1900). Accessed February 12, 2012. http://www.marxists.org/archive/lenin/works/1900/nov/tasks.htm.

Lenin, V.I. *What is to be Done? Burning Questions of our Movement* (1902). Accessed September 15, 2011. http://www.marxists.org/archive/lenin/works/1901/witbd.

Lenin, V.I. "Letter to Inessa Armand" (1913). Accessed January 12, 2012. http://www.marxists.org/archive/lenin/works/1913/dec/00ia2.htm.

Lenin, V.I. *State and Revolution: The Marxist Theory of the State and the Tasks of the Proletariat in the Revolution* (1917). Accessed February 12, 2012. http://www.marxists.org/archive/lenin/works/1917/staterev/index.htm.

Lenin, V.I. "Statistics and Sociology" (1917). Accessed February 12, 2012. http://www.marxists.org/archive/lenin/works/1917/jan/00d.htm.

Lepre, George. *Fragging: Why US Soldiers Assaulted Their Officers in Vietnam.* Lubbock, TX: Texas Tech University Press, 2011.

Lont, Cynthia M. "Between Rock and a Hard Place: A Model of Subcultural Persistance and Women's Music." PhD diss., University of Iowa, 1984.

Lowe, Frederick, and Derrick Blakley. "2nd Day of Humboldt Riots." *Chicago Tribune*, June 6, 1977, A1.

Lugones, Maria. "Structure/Anti-Structure and Agency Under Oppression." *The Journal of Philosophy* 87, no. 10 (October 1990).

Lumley, Robert. *States of Emergency: Cultures of Revolt in Italy, 1968–1978.* London: Verso, 1990.

Luthi, Lorenz M. *The Sino-Soviet Split: Cold War in the Communist World.* Princeton, NJ: Princeton University Press, 2008.

Mabee, Carleton, with Susan Mabee Newhouse. *Sojourner Truth: Slave, Prophet, Legend.* New York: New York University Press, 1993.

Mao Zedong. "Summary of Chairman Mao's talks with Responsible Comrades at Various Places during his Provincial Tour from the Middle of August to 12 September 1971," in *Chairman Mao Talks to the People: Talks and Letters: 1956–1971,* edited by Stuart Schram. New York: Pantheon Books, 1974.

Mao Zedong. "On Protracted War" (1938). Accessed February 12, 2012. http://www.marxists.org/reference/archive/mao/selected-works/volume-2/mswv2_09.htm.

Mao Zedong. *Quotations from Mao Tse-Tung.* Peking: Peking Foreign Languages Press, 1966.

Marqusee, Mike. *Redemption Song: Muhammad Ali and the Spirit of the Sixties.* New York: Verso, 1999.

Marx, Karl. *The Class Struggles in France, 1848–1850* (1850). Accessed September 15, 2011. http://www.marxists.org/archive/marx/works/1850/class-struggles-france/ch01.htm.

Marx, Karl. *Capital: A Critique of Political Economy.* (1867). Volume 1. Accessed September 15, 2011. www.marxists.org/archive/marx/works/1867-c1/ch32.htm.

Marx, Karl. *The German Ideology* (1846). Accessed September 15, 2011. http://www.marxists.org/archive/marx/works/1845/german-ideology/ch01b.htm.

Marx, Karl. *Grundrisse*, translated by Martin Nicolaus. New York: Penguin, 1973.

Marx, Karl. "Concerning Feuerbach" (1845), in Karl Marx, *Early Writings*. New York: Vintage Books, 1975, 423.

Matin-Asgari, Afshin. *Iranian Student Opposition to the Shah*. Costa Mesa, CA: Mazda Publishers, 2002.

McDonnell, Kevin. "Big Flame's Legacy: What is of Value and What Isn't" (2010). Accessed February 12, 2012. http://bigflameuk.wordpress.com/2010/01/18/opinions-about-big-flame-no-5-kevin-mcdonnell.

McGowan, Rory. "Claim No Easy Victories." *Northeastern Anarchist* 7 (2003).

McLellan, David, ed. *Karl Marx: Selected Writings*. New York: Oxford University Press, 1977.

Midnight Notes Collective. *Strange Victories: The Anti-Nuclear Movement in the US and Europe*. Boston and New York: Midnight Notes, 1979.

Moody, Kim. *An Injury to All: The Decline of American Unionism*. New York: Verso, 1988.

Moraga, Cherríe, and Gloria Anzaldúa, eds. *This Bridge Called My Back: Writings by Radical Women of Color*. New York: Kitchen Table, Women of Color Press, 1983.

Morgan, Mike. "Refusniks Down South" (2006). Accessed February 12, 2012. http://www.smokebox.net/archives/what/morgan1206.html.

Morgan, Robin. "Goodbye to All That," in *Dear Sisters: Dispatches From the Women's Liberation Movement*, edited by Rosalyn Baxandall and Linda Gordon. New York: Basic Books, 2000.

Morris, Dr. Colin. *Unyoung, Uncolored, Unpoor*. Nashville, TN: Abingdon Press, 1969.

Movimiento de Liberación Nacional. *The Time is Now! A Discussion Bulletin*. Chicago: MLN, n.d., but circa 1978.

Naison, Mark. *Communists in Harlem During the Depression*. Urbana, IL: University of Illinois Press, 1983.

Nappalos, S. "Defining Practice: The Intermediate Level of Organization and Struggle" (2010). Accessed February 12, 2012. http://anarkismo.net/article/16350.

Negri, Antonio. "Capitalist Domination and Working Class Sabotage" (1977), in *Working Class Autonomy and the Crisis*. London: Red Notes, 1979. Available online at http://libcom.org/library/capitalist-domination-working-class-sabotage-negri.

New York Committee Against Grand Jury Repression. *The Political Grand Jury: An Instrument of Repression* (n.d., but probably 1978).

Olesen, Thomas. "Globalizing the Zapatistas: From Third World Solidarity to Global Solidarity?" *Third World Quarterly* 25, no. 1 (2004): 255–267.

"117 Arrested in Arsenal Clash." *Moline Daily Dispatch*, Monday October 21, 1985, 1A.

"Oregon: Marxist From Multnomah." *Time*, October 13, 1967.

Outline History of Sojourner Truth (September 1972). Accessed September 15, 2011. http://www.marxists.org/history/erol/ncm-1/sto.htm

Padilla, Felix. *Puerto Rican Chicago*. Notre Dame, IN: Notre Dame University Press, 1987.

Painter, Nell Irvin. *Sojourner Truth: A Life, A Symbol*. New York: W.W. Norton, 1996.

Parkin, Rosa and Charley. "Peter Rabbit and the *Grundrisse*." *Theoretical Review* 17 (July–August 1980).

Pauline. "Critique of Noel's Portland Speech." Unpublished manuscript in author's possession (n.d., but circa 1973).

Patterson, Hayward, and Earl Conrad. *Scottsboro Boy*. New York: Collier Books, 1969 [1950].

"Payoff for Terror on the Road." *Time*, February 18, 1974.

Perry, Jeffrey B. "In Memoriam: Theodore W. Allen" (2005). Accessed September 29, 2011. http://clogic.eserver.org/2005/Perry.html

Peters, J. *The Communist Party: A Manual on Organization*. New York: Workers' Library Publishers, 1935.

Phelps, Linda. "More on 'Process,' or, How I Never Give Up." *Internal Discussion Bulletin* 17 (June 1980): 46.

Phelps, Linda. "Notes for a Discussion of the Personal as Political." *Internal Discussion Bulletin* 15 (February 1980): 37–38.

Piercy, Marge. "The Grand Coolie Damn." *Leviathan Magazine* (November 1969).

Porter, Bruce, and Marvin Dunn. *The Miami Riot of 1980: Crossing the Bounds*. Lexington MA: Lexington Books, 1984.

Potter, Will. "The Green Scare." *Vermont Law Review* 33, no. 4 (2009): 671–687.

Proletarian Unity League. "Proletarian Unity League: Where We Came From, What We Look Like, What We Do" (1981). Accessed October 18, 2011. http://www.freedomroad.org/index.php?option=com_content&view=article&id=237:family-tree-proletarian-unity-league&catid=171:our-history&Itemid=264&lang=en.

Radical America 5, no. 5 (September–October 1971), and *Radical America* 7, no. 2 (March–April 1973).

Ranney, Dave. "Some Notes on Faction and Factional Activity." Unpublished document in author's possession (1978).

Ranney, David. "Position on Splitting STO." Unpublished document in author's possession (1978).

Ransby, Barbara. *Ella Baker and the Black Freedom Movement: A Radical Democratic Vision*. Chapel Hill, NC: The University of North Carolina Press, 2003.

Realconditions. Accessed January 12, 2012. http://www.prairiegroup.org/communityprojects/communitywritingproject.html.

"The Reasons for the Split in STO: White Chauvinism in Practice." Unpublished document in author's possession (January 28, 1978).

The Right to Say No to a Crime Against Humanity: A Report on the Militarization of South Africa and the Right of Conscientious Objection. Brooklyn, NY: SAMRAF, 1979.

Romano, Paul, and Ria Stone. *The American Worker*. Detroit: Bewick Editions, 1972 [1947].

Rosemont, Franklin, and Charles Radcliffe, eds. *Dancin' in the Streets!: Anarchists, IWWs, Surrealists, Situationists and Provos in the 1960s, as Recorded in the Pages of* The Rebel Worker *and* Heatwave. Chicago: Charles H. Kerr Publishing Company, 2005.

Rothschild, Matthew. "European Anarchist Has to Cancel Trip to US." *The Progressive*, February 19, 2010.

Rubin, Gayle. "Thinking Sex: Notes for a Radical Theory of the Politics of Sexuality," in *Pleasure and Danger*, edited by Carol Vance. New York: Routledge, Kegan, and Paul, 1984.

Sakai, J. *Settlers: The Mythology of the White Proletariat*. Chicago: Morningstar Press, 1989 [1983?].

Sale, Kirkpatrick. *SDS*. New York: Random House, 1973.

"SAMRAF: Who We Are." *SAMRAF News & Notes* 3 (August/September 1981).

Savage, Jon. *England's Dreaming: Anarchy, Sex Pistols, Punk Rock and Beyond*. New York: St. Martin's Press, 1992.

Schapiro, Leonard. *The Communist Party of the Soviet Union*. New York: Vintage Books, 1964.

Schmidt, Michael, and Lucien van der Walt. *Black Flame: The Revolutionary Class Politics of Anarchism and Syndicalism*. Oakland, CA: AK Press, 2009.

Sheppard Jr., Nathaniel. "Four Freed Puerto Rican Nationalists Vow to Continue Fight; Sentenced for Terrorist Acts." *New York Times*, September 11, 1979, A16.

Singer, Daniel. *Prelude to Revolution: France in May 1968*. Boston: South End Press, 2002 [1970].

Sojourner Truth Organization (STO). *Toward a Revolutionary Party: Ideas on Strategy and Organization*. Chicago: STO, 1976 [1971].

STO. *The United Front Against Imperialism?* Chicago: STO, 1972.

STO. *The Insurgent Worker*. Various issues, 1971–1974.

STO. *Urgent Tasks*. Various issues, 1977–1983.

STO. *Internal Discussion Bulletin*. Various issues, 1978–1983.

STO. *Organizing Working Class Women*. Chicago: STO, n.d. but probably 1972.

STO. *Outline History of Sojourner Truth Organization*. Unpublished manuscript (1972).

STO. *Mass Organization in the Workplace*. Chicago: STO, 1972.

STO. *"Since When Has Working Been a Crime?" The Deportation of Mexicans Without Papers*. Chicago: South Chicago Workers Center [STO] (n.d., but circa 1977).

Sonnie, Amy, and James Tracy. *Hillbilly Nationalists, Urban Race Rebels, and Black Power: Community Organizing in Radical Times*. Brooklyn, NY: Melville House Publishing, 2011.

Special Sedition, November 1982.

Stalin, Josef. *Marxism and the National Question* (1913). Accessed December 23, 2011. http://www.marxists.org/reference/archive/stalin/works/1913/03.htm.

Staudenmaier, Michael. "The White Skin Privilege Concept: From Margin to Center of Revolutionary Politics" (2007). Available online at http://sojourn-ertruth.blogsome.com/2007/11/09/the-white-skin-privilege-concept-from-margin-to-center-of-revolutionary-politics/

Talkback. Various issues, 1972–1978.

Tendency Newsletter. Various issues, 1982–1983.

Terkel, Studs. *Hope Dies Last: Keeping the Faith in Difficult Times*. New York: The New Press, 2003.

"There Ain't No Justice … Just Us": An Account of a Wildcat Strike. Chicago: South Chicago Workers' Rights Center, 1978.

Tokar, Brian. "On Bookchin's Social Ecology and its Contributions to Social Movements." *Capitalism, Nature, Socialism* 19, no. 1 (March 2008): 51–66.

Torres, Andres, and Jose Velazquez, eds. *The Puerto Rican Movement: Voices From the Diaspora*. Philadelphia: Temple University Press, 1998.

Toward People's War For Independence and Socialism in Puerto Rico: In Defense of Armed Struggle: Documents and Communiqués from the Revolutionary Public Independence Movement and the Armed Clandestine Movement. Chicago: STO, 1979.

Tracy, James. *Direct Action: Radical Pacifism from the Union Eight to the Chicago Seven*. Chicago: University of Chicago Press, 1996.

Walker, J. Samuel. *Three Mile Island: A Nuclear Crisis in Historical Perspective*. Berkeley, CA: University of California Press, 2004.

Waller, Signe. *Love and Revolution: A Political Memoir: People's History of the Greensboro Massacre, Its Setting and Aftermath*. Lanham, MD: Rowman and Littlefield, 2002.

"We Have Nothing to Repent." *Time*. September 24, 1979.

We Want to Riot Not to Work: The 1981 Brixton Uprisings. London: Riot Not to Work Collective, 1982.

Wheaton, Elizabeth. *Codename Greenkil: The 1979 Greensboro Killings*. Athens, GA: University of Georgia Press, 2009 [1987].

Willis, Ellen. *Beginning to See the Light: Pieces of a Decade*. New York: Alfred A. Knopf, 1981.

Willis, Ellen. "Radical Feminism and Feminist Radicalism." *Social Text* 9/10 (1984): 91–118.

Woodward, C. Vann. *The Strange Career of Jim Crow*. New York: Oxford University Press, 2002 [1955].

Worchester, Kent. *CLR James: A Political Biography*. Albany, NY: State University of New York Press, 1996.

Wright, Steve. *Storming Heaven: Class Composition and Struggle in Italian Autonomist Marxism*. London: Pluto Press, 2002.

"You Don't Need a Weatherman to Know Which Way the Wind Blows," in *Weatherman*, edited by Harold Jacobs. San Francisco: Ramparts Press, 1970.

Young Lords Organization 1, no. 5 (January, 1970).

Zeskind, Leonard. *Blood and Politics: the History of the White Nationalist Movement from the Margins to the Mainstream*. New York: Farrar, Strauss and Giroux, 2009.

Index

A

A Call to Organize (leaflet), 66
Abalone Alliance, 249, 253
abolition movement, 134
abortion. *see also* reproductive rights movement
abortion, right wing response to, 292
Active Resistance, a Counter-Convention, 1
activists, young, 249, 252, 255. *see also* youth
    in STO, 298
Adams, Hal
    culture of STO, 198, 199, 218–219
    Dialectics Course, 221
    working-class intellectualism, 324–325
Adolphson, Cathy, 135, 208
Advance the Struggle, 333
adventurism, 297, 297n. 85
advertising and racism, 311n. 4
aesthetics, Marxist theories of, 194
affinity groups, 249, 301
affirmative action, 245, 312n. 7
Afghanistan, Soviet occupation of, 217
AFL-CIO, 16, 49, 75
Africa
    ancient civilizations, 202
    anti-authoritarians in, 321
    gay rights in, 326n–327n. 33
    nuclear power in, 242–243
    SAMRAF, 218, 243–244, 244n. 31
    STO's outreach efforts in, 320
    support from China, 130
African Americans, 19, 81–88, 85, 267. *see also* black militants, black nationalism, black liberation
African People's Socialist Party

(APSP), 110, 154
Afrikan People's Party, 143
ain't I a woman (quote), 135, 135n. 49
Alabama, 133
Albizu Campos, Pedro, 150, 187, 188n. 99
Ali, Muhammad and the draft, 19
alienation, 281, 297
All-People's Congress (APC), 256
Allen, Ted
    internal debate in STO regarding, 157–158
    on Weatherman, 92
    opposition to PL, 25–26
    solidarity work, 160–161
    theory of US history, 84
    white skin privilege, 47, 87, 88, 89–91, 311
    women and revolution, 136–140, 137n. 54, 138n. 61
Althusser, Louis, 203n . 45
Amalgamated Clothing Workers of America, 64
American dream, 192
American Federation of Labor, 16
American Indian Movement, 242
American Worker, The (pamphlet), 109
anarchism, 1
    Anarkismo, 321
    and restrictions on travel, 321
    antinuclear movement, 248n. 41
    critique of Leninism, 116n. 5
    Latin American, 331, 331n. 39
    punk rock music, 193
    revolutionary, 313
    tendency-building, 254
anarchist communism, 248n. 41
Anarkismo (web site), 321
anger, 192, 206
anonymity, 52, 207–208
anti-immigrant sentiment, 99–101
anti-imperialism, 86, 165. *see also* specific movements and groups
    and STO, 2, 124, 144, 218, 253–255, 319
    antinuclear movement, 234, 235–244, 238, 241–244

beyond solidarity work, 184
conferences, 45, 224
PFOC, 131, 131n. 36
student movement, 91
tendency-building, 280
women, 167
anti-intellectualism, 219
anti-intervention movement, 301, 305
anti-Klan organizing, 240–241, 271,
    292
anti-Leninism, 136, 157
anti-Marxism, 90, 91, 210n. 59
anti-parliamentarianism, 279
Anti-Racist Action, 106, 309, 322, 333
anti-secessionists in Mississippi, 228
anti-Stalinism, 155
    in STO, 27–28, 28n. 40, 92
antiabortion movement, 292
anticapitalism, 246
anticommunism, 16, 237
antifascist organizing, 289
    and STO, 132, 271, 291, 292, 322
    Anti-Racist Action, 309
    premature anti-fascism, 330n. 37
    punk rock music, 194
    secular crisis, 284
    tendency-building, 295
    United Front, 294
antiglobalization movement, 309
antinuclear movement, 165n. 41, 233
    Africa, 242–244
    arms race, 255–257
    CAWI, 192
    in Colorado, 235–238
    in Urgent Tasks, 132
    racism, 240–241
    radicalization, 183
antipolice violence, 296–298
antipoverty work, 14, 15
antiracist organizing
    and antinuclear movement, 239
    and Harold Washington
        campaign, 269–270
    and Ken Lawrence, 228
    and PL, 25
    and working class, 90
antiracists, white, 86, 96

antisocial behavior, 297, 298
antiwar organizing, 20, 31, 86, 256.
    see also antinuclear movement
    and STO, 258, 260
    groups, 235, 235n. 6
    rightward drift, 261n. 68
    working class, 18–20
apartheid, 242, 244
Apple, Inc., 312n. 6
Arab Spring, 309, 318
archaeology exhibits, 200–203
Argentina military police, 172
Armed Forces of National Liberation
    (FALN), 152
    arrests, 185
    attacks on, 217
    bombings, 169
    grand jury investigations, 162–163
    members, 173, 179
    seditious conspiracy charges,
        187–188
armed self-defense, 13
armed struggle
    in Namibia, 243
    OIPFG, 172
    Puerto Rican independence, 150,
        162, 162n. 33, 168
    urban, 174–175
arms race, opposition to, 256
arrests, 86
    antinuclear movement, 249, 250,
        253, 303–304
    of Puerto Rican radicals, 185–186
art, theories of, 194, 324. see also
    popular culture
assassinations, 172
Atlanta, 33–35, 269
Attica prison uprising, 54
authoritarianism, 288
authority in STO. see hierarchy,
    informal; power in STO
auto industry, 14, 31, 43, 286
autokoenony, 281n. 38
Autonomen, 279
Autonomia, 279
autonomism, 288

autonomist movement
  and STO, 123, 279–280
  Italian, 281, 282, 283, 283n. 45
  tendency-building, 280–281
Autonomous Zone, 1
autonomy, 5–6, 37–39, 262. *see also*
  autonomist movements
  and Big Flame, 73, 74
  and fascism, 289–290, 291, 294,
    322
  and international tendency-
    building, 280–281
  and Italian Hot Autumn, 44
  and STO, 56–57, 151, 274–275
  and STO recruitment, 126,
    329–331
  and STO's legacy, 310
  and the Harold Washington
    campaign, 272–273
  and the national question, 153, 157
  and the Rock Island protests, 302
  and workplace organizing, 96–98,
    286–287
  definitions of, 281, 281n. 38
  for black people, 275–276, 287
  for gay and lesbian activists,
    276–277
  for the Jewish Bund, 277–278
  for third world groups, 140–144,
    182, 242, 278
  for women, 134, 136, 166, 276
  for women in STO, 323
  for women revolutionaries, 137,
    139, 140
  for working class, 2, 280, 284–
    285, 287, 297, 302
  for youth, 296, 298
  importance of, 111, 288, 313–314
  within social movements, 3, 4, 4n

B

back-to-the-land movement, 246
Bacon's Rebellion, 85
Badiou, Alain, 6n, 317n. 13
Baker, Ella, 86, 86n.15
Balloon faction, 111–112

Barber, David, 13n. 3
barricades, 42, 303
Beltran, Haydee, 187n. 98
Berkeley Women's Music Collective,
  197
Berlin, 284
BHA. *see* Black Hills Alliance
Big Flame, 314n. 9
  and STO, 73–74, 281n. 37
  autonomy, 279, 313–314
  feminism, 323n. 26
  members, 327
  tendency-building, 280
biology and race, 88, 202–203
Black Belt, 153–154, 156, 157
black culture, 87, 107–109
Black Hills Alliance, 242, 242n. 26,
  253, 254
black history, 81–88
black liberation
  and STO, 102–103, 287
  autonomy, 288
  C.L.R. James, 105
  decline of, 13
  internal dynamics, 12–13, 12n. 1
  relationships with other groups,
    25, 26, 86, 94
  the national question, 154–155,
    154n–155n. 16
  Vietnam War, 19
black men and rape, 133
black nationalism. *see also* specific groups
  and black autonomy, 288
  and the national question, 153–
    154, 158–160
  and Weatherman, 93
  solidarity with Puerto Ricans, 178
  STO position on, 149, 159–160
Black Orchid Collective, 333
Black Panther Party (BPP), 11, 12,
  13, 14, 30
  influence, 13n. 3, 94, 152
  violence, 252
black people, 4 n. 2, 204n. 47. *see also*
  specific groups
  autonomy for, 276, 278
  in Chicago, 271

black power movement, 12, 279
black radicals, 252
    and state repression, 11
    C.L.R. James, 105
    in Detroit, 45
    in STO, 126
    influence on feminism, 134
    Maoist influence on, 110
    ties with STO, 97
Black Reconstruction in America: 1860-1880 (book)
    influence on STO, 89, 103–104, 103n. 60
    significance, 80–88
black soldiers, 20, 82
black women, 56, 134–136, 164
Black Worker, White Worker (speech), 103–106, 103n. 60
    autonomy, 275–276
    critique of, 106–112
black workers
    and STO, 96, 97–98
    anti-immigrant sentiment, 99–101
    caucuses in factories, 95
    in the colonial era, 84–85
    independent organizations for, 95
    racism, 17, 56, 79–80, 83
    slavery, 81–82
    solidarity, 90
    wildcat strikes, 37–39
Black Workers' Congress (BWC), 62, 96, 101–102
Blaut, James, 158
Boeing and solar power, 247
Bogart, Humphrey, 195
Boggs, Grace Lee, 224–225
Bolivarian revolution, 309
Bologna, Sergio, 280
Bolsheviks, 129, 220
    Jewish Bund, 277–278, 278n
    the national question, 153
bombings, 152, 169, 180, 292
Bookchin, Murray, 247n. 39, 248, 248n. 41, 283n. 42
bosses. *see* management
Boston Group, 119–121, 122

Boston, MA, 118, 245–246
Boulder, Colorado, 235
bourgeois legality compromise, 3
bourgeoisie. *see also* hegemony, bourgeois
    and parenthood, 213
    and the Occupy movement, 317
    critical thinking skills, 220
    in Marxist theory, 40
    in the antifascist movement, 294
    IWW rejection of, 49
    middle class, 244n–245n. 32
    role in capitalist society, 47
    taste in art, 202
    women, 22, 323
    working class, 5, 63, 245
BPP. *see* Black Panther Party
Bradley, Bill, 311n. 4
branches, STO, 287, 328. *see also* specific branches
Bread and Roses (newspaper), 53, 53n. 39, 98
Breakout! (newsletter), 52, 55
Breakthrough (journal), 166–167
Brennan, Peter, 245
Brezhnev, Leonid, 256
Bring the Ruckus, 309, 333
Britain, 127n. 23, 273, 284. *see also* Big Flame
    and autonomy, 279
    music, 193
    unions, 75
Brixton, England, 273, 284
Brown, John, 87
Brownmiller, Susan, 133–135
Brzotowski, Guillermo, 64–65, 77, 111
Buffalo, NY, 62, 151
Buhle, Paul, 87, 132
Bund. *see* Jewish Bund
bureaucracy
    and people of color, 290
    in STO, 70, 258
    in the Soviet Union, 129
    in unions, 16, 18, 18n. 17, 43–44, 54

working class reliance on, 275
bylaws, STO's lack of, 328
Byrne, Jane, 268
Byster, Leslie, 255, 265

C

C&D Printshop, 130. *see* Printshop, C&D
    after STO disbanded, 1, 128n. 25
    and No Easy Answers Left conference, 265
    and STO's solidarity work, 163, 163n. 36, 186
    jobs for STO members, 127–128
    support for SAMRAF, 244n. 31
    workplace organizing, 39, 58, 60
Cagney, James, 195
California, 253, 312n. 6
Call to Organize, A (leaflet), 32–33, 49, 66
Calumet Insurgent Worker, 54
Cambodia, bombing of, 26
Campaign Against White Chauvinism, 215n. 79
campaigns, mayoral, 267–273
campaigns, presidential, 268
Cancel Miranda, Rafael, 150, 215
capitalism
    and antinuclear movement, 246
    and fascism, 290, 291, 294, 322
    and union reform, 284
    and white pacifists, 251
    and white supremacy, 312
    and women, 21–22, 138, 139
    and working class, 5, 46, 275
    contradictions, 222, 313
    effect of strikes on, 61
    in Marxist theory, 40
    in the Soviet Union, 128–129
    international, 308
    law of value, 282
    overthrow of, 15
    secular crisis, 266
    slave holders, 84
    systems of oppression, 133
Capitol, United States, 151n. 6

Carter, Jimmy, 178–179, 217, 226
Castro, Fidel, 177, 177n. 72
Catfish Alliance, 249
caucuses, 95, 136, 141–145
Central America, 256, 260, 301. *see also* specific countries
Central Committee of STO, 124
    communication problems, 257–259, 258n. 60, 287
    internal discipline, 205
    members of, 271
    Phantom Pheminists letter, 207
Central Intelligence Agency (CIA), 16, 171
Central Park antiwar rally, 1982, 260
Central YMCA Community College, 172–173
centralization, 119–120
centrism, political, 269
chants at rallies, 241
Chaplin, Charles, 195
charla, 178
Chiapas, Mexico, 320
Chicago branch of STO, 62, 125, 257. *see also* Central Committee
    antinuclear work, 238
    far right groups, 292
    mayoral election, 271
Chicago Police Department, 173
Chicago Seven, 29
Chicago, IL
    attacks on ISA members, 172–173, 173n. 60
    black community, 154
    bombings, 180
    deindustrialization, 307, 309
    factory organizing in, 50, 55
    grand juries in, 163
    Latino population, 98–101, 147, 151, 169
    mayoral election, 267–271
    race relations, 103–104
    radical movements, 1, 27, 118, 256
    rallies, 178
Chicano activists, 162, 235

children, 212, 214n. 75, 215
Chile, 172
China, 128, 130, 308. *see also* Maoism
China Syndrome, The (movie), 238n. 16
Church Commission, 207
Churchrock, NM accident, 241
Churgin, Ira, 183, 219, 227
    Washington campaign, 270, 271
Cicero, IL., 37–39, 57–59
circle discussion, 221
civil disobedience, 249, 250, 303, 304
civil liberties, defense of, 318
civil rights movement, 21
    and labor, 16
    as training ground, 17, 33
    black autonomy, 276
    conflicts within, 12
    origins of, 85
Civil War, 81–82, 90, 228, 309
civilians, 302
Claiborne County, Mississippi, 238–240
Clamshell Alliance, 245–246, 248n. 41, 253, 256
    and nuclear weapons, 255
    energy sources, 246n. 36
    nonviolence, 250
    Seabrook Nuclear Plant, 249
clandestine groups
    and Puerto Rican independence, 152, 162, 180
    illegality, 297
    in Iran, 172
    in Russia, 220n. 91
Clark, Mark, 13
Clarke, Kingsley
    on working-class culture, 65
    organizing in Humboldt Park, 170
    rejoining of STO, 300
    Rock Island protests, 303
    solidarity work, 97
    workplace organizing, 58, 76
Clash, the, 193
    and the Rock Island protests, 303
    and younger activists, 255
    political lyrics, 195, 296

class consciousness, 212, 248n. 40, 274, 331
class struggle
    and Anarkismo, 321
    and enlisted men, 19
    and Ignatin's critique of Weatherman, 94
    and revolutionary theory, 313
    and STO's legacy, 325–328
    and unions, 75
    and unity, 102–105
    and working class organizing, 290–291
    and workplace organizing, 65
    in ancient Egypt, 201
    in the antinuclear movement, 244–248
    overthrow of bourgeoisie, 47
    within STO, 212
classical music, 198–199
classism, 326
Cleaver, Eldridge, 13
closures, factory, 57–59
coal power, 246–247, 246n. 36
Coalition. *see* Midwest Federation
Coalition for a Non-Nuclear World, 240–241
coalitions, international, 280
code of silence, 39
Coe Resolutions, 124–126, 140–142
COINTELPRO, 12, 12n. 2
    and paranoia on the left, 180
    anonymity, 207, 208
    targeting of far right groups, 292
Collazo, Oscar, 150, 150n–151n. 6
collectives, 1, 118–124
Collins, Jasper. *see* Lawrence, Ken
colonial period, 84–85
Colorado, 238, 245
Colorado Committee Against Repression (El Comite), 235
Columbia University, occupation of, 42
Committee Against Nuclear Imperialism, 236
Committee Against War and Imperialism (CAWI), 191–193, 260

Committee in Solidarity with the
    People of El Salvador, 260
Committee in Solidarity with the
    Revolutionary Movement in Iran,
    173–174
Committees Against Grand Jury
    Repression, 163–164
communication
    international, 320–321
    problems in STO, 257, 287, 328
    technology and, 308
communism, anarchist, 248n. 41
communism, libertarian, 313
Communist League, 97
communist movement. *see* New
    Communist Movement
communist movement, international,
    115–117
Communist Party (Marxist-Leninist),
    33–35
    and Puerto Rican independence, 151
    and STO "Crisis" faction, 110
    collapse of, 215n. 79
    comparison with STO, 218
    creation of, 48
    demise of, 305
Communist Party of France, 43
Communist Party of Italy, 46
Communist Party of the Soviet
    Union, 129, 259n. 63, 277
Communist Party USA, 15
    and international tensions, 115
    and sexual violence, 133
    disillusionment with, 109
    FBI targeting of, 207
    former members, 32, 115, 117
    impact on STO, 143, 328
    internal discipline, 204, 204n. 47
    members of, 31
    national question, 153–154
    offshoots, 25, 27n. 37, 84
    party-building, 274
    support for black liberation,
        155–156
Communist Workers Party, 289
communists. *see* revolutionaries;
    specific organizations and

individuals
communities of color, 237, 238–240.
    see also specific groups
community, 281n. 38
community colleges, 14
community organizing, 15, 35, 169, 279
    and STO, 95
community, Puerto Rican, 151–152
condescending saviors, 4, 4n
Confederate Army deserters, 227–228
Confederation. *see* Midwest
    Federation
conferences, 257. *see also* specific
    events
    at Coe College, 124
    educational, 224
    of independent Leninists,
        117–118
    RYM II, 26, 33–35
    tendency-building, 262, 264–265
conflict. *see* internal conflict
Congress of Industrial Organizations
    (CIO), 16, 31, 85, 91
Congress of Racial Equality, 12
congress people, 268, 311n. 4
connections, personal, 257
consciousness, dual. *see* dual
    consciousness
consciousness, Gramsci's analysis of, 285
consciousness, revolutionary. *see*
    revolutionary consciousness
consensus process, 237, 241, 249
constitution, IWW, 33
constitution, STO's lack of, 328
Constitution, United States, 318
construction industry, 245
conventions, 25, 32, 86n. 15
Cook County Jail, 31
corporations opposing Proposition
    Eight, 312n. 6
Corretjer, Juan Antonio, 178
corruption, political, 267–268
corruption, union, 16, 49, 68, 145
    and shop sheets, 52
    Hamerquist on, 75
    of shop stewards, 55n. 43

costumes at protests, 303
counterculture, 87, 165n. 41, 196n.
    14. *see also* culture, popular; punk
    rock music
coups, 32, 171
courses offered by STO, 220–223,
    220n. 91. *see also* Dialectics Course
CPUSA Manual on Organization, 204
Creamer, Janeen, 283n. 45, 286, 299
    workload, 218. *see also* Janeen
        Porter
criminal records, 180. *see also* arrests
Crisis in STO (paper), 69–72, 74–76,
    107
crisis, cyclical, 293–294
crisis, secular, 282–284, 293–294, 299
Crisis, The (magazine), 80
crisis, theory of, 223
criticism, value of, 318, 320
criticism/self-criticism, 203–204
Crosscurrents Cultural Center, 226
Cruz, Rafael, 169
Cuba, 86, 128, 177, 177n. 72
    revolution in, 151
cultural feminism, 23n. 28
culture, popular, 64–65, 87
    and consciousness, 195–196,
        195n. 11
    and social struggle, 192
    and STO, 198–200, 226–227, 324
    importance of, 229
    in radical movements, 92
culture, Puerto Rican, 169
culture, working class, 108, 192–193,
    324, 325–326
Cunningham, David, 12n. 2
curriculum, dialectics course, 220–
    223, 220n. 91
cynicism of STO members, 259–260
Czechoslovakia, invasion of, 32

D

Daley, Richard J., 267, 268
Daley, Richard M., 268
Dalla Costa, Mariarossa, 280

dance parties, STO, 64–65
dancing, 194–195, 198–200, 296
Danville, IL, 118
Darnovsky, Marcy, 253n. 52
Davidson, Carl, 14, 15n
Days of Rage, 20, 20n. 22, 297n. 85
de Gaulle, Charles, 43
debate, external, 122, 128, 149
    at No Easy Answers Left
        conference, 265
    over nonviolence, 250–252
    problems with, 182
    tendency-building, 234
    the national question, 155–158
debate, internal, 218–220, 226, 315
debates, political, 268, 311n. 4
defense industry, 51, 299, 301–305.
    see also military
Dehghani, Ashraf, 174n. 65
deindustrialization
    and unions, 233
    collapse of STO, 308
    in Chicago, 307
    in the Quad Cities, 302
    unemployment, 285
    workplace organizing, 216, 247
democracy, 208n. 56, 289–290
Democracy and Hip-Hop Project, 324
democracy, direct, 241
democracy, social, 305
democratic centralism, 120–125, 143
Democratic Party
    and Vietnam War, 20–21
    Chicago, 267, 268–270
    national conventions, 1, 27, 28
    New Deal, 31
    primaries, 268, 270, 311n. 4
democratic rights struggle, 277
demographics, 244–245
    of STO, 94–98, 125–126, 140–
        142, 329–331
demonstrations, 170, 235, 256
Denmark, autonomist movement in,
    279
Denver STO branch, 125, 235
    antinuclear organizing, 235

international organizing, 242
members with children, 214
Puerto Rican solidarity, 178
deportation, 99, 218
depression of STO members, 259–260
deserters
Confederate army, 227–228
South African, 218, 243
Vietnam War, 18, 19
Detroit
All-People's Congress, 257
black organizations in, 14
local elections in, 269
NAWF members in, 256
radical groups in, 42
radical organizations in, 2–3
similarity to Gary, Indiana, 62
steel workers in, 62
Tigers fans, 199
Diablo Canyon, 253
Dialectics Course, 220–223, 285, 314
and internal debate, 315
and STO's reputation, 263
informal hierarchy, 329
resurrection of, 309–310
study guides, 132
dictatorship, 82, 82n. 6, 116, 171
fascist, 291
military, 172
direct action
against Fugitive Slave Act, 100–101
against Vietnam War, 18
and *Autonomia,* 279
and civil rights movement, 85–87
and Puerto Rican independence, 168
and revolutionary consciousness, 316
antifascist, 289, 293, 322
antinuclear movement, 249–250, 253
STO, 2, 3, 298–299, 300–301, 305
workplace, 67–68, 79–80, 99
Disarm Now Action Group, 301–305
disarmament, nuclear, 256
discipline
in Leninist party-building, 122
within STO, 111, 117, 142,

203–206
dissidents, pro-Union, 228
diversity of tactics, 302, 302n. 94
divorce, STO members, 323
Dixon, Marlene, 29
Dodge plant, 14
Dodge Revolutionary Union Movement, 14
double consciousness. *see* dual consciousness
Doyle, Tony, 1
draft resisters, 18, 19, 243
drag queens. *see* gay rights
DRUM, 18, 62
Du Bois, W.E.B., 86, 89, 89n. 22
double consciousness, 4 n. 2
influence on STO, 27, 80–88, 103–104, 103n. 60, 221, 315
white privilege, 5
dual consciousness theory, 32, 74, 252, 313
and hegemony, 46
and STO's legacy, 310, 312–313
and tendency-building, 235
capitalism, 222
examples of, 103–104
refutation of, 70–71
STO's internal conflict over, 106
working class, 4–5, 4–5 n. 2, 274–275
Duggan, Bob, 29, 29n. 47
Dunayavskaya, Raya, 110n. 80
Dworkin, Andrea, 211
Dylan, Bob, 92

E

Echols, Alice, 23n. 28
ecology movement. *see* environmental movement
economic factors
fascism, 293
global economy, 308
in Puerto Rico, 150
in the Soviet Union, 129
inflation, 59, 59n. 52, 60

of women's liberation, 138, 139
organizing around, 286
Rock Island protests, 302
secular crisis, 283
education, 104
public schools, 82, 268
Puerto Rican activism, 148, 152
education, formal, 314, 314n. 10
education, internal, in STO, 3, 73
and workload of STO members, 218
commitment to, 124, 193
Dialectics Course, 220–223
downsides to, 199
for women, 210
IDB, 226
organization of, 223, 223n. 99
power structures, 329
Edwards, Allison
critique of radical feminism, 323
critique of Susan Brownmiller, 133
male supremacy, 139–140
Phantom Pheminists letter, 207–208, 211–212
revolutionaries as parents, 213
Egyptian artifacts, 200–203
El Comite
see Colorado Committee Against Repression
El Obrero Insurgente. see Insurgent Worker
El Paso, Texas, 63–64
El Salvador, 192, 256, 301, 309
Elbaum, Max, 199, 203, 318
elected leaders in STO, 124–125
elections
antinuclear movement, 254
mayoral, 267–273
presidential, 311n. 4
race, 20, 83
veteran activists, 261
elections, union, 55, 55n. 43
Emancipation Proclamation, 81
emergency response mode, MLN, 170, 170n. 53, 186, 214, 216
employment. *see* jobs
energy policy, 59, 246–247
Engels, Friedrich, 221, 225,

244n–245n. 32
environmental impact of imperialism, 150
environmental movement, 164n. 37, 233, 237, 246, 308
social ecologists, 254
Episcopal Church, 152, 162
Epstein, Barbara, 253, 253n. 52, 255–256
Epton, Bernard, 270, 272
equality
for women, 138, 139
of ideas, 221
racial, 102–103
the national question, 153, 154, 154n–155n. 16, 157
escaped slaves, 99–101
especifismo, 331, 331n. 39
Eurocentrism and socialism, 154
Eurocommunism, 315
Europe, 296. *see also* specific countries and groups
autonomist movements, 273, 279–280
fascism in, 292
STO outreach, 320
Evanston FALN arrests, 185, 216
events, STO, 64–65
Executive Committee, STO, 214
expansion of STO, 218, 259–260, 329–331
Exxon, 202
EZLN. *see* Zapatista Army of National Liberation

F

facilitation, ineffective, 265
Facing Reality Organization (FRO), 32, 33
factions in left groups, 69–72, 96, 121, 162
factories. *see also* jobs; working class; workplace organizing; specific factories

alternative media in, 35
and Marxist theory, 40–41
jobs for STO members, 50–51,
   124, 144
Quad Cities, 302
racism, 17
wildcat strikes, 14, 18, 37–39, 145
workers, 64–65, 67, 109–110
FALN. *see* Armed Forces of National
Liberation
families, interracial, 228
family life and political work, 65
family planning, 164. *see also*
reroductive rights movement
Fanon, Franz, 252, 316, 316n. 12
far-right, 286. *see also* right wing
movements; specific movements and
groups
   and women, 134
   divisions in, 291–292, 294
   in Italy, 43–44
   STO's analysis of, 322
Farah Manufacturing Company
strike, 63–64, 101, 111–112
farms, 302
fascism, 132, 203n. 45
   and the secular crisis, 282
   anti-Semitism, 295
   autonomy, 288–289
   definitions of, 291
   Harold Washington campaign, 272
   imminent fascism theory, 291
   in Italy, 43–44
   punk rock music, 193, 195
   relationship with government, 293
   white youth violence, 298
fatherhood and political work, 213
Federal Bureau of Investigation (FBI),
11, 172, 207
Federal Energy Administration, 60
federalism, 120
Federation. *see* Midwest Federation
Fein, Sinn, 298
feminism, 21–24, 209n
   agency of the oppressed, 210n. 59
   Big Flame and, 323n. 26
   Brownmiller, 133–135

in PFOC, 165–167, 166n. 46
in SDS, 24
mass sterilization, 164–165
music, 197
pro-sex, 208–209, 209n, 211
STO and, 225, 322–323, 324
feminist radicalism, 21, 21n, 23–24,
23n. 29, 29–30
   and STO publications, 63
   goals, 22
feminists, Iranian, 218
feudalism, 40
Fiat factory, 43–44
fight the people (slogan), 16, 16n. 13
Figueroa Cordero, Andres, 150,
   178–179
First of May Anarchist Alliance, 333
Five, the, 150, 173, 178–179, 215
Flint Sit-Down Strike, 31, 275n. 27
Flores, Irving, 150
folk music, 200
food, 324
foreign aid and imperialism, 326n. 33
foreign policy, 130, 171, 286
Forest, F., 110n. 80
Fortune 500 companies, 312n. 7
fragging, 18, 18n–19n. 18, 20
Free State of Jones, 228
Free the Five campaign, 178–179
Freedom Road Socialist Organization,
   119n. 9
French General Strike of 1968, 42–43
French, Lynn, 30–31, 94, 95
friendships in STO, 199, 199n. 28
Fugitive Slave Act, 100–101
fun at STO meetings, 199
fundamentalism, religious, 175, 176
fundraising, 63, 64, 178, 321
future of STO, 262, 263. *see also*
expansion of STO

G

Gambino, Ferruccio, 280
Gandhi, Mohandas, 251–252, 251n.
   47, 251n–252n. 48, 253

gangs, Puerto Rican, 151
gardener approach, 107–111
garment worker strikes, 63–64
Garvey, John, 332
Garvey, Marcus, 154
Gary, Indiana branch of STO, 96,
    273n. 21
    1974 truckers' strike, 60
    Calumet Insurgent Worker, 54
    solidarity work, 97–98
    working-class culture, 65–66
    workplace organizing, 50
Gasoline Alley, 195
Gateway Industries factory, 57–59, 101
gay rights, 132, 210n. 59, 276
    and Stonewall, 24
    in Africa, 326n. 33
    marriage, 312n. 6
Gdansk, Poland, 284
General Confederation of Labor
    (CGT), 43
General Electric, 247
General Membership Meetings, STO
    authority of, 141
    culture, 199
    internal discipline, 205
    organizational structure, 124,
        142, 328
    reframing of STO's priorities,
        183–184
    response to fascism, 293
    the national question, 158
general strikes, 42–43, 50, 82, 317
Geneva Conventions, 185
Genoa protests, 309
genocide, 164, 236, 241–242, 282
geographical reach of STO, 3, 125,
    257–258, 329, 329n
Georgia Communist League, 34
Germany, 279
get rich quick scheme, 260
ghetto rebellions, 14
Glaberman, Martin, 32
global warming, 308
globalization, 302n. 94, 308, 312
Goldfield, Evie, 28, 29–30

Goldfield, Michael, 28, 69–72, 69n.
    81, 76
Google, 312n. 6
Gore, Al, 311n. 4
Gould, Randy, 193, 293
    criticisms of Central Committee,
        258, 258n. 61
    departure from STO, 296
    STO's internal hierarchy, 257
governance of Puerto Rico, 150
governance, STO, 124–125, 328. *see
    also* hierarchy, informal
    by the Third World Caucus,
        141–143
    internal discipline, 203–206
government, Iranian, 175
government, United States, 276. *see
    also* state repression
    and labor, 16, 60, 61
    and nuclear power in Africa, 242,
        243
    and white skin privilege, 88
    antifascism, 293
    attacks on national liberation
        movements, 256
    corruption in Chicago, 267–268
    during Reconstruction, 82
    interference with the left, 180,
        321, 321n
Grailville Conference, 117–118
Gramsci, Antonio
    influence on STO, 32, 109, 221, 315
    organic intellectuals, 324–325
    working class, 4, 4 n. 2, 41,
        45–46, 274
    writings on consciousness, 285
grand juries, 162–163
grassroots organizing, 14
Gray, Maryon, 261
Greason, David, 176
Great Lakes Naval Base, 305
Great Migration, the, 154
Green Scare, 164n. 37
Green, Joe, 95
Greensboro massacre, 289, 289n. 58
Greensboro, N.C., 240, 289, 289n. 58
Greyhound Bus Company, 305

grievance procedures, 38, 79–80, 206
Grito de Jayuya uprising, 150n–151n. 6
Grossman, Zoltán, 242n. 26
Grundrisse (manuscript), 281, 282, 282n. 41
Guardian (newspaper), 90–91
Guatemala, 256, 301
guerrillas, Iranian, 172, 174–175, 174n. 65
guilt, white, 311
Guthrie, Woody, 255

H

Halk, Macee, 97, 287
Hall, Gus, 32
Hamer, Fannie Lou, 269
Hamerquist, Don
  and Gramsci's theories, 45–46
  and international communist movement, 115–117
  and No Easy Answers Left conference, 266
  and the national question, 155–158, 159–160
  and unity within STO, 200
  background, 31–32, 207, 314
  C&D Printshop, 1, 163
  call for Chicago general strike, 50
  critique of Boston Group, 119n. 10, 120–122
  debates, 234–235, 315–316
  dual consciousness theory, 4–5 n. 2, 70
  fascism, 289–291, 322
  leadership in STO, 78, 124–125
  multiracial organizations, 140
  on get rich quick scheme, 260
  on revolutionary movements, 6, 6n
  on seeds of socialism theory, 109
  on shop sheets, 52
  on the Jewish Bund, 277–278
  power in STO, 143, 144, 219, 328–329
  problems in STO, 74–76
  problems with Third World autonomy, 182
  rejection of Stalinism, 122–123
  STO strategy, 66–68, 149, 183–184
  tendency-building, 258
  three way fight analysis, 176n–177n. 71
  ties to Italian autonomists, 280
  writings, 128, 228
Hampton, Fred, 13, 30, 297n. 85
Hard Hat Riot, 245
Harlem, 204n. 47, 241, 311n. 4
Harlem Fight Back!, 254
harmonica music, 199
harness the energy approach, 297, 298
Harpers Ferry Organization, 15
Harpers Ferry, WV, 87
Harrisburg, PA, 238
Hartford, CT, 151
Harvester Plant. *see* International Harvester Plant
Hatcher, Richard, 273n. 21
Hawthorne Works. *see* Western Electric Hawthorne Works factory
Haymarket Organization, 123, 123n–124n. 19
Hayse, Carol, 223, 254
Haywood, Harry, 154
Hayworth, Rita, 195
health care, 82
hearings, CPUSA, 204
heavies, intellectual. *see* intellectual culture in STO
Hegel, Georg Wilhelm Friedrich, 220, 221
hegemony, bourgeois, 224, 307
  and dual consciousness, 274, 313
  Gramcsi's theory of, 46
Hella Occupy! (pamphlet), 318
Hendrix, Jimi, 255
Henson, Beth, 58–59, 135, 174–175
hierarchy and oppression, 326
hierarchy, informal, 73, 77–78, 124–125, 219
  during APC, 257
  organizational structure, 328–329
  racial tensions, 143

Hill, Lance, 212, 215, 217
Hinton, William, 70n. 84
hip-hop music, 324
hippies, 11
hiring practices, racist, 103–104
history
    according to STO, 84, 132, 225
    ancient Egypt, 201
    Marxist theory of, 40–42, 40n. 6
    of communism, 115–117
    of nonviolent action, 252
    primary sources, 85
    Puerto Rico, 150–152
    purpose of, 308
    the national question, 155
    United States, 80–88
    women's movement, 134
Hoagland, Sarah Lucia, 281n. 37
Holstein, Lee, 198
    agency of the oppressed, 210–211
    and dual consciousness, 313
    and working class autonomy,
        284–285
    critical Marxists, 216
    democratic resistance in STO,
        208n. 56
    internal discipline, 206
    Puerto Rican solidarity, 184n. 91
    punk rock music, 194
    self-esteem, 210n. 60
homosexuality, 276–277, 312, 326n.
  33. see also gay rights
    terminology, 277n. 29
hootenannies, 200
hostage crisis, Tehran, 175
Hot Autumn, 42, 43–44
    impact, 73, 75, 279
Hotpoint factory, 97
housing discrimination, 151
Humboldt Park, Chicago, 147, 169,
  268–269, 270
humor, 226–227
Humphrey, Hubert, 20

I

IBEW. see International Brotherhood
of Electrical Workers (IBEW)
identity politics, 326
Ignatiev, Noel. see also Noel Ignatin
    analysis of white skin privilege,
      311
    and international communist
      movement, 115–117
    and Left-ISA, 171n. 56
    and working-class culture, 65–66,
      325–326
    education, 314, 314n. 10
    on get rich quick scheme, 260
    on STO, 216, 307, 327
Ignatin, Noel, 62, 221. see also Noel
Ignatiev
    and autonomy, 275–276
    and C.L.R. James, 200n–201n. 34
    and Internationale translation,
      4 n. 1
    and STO publications, 66
    and tendency-building, 262, 263,
      280–281, 281n. 37
    and theoretical debates, 315–316
    and Urgent Tasks, 131, 132, 203n.
      45
    and white skin privilege, 5
    and white supremacy, 80,
      102–104
    and women, 138–139
    Black Worker, White Worker
      speech, 103–112, 103n. 60
    critique of Boston Group, 120
    critique of socialist governments,
      128–130, 177, 177n. 72
    critique of Stalinism, 32
    critique of Weatherman, 92–94
    departure from STO, 300
    founding of STO, 27
    friendship with Ted Allen, 136
    history, theory of, 87, 91
    on STO and the left, 6, 7
    on white skin privilege, 88
    opposition to PL, 25–26
    power within STO, 78, 124–125,
      143, 144, 219, 328–329
    problems in STO, 258n. 60
    seeds of socialism theory, 109–
      111

solidarity work, 99–100,
    99n–100n. 54, 147n–148n.
    1, 149
The White Blindspot, 89–91
theory, dual consiousness, 313
workplace organizing, 50
writings on autonomism, 288
writings on fascism, 289n. 59,
    291, 294–295
illegality, 316
    and STO, 298–299
    and the secular crisis, 284
    antinuclear movement, 249–250
    clandestinity, 297
    far-right, 292
    NGOs, 319
    state repression, 317
immigrants, 88, 308
    solidarity work, 169
    workers, 99–100
    writings by, 325
Immigration and Naturalization
    Service (INS), 99
imminent fascism theory, 289–291,
    293–294
immunity and testimony, 162
imperialism
    Cuban struggles against, 177
    during WWI, 156
    energy policy, 247, 247n. 39
    fascism, 291
    foreign aid, 326n. 33
    in Puerto Rico, 150
    Kohmeini regime, 176
    nuclear power, 235, 236, 241–
        242
    racism, 87, 93
    social, 130
    united front against, 101–102
    Vietnam War, 11, 20
    weapons industry, 301
incidental function, 137–138, 140
indentured servitude, 84–85
independence
    and autonomy, 276
Independent Marxist Collectives. see
    Midwest Federation

Independent Marxist-Leninist
    Organizations. see Midwest
    Federation
independent workers' organizations,
    49, 74, 96–98, 286
    limitations of, 75–76
India, people's war in, 187n. 97
Indiana. see Gary, Indiana branch of
    STO
individualism, 259–260, 281, 281n. 38
individuals and white skin privilege, 312
individuals, autonomy for, 278, 281
Industrial Workers of the World (IWW)
    influence on STO, 32–33, 49–50,
        333
    shortcomings, 109
    textile strike of 1912, 53
    working class consciousness, 327
industry, heavy, 40–42, 285
inflation, 59, 59n. 52, 60. see also
    economic factors
informers, government, 180–181
instrumentalism, 324
Insurgent Worker (newspaper), 54
    and working class unification, 90
    Spanish language in, 98
    workplace organizing, 38, 62, 79
insurrectionalism, 279
integration, workplace, 17
intellectual culture in STO, 218–220,
    310
    "intellectual heavies," 219, 226,
        315, 328–329
intellectuals, organic, 314, 324
intermediate level, 319
internal conflict, STO, 3, 12, 96,
    103–112, 149
    national liberation, 159
    size of organization, 219, 259
    third world members, 140–145
Internal Discussion Bulletin (IDB)
    (newsletter), 206
International Brotherhood of
    Electrical Workers (IBEW), 37–39,
    75
International Brotherhood of

Teamsters, 185
International Harvester Plant, 28
    black leadership, 96
    closure of, 35
    Melrose Park location, 50, 52
    solidarity work, 79–80
    STO, 29, 68–70
    STO organizing in, 95
International Libertarian Solidarity
    Network, 321
International Socialists, 118, 217,
    284, 286
International Workingmen's
    Association, 18n. 17
Internationale (song), 4 n. 1, 199
internationalism, 235, 292, 320
interracial families, 228
intersectionality, 326, 326n–327n. 33
Iowa, 123, 301, 303
Iran
    and nuclear power, 236, 236n.
        10, 243
    conflict with US, 217
    resistance to the Shah's regime,
        171–177, 172n. 57
    revolution in, 124, 236n. 10
    STO's outreach efforts in, 320
Iranian student movement, 3, 149,
    171, 173, 177
Iranian Students Association (ISA),
    171, 177
Ireland, 218, 280, 297, 298
Irish Republican Army, 298
Iskra, 130
Islam, 172, 175–176
Islamic Republic, 236n. 10
Israel, 236, 301
Israel/Palestine conflict, 295–296
Italy, 45, 75. *see also* Hot Autumn
    autonomist movement in, 279–
        280, 332
    rebellions in, 43–44

J

Jackson, Jesse, 268
Jackson, Miss., 228, 239

Jaggar, Alison, 21n
James, C.L.R.
    and autonomist Marxism, 123
    anti-Stalinism, 27–28
    background of, 105
    correspondence with STO, 203n.
        45
    critique of Stalinism, 32
    in Black Worker, White Worker,
        107–109
    influence on Ignatin, 109, 111, 128
    influence on STO, 73, 74,
        200n–201n. 34, 221, 315
    Johnson-Forest Tendency, 110n. 80
    on culture, 195, 200–201, 324
    organizing strategy, 5
    split from Grace Lee Boggs, 224
    Urgent Tasks issue on, 132
Jamestown, sacking of, 85
Jewish Bund, 140, 277–278
Jim Crow, 82–83
jobs. *see also* deindustrialization
    and energy policy, 246
    and white skin privilege, 87–88
    discrimination, 151
    during recessions, 192
    for black people, 103–104
    for Puerto Ricans, 151
    for STO members in factories,
        50–51
    for women, 21–22, 138
    in weapons industry, 302
    nuclear power industry, 239, 245
    workers' pride in, 109–110
Johnson, J.R. *see* C.L.R. James
Johnson, Lyndon, 11, 20
Johnson-Forest Tendency, 110n. 80
Journal of Ordinary Thought, 325

K

Kansas City branch of STO, 125
    1981 Springsteen concert,
        191–193
    antifascist organizing, 295
    children, 214
    deindustrialization, 309
    departure from STO, 296

far-right, 292
Leninist groups in, 118
Marxist groups in, 123
NAWF, 256, 257
organizational structure, 328
solidarity work, 178
Special Sedition, 296–298
union reform, 285
workload of members, 217–218
workplace organizing, 161, 185
Kant, Immanuel, 281, 281n. 38
Kasama Project, 333
Katsiaficas, George, 281, 281n. 38
Katz, Marilyn, 28, 271–272, 272n. 16
Kemper Arena, 191–193
Kennedy, Ted, 226
Kent State University, 245
Kerensky, Alexander, 175
Khomeini, Ruhollah, 175, 176–177
Khruschev, Nikita, 115–116, 128–129
King, Martin Luther Jr.
   and racism in Chicago, 267,
      267n–268n. 2
   assassination of, 12
   influence, 253
   nonviolence, 251–252
   opposition to Vietnam War, 19
Kinman, Tony, 194, 197, 200
Ku Klux Klan (KKK), 286
   autonomy, 292
   harrassment, 289, 291–292
   resurgence, 239
Kuhn, Gabriel, 321n
Kurds, 175
Kushite civilization, 202

L

labor movement, 15–16, 16n, 25, 43.
   see also unions
   autonomy, 276
   changes to, 16
   failure of, 89
   in Chicago, 3
   law of value, 282
   right wing forces in, 245
   STO rejection of, 3

support for coal power, 246–247
wages for women, 139
white skin privilege, 93–94
white supremacy, 91
Lamme, Bill
   culture of STO, 198, 219, 221
   debate in STO, 182, 264
   demise of STO, 300–301, 306
   liberal politics, 272
   militant direct action, 298–299
   recruitment of, 223
   Rock Island protests, 301, 302
   Washington campaign, 270
Latin America, 308, 320, 321. *see also*
   specific countries
latino workers. *see also* Puerto Rican
   workers, Mexican workers
   and white supremacy, 98–101
   at Gateway factory, 57–59
   class unity, 90
   factory closures, 57–59
   racism, 17
   strikes, 63–64
   wildcat strikes, 37–39
latinos
   activists, 126, 152
   and Chicago's mayoral campaign,
      268
   and the Harold Washington
      campaign, 270
   feminism, 30
   soldiers, 20
law. *see* legality, illegality
law of value, 132, 282–284
Lawrence, Ken
   and C.L.R. James, 195n. 11,
      200n–201n. 34
   anti-fascist organizing, 292, 293
   antinuclear organizing, 238–240,
      238n. 19
   background, 32
   Dialectics Course, 220, 221
   education, 314
   Jasper Collins pseudonym, 140n.
      70, 227–228, 228n. 117
   mentoring of Allison Edwards, 135
   musical preferences, 200
   No Nukes Left!, 254

Phantom Pheminists controversy, 207, 227
power in STO, 143, 144, 219, 328–329
reponse to *Special Sedition,* 297–298, 297n. 85
SNCC, 86n. 15
state repression, 317–318, 317n–318n. 14
STO founders, 27
STO governance, 141
the middle class, 244n–245n. 32
theoretical debates, 315–316
threats from the KKK, 291–292
Urgent Tasks issue on James, 132
Lawrence, KS, 218
Lawrence, Massachusetts, 53
lawyers, 38, 135, 289
leadership
autonomy, 275, 276, 298
by Third World revolutionaries, 181–182
women in PFOC, 166
leadership, STO, 77–78
and Israel/Palestine conflict, 296
and the Third World Caucus, 141–143
and third world autonomy, 278
by multiple people, 219
by women, 323
during APC, 257
informal, 143–144, 328
reliance on, 259
leaflets, 66, 127. *see also* specific publications
at rock concerts, 191–193
bilingual, 98–99
Rock Island protests, 302, 304
STO, 268–271
League of Revolutionary Black Workers (LRBW), 2–3, 13–14
and labor struggles, 18
in Chicago, 97
influence, 33, 42, 45
Maoist influence, 110
successors to, 62
Lebanon, 301

Lebron, Lolita, 150
left work *versus* mass work, 263, 318
left, the. *see also* new left
history of, 7
influence of black liberation, 13, 13n. 3
interracial rape, 133
old left, 33, 143, 328
punk rock music, 193–198
relationship with STO, 6
Left-ISA, 171, 177
legal clinics, 57–58
legal issues, 35
arrest of activists, 86, 86n. 15
Brownmiller's solutions to rape, 133–134
constitutional rights, 318
escaped slaves, 100
grand juries, 162, 163
Iranian students, 173
Joe Green, 95
John Strucker, 51
limits on organizing, 47
LRBW, 14
suspected FALN members, 186–189
systemic racism, 83
the Chicago Seven, 29
the Panther 21, 13
undocumented workers, 99
wildcat strikes, 38–39
legality
and STO's critique of electoral politics, 272–273
IWW rejection of, 49
STO rejection of, 262
working class reliance on, 275
legislation, antinuclear, 254
Lenin, Vladimir
and the Jewish Bund, 140, 277, 278n
capitalism in the Soviet Union, 129
critical thinking skills, 220n. 91
critique of trade unions, 4–5 n. 2
industrial working class, 41
influence on STO, 130, 221, 225, 315
legacy of, 316

Leninism, 7, 33
  "The Crisis in STO" paper, 69
  and Islam, 172
  Black Worker, White Worker, 106
  criticism from STO members, 300
  Hamerquist, 48
  homosexuality, 277
  Ignatin, 115
  in Iran, 174
  Israel/Palestine conflict, 295
  Jamesian approach to, 108
  nationalism, 149, 154
  organizing strategy, 5
  party-building, 122
  perceptions of Kruschev, 116
  recruitment, 56–57
  STO's unorthodox version of,
    315–316
  the national question, 153, 155–158
  the United Front, 294
  theory of consciousness, 47–48,
    48n. 26
  union reform, 70–71
  working class, 74
  working class autonomy, 44
Leninists, independent, 117–118
lesbian rights. see gay rights
lesbian separatists, 21
Letelier, Orlando, 172
Lexington, Miss., 239
liberal feminism, 21, 21n, 23
liberalism, 23
  antifascist movement, 294
  antinuclear movement, 237
  appeal to revolutionaries, 272
  Occupy movement, 317
liberals, 20, 163–164, 251, 311–312
liberation movements, dearth of,
  319–320, 319n. 19
libertarian communism, 313
libertarians, civil, 163, 164
Liga Socialista Puertorriquena (LSP),
  178
line educationals, 223
liquidators, 220, 220n. 91
literary criticism, Marxist, 226–227
Literature Committee, STO, 106–

107, 111
Liverpool, 73
Logan Square, Chicago, 147
London, STO pamphlets in, 127n.
  23
Lopez, Jose, 148, 161–162, 162–163
Lopez, Oscar, 148
Loretz, Carol, 257, 258
Los Angeles, 154
Lotta Continua (Continuous
  Struggle), 44
Louisville, KY, 118
Lousisiana, 154
Love and Rage Revolutionary
  Anarchist Federation, 333
low-income communities. see poor
  people
LRBW. see League of Revolutionary
  Black Workers
Lugones, Maria, 210n. 59
Lukacs, Gyorgy, 221
lull, the, 124, 196
  optimism during, 317
  STO re-examination of, 183
  STO response to, 127, 148
Luxemburg, Rosa, 221

M

machine, the, 267–268, 267n–268n. 2
machines replacing humans, 282–283
Madison, Wisconsin, 255
mafia ties to labor unions, 16
majority rule, 121, 141
Malawi, 326n. 33
male supremacy, 139, 211, 259–260
  autonomy for women, 276
  challenges to, 11, 21, 134–135
  comparison with white
    supremacy, 166–167, 166n. 46
  definition of, 211
  economic factors, 139
  in STO, 205, 211, 259–260, 323
  on the left, 22
  Phantom Pheminists letter,
    206–207

resistance within STO, 210
sexuality, 208–209
STO internal discipline, 205
study of, 138
within STO, 215–216
management
    at Gateway factory, 58
    campaigns against, 54
    concessions, 44
    criticism of, 52
    racism, 79–80, 103–104
    Stewart-Warner INS raid, 99
    union bureaucracy, 43
manipulation in STO, 328
Mao Tse-Tung, 42, 116
Maoism, 25, 119, 289
    and STO, 315
    criticism/self-criticism, 203,
        203n. 46
    critique of Soviet Union, 128
    Hamerquist's critique of, 119n. 10
    in Nepal, 309
    in the black movement, 110
    people's war, 187n. 97
    social imperialism, 130
    STO factions, 70
    workplace organizing, 47–48
March 1 Bloc, 161–162
March on Washington Movement, 85
marriage, gay, 312n. 6, 326n–327n. 33
Martin, Steve, 201n. 35
Marx, Karl
    and the law of value, 282
    and the middle class, 244n–245n.
        32
    definition of autonomy, 281
    influence on Ignatin, 89–90
    influence on STO, 221, 225, 315
    quotations, 308
    theory of history, 40–42, 40n. 6
Marxism
    analysis of fascism, 289–290
    analysis of slavery, 84
    and authoritarianism, 288
    and Holstein's critique of Moody,
        285
    and homosexuality, 276–277
    and punk rock music, 193

and the national question, 153
and wildcat strikes, 18
autonomist, 123
competing versions of, 222
influence on Ignatin, 89–90
influence on STO, 3, 132
practical applications of, 220
scientific character of, 122
theories of art and aesthetics, 194
theory of consciousness, 47
theory of history, 40–42, 40n. 6
varieties of, 92
Marxists. *see also* specific individuals
    and groups
    and founding of STO, 33
    and liberal feminism, 22
    French, 203n. 45
    in STO, 216
    in the Middle East, 172
    organizing strategies, 5
    reaction to truckers' strike, 61
    reaction to White Blindspot,
        90–91
    relationship with workers, 38
    response to French General
        Strike, 43
    response to Russian Revolutions, 42
    W.E.B. DuBois, 80–88
mass movements
    and dual consciousness theory, 5
    and fascism, 294
    and revolutionary consciousness,
        316
    and socialism, 48–49
    and STO, 57–61, 63–64
    and the antinuclear movement,
        249, 255–256
    and the arms race, 256–257
    and the Federation, 118
    dissipation of, 76
    importance of, 4, 258
    in daily life, 108
    in Northern Ireland, 297
    role of the party in, 247–275
    sudden emergence of, 317, 317n. 13
    tendency-building within, 234
Mass Organization in the Workplace
    (pamphlet), 66

mass organizing, 35, 69–70
  by independent STO members,
    144, 263, 318–319
  STO emphasis on, 68, 69, 69n. 81
May 19th Communist Organization,
  161, 161n, 174, 182, 183
May Day, 50
May, Lowell, 173, 200, 287
mayors, black, 273n. 21
McDonnell, Kevin, 127n. 23, 313–
  314, 327
media, alternative
  feminist radicals, 29–30
  in factories, 35, 52–54
  labor struggles, 39
  LRBW, 14, 15
  Rock Island protests, 302
media, mainstream, 226, 253, 301, 302
meetings, evaluation of work, 66–68
Melrose Park, Chicago, 50, 52,
  68–70, 79–80
membership, STO. see also expansion,
  recruitment
  and power structures, 143, 211,
    257, 328–329
  changes in, 35
  demographics of, 94–98, 125–
    126, 140–142, 329–331
  rebuilding after split, 118
  size of, 329
  third world revolutionaries,
    140–142
Menshevik faction, 277
mergers, 123, 264
Mexican activists in MLN, 162
Mexican women workers, 57–59,
  63–64, 101
Mexican workers, 98–101
Mexican-American revolutionaries, 170
Mexico, 308, 309, 320
Meyer, J. see C.L.R. James
Miami Autonomy and Solidarity,
  319, 333
Miami, FL, 273, 284
Michigan, 14, 69–72
middle class activists

antiwar movement, 19
feminists, 21–22, 23
in antinuclear movement, 237, 244
workplace organizing, 51–52
middle class, definitions of,
  244n–245n. 32
Middle East, 59, 171, 192, 301
Midnight Notes Collective, 245–246
Midwest Action League (MAL),
  145–146, 161
Midwestern United States, 118, 305
Milan, Italy, 43
militancy
  antifascism, 322
  at Rock Island Two, 304
  Chicago DNC, 27
  Europe, 43–44, 75
  gay rights, 24
  in antinuclear movement, 241, 249
  in far right groups, 292
  in Puerto Rican independence
    movement, 148, 150
  in STO, 211, 298–299
  Special Sedition, 296–298
  workers, 17, 38, 45, 50–51
military. see also defense industry
  arms race, 256
  crackdown on protesters, 43, 61
  direct action against, 299,
    301–305
  occupation of Puerto Rico, 150
  racial discrimination, 85
  recruitment, 18
  resistance within, 18, 18n–19n. 18
  struggle against oppression, 252
militias, 85
millenarianism, 282, 299, 316, 327
mining industry, 246–247
mining, plutonium, 236
mining, uranium, 236, 242–243, 246
ministers, radical, 251
minorities, national, 153, 157, 175
Mississippi, 228, 238–340, 291–292
Mississippi Freedom Democratic
  Party, 269
Mississippi Power and Light, 240
Mississippi River, 238–240, 301–305

Mississippi State University, Starkville, 174n. 65

MLN. *see* Movement for National Liberation

Mobe, the, 301

Mobil, 247

Mobilization for Survival, 235

monogamy in STO, 205, 209

Moody, Kim, 284–285

Morales, Guillermo, 179, 179n–180n. 78

Morgan, Mike, 243n. 29

Morris, Colin, 251–252, 251n.–252n. 48

Mosaddeq, Mohammed, 171

mothers, single, 213

Motorola factory, 50, 55

Motorola Organizing Committee, 55

Movement for Independence (MPI), 151

Movement for National Liberation (MLN)
    and FALN, 186–187
    and STO, 163, 163n. 36, 184, 320
    Chicago mayoral election, 268–269, 268n. 4
    critique of PRSC, 162
    emergency mode, 170, 186, 214
    founding of, 162n. 32
    support for FALN, 179

movementism, 318–319

movies about nuclear accidents, 238

multiracial organizations, 330, 330n. 36

music, 4n. 1
    and STO, 198–200
    as an organizing tool, 191–193
    black culture, 87
    Bob Dylan lyrics, 92
    hip-hop, 324
    James' analysis of culture, 324
    King Tut song, 201n. 35
    punk rock, 165n. 41, 193–198, 201, 296–298, 303
    rock and roll, 194
    working-class culture, 65

Mussolini, Benito, 46

N

Namibia, 242–244, 253

Nappolis, S., 319

National Anti-Klan Network (NAKN), 292–293

National Anti-War Fraction (NAWF), 256–257, 260

National Association for the Advancement of Colored People (NAACP), 80, 239

National Basketball Association (NBA), 311n. 4

National Commission on Hispanic Affairs, 152

National Committee, STO
    and Israel/Palestine conflict, 296
    authority of, 141
    dissolution, 300
    election of, 144
    organizational structure, 124, 328
    reports, 226
    workload of members, 218

National Guard, 61

National Labor Conference for Safe Energy and Full Employment, 233–234, 241

National Labor Relations Board, 51, 54

National Lawyers Guild, 38, 289

National Liberation Front, 20, 20n. 22, 21

national liberation movements. *see also* specfic movements and groups
    and nationhood, 156
    decline of, 309
    nuclear weapons, 236
    Reagan administration, 256
    role of white radicalism, 160
    solidarity, 3, 152, 157–158, 181–182
    STO, 126, 127, 167, 224
    STO suboordination to, 184
    tendency-building, 235

white skin privilege, 159
national minorities, 153, 157, 175
National Mobilization Committee to
  End the War in Vietnam, 31
national organizing, 293
national question, the, 149, 153–159,
  223
national-colonial theory, 155–157
nationalism, 25, 149, 288, 319–320
Nationalist Party in Puerto Rico, 150
nationhood, definition of, 153–154
Native Americans
  and nuclear plants, 236
  and STO, 98
  nuclear plants and, 241
  self-determination for, 233–234,
    233n
  solidarity work with, 255
  women, 164
Navajo Indians, 241
NAWF, 256–257, 260
NCM. *see* New Communist
  Movement
negotiations outside unions, 38, 39
Negri, Antonio, 280, 283, 283n. 45,
  299
neo-Nazis, 292, 295
neoliberalism, 308
Nepal, 187n. 97, 309
Netherlands, 279
networking, 257, 263
New Communist Movement (NCM),
  33, 111, 117–123, 199. *see also*
  specific groups
  and feminism, 165
  and internal conflict, 203
  and PFOC, 131n. 36
  and Puerto Rican solidarity, 178
  and STO, 131, 136, 144
  and working class, 47–48
  Farah strike, 63
  members, 15n
  offshoots of, 289
  opposition to armed struggle,
    162, 162n. 33
  reaction to Hot Autumn, 44

  recruitment, 56–57
  STO's place in, 127
  united front, 101–102
  workplace organizing strategy, 76
New Deal liberalism, 91
New Economic Policy, 129
New England, 245–246
New Hampshire, 249
new left, 11, 87, 117
  and feminism, 21–23
  and founding of STO, 15–18, 27,
    33, 115–117
  and youth culture, 87
  influence on STO members, 32
  Maoist tendencies, 116
New Movement in Solidarity with
  Puerto Rican Independence, 184
new right, rise of, 273
New State Repression, The, 317–318,
  317n–318n. 14
New York City
  black community in, 154
  Columbia University occupation,
    42
  grand juries in, 163
  Hard Hat Riot, 245
  Leninist groups in, 118
  Panther 21, 13
  Puerto Rican nationalists, 30, 180
  radical groups, 15n
  rallies in support of the Five, 178
  SAMRAF, 243
  Second Special Session on
    Disarmament, 260
  STO, 125
  Stonewall, 24
Newark, NJ local elections, 269
newsletters, 52–53, 218. *see also*
  specific publications
newspapers, agitational, 53, 53n. 39,
  96, 98. *see also* specific publications
Newton, Huey, 13
NGOs, 319
Nicaragua, 187n. 97, 256
Nixon, Richard, 11, 20–21, 245
  economic strategy, 54, 60
No Easy Answers Left (conference),

262, 264–265, 282n. 41, 299
No Nukes Left!, 253n. 52, 254
non-government organizations
    (NGOs), 319
nonconfrontational protests, 28
nonmembers, involvement of, 223,
    223n. 99, 227, 227n. 114
nonprofit industrial complex, 319
nonunion factories, 55, 57–59
nonviolence, 249, 250–254, 303
Northern Ireland, 297, 298
Northrop, 305
Northwest branch of STO, 125, 257,
    272, 297, 300, 328
nuclear power, 255–256
    and imperialism, 235, 242–243
    waste, 233–234, 233n
nuclear weapons, 236, 255–256

O

Oakland General Strike, 317
Obama, Barack, 244n–245n. 32
occupations, campus, 29, 42
occupations, factory, 18, 42, 44
occupations, nuclear plant, 249, 250,
    253
Occupy movement, 308n. 2, 309,
    317, 318
October League (OL), 117
    and STO, 130, 144
    recruitment, 56
    successors, 48
    the national question, 154
    workplace organizing, 49, 54,
        76, 95
oil, 171
OIPFG. *see* Organization of Iranian
    People's Fedayee Guerrillas
old left, STO members in, 33, 143, 328
operaismo, definition of, 44, 44n. 15
Operation Condor, 172
oppression
    agency among victims, 210
    and nonviolence, 251–252
    and privilege, 311n. 5

capitalism, 73
    of third world people, 290
    of women, 22, 29–30, 133–135,
        136–140, 166, 167
    the national question, 156–157, 158
    working class, 56, 325
optimism, 283–284
Organization Bureau, 259n. 63
Organization of Iranian People's
    Fedayee Guerrillas (OIPFG), 172,
    174, 175
organizational drift, 288
organizations, membership, 262–263
organizations, white. *see* white
    organizations
organizations, workers'. *see*
    independent workers' organizations
Organizing Committee for an
    Ideological Center (OCIC), 215n. 79
Organizing Working Class Women
    (pamphlet), 63
organizing, workplace. *see* workplace
    organizing
Oscar Mayer factory, 233
Osorio, Julio, 169
owner-operator strikes, 59–61
Oystershell Alliance, 249

P

pacifism, 19
    in antinuclear movement, 237,
        249, 250–253
    STO's rejection of, 316
Palestine, STO stance on, 295–296
pamphlets. *see also* specific pamphlets
    and Mexican workers, 99–100,
        99n–100n. 54
    STO, 4 n. 1, 62–63, 66, 127–
        128, 169
Pan y Rosas (newspaper), 53, 53n.
    39, 98
Panther 21, 13
paranoia, 180–181, 207
parenting, 65
    by revolutionaries, 213n. 68

in STO, 323
single, 213, 324
STO's attitude toward, 212–216
Paris Commune, 43
parties, vanguard, 318
party-building, 5, 69, 109, 122–123, 274–275
and geographical expansion, 125
and mass struggle, 318
BWC, 62
people of color in STO, 144
recruitment, 56–57
versus tendency-building, 258
passive resistance, 251–252, 251n. 48
patents, 247
patriarchy, 133, 135. *see also* male supremacy
patriotism, 20
Pauline, 106–107, 110, 111
Peniel, Joseph E., 12n. 1
People Against White Supremacy (PAWS), 240n
people of color. *see also* specific groups or individuals
autonomy, 5–6
oppression of, 290
relationship with STO, 278, 330
workers, 51, 56
People United Against Government Repression and the Klan and Nazi Coalition, 292
People's Anti-War Mobilization (PAM), 256, 301
People's Fedayee Guerrillas, 174n. 65
People's Republic of China, 115
people's war, 187, 187n. 97, 188–189
personal as political, 323, 323n. 25
personal lives of STO members, 125, 193, 198–200, 205, 323–324
and children, 212–216
Peru, 187n. 97
Peter Rabbit and the *Grundrisse,* 226–227
Petrograd, 41
PFOC. *see* Prairie Fire Organizing Committee

PG&E, 253
Phantom Pheminists (letter), 206–212, 215–218, 227
Phelps, Linda, 135, 207–208, 211–212, 323n. 25
Philadelphia Workers' Organizing Committee (PWOC), 154, 154n–155n. 16, 215n. 79, 305
STO critique of, 131, 140
Philadelphia, PA, 125, 151
Philippines, 187n. 97, 235, 236
picket lines, 268
Piercy, Marge, 22, 22n–23n. 27
Pirelli factory, 43–44
Pittsburgh, 233–234, 241
plants. *see* factories
plutonium mining, 236
pogo dancing, 194–195, 296
point-of-production work. *see* workplace organizing
Points of Agreement, 262–263
Poland, 273
police, 317–318
and autonomy for black people, 276
and the Harold Washington campaign, 272
and white skin privilege, 88
at antinuclear protests, 303, 304
at Stonewall, 24
attacks on black radicals, 11, 13
brutality, 151, 169–170, 192, 239, 250
collaboration with far-right groups, 293
female, 134
foreign forces in the US, 172–173
in Europe, 42
kindness of, 266
raids on punk rock clubs, 197
violence against, 273, 296
Police Board, 173, 173n. 60
police, military, 303
police, secret. *see* SAVAK
political economy, STO courses in, 223
politicians, 311, 311n. 4

politicians, black, 269, 273n. 21
politicians, Jewish, 272
politics in command, 70, 70n. 84
poor people, 151, 251–252,
    251n–252n. 48, 325
popular culture. *see* culture, popular
pornography, conflict over, 209
Port Gibson, Miss., 238–240
Porter, Janeen, 1, 212, 265, 271, 301.
    see also Janeen Creamer
Portland speech. *see* Black Worker,
    White Worker
Portland, Oregon, 103–112,
    103n. 60, 125, 178, 257. *see also*
    Northwest branch
Postal Service, United States, 305–306
posters, 60
posturing, 65–66
Potere Operaio (Workers' Power),
    44, 279
poverty. *see* poor people
power in STO, 143, 211, 257,
    328–329
pragmatism, 264, 316
Prairie Fire Distribution Committee,
    165–166
Prairie Fire Organizing Committee
    (PFOC), 131n. 36
    and STO, 131, 144, 161, 323
    and working class, 183
    grand jury resistance, 163
    origins of, 161n, 165–166
    Puerto Rican solidarity, 145, 167
    solidarity work, 174, 182
pranks at protests, 303
prayer services, 301, 303
premature universalism, 330, 330n. 37
pressure groups, 241
primary relationships, 209
printshop, STO. *see* C&D Printshop
Prison Notebooks, The, 46
prison sentences, 162–163
prison uprisings, Attica, 54
prisoner abuse, 31
prisoner of war status, 185, 188

prisoners, political, 173, 240
    in Italy, 299
    the Five, 150, 150n–151n. 6,
        152, 178–179
pro-sex feminism, 208–209, 209n, 211
procapitalism, 319
production, 18, 40–41, 58, 282–286,
    325
    and slavery, 84
Production Fraction, 286
production, point of. *see* workplace
    organizing
Progressive Labor Party (PL), 25–26,
    25n. 33, 90–91
progressives, religious, 163, 164
Proletarian Unity League (PUL). *see*
    Boston Group
proletariat. *see* working class
pronuclear organizing, 245
propaganda. *see also* publications
    and workplace organizing, 52
    for No Easy Answers Left
        conference, 265
    in solidarity work, 168, 178,
        185–186
property, destruction of, 61, 250, 298
Proposition Eight, 312n. 6
protests against mass sterilization, 168
protests, antinuclear, 238–240, 245,
    301–305
Provisional Organizing Committee,
    84, 143
PSP. *see* Puerto Rican Socialist Party
Ptolemy, Claudius, 225
publications, antinuclear movement,
    254, 256
publications, STO. *see also* specific
publications, C&D Printshop
    and revolutionary theory, 315
    Black Worker, White Worker, 112
    Call to Organize, 32–33
    during the lull, 127–128
    final issues of *UT* and *IDB,* 300
    IWW influence on, 49–50
    magazines, 130–132
    newspapers, 53–54, 53n. 39

pamphlets, 62–63
shop sheets, 52–53
Puerto Rican community, Chicago,
188–189, 268, 270
Puerto Rican independence
movement, 30
and struggle against forced
sterilization, 167
and the national question, 158
autonomy, 278
bombings, 180
debate over armed struggle, 162,
162n. 33
history of, 150–152
political prisoners, 185–189
publications, 145
response to Humboldt Park riots,
170
solidarity with Iranian students, 173
STO support for, 3, 124, 147–
149, 160, 216, 253
successes of, 178–179
Puerto Rican Socialist Party (PSP), 161
impact on US left, 147
in Chicago, 148, 152, 268n. 4
local chapters, 151
members of, 158
Puerto Rican Solidarity Committee
(PRSC), 161–162
Puerto Rican women, 56, 135, 164
Puerto Rican workers, 51, 53,
98–101
Puerto Rico, 242, 309
punk rock music, 165n. 41, 193–
198, 201, 296–298, 303
purging, organizational, 121–122, 124
puritanism on the left, 196

Q

Quad Cities, 301, 302–303
Quakers, radical, 249
Quebec City, 302n. 94
queer terminology, 277n. 29

R

R&B music, 193
race relations. see solidarity,
multiracial
Race Traitor (Journal), 333
race, lack of biological basis for, 88,
202–203
racism, 12–13
against Puerto Ricans, 150
and Chicago politics, 267–268,
267n–268n. 2, 268–270
and interracial rape, 133–135
and nuclear power, 237, 240, 254
and police, 272, 273, 296
and reproductive rights, 164
and the Vietnam War, 19
as an inherent quality, 88
in advertising, 311n. 4
in the workplace, 17, 56, 79–80
institutional, 148
Jim Crow, 82–83
on the left, 20, 157, 241, 260
within CPUSA, 204
within SDS, 91–92
within STO, 142
Radical Education Project, 29
radical feminism, 21–23, 21n, 22n. 26
and STO's tendency building, 254
Edwards' critique, 133–135, 323
radicalization, 286
and grand jury resistance, 163–164
in the antinuclear movement,
183, 236, 245, 256–257
of mass movements, 6
punk rock music, 196
radicals, 218, 280
raids, INS, 99
Rainbow Coalition, 268
rallies, 173, 240–241, 292
Ramones, 196
Randolph, A. Phillip, 85
Ranney, David, 143–144, 145, 171n.
56, 181
rape, 133, 135–136, 208
Rausch, Alan, 123n–124n. 19, 253n.
52, 254, 256

departure from STO, 300
relationship between Marxism
    and homosexuality, 276–277,
    277n. 29
solidarity work, 233–234, 233n,
    241–242, 253
Rawick, George, 195n. 11, 221
Reagan, Ronald, 192, 256, 273, 304
    era of, 229, 261, 308
Realconditions (Journal), 325
realism, socialist, 324
recession, organizing during, 191–
    192
Reconstruction period, 81–83, 132,
    156, 290
record industry, 197
recruitment, STO
    and autonomy, 287–288
    and punk rock music, 194
    at conferences, 224
    from antinuclear movement, 255
    of people of color, 95–98, 125–126
    of working class, 56–57, 168
    STO dialectics course, 223
Red Notes Collective, 280n
red-diaper babies, 214, 214n. 75
reformism
    and unions, 68–69, 71, 284–286
    and veteran activists, 261
    and working class, 47–48
    antinuclear activism, 234, 251,
        253, 254
    critique of STO, 160
    in far right groups, 292
    instead of revolution, 12, 273, 305
    resistance to, 299
    STO support for, 185
refugees, African, 243
refusal, strategy of, 299
regroupment, 217, 263, 264
religion and oppression, 252
religious activists, 301
Renewing the Anarchist Tradition
    Conference, 311n. 5
repression, 105, 290. *see also* state
    repression
reproductive rights movement

and sterilization of Puerto Rican
    women, 164–165, 165n. 40
and STO, 135, 215, 271
antiabortion movement, 292
Reproductive Rights National
    Network, 323
Republic of New Afrika, 124
    and black nationalism, 93, 154
    and black power, 12
    and STO, 143, 149
    Maoist influence, 110
    political prisoners, 240
Republican Party, 270
reputation of STO, 149, 263
resistance
    and punk rock, 196
    and STO's legacy, 327
    democratic, 208n. 56
    role in the national question,
        156–157, 158
    to capitalism, 284–285
    to grand jury subpoenas, 162–164
    to Iranian Shah, 171–177, 172n. 57
    to victimization, 210
    within military, 18, 18n–19n. 18,
        19, 20
retreats, STO, 221
revolution
    and feminism, 22, 24
    and reformism, 273
    and truth, 6–7, 6n, 7n
    and unions, 75
    changing notions of, 309
    difficulty of, 105
    in China, 42
    in Cuba, 177
    in Iran, 124, 236n. 10
    in Marxist theory, 40
    in Russia, 41–42, 41n. 11, 129
    inevitablity of, 316–317
    nonviolent, 251, 253n. 52
revolutionaries
    and Chicago politics, 267–268
    and STO, 263–264, 332
    appeal of liberal politics to, 272
    black people as, 279
    involvement in mass movements,
        319

relationship with the Occupy
movement, 317
threats from the KKK, 291
with children, 212–216, 213n. 68
Revolutionary Action Movement, 12
revolutionary anarchism, 313
Revolutionary Communist Party
(RCP), 48, 218
revolutionary consciousness, 237
and black liberation, 159
and direct action, 316–317
and fascism, 292
and labor struggles, 17
and party-building, 274–275
and working class, 48
and workplace organizing, 287
development of, 107
in Puerto Rican community, 148
in the antinuclear movement,
251, 253, 254
in the women's movement,
134–135
Lenin's theory of, 70–71
of black people, 108–109
see also tendency-building
within social movements, 3
revolutionary movements, 94, 261
and autonomy for black people,
276
and STO, 2, 143
history of, 7
natural lifespan of, 327
role of, 331–332
STO criticism of, 177
the role of women in, 136
revolutionary social bloc, 275, 280
Revolutionary Struggle (group), 280
revolutionary theory. see theory,
revolutionary
Revolutionary Union (RU), 48, 117
party-building, 274
recruitment, 56
successors, 62
tokenism in, 126
united front, 101–102
Revolutionary Union Movements
(RUM), 42, 45

Revolutionary Youth Movement
(RYM), 25, 26
Revolutionary Youth Movement II
(RYM II), 26, 28, 30, 33–35
right wing movements, 177, 193,
291, 309. see also far-right; specific
movements and groups
rightward drift, 261, 271
riot gear, 303
riots, 24, 151, 151n. 10, 169–170
Roberto Clemente High School,
268–269, 270
Robinson, Edward G., 195
Rock Against Racism, 194
rock and roll music, 193
Rock Island Arsenal
STO actions at, 301–305
Rock Island Two protest, 304
Rocky Flats, 245
Romano, Paul, 109–110
romanticization of oppressed groups,
107–109, 160, 196–197, 225, 288
Rome, 45
Rossing Uranium Mine, 243
Rothenberg, Marcia, 212
Rothenberg, Mel, 65, 65n. 70,
69–72, 212
RU. see Revolutionary Union
Rubin, Gayle, 209n
Rubio, Paula, 198n. 22, 213–214
Rubio, Phil, 198n. 22
and alternative energy, 247
and STO's culture, 199, 212
antinuclear organizing, 237–238,
241, 250–253, 251–252n. 48
parenting, 213, 215
ruling class, 47, 244n–245n. 32,
289–290, 295
power of, 88–89
rural areas, 236, 240, 246
Russia, 175. see also Soviet Union
Russian empire, 153
Russian Jews, autonomy for, 277–278
Russian Revolution. see revolution
Russian Social Democratic Labor

Party, 277, 328

RYM. *see* Revolutionary Youth Movement

S

sabotage, 61

sadomasochism, 209n

SAMRAF, South African Military Refugee Aid Fund

San Francisco, CA, 237

San Juan, 150

sanctions, 205

Saturdy Night Live, 201n. 34

SAVAK, 171–173, 172n. 57

scab labor, 61, 305

schools. *see* education

scientistic Marxism, 92, 122

Scottsboro case, 133

SDS. *see* Students for a Democratic Society

Seattle, 257, 302n. 94, 309. *see also* Northwest branch of STO

Second Special Session on Disarmament, United Nations, 260

secrecy, 68
    and Rock Island protests, 301
    in STO, 180–181, 180n–181n. 81, 227, 238n. 19

Secret Supplement of *IDB,* 227, 227n. 114

sectarianism, 174, 265, 293

secularism in Israel/Palestine, 295

security in STO, 181, 227–228, 303

seditious consipiracy charges, 187–188

seeds of socialism theory, 107–111

Seeger, Pete, 196

segregation, racial, 267

self-activity and autonomy, 285–286

self-defense, armed, 13

self-deprecation in STO, 287

self-determination. *see* autonomy

self-determination for Native Americans, 233–234, 233n

September 11, 2001 attacks, 309

Sex Pistols, 193, 197

sexism. *see also* feminism
    and sexual advances, 208–209
    in CPUSA, 204
    on the left, 22
    Phantom Pheminists letter, 206–207
    within STO, 205, 217

sexual violence, Susan Brownmiller on, 133

sexuality, 87, 208–209, 211, 323

Shadrach, 100

Shah Pahlavi, Mohammad Reza, 171

shop sheets, 52–53, 54, 54n. 41
    and black workers, 96
    and Farah strike, 63
    and shop steward elections, 55
    bilingual, 98–99

shop stewards, 55, 75, 79–80
    STO members as, 68–71, 77

Simon, William, 60

single-issue organizing, 241

single-party states, 129

Sino-Soviet conflict, 115

size of STO, 218, 259–260, 329–331

skill-sharing in STO, 210

skits, 199, 303

slavery, 81–82, 84, 89–90, 99–101

slogans, 247
    about white skin privilege, 311–312, 312n. 6
    and antinuclear movement, 241
    anti-Klan, 293
    Weatherman, 16, 16n. 13

SNCC. *see* Student Nonviolent Coordinating Committee

Social Democracy, 264

Social Democratic Labor Party, 220n. 91

social ecology. *see* environmental movement

social imperialism, 130

social movements. *see* specific movements and groups

socialism, 27–28, 48–49
    and socialist realism, 324
    and working class autonomy, 104, 262

in the Soviet Union, 128–129
    paths to, 107
Socialist Workers Party, 15, 110n. 80,
    194, 274
societies, communist, 282–283
Sojourner Truth Communist
    Organization. *see* Sojourner Truth
    Organization
Sojourner Truth Organization
    (STO). *see also* Central Committee;
    Dialectics Course; General
    Membership Meetings; National
    Committee; white skin privilege;
    Women's Commission; workplace
    organizing
        and women's liberation, 133–140
        anti-imperialism, 2, 125, 144,
            218, 253–255, 319
        antifacism, 132, 271, 291–292, 322
        areas of work, 2–6
        debate over national question,
            155–158
        demise of, 305–306
        demographics of members,
            94–98, 125–126, 140–142,
            329–331
        early members, 27–33
        expansion of, 218, 259–260,
            329–331
        founding of, 12, 27
        geographical reach of, 3, 125,
            236, 241–242, 282
        intellectual culture, 218–220,
            226, 310, 315, 328–329
        internal conflict, 96, 103–112,
            149, 159, 219, 259, 312
        internal discipline, 203–206
        merger with Workforce, 123
        naming of, 31
        organizational structure, 328–329
        power structures in, 143, 211,
            257, 328–329
        priorities, 260–261
        rebuilding of after splits, 78
        schisms within, 68–72
        security in, 181, 227–228, 303
        size of organization, 218, 259–

        260, 329–331
        solidarity work, 64, 149, 171–
            180, 242
        splinter groups, 118
        splits, 3, 72, 97, 111–112, 145, 278
        third world members in, 140–145
        use of music in organizing, 191–193
STO(X), 118–123
solar power, 246, 247
soldiers, South African, 218, 243–
    244, 244n. 31
solidarity coalitions, 234
        after Humboldt Park riots, 170
        and grand jury resistance, 162–163
        and Iranian students, 174
        Puerto Rican, 164, 184
solidarity work, 5, 26, 52, 79–80,
    103–104
        and anti-authoritarianism, 321
        and arrests of suspected FALN
            members, 185–188
        and black nationalism, 159
        and Chicago's mayoral election, 270
        and immigrants, 99
        and national liberation
            movements, 127
        and STO internal struggles, 96
        and STO's legacy, 319–320
        and tendency-building, 235
        and unconditional support,
            181–182
        and Weatherman, 92
        and white skin privilege, 88
        and women, 167
        ciriticism of STO, 159–161
        for the Five, 178
        groups involved in, 161–162
        in factories, 95–98
        justification for, 157–158
        limitations of, 184
        potential for, 297
        STO events, 64
        STO focus on, 102–105, 149, 242
        with Iranian resistance, 171–178
solidarity, international
        STO's efforts towards, 320–321
solidarity, working class
        and parenthood, 215

and Rock Island protests, 302
Solidarnosc, 273
songs. *see* music
South Africa, 253, 309
    nuclear power in, 236, 242–243
South African Military Refugee Aid
    Fund (SAMRAF), 218, 243–244,
    244n. 31
South America, 172, 174
South Chicago, 101
South Dakota, 242
South West Africa. *see* Namibia
South West African People's
    Organization (SWAPO), 243–244
Southern Christian Leadership
    Conference, 12
Southern United States
    and black nationalism, 93, 159
    and Jim Crow, 82–83
    and slavery, 81–82
    and the Fugitive Slave Act, 100
    and the national question, 153–154
    antinuclear movement in, 238–240
    democracy in, 290
    support for Nixon, 20
    violence toward revolutionaries
        in, 289
Southwestern United States, 152,
    162, 236, 241
Soviet Union, 224
    and the arms race, 256
    and the Jewish Bund, 277–278
    capitalism in, 308
    collapse of, 308
    foreign policy, 116, 130, 217
    international communist
        movement, 115
    invasion of Czechoslovakia, 32
    legacy of, 315
    STO critique of, 128
Spanish language, 53, 64, 98
Spanish-American war, 150
Sparticist League, the, 271
speaking tours
    anarchist, 321n
    and STO solidarity work, 168,
        181, 244, 320

and workload for STO members,
    218
    importance of, 321
    of Europe, 265
Special Sedition (magazine), 296–298,
    300
Special Supplement (newsletter), 227,
    227n. 114
speed-ups, 37–39
Speedwell, Vic, 1
spills, nuclear, 241
splinter groups, STO, 118
splits
    in Federation, 123
    within STO, 3, 72, 97, 111–112,
        117, 145, 278
sports, 87, 198, 199, 324
Springsteen, Bruce, 191–193
squatting, 273
St. Louis, MO, 118
Stalin model, 117
Stalin, Joseph
    and Organization Bureau, 259n. 63
    and the national question, 153–155
    and the single-party state, 129
    and Trotskyists, 116n. 5
    China's embrace of, 116, 116n. 3
    successors to, 115–116
Stalinism
    and critique of Black Worker,
        White Worker, 108
    and democratic centralism debate,
        121
    and Ignatin, 92–93, 115
    and informal hierarchy in STO, 328
    and party-building, 5
    and sexuality in STO, 209–210
    critique of, 32
    in the black movement, 110
    in the Communist Party, 27n. 37
    rejection of by left groups, 264
    STO rejection of, 3, 6, 116–117,
        122–123, 143, 315
    supporters of, 27, 27n. 37
state capitalism, 128, 129, 138
State Department, US, 326n. 33
state oppression

in Iran, 171–172
of Puerto Rican community, 169–170
state repression
and antifascist direct action, 322
and MLN, 162
and pacifism, 251
and punk rock music, 197
fear of, 180–181, 297, 317
grand juries, 162–164
in Iran during Khomeini regime, 177–178
in Italy, 43–44
in Puerto Rico, 150
of black radicals, 11, 12, 13, 15
restrictions on travel, 321, 321n
the KKK as, 291
state, challenges to the, 298
Staudenmaier, Peter, 330n. 37
steel mills, 54, 62, 101, 169
sterilization of Puerto Rican women, 135, 150, 164–165, 165n. 40, 167
stewards, shop, 55, 68–71, 75, 77, 79–80
Stewart-Warner factory
and union representation, 54–55, 55n. 43, 68
INS raid, 99
racist pay structure, 56
site of, 307
STO organizing in, 50, 51–52, 51n. 34
STO. see Sojourner Truth Organization
STO(X), 118–123
Stone, Ria, 109
Stonewall, 24
strategy of refusal, 299
strategy, revolutionary, 299
street fights, 42, 273, 304
strike-breaking, 305
strikes, 31. see also wildcat strikes; specific strikes
at Farah Manufacturing Company, 63–64, 101, 111–112
Flint Sit-Down Strike, 31, 275n. 27
garment workers, 63–64
general strikes, 42–43, 50, 82, 317

in Europe, 17
revolutionary potential of, 67
Strucker, John, 51, 51n. 34, 65, 99, 147–148
student movements, 14. see also specific groups
after SDS, 24–25
and anti-imperialism, 91
and Autonomia, 279
and Puerto Rican independence, 152
attacks on, 245
direct action by, 42
downfall of, 26
Iranian, 171
limitations of, 11
radicalization of, 19
Student Nonviolent Coordinating Committee (SNCC), 85, 86, 200, 252
Students for a Democratic Society (SDS)
and white supremacy, 91–92
anti-PL sentiment, 26
as a training ground, 24, 28
collapse of, 11
Days of Rage, 297n. 85
dominance of, 15
factions within, 25
national office, 27, 27n. 36
publications, 91
ties to Black Panthers, 13, 30
Sudan, 202
super-nationalism and fascism, 292
Supreme Court, United States, 312n. 7
surveillance, 13, 303
Switzerland, 279
syndicalism, 107
systems of oppression, 326–327, 326n.–327n. 33

T

Talk Back (newsletter), 52–56, 60
Teamsters for a Democratic Union (TDU), 185, 218, 285–286
technique in command, 70, 70n. 84
technology, 282, 283, 320–321
Tehran hostage crisis, 175

Tendency Newsletter (magazine), 262, 263, 264
tendency-building
    and networking, 257
    and STO, 2, 261–265
    anti-fascist organizing, 295
    in antinuclear movement, 233–234, 239, 249, 253–255
    international, 280
    problems with, 258
territory, 153–154
terrorism, 43–44
Texas, 173
textile industry strikes, 53
Thatcher, Margaret, 256
theory, revolutionary
    and class struggle, 325
    and critical thinking, 220
    and dual consciousness, 313
    and mass struggle, 48–49
    and revolutionary strategy, 299
    and STO, 70, 310, 314–316
    and STO's dialectics course, 223
    connection with practice, 264
    distaste for, 314n. 9
theses, STO, 131
    on fascism, 293–296
    on the national question, 158–159, 158n–159n. 26
thinking, critical, 220–222, 220n. 91
Third International, 153–154
Third World Caucus of STO, 141–143, 330
third world people
    and white supremacy, 91
    anti-imperialism, 86
    communist parties, 125–126, 130
    STO support for, 124
    workers, 56, 248
Thirteenth Plenum of the Executive Committee of the Comintern, 291
Thompson, E.P., 256
threats against revolutionaries, 291
Three Mile Island accident, 237, 238, 241
Three Way Fight (web site), 322
three way fight analysis, 176n–177n.

71, 322
tokenism, 126
Toward a Radical Movement (pamphlet), 29–30
Toward a Revolutionary Party (pamphlet), 46–47, 46n. 21
Tracy, Dick, 195
trade unions. *see* unions
transgender terminology, 277n. 29
transportation industry strikes, 59–61
travel, 249, 249n. 44, 321
Travis, Bob, 31
Travis, Carole
    and C&D Printshop, 163
    and STO, 78, 200, 259–260
    background, 30, 31
    critique of PFOC, 165–167, 323
    feminism, 23n. 30, 135
    power within STO, 143, 144, 328–329
    workplace organizing, 15–16, 60–61, 286–287
Treasures of Tutankhamun (exhibit), 200–203, 201n. 35
Tronti, Mario, 332
Trotskyism
    critique of Stalin, 116n. 5
    influence on STO, 109–110, 254, 315
    workplace organizing, 47–48
Trotskyist groups, 271. *see also* specific groups
    alternatives to, 118
    and punk rock music, 194
    STO relationship with, 217
    support for Khomeini, 176
    union takeover attempts, 49
truck drivers' strike, 59–61, 111–112
Truman, Harry S., 150n–151n. 6
truth in revolutionary movements, 6–7, 6n, 7n
Truth, Sojourner, 31, 94
    "ain't I a woman" quote, 135, 135n. 49
    choice of STO's name, 330
Twain, Mark, 221

U

underground. *see* clandestine groups
Underground Railroad, 94
undocumented workers, 99–100
unemployment, 54
    and black people, 14
    and deindustrialization, 302
    and factory closures, 57–58
    organizing around, 192, 286
    racial differences, 17n. 16
unions. *see also* labor movement;
  specific organizations
    and bourgeois consciousness, 47
    and deindustrialization, 233
    and women workers, 53
    and working-class culture, 65, 66
    autonomy for, 284
    caucuses, 69
    contracts, 109–110
    corruption in, 11
    elections, 68–69
    evolving STO attitude toward,
      74–75
    in Europe, 43–44
    IWW attitude toward, 109
    organization of members, 163, 164
    PO's rejection of, 279
    popularity of, 285
    reform, 71, 76
    STO rejection of, 49, 54–55, 64
    wildcat strikes by members,
      37–39
    workerist faction in STO, 77
United Auto Workers (UAW), 69,
  79–80
United Front, 294
united front against imperialism
  STO rejection of, 101–102
United League, 239
United Mine Workers (UMW), 246
United Nations, 243–244, 260
United States Treasury, 60
Unity and Struggle, 333
unity, working class, 159, 275
universities, 19, 24, 29, 42, 312n. 7
University of Chicago, 29

University of Michigan, 312n. 7
uranium mining, 236, 242–243, 246
Urgent Tasks (magazine), 130–132,
  135, 174, 200–203, 201n. 35
Uruguay, 172
US Steel South Works, 169

V

Valentin, Carmen, 173
value, law of, 132, 282–284
Vasquez Ignatin, Hilda, 30, 30n. 52,
  72, 98, 147n–148n. 1
Venezuela, revolution in, 309
veterans, Vietnam, 152
victimhood, 210
Vietcong, 20, 20n. 22, 21
Vietnam War, 17, 54, 86
    nonviolent protest, 252
    resistance to, 18–20
    support for, 16, 245
Vietnamese people, 20
violence, incitement of, 296–298
Virginia, 84–85, 154
Voci, Ed, 171n. 56, 173, 186,
  226–227
*Voice of the Women's Liberation
  Movement, The* (newsletter), 30

voting rights, 82. *see also* elections

W

wages, 44, 56, 139
wages, psychological, 83, 85, 87–88
walkouts. *see* strikes
Waller, Signe, 289n. 58
war, 186. *see also* specific wars
war, nuclear, 255–256
Warner Brothers, 197
Washington, D.C., 150, 172
Washington, Harold, mayoral
  campaign of, 268, 269, 292, 300
waste disposal, nuclear, 236
wealth, 282
Weather Underground Organization

(WUO), 161n, 165–166, 167. *see also* Weatherman

Weatherman. *see also* Weather Underground Organization
  and labor unions, 16
  and SDS split, 26
  critiques of, 28, 107
  Days of Rage, 297n. 85
  response to Vietnam War, 20, 20n. 22, 21
  white skin privilege analysis, 92–94

West Town, Chicago, 147, 151, 173

Western Electric Hawthorne Works factory
  and latino workers, 99
  black leaders at, 95–96
  organizing in, 50, 57–59
  wildcat strike, 37–39

Westside Chicago branch of STO, 68–69, 75

white activists
  and black liberation, 13, 14–15
  commitment to pacifism, 251
  departure from SNCC, 86
  in antinuclear movement, 183, 236
  priorities of, 160–161

white blind spot, 225

White Blindspot, The (letter), 25–26, 25n. 34, 89–91

white organizations, 32, 45–46, 287
  STO's identity as, 95–98, 330–331

white people, 88, 194, 268, 269–270

white skin privilege
  and STO's legacy, 310–312, 311n. 4, 311n. 5
  and autonomy for black people, 275
  and class struggle, 325
  and identity politics, 326
  and imperialism, 93–94
  and nationalism, 149
  and revolutionary strategy, 34
  and the Federation, 118
  and working class, 26, 47
  definition of, 87–88
  disadvantages to white people, 106–107
  Ignatin's analysis, 112
  in Chicago's political machine, 268
  in colonial Virginia, 85
  in South Africa, 243, 243n. 29
  internationally, 91
  rejection of, 89, 90, 104
  relationship with fascism, 290
  role in US history, 155–156
  STO emphasis on, 5, 78, 262
  STO's internal conflict over, 96–98, 111

white supremacy, 5
  actions against, 79–80
  and ancient civilizations, 202–203
  and anti-immigrant sentiment, 100
  and bourgeoisie consciousness, 47
  and capitalism, 4, 133
  and dual consciousness theory, 4 n. 2
  and DuBois' influence on STO, 80–88
  and enlisted men, 19
  and feminists, 276
  and Jim Crow, 82–83
  and nationalism, 149
  and nuclear waste disposal, 236–237
  and tendency-building, 235
  and the national question, 155
  and Vietnam War, 19, 20
  and white skin privilege analysis, 88, 311
  and working class, 53, 275
  comparison to male supremacy, 137, 138
  future of, 312
  importance of struggle against, 160
  in CPUSA, 204
  in SDS, 91–92
  links to other struggles, 165
  opposition to, 28

origins of, 84
relationship with fascism, 290–291
STO analysis of, 101–103, 127
STO opposition to, 26
white women, 21–22, 133, 165–167
white working class, 245
    and 1974 truck driver strike, 59–61
    and black nationalism, 158
    and tendency-building, 235
    and white skin privilege, 82–83, 89, 90, 93, 106
    anti-immigrant sentiment, 99–101
    anti-racist actions, 79–80
    betrayal of black workers, 224
    causes of racism, 107
    in colonial times, 84–85
    jobs in the nuclear industry, 245
    multiracial solidarity, 91, 92, 102–105
    organizing of, 286
    STO focus on, 94, 96
whiteness
    and bourgeois class status, 248
    and the women's movement, 323
    as a political category, 88
    betrayal of, 311–312, 312n. 6
    of Egyptians, 202–203
Whitman, Steve, 269–270
Whitney, Ted, 298
wildcat strikes. see also strikes
    and labor movement unrest, 16
    and the collapse of SDS, 11
    and truck drivers, 59–61
    and younger workers, 17–18
    at Chicago lard factory, 145
    at Dodge plant, 14
    at Hawthorne Works, 37–39
    black leaders of, 95–96
    build-up to, 168
Wilkins, Fred, 100
Willis, Ellen, 21n, 209n
wobblies. see Industrial Workers of the World
women. see also Women's Commission of STO; women's

liberation movement
    autonomy for, 276
    in Iran, 175
    in STO, 210–211, 225
    leadership roles for, 166, 262
    mass sterilization in Puerto Rico, 135, 150, 164–165, 165n. 40, 167
    organizing of, 218
    violence against, 164
    working class, 23, 29–30, 53, 63
women of color, 23, 29–30, 165, 326. see also specific groups
women workers, 51, 53, 56, 57–59
Women's Commission of STO
    and male supremacy, 323
    and Phantom Pheminists letter, 207–208
    and STO internal discipline, 205
    and STO's feminist stance, 136
    call for greater militancy, 211
    workload of members, 218
women's liberation movement
    and Boggs' critique of STO, 225
    and labor movement, 16, 58–59
    and middle class STO members, 212
    as a byproduct of revolution, 137–138
    autonomy for, 276
    conflict with STO, 207
    factions, 21–24
    growth of, 11
    right wing tendencies in, 134
    rightward drift of, 261n. 68
    STO's relationship with, 183, 322–324
    writings, 29–30
Women's Wing. see Women's Commission
Woods, Dessie, 135–136
work stoppages. see strikes
Worker Student Alliance, 25
workerism, 44n. 15, 65–66, 70, 77
Workers Party, 110n. 80
Workers World Party, 256
workers' organizations, independent.

see independent workers' organizations
Workers' Power, 217
Workers' Rights Center, South Chicago, 57–58, 101, 145
Workers' Voice (newsletter), 52
Workers' Voice Committee, 69
Workers' Voice Organization, 289
Workforce merger with STO, 123
working class
    activists, 31
    and dual consciousness, 4–5, 4–5 n. 2
    and fascism, 292
    and Italian autonomists, 280
    and labor struggles, 17
    and multiracial solidarity, 5
    and PL, 25
    and racism, 19
    and STO, 35, 183
    and the contradiction of capitalism, 222
    and the shift toward technology, 282–283, 283n. 42
    and Tutankhamun exbibit, 201
    and white skin privilege, 290–291, 312
    and white supremacy, 26, 87–89
    as ruling class, 81
    autonomy for, 284–285
    benefits of black liberation to, 157
    black workers, 14
    conflict within, 18
    culture, 64–66
    importance to revolutionary groups, 327–328
    in European struggles, 42–44
    in Iran, 176
    in Marxist theory, 40–41, 40n. 7, 122–123
    in Poland, 273
    industrial, 45, 49
    latino workers, 98–101, 150
    membership in STO, 331
    multiracial solidarity, 26, 102–105
    Puerto Rican, 150

    racism in, 82–83
    radicalization of, 67
    recruitment of, 34, 56–57, 168
    role in socialism, 262
    STO organzing outside unions, 3
    support from RYM II, 28
    unification of, 89, 90
    unionized, 244n–245n. 32
working conditions, 54, 56
working mothers, 53
workload of STO members, 217–218
workplace organizing, 3, 15, 28, 29
    and anti-imperialism, 183–184
    and *Autonomia,* 279
    and early STO, 35
    and environmental issues, 237
    and radicals, 16
    and solidarity work, 185
    and STO, 2, 3, 31, 97
    and STO internal conflict, 66–78
    and the LRBW, 14
    by Big Flame, 73
    by independent STO members, 144
    comparison with solidarity work, 168
    effects of Hot Autumn on, 44
    in Detroit, 45
    in Kansas City, 161
    in *Urgent Tasks,* 132
    of Italian working class, 44
    problems with, 73
    role in Hot Autumn, 43–44
    STO approach to, 37–39, 49–64, 72, 95
    STO departure from, 124
    STO's changing tactics, 285–287
    STO's return to, 216, 233, 261
    use of shop sheets, 52–53
    wildcat strikes, 37–39
    workerism, 65
Workplace Papers (Journal), 216
World War II, 85
Wright, Steve, 283, 283n. 45

Y

Yokinin, August, 204
Young Lords Party, 30, 30n. 52,
    147n–148n. 1, 151–152
Young Patriots, 30
Young, Ethan, 160, 162
youth
    activists, 17
    and black culture, 87
    and Puerto Rican independence,
        152, 162
    and SDS, 25
    and the Occupy movement, 317
    at Rock Island protests, 303
    culture, 193, 200, 296
    in CPUSA, 32
    organizing of, 297
    potential for solidarity work, 167
    STO involvement with, 165n. 41

Z

Zapatista Army of National
    Liberation (EZLN), 309, 320
Zeskind, Elaine, 135, 136, 194–8,
    196n. 14
Zeskind, Leonard, 295, 296, 322n.
    24
Zwierzynski, Elias, 77, 111

Support AK Press!

AK Press is one of the world's largest and most productive anarchist publishing houses. We're entirely worker-run and

democratically managed. We operate without a corporate structure—no boss, no managers, no bullshit. We publish close to twenty books every year, and distribute thousands of other titles published by other like-minded independent presses from around the globe.

The Friends of AK program is a way that you can directly contribute to the continued existence of AK Press, and ensure that we're able to keep publishing great books just like this one! Friends pay a minimum of $25 per month, for a minimum three month period, into our publishing account. In return, Friends automatically receive (for the duration of their membership), as they appear, one free copy of every new AK Press title. They're also entitled to a 20% discount on everything featured in the AK Press Distribution catalog and on the website, on any and every order. You or your organization can even sponsor an entire book if you should so choose!

There's great stuff in the works—so sign up now to become a Friend of AK Press, and let the presses roll!

Won't you be our friend? Email friendsofak@akpress.org for more info, or visit the Friends of AK Press website: http://www.akpress.org/programs/friendsofak